The State of Black Michigan, 1967–2007

The State of Black Michigan, 1967–2007

EDITED BY

Joe T. Darden • Curtis Stokes • Richard W. Thomas

Michigan State University Press • *East Lansing*

∞ The paper used in this publication meets the minimum requirements of ANSI/NISO Z39.48–1992 (R 1997) (Permanence of Paper).

Michigan State University Press
East Lansing, Michigan 48823-5245

1947 · CELEBRATING 60 YEARS of SCHOLARLY PUBLISHING · 2007

Printed and bound in the United States of America.

14 13 12 11 10 09 08 07   1 2 3 4 5 6 7 8 9 10

LIBRARY OF CONGRESS CATALOGING-IN-PUBLICATION DATA

The state of Black Michigan, 1967–2007 / edited by Joe T. Darden, Curtis Stokes, Richard W. Thomas.
p. cm.
Includes bibliographical references.
ISBN 978-0-87013-827-0 (pbk. : alk. paper)
1. African Americans—Michigan—Social conditions—20th century. 2. African Americans—Michigan—Social conditions—21st century. 3. African Americans—Michigan—Economic conditions. 4. African Americans—Michigan—Politics and government. 5. Michigan—Race relations—History—20th century. 6. Michigan—Race relations—History—21st century. 7. Michigan—Social policy. I. Darden, Joe T. II. Stokes, Curtis. III. Thomas, Richard Walter, 1939-
E185.93.M5S734 2007
305.896'073077409045—dc22

2007023790

Book and cover design by Sharp Des!gns, Inc., Lansing, MI

green press INITIATIVE

Michigan State University Press is a member of the Green Press Initiative and is committed to developing and encouraging ecologically responsible publishing practices. For more information about the Green Press Initiative and the use of recycled paper in book publishing, please visit *www.greenpressinitiative.org.*

Visit Michigan State University Press on the World Wide Web at *www.msu.edu/msupress*

*This book is dedicated to the former faculty,
students and staff of Urban Affairs Programs,
who witnessed the release of the annual
State of Black Michigan reports
from 1984–1993.*

Contents

Acknowledgments ix

Foreword to *The State of Black Michigan, 1967–2007* xi

Preface xv

PART 1: INTRODUCTION AND OVERVIEW

Introduction and Overview Racial Disparities Persist in Michigan 40 Years After the Civil Disorders of 1967, *Joe T. Darden* 3

PART 2: ECONOMIC CONDITIONS

1 Trends in the Economic Status of Michigan Blacks Since 1967, *Karl D. Gregory* 15

2 Black-Owned Businesses in Michigan, 1982–1987, and the Top 31 in 1989, *Karl D. Gregory* . . . 37

3 Black Business Development in Michigan, 1987–2002, *Joe T. Darden* 69

4 Black Self-Help in Michigan, *Richard W. Thomas* 81

5 The Black Self-Help Tradition in Michigan, 1967–2007, *Richard W. Thomas* 97

PART 3: SOCIAL CONDITIONS

6 **The Housing Situation of Blacks in Metropolitan Areas of Michigan,** *Joe T. Darden* 113

7 **Residential Segregation of Blacks in Metropolitan Areas of Michigan, 1960–1990,** *Joe T. Darden* 129

8 **Changes in Black Residential Segregation in Metropolitan Areas of Michigan, 1990–2000,** *Joe T. Darden* 147

9 **The Health of Black Michigan,** *Clifford L. Broman* 161

10 **The Health of Black Michigan, 2006,** *Clifford L. Broman and Renee B. Canady* 171

11 **The Young Black Offender in Michigan,** *Homer C. Hawkins* 179

12 **Black Crime in Michigan: Past and Present,** *Homer C. Hawkins* 217

13 **Black and White High School Dropout Rates in Michigan: The Inequality Persists,** *Percy Bates* 231

14 **Blacks in Michigan Higher Education,** *Walter R. Allen* 243

15 **Racial Disparities in Michigan's Educational System in 2006,** *Joe T. Darden* 269

PART 4: POLITICAL CONDITIONS

16 **Black Political Participation in Michigan,** *Curtis Stokes* 277

17 **Black Political Participation in Michigan, 15 Years Later,** *Curtis Stokes* 289

PART 5: CONCLUSIONS AND RECOMMENDATIONS

18 **Summary of Past Conclusions and Recommendations to Improve Black Michigan, 1985–1993,** *Joe T. Darden, Curtis Stokes, and Richard W. Thomas* ... 297

19 **Assessment of the Michigan Legislature Response to Past Recommendations and Future Actions Needed,** *Joe T. Darden* 343

About the Authors 353

Index 355

Acknowledgments

This book is based on the contributions of a variety of individuals. Without their support, the book could not have been compiled. We owe a great debt to all of them. First, we thank the interdisciplinary group of researchers from higher-education institutions and organizations in Michigan who contributed chapters to the original *State of Black Michigan* reports and whose chapters we use in this volume.

Although conceptualized by the editors, this book could not have become a reality without the support of key administrators at Michigan State University. We thank President Lou Anna K. Simon for her continued support of the *State of Black Michigan* project. We also thank the various unit administrators who agreed to provide financial support to ensure that the book receives widespread distribution to members of the state legislature, governmental officials, policy makers, and community leaders. We owe much to Marietta Baba, Dean, College of Social Science; Sherman Garnett, Dean, and Norman A. Graham, Acting Dean, James Madison College; Richard Groop, Chairperson, Department of Geography; Mark Kornbluh, Chairperson, Department of History; and Gloria Smith, Acting Director, African American and African Studies Interdepartmental Program.

We also appreciate the contributions of graduate students LaToya Tinean Brackett, African American and African Studies Interdepartmental Program, and Lisa Eldred, Department of Rhetoric and Writing, College of Arts and Letters. LaToya provided much needed assistance with the research on Public Acts of the Michigan Legislature and Lisa provided important editorial assistance with the updated chapters in the book.

Finally, we thank Julie Loehr, Associate Director of Michigan State University Press, for understanding the significance of this book and for making it a part of the Michigan State University Press collection.

Foreword to *The State of Black Michigan, 1967–2007*

Forty years ago, Detroit, like many cities across the country, erupted in extended violence after a conflict between the police and black residents. That the precipitating event seemed comparatively minor when viewed against the ensuing riots focused thinking in the aftermath on causes of the events. The first formal study asking such questions as what happened and why—as well as seeking means to prevent recurrence—was commissioned by President Lyndon Johnson. His National Advisory Commission on Civil Disorders concluded that racism as manifested in segregation and discrimination against blacks in employment, housing, and education was the basic cause. Later studies added police brutality and economic inequality to the growing list of explanations.

These nationwide events as well as Johnson's study demonstrated the need for thoughtful analysis of racial, social, and economic conditions in American cities, an area of study mostly neglected until that time. At Michigan State University (MSU), where the land-grant tradition supports research on critical issues that affect society and finding solutions to improve the conditions of all population groups, this need was addressed through the founding of the Center of Urban Affairs in 1969. As the first unit at MSU focused on cities and their demographics, Urban Affairs attracted faculty and students driven to understand the reasons behind the riots in Detroit and other American cities. Timely and relevant, the center became a hub for examining such questions and was very popular. To address the growing breadth and depth of the field ignited by the center, in 1974 MSU established the College of Urban Development, home to the Department of Urban and Metropolitan Studies, the Department of Racial and Ethnic Studies, and the Center of Urban Affairs. These academic units focused their research not only on understanding and addressing the defined causes of the riots in 1967 but also on the racial, social, and economic challenges that garnered attention because of the riots.

As part of their research into this field, in 1984, faculty of MSU's Urban Affairs Programs, the successor to the College of Urban Development, in cooperation with the Michigan Council of Urban League Executives, decided to publish an annual report on *The State of Black Michigan* to present their research findings on factors that impact specific life conditions affecting black citizens of the state. Additionally, they made suggestions as to how these factors could be addressed by policy makers, program managers, and interested citizens. The report was well received in both academic and public service circles, and has often been credited as the impetus behind legislative action to address social inequality in Michigan. Based on the National Urban League's annual report, *The State of Black America,* begun in 1977, *The State of Black Michigan* reports were published through 1993.

This book, *The State of Black Michigan, 1967–2007,* was published not only to remember the events that led to the recognition that social and economic events in cities could not be ignored—by political leaders or academics—but to examine whether society, 40 years later, has actually evolved and grown since those turbulent times.

The research in this book, based on the most up-to-date data, reminds us that the challenge of removing the racial divide and achieving equality between blacks and whites in Michigan remains unmet. The book investigates key questions that concern us all.

Do the ingredients of the explosive mixture in cities that were present in 1967 still exist in Michigan today? What difference has 40 years made? Is Michigan a state with two separate and unequal societies—one black and one white? Has the socioeconomic condition of blacks improved relative to the condition of whites?

It would be a pleasure if I could say that Michigan has met the challenge of the color line and that today, relative to 1967, the condition of blacks relative to whites has improved. However, based on the evidence provided in this book, the social and economic gap based on most indicators has widened since the civil disorders of 1967. These realities demand our attention and should not be ignored, as they were in the years preceding the 1967 riot (which was actually foreshadowed by similar events that culminated in a social uprising in 1943), or dismissed as remnants of our past about which we are now enlightened.

This book is very timely in that its publication follows the passage of Proposal 2, a state amendment to ban Affirmative Action programs that give preferential treatment to groups or individuals, based on their race, gender, color, ethnicity, or national origin, regarding public employment, education, or contracting purposes. The passage of Proposal 2 has effectively eliminated Affirmative Action, an event that has many Michigan residents concerned about the ongoing effort to achieve racial equality in the state.

Topics in the book include trends in the economic status of blacks since 1967, including particulars on business ownership over 5- and 15-year periods; housing and segregation of blacks in metropolitan areas—and the changes that have occurred during these 40 years; health disparities and concerns; crime and punishment of blacks, particularly of young black men; education and dropout rates; and changes in black participation in the political process.

Because many of these topics have been examined in earlier annual *State of Black Michigan* reports, including recommendations for specific actions to be taken to address disparities, the researchers have provided a detailed chapter summarizing their past conclusions and recommendations for addressing them, noting which recommendations were initiated and which remain in legislative limbo. We must use our energy and our creative powers to address the specific, quantifiable issues that hinder the progress of the black community. The data are there. Readers can reach their own conclusions, based on fact, not just rhetoric.

Additionally, like earlier *State of Black Michigan* reports, this book provides recommendations for improving the condition of blacks based on the measured, statistical extent of racial inequality. Recommendations are presented for improving the quality of public schools, reducing dropout rates, and providing greater access to institutions of higher education. Other recommendations include ways to reduce crime and recidivism and to increase black business development.

This book is a valuable resource for policy makers, researchers, students, and all residents of Michigan. It should lead to more informed discussions and debates related to the critical issue of the racial divide and, in the land-grant tradition of applicable research, to addressing—maybe even solving—some of the state's racial disparities.

Throughout the years since the Detroit and related riots drew much needed attention to the plight of underrepresented minorities in the United States, MSU has been a leader in the support of efforts to better understand the persistent problem of the color line. This book is the latest contribution to that effort.

LOU ANNA K. SIMON
President, Michigan State University

Preface

This book is an update of the *State of Black Michigan* reports that were published annually from 1984 to 1993 by Michigan State University's Urban Affairs Programs, in cooperation with the Council of Michigan Urban League Executives. The reports examine the status of blacks in Michigan in a variety of areas, including housing, unemployment, education, business development, health, crime, political representation, civil rights, and the media.

From its inception, Joe T. Darden, one of the co-editors of this volume, was both the Dean of Urban Affairs Programs and the Coordinator of the *State of Black Michigan* project. As coordinator, Darden recruited scholars from higher-educational institutions and organizations in the state to conduct research and write chapters for the annual reports.

These reports were patterned on the annual National Urban League's *State of Black America* reports, which have been published since 1977.

The *State of Black Michigan* reports were the only annual reports on the status of blacks at the state level. Each report contained chapters written from a variety of perspectives, and more importantly, each author presented recommendations, based on research, to improve the socioeconomic and/or political condition of blacks in Michigan.

On each publication date, there was a major press conference attracting reporters from around the state, with occasional national attention. Following the press conference, the annual reports were distributed to policy makers, elected officials, and community leaders throughout the state with the expectation that they might impact legislation to improve the condition of blacks. Indeed, governors and members of the state legislature anticipated receiving these reports from Michigan State University.

This book selects some of the original essays from various *State of Black Michigan* reports and provides new data and analyses to inform the reader about the state of black Michigan today, 40 years after the civil disorders of 1967. The book addresses key questions: (1) What is the extent of disparities in the socioeconomic status of blacks and whites in Michigan today? (2) Given some degree of black political progress via the electoral process, what are the reasons for any persistent racial gaps in the overall quality of life between blacks and whites in Michigan? and (3) Given the numerous past recommendations and the policy makers' response to them, what additional recommendations must be implemented today if blacks in Michigan are to achieve parity with whites?

Reissuing selected essays from the original *State of Black Michigan* reports combined with original essays focusing on the present state of black Michigan should contribute both to a better understanding of the persistent problem of race and to strategies and policies to address the problem of racial inequality in Michigan. The book should serve as a magnet for conversation and debate and, hopefully, action.

JOE T. DARDEN

CURTIS STOKES

RICHARD W. THOMAS

PART 1

Introduction and Overview

Racial Disparities Persist in Michigan 40 Years After the Civil Disorders of 1967

Joe T. Darden

Introduction and Overview: Racial Disparities Persist in Michigan 40 Years After the Civil Disorders of 1967

Mid-July 2007 marks the 40th anniversary of 1967's civil disorders in Michigan's cities. This volume examines changes in the conditions of Michigan's black population and the extent of racial inequality that has persisted since that time.

During the summer of 1967, cities across America were disrupted by severe racial disorder, leading to shock, fear, and bewilderment. Detroit (Michigan's largest city) was the scene of one of the two worst upheavals in the entire nation (National Advisory Commission on Civil Disorders 1968). During a two-week period of rioting, which began on July 23, property was destroyed, hundreds were wounded, and 43 people were killed.

On July 28, 1967, President Lyndon Johnson established a National Advisory Commission on Civil Disorders and directed the commission to answer three questions: (1) What happened? (2) Why did it happen? and (3) What can be done to prevent it from happening again?

The Commission's basic conclusion was that "our nation is moving toward two societies, one black, one white—separate and unequal. White society is deeply implicated in the ghetto: white institutions created it, white institutions maintain it and white society condones it" (National Advisory Commission on Civil Disorders 1967). White racism, according to the Commission, was essentially responsible for the chain reaction of racial violence in the summer of 1967. Among the ingredients of the white racism were segregation and pervasive discrimination in employment, education, and housing.

This volume investigates the following questions about the status of blacks in Michigan today: (1) Are the ingredients of the explosive mixture still present? (2) What difference has

40 years made? (3) Is Michigan a state with two separate and unequal societies—one black and one white? and (4) Have the socioeconomic conditions of blacks improved relative to the conditions of whites?

The editors of this volume have been part of a research team that has raised these questions in the past and has published their findings in a series of 10 annual reports entitled *The State of Black Michigan*. These reports were authored by researchers from leading Michigan universities and institutions and were published by the Urban Affairs Programs at Michigan State University in cooperation with the Michigan Council of Urban League Executives. They address a wide variety of socioeconomic and political topics, including children, youth, families, civil rights, crime, economic issues, education, employment/unemployment, health disparities, housing and residential segregation, the media, and political participation and representation. Regardless of the topic, the conclusion has been the same—racial disparity between blacks and whites in Michigan remains a serious problem, and the gap is widening.

This volume updates these previous reports and addresses the question of black-white inequality since 1967 using the most recent data available. It examines the extent to which racial disparities have been reduced, remained the same, or increased. A variety of social, spatial, economic, and political topics has been selected, including overall socioeconomic inequality, black self-help, black business development, residential segregation, crime, health, and political representation.

Overview of This Book

This first, introductory chapter briefly establishes the foundation for understanding the historical events that led to the civil disorders in Michigan cities during 1967. This is followed by an overview of the present racial disparities in quality of life that still persist. The Conclusion examines the political climate in Michigan from which any public policies must be developed to address the disparities.

Chapter 1, written by Karl Gregory, examines trends in the economic status of Michigan's blacks from 1967 to 1982. In Chapter 2, Gregory measures the progress blacks in Michigan made in the area of black business ownership from 1982 to 1987. In Chapter 3, Joe T. Darden updates Gregory's research by examining the changes in black-owned businesses in Michigan from 1987 to 2002.

A key component of the black struggle for parity has been black self-help. Richard Thomas describes black self-help in Michigan during the eighties in Chapter 4 and updates the efforts by blacks in the area of self-help today in Chapter 5.

Housing and black residential segregation are examined by Darden. In Chapter 6, he assesses the housing situation of blacks in Metropolitan areas of Michigan from 1960, before the civil disorders, and measures any progress between 1960 and 1980. In Chapter 7, Darden focuses specifically on the residential segregation of blacks from whites in metropolitan areas of Michigan from 1960 to 1990. He then updates the data and analysis on black residential segregation by examining the changes from 1990 to 2000 in Chapter 8.

Black health from 1965 to 1985 is examined by Clifford Broman in Chapter 9. Broman, in Chapter 10, teams up with Renee Canady to assess any changes in the health of blacks since 1985.

In Chapter 11, Homer Hawkins examines the data on young black offenders for the period between 1978 and 1987. Hawkins updates the extent to which blacks are impacted by crimes in Chapter 12, in which he examines data for the period from 1972 to 2004.

Chapter 13 focuses on the problem of black and white high school dropouts. Twenty years after the civil disorders, Percy Bates concludes that the racial disparities in high school dropout rates are persistent. These disparities persist not only in secondary schools, but also in institutions of higher education. This is revealed by Walter Allen in Chapter 14. The state of black education in Michigan's public schools, including the topics of high school dropouts, black representation in higher-education institutions, and degrees awarded to blacks, is updated by Darden in Chapter 15.

If progress is to be made in Michigan, some attention must be given to black political participation. Curtis Stokes examines black political participation in Michigan in 1990 in Chapter 16 and, in Chapter 17, updates the extent to which blacks are using the political system for black gains 40 years after the civil disorders.

The final two chapters (18 and 19) focus on past recommendations made by researchers in the *State of Black Michigan* reports, the extent to which they have been implemented directly or indirectly by the state legislature, and whether the state legislature has passed other laws that have been beneficial to black progress toward racial equality. The final chapter also presents new recommendations that must be put into public policy in the future if blacks are ever to achieve parity with whites in Michigan.

Given the state's recent passage of Proposal 2, which eliminates Affirmative Action, the struggle for black equality with whites has become much more difficult. The next section examines the state of overall socioeconomic inequality between blacks and whites since 1967. The discussion begins by providing a summary of the overall socioeconomic inequality between blacks and whites in Michigan, past and present.

Black-White Overall Socioeconomic Inequality, Past and Present

This section examines the extent of persistent black-white inequality in Michigan based on the most recent census data. Among the social and economic indicators considered are unemployment, occupational status inequality, income and poverty, educational attainment, age of housing, value of housing, gross rent, and vehicles available.

Unemployment Rate Differences between Blacks and Whites

Since the 1960s the unemployment rate gap between blacks and whites has varied. The black rate of unemployment has consistently been *twice* the rate for whites throughout most of this period (1967–2004). In 2004, the black rate of unemployment was 14.4%, compared to the white rate of 5.8%. Thus the black unemployment rate was 2.48 times the rate for whites. The black male unemployment rate was higher than the rate for black women. The unemployment rate for black men was 16.4%, compared to 12.7% for black women. When the black unemployment rate is compared to the white unemployment rate, there is even more racial disparity. The black male rate of 16.4% was 2.56 times the rate of 6.4% for white males (U.S. Department of Labor 2006). The next section examines the positions that blacks and whites hold when both groups are working.

Racial Inequality in the Occupational Structure

Since the 1967 civil disorders, the question here is whether racial inequality still exists in the distribution of jobs. Are black workers underrepresented in high-paying, high-status jobs, such as managerial and professional specialty occupations, and in technical, sales, and administrative support occupations? Are blacks also underrepresented in such skilled trades as precision production, craft, and repair occupations?

In other words, are blacks still highly concentrated in the lowest-skilled and lowest-paying occupations, such as service, operations, fabrications, and labor, as they were in 1967? These jobs often involve substandard wages, great instability, uncertainty of tenure, extremely low status in the eyes of both employer and employee, little or no chance for meaningful advancement, and unpleasant or exhausting duties. Is the distribution of jobs still unequal?

To determine the extent of the racial inequality in the occupational structure, the index of dissimilarity (Darden and Tabachneck 1980) was computed for jobs occupied by blacks and whites in 2000. The index assesses the percentage of the employed black population in a given occupation compared to the percentage of the employed white population in the same occupation. The derived values, which range from 0 to 100, indicate the percentage of either race that would have to change occupations to make the percentages equal.

The results of the analysis of racial inequality in the occupational structure in 2000 are revealed in Table I-1. Blacks were underrepresented in management and professional

Table I-1. The Distribution of Occupations between Blacks and Whites in Michigan, 2000

Occupations	Number of Blacks	% of Total Blacks	Number of Whites	% of Total Whites	Difference
Management, professional, and related	118,392	23.4	1,261,138	32.4	–9.0
Service	108,181	21.4	539,742	13.9	7.5
Sales and office	134,647	26.6	1,086,715	25.8	0.8
Farming, fishing, and forestry	513	0.1	17,235	0.4	–0.3
Construction, extraction, and maintenance	27,278	5.4	379,812	9.8	–4.4
Production, transportation, and materials moving	117,151	23.1	690,530	17.7	5.4
Total	506,162	100	3,895,172	100	27.4

Index of dissimilarity = one-half the absolute difference of 27.4 = **13.7.**

SOURCE: Computed by the author from data obtained from U.S. Census Bureau (2000).

occupations compared to whites. While 23.4% of all blacks employed in Michigan in 2000 were in positions of management, professional, and related occupations, 32.4% of all whites employed held these high-status positions. Blacks were also underrepresented in construction, extraction, and maintenance occupations. Whereas only 5.4% of all employed blacks held these types of positions, 9.8% of all employed whites were occupying these positions. Instead, blacks were overrepresented in the lower-paying service positions (21.4%, compared to 13.9% of all employed whites). Blacks were also overrepresented in production, transportation, and materials-moving occupations (23.1%, compared to 17.7% for all employed whites). The index of dissimilarity measuring the extent of racial inequality in the occupational structure was 13.7 (Table I-1).

Racial Disparities in Family Income and Poverty Rates

Table I-2 reports the extent of racial inequality in family income in 2000. The differences are revealing. Whereas 14% of all black families earned less than $10,000 in 2000, only 3.2% of all white families experienced this very low level of income. On the other hand, white families were 2.25 times more likely than black families to be at the very high income level ($200,000 or more). The percentages of black and white families were almost equal at the $25,000–$34,999 income level. The index of dissimilarity, which measures the extent of racial differences in family income, was 23.7. This index demonstrates that there is increasing racial inequality in family incomes. Take 1980, for example. The index of dissimilarity based on black and white family incomes in Michigan was 22.9. Moreover, the median family income of whites in 1980 was $24,167, compared to $15,860 for blacks, a difference of $8,307 (Darden 1984). In 2000, the median family income of whites in Michigan had increased to $56,320, more than doubling since 1980. However, while the median family income of blacks also more than doubled (increasing to $31,720 by 2000), the *gap* in median family income in real dollars *widened*, increasing from $8,307 in 1980 to $20,784 in 2000.

Table I-2. Differences in Income between Black and White Michigan Families, 2000

Family Income	% of Total Black Families	% of Total White Families	Difference
Less than $10,000	13.9	3.2	10.7
$10,000–$14,999	7.5	2.8	4.7
$15,000–$24,999	15.2	8.7	6.5
$25,000–$34,999	12.8	11.0	1.8
$35,000–$49,999	14.6	17.1	–2.5
$50,000–$74,999	17.1	24.7	–7.6
$75,000–$99,999	9.3	15.1	–5.8
$100,000–$149,999	6.9	11.8	–4.9
$150,000–$199,999	1.6	2.9	–1.3
$200,000 or more	1.2	2.7	–1.5
Median family income	$35,536	$56,320	47.3

The index of dissimilarity = one-half the absolute difference of 47.3 = **23.7**.

SOURCE: Computed by the author from data obtained from U.S. Census Bureau (2000).

Disparities in black-white poverty rates contributed to the civil disorders in 1967. In 1969, just two years after the civil disorders, the black poverty rate was 20.6 (Darden 1984). The rate for whites was only 5.7, resulting in a black poverty rate 3.6 times the rate for whites. However, by 2000, the black poverty rate in Michigan had increased to 21.1%, compared to a white poverty rate of 5.0%, down slightly from 5.7 in 1969. Thus the racial inequality gap between black and white families in poverty *widened* between 1969 and 2000. Instead of a black poverty rate 3.6 times the rate for whites, by 2000 the black poverty rate was 4.22 times the rate for whites.

Racial Disparities in Educational Attainment

Educational attainment is measured here in terms of blacks and whites who have received a bachelor's degree or higher level of education. In 1970, only three years after the civil disorders, 2.8% of blacks in Michigan had attained four or more years of college, compared to 7.2% of whites, a gap of 4.4 percentage points. In 2000, the percentage of blacks with a bachelor's degree or higher had increased to 12.8%. However, the percentage of whites with a bachelor's degree or higher had *increased* to 22.6%. Thus, the gap between blacks and whites with bachelor's degrees or higher *widened* between 1970 and 2000, from 4.4 to 9.8 percentage points (U.S. Census Bureau 2004).

Racial Differences in the Age of Housing

The age of housing occupied by blacks differed from the age of housing occupied by whites in 2000. Forty-two percent of all blacks in Michigan occupied housing that was built between 1940 and 1959 and 21.8% occupied housing built in 1939 or earlier. In other words, 64% of all blacks in Michigan lived in housing built in 1959 or earlier. On the other hand, only 25% of all whites lived in housing built between 1940 and 1959, and only 16% lived in housing built in 1939 or earlier. Whites were three times more likely than blacks to live in housing built between 1990 and 2000 (Table I-3).

Table I-3. Black-White Differences in the Age of Housing in Michigan, 2000

Year Structure Was Built	% of Total Black Occupants	% of Total White Occupants	Difference
1990–March 2000	0.7	1.9	−1.2
1995–1998	2.3	7.1	−4.8
1990–1994	2.0	6.9	−4.9
1980–1989	4.9	11.3	−6.4
1970–1979	11.4	18.1	−6.7
1960–1969	14.9	14.1	0.8
1940–1959	42.0	24.5	17.5
1939 or earlier	21.8	16.0	48.1
Total	100	100	48.1

The index of dissimilarity = one-half the absolute difference of 48.1 = **24.**

SOURCE: Computed by the author from data obtained from U.S. Census Bureau (2000).

Table I-4. Black-White Inequality in the Value of Housing in Michigan, 2000

Housing Value of Owner-Occupied Units	% of Total Blacks	% of Total Whites	Difference
Less than $50,000	30.4	7.4	23.0
$50,000–$99,999	44.7	29.9	14.8
$100,000–$149,999	13.3	29.3	–15.0
$150,000–$199,999	6.0	16.0	–10.0
$200,000–$299,999	3.8	11.9	–8.1
$300,000–$499,999	1.4	4.9	–3.5
$500,000–$999,999	0.3	1.3	–1.0
$1,000,000 or more	0.1	0.3	–0.2
Total			75.6
Median value	$69,700	$121,300	$51,600

Index of dissimilarity = one-half the absolute difference of 75.6 = **37.8.**

SOURCE: Computed by the author from data obtained from U.S. Census Bureau (2000).

Racial Inequality in the Value of Housing

The wealth of most residents of Michigan is related in large part to the ownership and value of their housing. Among the black residents in Michigan, only 48.2% were homeowners in 2000, compared to 75% of white residents, a difference of 26.8 percentage points. In other words, whites were 1.5 times more likely than blacks to own their homes. The homes occupied by whites were also of greater value than the homes occupied by blacks. The median value of white-occupied homes was $121,300, which was 1.74 times the $69,700 median value of homes occupied by blacks, a difference of $51,600.

Table I-4 reports the racial difference in the distribution of housing values of blacks and whites in 2000. While 30.4% of all blacks lived in housing valued at less than $50,000, only 7.4% of all white homeowners lived in such low-valued housing. In other words, blacks were four times more likely than whites to reside in such housing. Moreover, 75% of all black homeowners lived in housing valued at $99,999 or less, compared to only 37.3% of all whites. In other words, blacks were twice as likely as whites to reside in such housing (Table I-4). Whites were three times more likely than blacks to live in housing valued at $200,000 to $299,999 and 3.5 times more likely than blacks to live in housing valued from $300,000 to $499,999.

Racial Inequality in Levels of Rental Housing

Unlike whites, 51.8% of blacks in Michigan were renters in 2000, as opposed to 25% of whites. Moreover, the cost of rental units occupied by whites differed from the cost of units occupied by blacks. The median rent paid by whites was $555 per month, compared to $511 for blacks. Table I-5 reports the racial difference in gross rent paid by blacks and whites in 2000. It is important to note that the racial gap in median gross rent was not very wide. Blacks on average paid only $44 less than whites for rent.

Table I-5 shows that 46.5% of all black renters paid less than $500 per month rent, compared to 37% of all white renters. The index of dissimilarity between the gross rent paid by

Table I-5. Black-White Inequality in the Gross Rent of Units in Michigan, 2000

Gross Rent for Renter-Occupied Units	% of Total Blacks	% of Total Whites	Difference
Less than $200	7.3	5.1	2.2
$200–$299	6.3	5.1	1.2
$300–$499	32.9	26.8	6.1
$500–$749	36.6	38.5	–1.9
$750–$999	10.5	13.0	–2.5
$1,000–$1,499	3.1	4.8	–1.7
$1,500 or more	0.4	1.6	–1.2
No cash rent	2.9	5.1	–2.2
Total			19.0
Median gross rent	$511	$555	

The index of dissimilarity = one-half the absolute difference of 19.0 = **9.5.**

SOURCE: Computed by the author from data obtained from U.S. Census Bureau (2000).

blacks and that paid by whites was 9.5, far less of a difference compared to the value of black versus white owner-occupied housing, with an index of dissimilarity of 37.8 (Table I-4). Since there was a gap in the age of housing occupied by blacks versus whites (Table I-3), the difference in the level of rent paid by blacks and whites does not seem to be completely reflected in the differences in age of housing between the two racial groups. Compared to whites, blacks seemed to be paying higher rent for older housing.

Racial Inequality in Vehicles Available

Having a vehicle available (if it runs) is an important resource. It enables a family to go to and from work, to shop at a greater variety of places, and to have greater security in case of a medical emergency. A vehicle is especially important in Michigan, a state that is deeply automobile dependent, as rapid public transit is virtually absent. Table I-6 reports the racial disparity in vehicles available to black and white households in 2000. Almost 20% of all black

Table I-6. Black-White Inequality in Vehicles Available for Michigan Households in 2000

Vehicles Available	% of Total Blacks	% of Total Whites	Difference
None	19.7	5.7	14.0
1	43.8	32.0	11.8
2	26.3	43.1	−16.8
3 or more	10.2	19.2	−9.0
Total			51.6

The index of dissimilarity = one-half the absolute difference of 51.6 = **25.8.**

SOURCE: Computed by the author from data obtained from U.S. Census Bureau (2000).

households had no vehicle available to them, compared to only 5.7% of all white households. In other words, black households were 3.5 times more likely than white households to have no vehicle available. White households were 1.6 times more likely than black households to have two vehicles available. Whereas 43.8% of all black households had one vehicle available, 43.1% of all white households had two vehicles available (Table I-6). The index of dissimilarity between vehicles available to black and those available to white households was 25.8 in 2000.

Conclusions

Forty years after the civil disorders in 1967, racial disparities persist. Some indicators reveal that the socioeconomic gap between blacks and whites in Michigan has actually *increased.* This conclusion is based on an analysis of the most recent census data to assess the social and economic status of blacks and whites in Michigan. The black unemployment rate in 2004 was 2.48 times the rate for whites. The black male rate of unemployment was 2.56 times the rate for white males.

In 2000, as in 1967, blacks were still underrepresented in high-level jobs such as management, professional, and related occupations compared to whites. However, blacks have remained overrepresented in the lower-status service positions. Such low-status positions pay lower wages. Thus, whereas 14% of all black families earned less than $10,000 in 2000, only 3.2% of all white families earned such low incomes. The median family income of whites was $20,784 more than the median family income of blacks. The gap in median family income in real dollars increased from $8,307 in 1980 to $20,784 in 2000.

Although the poverty of blacks was a contributing factor to the civil disorders in 1967, the racial inequality gap between black and white families in poverty increased between 1969 and 2000. Like poverty rates, the gap between blacks and whites with bachelor's degrees or higher also increased between 1970 and 2000.

As in 1967, blacks have remained in older housing to a much greater extent than whites. The evidence shows that 64% of all blacks in Michigan resided in housing that was built in 1959 or earlier. On the other hand, only 40.5% of all whites lived in housing built in that same time frame.

Most blacks have not become homeowners, while 75% of all whites in Michigan own their homes. Moreover, the median value of white-owned homes was 1.74 times the median value of black-owned homes. While blacks were four times more likely than whites to live in low-value housing (less than $50,000), whites were three times more likely than blacks to live in high-value housing ($200,000–$299,999).

Unlike housing value, the racial gap in the gross rent paid by black versus white families was not very wide, that is, only $44. Finally, black households were 3.5 times more likely than white households to have no vehicle available in 2000. This chapter along with the remainder of the book demonstrates that 40 years after the civil disorders of 1967, not only has the socioeconomic gap between blacks and whites persisted, but the gap has actually *increased* based on most indicators.

REFERENCES

Darden, J. T. (1984). Racial disparities persist in Michigan. *The state of black Michigan, 1984* (pp. 173–189). F. Thomas, ed. East Lansing: Michigan State University Urban Affairs Programs.

Darden, J. T., and Tabachneck, A. (1980). Algorithm 8: graphic and mathematical descriptions of inequality, dissimilarity, segregation, or concentration. *Environment and Planning A* 12:227–234.

National Advisory Commission on Civil Disorders (1968). *Report of the National Advisory Commission on Civil Disorders.* Washington, DC: Government Printing Office.

U.S. Census Bureau (2004). *2000 summary file 4 (SF4). Sample data. Michigan.* Washington, DC: USCB.

PART 2

Economic Conditions

CHAPTER 1

Trends in the Economic Status of Michigan Blacks Since 1967

Karl D. Gregory

Chapters in the previous annual reports of the *State of Black Michigan* dealing with economics have focused on a wide range of issues. In 1984, the widespread and persistent economic disparities between blacks and whites were documented. Also presented was an overview of the then current economic condition of Michigan's black citizens (Gregory, 1984). In the following year, a strategic process for economic development in the black community was delineated (Gregory, 1985). In 1986 the series progressed with a detailed report on the trends and then current status of black business development and a description of the technical support services available to these businesses (Gregory and McMurtry, 1986A).

Because 1987 is the 20th anniversary of the rebellion in Detroit, we analyze this year the economic trends since that event. The tracing of changes in the economic status of blacks since 1967 should not be interpreted to mean that all of the trends observed are due to the uprising which began in July of 1967. It started on Twelfth Street and Clairmount in central Detroit as rumors circulated widely concerning alleged police brutality during and after a police raid on a "blind pig" (a place of entertainment which served drinks after the legal hours to do so). According to reports, 43 people were killed and more than 600 were injured. Over $40 million worth of property was destroyed by arson (Kerner, 1968). The arson burned completely the housing of many families, destroyed businesses (or at the very least forced them to relocate or to become engaged in substantial rebuilding and renovation expenses), and reduced the tax base for supporting public services. Gargantuan increases in insurance costs followed when such insurance was available; often it was not.

Previously existing trends in the migration of businesses and households out of Detroit accelerated. Persons who were able to do so often moved, leaving behind a disproportionate share of those with an inability to contribute much to the cost of public services and with a large need for such services. The outward migration also had its impact in reducing the leadership and professional skills available in the central city, as well as the buying power of the remaining residents of the city. These factors also made it easier to rationalize massive disinvestment in residential and productive endeavors, redlining by financial institutions (Bradford and Rubinowitz, 1975), and the seeking of newer homes and other facilities elsewhere in areas that were perceived to have better amenities.

The outward migration of households markedly increased the proportion of the residents of Detroit who were black. This gave rise to a substantial increase in the representation of blacks among elected officials and local government employees. The proportion of blacks on the Detroit Common Council increased, and a black mayor was elected for the first time. Black representation on the Wayne County Commission and the Detroit School District Board also increased.

The net impact of these political developments is unclear. Greater power in public decision-making can be offset by increased unmet needs for public services, as the number rises of the aged and the underclass with a diminished ability for financing public services through taxation.

Care must be taken in reviewing trends since 1967 to avoid attributing too much in a causative fashion to the events of that summer. There have been several other shocks from external sources to the social, political, technological, and economic interactions that have impacted on developments in the last 20 years (Gregory, 1986B). These shocks must also be factored into the historical dynamics of Detroit and the State of Michigan. In addition, there were large cutbacks in federal revenue-sharing and other grant programs.

General Trends

The following general trends are among the factors contributing to the present circumstances of blacks in Michigan. It is difficult to separate the impact of these factors from that due to the events of July 1967; no attempt is made to do so in this chapter.

1. The boycott in the shipping of oil in the Middle East in November 1973 and a related similar reduction in oil supplies in the late 1970s helped to precipitate two major periods of inflation and recession in the United States. This led to modest depressions in the state as a whole, but to severe depressions in the cities of Detroit and Flint and some other Michigan communities with a heavy concentration in durable goods production and a large black population.
2. A significant number of central-city business firms relocated elsewhere, some to the Sunbelt and to the West. Among the reasons for these moves were: to take advantage of the warmer climate, to gain from lower wage rates, and to take advantage of a perceived better business climate. One effect was a reduction in job opportunities for inner-city blacks in Michigan.
3. The overvalued U.S. dollar for several years in this period made U.S. exports very unattractive abroad and induced Americans to increase their consumption of foreign goods. This helped to export U.S. jobs, contributing to high rates of unemployment in Michigan. Blacks were disporportionately affected.

4. Competition increased in the early part of the period, primarily from Japan and some European countries. In the latter part of the period, the increased competition spread to countries like Korea, Taiwan, Singapore, other Pacific Basin countries, Mexico, and a few countries in Latin America. A significant number of blacks are employed in export industries and are impacted substantially by the negative trade balance produced by these and other circumstances.
5. In order to reduce costs and improve product quality, some private firms reacted to these developments by increasing their use of technology. This often resulted in further disporportionate displacement of black workers.
6. A substantial shift took place politically from a liberal and a middle-of-the-road orientation among elected officials in Washington D.C. and elsewhere to positions somewhat to the right, evidencing a more conservative posture. This shift has reflected itself in a greater emphasis on restraining domestic expenditures while expanding outlays for defense and outer space. In addition, more functions have been shifted from the federal government, with its progressive tax structure, to state and local governments with their regressive tax structures. This move has disproportionately affected blacks, who usually have lower incomes than whites.
7. A greater focus was placed on deregulation, including watering down public efforts in support of both affirmative action and minority business development. These deregulation measures reduced black employment and business development opportunities (Swinton, 1987).
8. High levels of residential segregation in 80 percent of the metropolitan areas in Michigan have kept blacks concentrated in central cities (Darden, 1985), away from most of the job opportunities that have moved to the suburbs. Compounded by frequently inadequate public transit systems, the result has been high levels of black unemployment.
9. The status of black students in higher education in Michigan institutions has retrogressed (in terms of access and retention) at a time when the state's economy needs a better educated citizenry. Many of Michigan's public schools fail to provide adequate educational services for both college-bound students and those who enter the workforce directly.
10. Increasingly, major commercial establishments and shopping centers have been located just outside the city boundaries of Detroit and other central cities, resulting in reduced opportunities for black employment. Many large shopping areas have siphoned off the purchasing power from the central city, reducing the number of times that dollars earned by black central-city residents turn around in their own communities, creating jobs and personal income. The result has been to build tax bases, jobs, and income outside the central city, where most blacks live, depriving it of the ability to provide adequately for much needed public services.
11. Plant closings have risen, resulting in a disproportionate impact on black unemployment. The effects of these closings are severe and prolonged because of the lack of adequate retraining programs, health care coverage, and extended unemployment benefits.
12. A powerful collaboration, the white power structure in Detroit, has launched long-range strategic planning without adequate participation at the outset of either authentic black

leadership or female leadership of any race. When the white "haves" are well organized, and the black and female "have-nots" are both poorly organized and uninvolved at the outset, the resultant long-range planning often reinforces the power of the "haves" and continues the "have-nots" in their subordinate status. This circumstance has created the potential for worsening relations between blacks and whites, and between white males and females of all races.

13. Despite the negative trends, the number of black upwardly mobile professionals (BUMP-ies) in Michigan has grown significantly. They have gained from the civil rights movement and its successes, such as the civil rights laws and affirmative action programs. As yet, however, they have not used their skills and high energies to address the problems of a substantially expanded black underclass.

Although these general trends have occurred since 1967, care must be taken to avoid overgeneralizing the impact of what the Kerner Commission referred to as the "Civil Disorder" of 1967 (Kerner, 1968). Other, more specific, trends are discussed in the following sections, and some highlights of the Kerner Commission Report are briefly reviewed.

Specific Trends

Numerous data exist that permit us to review some of the major economic trends since 1967.

Population Growth

Rates of population growth differ greatly by race in Michigan. As shown in Table 1-1, the black population of the state rose by 38 percent to 991,000 persons in the ten years ending in 1970, and then expanded by another 21 percent in the ten years ending in 1980. In contrast, the white population grew by 10 percent in the decade ending in 1970, but remained almost constant in the next decade. Although many factors contributed to this, including differences in birth rates, length of life, and experience with homicide (particularly for young males), the dominant causal factor was the great net outmigration of whites from the state, especially after the 1975 depression. This outmigration continued through 1983. When jobs are not available, persons who have opportunities elsewhere and can afford to move often do so. Compared to whites, blacks had less opportunities to change locale.

Table 1-1. Population in Michigan by Race, 1960, 1970, and 1980, and the Percentage Change

				Percentage Change	
Race	1960 (1,000)	1970 (1,000)	1980 (1,000)	1960–70	1970–80
Black	718	991	1,199	38.0	21.0
White	7,086	7,843	7,872	10.7	0.4

SOURCES: U.S. Department of Commerce, Bureau of The Census, U.S. Census of Population: 1960 Final Report PC (1)-248, *General Population Characteristics Michigan*; 1970 Census of Population, *General Social and Economic Characteristics; Statistical Abstract of the United States, 1970*; 1980 Census of Population, *General Population Characteristics; State and Metropolitan Area Data Book 1986*, U.S. Government Printing Office, 1986.

Income and Its Distribution

The median income and the distribution of income are important measures of how well-off families and unrelated individuals are. Table 1-2 presents data for Michigan for the years 1959, 1969, and 1979. While the number of white families increased from 1959 to 1979 by 17 percent, the number of black families rose by 75 percent. The median income, unadjusted for inflation, rose during the two decades by roughly the same percentage for families of both races—about 260 percent. However, the ratio of nonwhite to white median income, at 68 percent in 1959, rose to 75 percent in 1969, and returned to virtually its 1959 level in 1979 when the ratio stood at 69 percent. Hence, the gains made in the 1960s in increasing the ratio of nonwhite to white income were offset in the 1970s.

Between 1969 and 1979, the Census Bureau, which provides these data, shifted from a nonwhite to a black classification. The term "nonwhite," used in earlier years, includes, in addition to blacks, Aleuts, Asians, and a few other groups, although blacks accounted for over 90 percent of nonwhites. In more recent years blacks have been shown separately.

Table 1-2. The Number of Families and Unrelated Individuals in Michigan, Median Income, and Income Distribution, 1959, 1969, and 1979, and Change in Percents

	1959		1969		1979		Percentage Change 1959 to 1979	
	White	Non-white[2]	White	Black	White	Black	White	Black
Families:								
Total number (000)	1,784	160	1,962	219.9	2,088	279.7	17.0	74.8
Median income, $	6,442	4,407	11,303	8,501	22,841	15,817	254.6	258.9
Percent:								
Below $5,000	31.0	59.0	13.2	26.9	4.7	16.2	−84.8	−73.0
$5,000 to 9,999	50.6	35.2	27.5	33.9	10.7	18.5	−78.9	−47.4
Over $9,999[1]	18.4	5.8	59.2	39.2	84.7	65.4	360.3	1027.6
Over $50,000	NA*	NA*	0.9	0.2	6.9	3.2	NA*	NA*
Unrelated individuals:								
Total number (000)	424	59	609.7	89.3	952.4	154.3	124.6	161.5
Median income, $	1,612	1,476	2,629	2,839	7,209	5,638	347.2	282.0
Percent:								
Below $5,000	83.8	89.5	69.1	65.8	37.5	47.1	−55.3	−47.4
$5,000 to 9,999	14.3	10.1	21.7	28.7	24.0	18.4	67.8	82.2
Over $9,999[1]	1.9	0.4	9.2	5.5	38.5	34.4	1926.3	7600.0
Over $50,000	NA*	NA*	0.1	0.1	0.6	0.2	NA*	NA*

SOURCE: David Verway, ed., *Michigan Statistical Abstract*, 7th ed., 11th ed., and 18th ed., 1968, 1976, and 1984, published by Michigan State University Graduate School of Business Administration, and more recently by Wayne State University Bureau of Business Research.

*Not Available

[1]The over $9,999 category is also included in the over $50,000 category. Hence, the sum of the percent of the income distribution will exceed 100, for the families over $50,000 are counted twice.

[2]In 1959, data for blacks were not shown separately. Blacks were over 90% of nonwhites. Among the groups included in the nonwhite category are American Indians, Japanese, Chinese, Aleuts, Asian Indians, Eskimos, Filipinos, Hawaiians, Indonesians, Koreans, and Polynesians. Bureau of the Census, *Statistical Abstract of the United States*, 1979, p. 35.

Another caution should be observed in interpreting these data. The income data represent money income—that is, cash actually paid out to families and unrelated individuals. In the last couple of decades, there has been a growth in "in-kind" programs, through which subsidies are provided in forms other than cash—for example, food stamps, housing allowances, school lunches, and other forms of assistance. It should therefore be recognized that money income does not reflect all of the resources received by people. On the other hand, it should also be observed that money income does not reflect all of the potential resources that the well-to-do have. Employer-provided fringe benefits, unrealized earned capital gains, and stock options are excluded from the money income of the well-to-do. Also, underreporting of income is much more serious among higher income groups. The money income data are still useful, despite the partially offsetting biases.

The percentage of white families with incomes below $5,000 declined by 85 percent from 1959 to 1979, while the percentage of blacks declined by a smaller proportion, 73 percent. Viewed in another way, nonwhites had twice as large a proportion of families in the income class below $5,000 as whites in both 1959 and 1969; by 1979, however, the situation had worsened. Blacks then had over three times as large a proportion in the income class under $5,000.

Similarly, with the income group between $5,000 and $9,999, white families in the two decades decreased their representation by 79 percent. Blacks decreased theirs by only 47 percent.

Higher up on the scale, the proportion of blacks with family incomes above $9,999 grew more rapidly than that of whites from 1959 to 1979. The larger percentage gain for blacks reflects the very small number of black families above this income bracket in 1959, as well as the increasing black middle class occurring simultaneously with a larger black underclass. Nonetheless, while nonwhites were gaining in the lower middle class, whites were moving into the upper middle class and into groups higher than that. For example, in 1959 there was a 12.6 percentage point gap in family income between blacks and whites in the income class above $9,999. This gap rose to 20 percentage points in 1969 and remained roughly at that level, at 19.3 percent, in 1979. Further, among families with income over $50,000, the proportion for white families rose 6 percentage points from 1969 to 1979, while the proportion for black families rose by only 3 percentage points.

Although the differences are not as great for the incomes of unrelated individuals, the general trends for these individuals are similar to those of families. From 1959 to 1979, the median income for white unrelated individuals rose by more than that for black unrelated individuals, in contrast to a near-equality for families. For both families and unrelated individuals, the proportion of persons with money incomes below $5,000 fell by a smaller percent for blacks than for whites. In the $5,000 to $9,999 income class, however, black unrelated individuals experienced a larger percentage increase than unrelated white individuals.

Little or no progress has been made in this twenty-year period in narrowing income differentials by race, except in the lower middle-class. At the highest income levels, circumstances have worsened considerably. Economic empowerment is a more distant dream than it was 20 years earlier. The *Black Power Imperative* remains (Cross, 1969 and 1985).

Table 1-3. Percentage of Persons Below the Poverty Level,* by Family Status, Aged 65 and Over, and by Race in Michigan, 1969, 1979

	All		White		Black	
Age and Family Status	1969	1979	1969	1979	1969	1979
Persons in poverty status	9.4	10.4	7.8	7.9	22.2	25.8
65 years and older	24.1	12.2	23.0	10.9	36.4	23.5
In Families	7.4	8.7	5.7	6.2	20.6	24.3
Unrelated individuals	35.6	24.1	35.0	21.9	39.2	36.0
65 years and older	49.8	26.0	48.4	23.8	66.1	45.1

SOURCE: U.S. Department of Commerce, Bureau of the Census, *Characteristics of the Population, 1980*, Section 1 of 2, V. 24–108.

*The poverty threshold for a family of four in the U.S. was $9,862 in 1982, $9,287 in 1981.

Reproduced from Karl D. Gregory, "The Economic Status of Blacks in Michigan," *State of Black Michigan:* 1984, Urban Affairs Programs at Michigan State University; and Michigan Council of Urban League Executives, 1984.

Poverty

Another way to observe the lower segment of the income distribution is to review the poverty status of families and unrelated individuals. In Table 1-3, data are shown for persons in poverty by family status and aged 65 and older.

The federal government defines the poverty threshold. It varies from year to year depending on family size, inflation, and other factors. The threshold for a family of four in 1981 was $9,287 and was increased to $9,862 in 1982, an amount that was then three times the average public assistance amount per household in Michigan (Gregory, 1984).

The percent of whites who were below the poverty threshold in 1969 and 1979 remained fairly constant at rates slightly below 8 percent. For blacks, the poverty rate rose from 22.2 percent in 1969 to 25.8 percent in 1979.

Poverty rates by race and state are not available for years between the two censuses. However, poverty rates at a national level show that the number of blacks below the poverty threshold has increased each year from 1978 through 1983. In 1984, the poor declined modestly (U.S. Department of Commerce, August 1985).

Between 1969 and 1979 poverty rates for whites aged 65 and older were cut by more than one-half. For blacks, the rates for these senior citizens were reduced by a more modest one-third. This is an example of a positive impact from governmental intervention, this time in the form of Social Security. It is also an example of how government policy that is aimed at the total population without factoring in the reduction of racial differentials can be successful in its goals while not reducing racial differentials. The percentage point spread between the poverty rates of blacks and whites aged 65 and older remained at about 13 percentage points between 1969 and 1979; but for the aged unrelated individuals, the spread rose from 17.7 percentage points to 21.3 percentage points.

For all unrelated individuals also, the poverty rates for blacks were reduced to a much lesser extent than the poverty levels for whites between 1969 and 1979. The same is also true for senior citizens who were unrelated individuals.

The proportion of blacks in poverty was 2.8 times the proportion of whites in a poverty status in 1969. This ratio rose to 3.3 in 1979. Given the pace of current economic development in central cities where blacks are concentrated, it is likely that the ratio of blacks in poverty to that of whites in poverty will also be higher in 1989 than it was in 1979.

Clearly, the gap between the poverty statuses of blacks and whites appears to have worsened and may still be worsening. The size of this gap would probably be reduced, if there were adjustments available to factor in food stamps, housing allowances, and other in-kind public assistance. The negative trend in relative status would likely persist, however.

Labor Force Participation Rates

The gross deterioration of the relative labor force participation of blacks, particularly black males, is shown in Table 1-4. These participation rates are defined as the sum of the persons who are employed and those who are seeking work but are unemployed, aged 20 years or older, divided by the total population aged 20 or over. The ratio measures roughly the proportion of the population who are working, or actively seeking work if they are not currently working. The participation rate for black males in the state declined by 19 percent from 1970 to 1985. For white males, the decline in the same period was less than 6 percent, or about one-third as much.

Black females have always participated significantly in the work force. Their participation rate has increased modestly during the 15-year period. In contrast, white females, who in earlier decades did not participate in the labor force as much as did black females, increased their participation rate substantially, by 28 percent.

Table 1-4. Labor Force Participation Rates[1] (Percentage) by Race and Sex, 20 Years and Older, Michigan and the Detroit SMSA, 1970, 1980, and 1985

Year	1970	1980	1985	Percent Change 1970 to 1985
Michigan				
Black and other races:				
Males	83.5	71.1	67.6	−19.0
Females	51.5	50.6	52.9	2.7
White:				
Males	82.8	79.6	78.2	−5.6
Females	41.4	49.6	53.0	28.0
Detroit SMSA				
Black and other races:				
Males	83.9	67.7	65.6	−21.8
Females	50.7	51.2	50.4	−0.6
White:				
Males	82.1	81.2	80.1	−2.5
Females	39.1	48.8	53.4	36.6

SOURCE: David Verway, ed., *Michigan Statistical Abstracts*, 1981, 1982-83, pp. 139-140, published by Michigan State University Graduate School of Business Administration, and more recently by Wayne State University Bureau of Business Research; and data from worksheets from the Michigan Employment Security Commission, 7310 Woodward Ave., Detroit 48202.

[1]Defined as the percentage of persons twenty years and older working or actively seeking work.

In summary, for the state as a whole, the participation rate of all males declined, but the decrease was more than three times as great for black males as for white males. The labor force participation rates for females rose for each group; but for white females, starting from a lower level of participation, the increase was 10 times that for black females. Hence, labor force participation is becoming increasingly a white phenomenon in the state, reflecting all of the external shocks to the socioeconomic system that have been previously discussed. Public and private policies have, for the most part, ignored these developments.

The data on labor force participation in the Detroit Standard Metropolitan Statistical Area are comparable to those of the state at-large, with some exceptions. The decline in the male participation rate was larger for black males and smaller for white males than at the state level.

For females, the participation rate for blacks declined modestly, while that for white females expanded at a much larger rate than for the state at large. Looked at in another way, the labor force participation rate for blacks, regardless of gender, was lower in 1985 for the Detroit-metropolitan area than for the state. On the other hand, the participation rate for whites was higher in the Detroit metropolitan area than it was for the state at large. Whites appeared to be doing better in the Detroit metropolitan area than in the state, and blacks appeared to be doing worse in the Detroit metropolitan area than in the state at large. This is partially explained by the disproportionate presence of blacks in the central cities of Detroit and Pontiac, where fewer jobs exist for the unemployed.

Unemployment Rates

The bleak pattern in Michigan regarding the labor force participation of blacks is reinforced by their employment experience in the post-1967 period. A catastrophic black employment experience is shown in Table 1-5 for two nine-year periods. The first is from 1967 to 1976; and the second, from 1976 to 1985. Again, there is a discontinuity in that, prior to 1982, the data relate to nonwhites, of which, as we have previously noted, over 90 percent are black. Beginning in 1982 and continuing thereafter, the data relate to blacks only.

Table 1-5. Unemployment Rates by Race, Persons 16 and Over, Michigan, Detroit SMSA, and the City of Detroit (Percent) 1967, 1976, 1985

	Michigan			Detroit SMSA			City of Detroit		
Year	Total	White	Nonwhite	Total	White	Nonwhite	Total	White	Nonwhite
1967	4.1	3.3	11.0	4.5	3.2	10.9	5.2	2.9	9.8
1976	9.4	8.8	14.2	8.9	8.2	14.1	11.1	11.3	15.0
1985[1]	9.9	7.6	27.8	10.1	6.5	28.9	24.6	13.3	30.7

SOURCE: Michigan Employment Security Commission, Research and Statistics Division, U.S. Department of Labor, Bureau of Labor Statistics, *Current Population Survey*, annually. Data for 1967 and 1985 are unpublished data from the same source.

[1]Blacks only, not other nonwhites, in 1982 and thereafter. Among the groups included in the nonwhite category are American Indians, Japanese, Chinese, Aleuts, Asian Indians, Eskimos, Filipinos, Hawaiians, Indonesians, Koreans, and Polynesians.

In 1967, the unemployment rate for nonwhites in the state was 11 percent, slightly higher than that for nonwhites in the Detroit metropolitan area, and roughly a percentage point above that for nonwhites in the City of Detroit. The nonwhite rate was over three times that for whites at all three levels within Michigan in 1967.

By 1976, the unemployment rate for whites had gone up by 5 to 8 percentage points; and that for nonwhites, by 3 to 5 percentage points. Hence, differentials narrowed.

In the period ending in 1985, the unemployment rate for whites in the state fell by 1.2 percentage points to 7.6 percent, while the rate for blacks almost doubled to 27.8 percentage points. The black/white ratio rose from 1.6 in 1976 to 3.7 in 1985. At the Detroit metropolitan level, the unemployment rate for whites fell by 1.7 percentage points, and for blacks rose by 14.8 percentage points—more than in the state during that same period of time.

In the City of Detroit, the unemployment rate for whites rose by 2 percentage points in the most recent nine-year period. It doubled for nonwhites, going from 15.0 to 30.7 percent. Despite the reported recovery in the state's economy, the unemployment rate for blacks in the City of Detroit has remained at 30 percent or above each year from 1982 to 1985. This unemployment rate is 5 percentage points higher than that which existed for the entire labor force in the nation during the depth of the Great Depression in 1932 (Gregory, 1984).

In the most recent year, 1986, the unemployment rate for whites in the state fell by 0.5 percentage points to 7.1 percent; that for blacks declined by 5.5 percentage points to 22.3 percent. A long recovery can make a difference in the absolute levels of unemployment. In addition to a sustained recovery, targeted policies are required to reduce substantially unemployment rate differentials.

These already high unemployment rates for blacks would be disproportionately higher, if unemployment data were refined to include persons who are working part-time but wish full-time jobs, or who have ceased looking for jobs but would take jobs were they available. This is particularly true in the central city for persons who have ceased looking for jobs either because they believe there are none available, or because there is no transportation to get to those jobs that are available. Such persons frequently stop looking for work due to their discouragement, and then are not counted as being in the labor force and being unemployed. This circumstance results in the extent of real unemployment being greatly understated.

Another bleak circumstance is revealed by the unemployment rates for teenage youths. We have not reproduced these rates, because they are such a small proportion of a sample from the *Current Population Surveys* that the error rate in the numbers is quite large. It is widely believed that in the City of Detroit the unemployment rate for black persons aged 16 to 19 is above 50 percent, not adjusting for the involuntary part-time and discouraged worker. An appropriate adjustment for those two biases would probably elevate this rate substantially above 50 percent.

The concentration of black youths within central cities, combined with a grossly inadequate transportation system, creates a dual labor market. This appears to elevate wages for white suburban youths by creating an artificial scarcity in the labor supply. It also depresses wage rates for black youths in the city. An example is given by the fast-food industry. In the suburban areas, fast-food operators have to pay wages above the minimum wage and to employ many part-time workers, senior workers, and handicapped persons, some of whom they would not have otherwise employed. Such employers frequently complain about the difficulty in filling positions, even with wage scales above the minimum wage.

In the central city, so many black youths seek jobs that employers can pay the minimum wage and do not have to worry about filling positions. There is such an excess of young, willing, and able teenage workers that many employers have not recruited older workers or the handicapped. The breaking down of this dual labor market with its built-in apartheid would be in the best interests of the metropolitan community: central city and suburbs. Discrimination and segregation have high economic and social costs. In the absence of legitimate job opportunities, it is not surprising that some city youngsters turn to car theft, selling drugs, and other illegitimate activities. Since 1967, black teenage unemployment has increased substantially, as has unemployment for black adults.

Black Business Development

Prior to viewing the trends since 1967 in occupational status by race, it would be appropriate to review black business development. This is done much more briefly than the importance of the subject warrants, for this matter was the subject of an extensive study in last year's *State of Black Michigan* report (Gregory, 1986A).

There are two sources of data on black business firms. Neither gives the data that we would like to have on profits, losses, and net worth. The Census Bureau publishes the most comprehensive data, commencing with 1969, but its findings are swamped by the impact of a large number of "ma and pa" establishments. The *Black Enterprise* magazine traces the largest firms annually from 1972 to date.

As discussed in last year's report, the total number of black-owned firms increased from 1969 to 1982, by an annual average of 4.5 percent. This was accounted for, however, entirely by the firms without paid employees. Those with paid employees declined by an annual average of 3 percent. The sales of all firms rose by 4.4 percent on an average annual basis. Firms with paid employees, however, had sales increases of only 2.8 percent. All of these increases in sales were less than the 7.6 percent average annual increase in the Consumer Price Index. One can safely conclude from these fairly comprehensive data that there has been no progress in black business development, viewed on an aggregated basis.

This, however, suppresses a success story which is lost in all of the numbers that are dominated by the 88 percent of firms in 1982 without paid employees and by approximately 1,400 more firms with a relatively small number of employees. This bias in the census data is overcome in part by the *Black Enterprise* magazine annual report. *Black Enterprise* lists annually the top 100 black nonfinancial and nonpersonal service industries. Michigan had seven such firms in 1972, with the largest firm having $18,500,000 in sales, and employing 110 persons (Gregory, 1986A). By 1986 there were 11 firms, with the largest firm having $49.7 million in sales and 880 employees ("Top Black 100 Businesses," 1987). The number of firms fell from 1972 to 1974 when it reached a bottom of 4 during that depression period in Michigan; the number has since risen to 11. The high volatility of the state's business cycle is difficult for all firms, and particularly for black-owned firms.

Given the activity currently taking place in black business development, it is anticipated that the list of Michigan firms within the *Black Enterprise* 100 will continue to expand. Further, there are several other Michigan firms that surpass the $16.6 million threshold of sales for the top ranking 100 firms in 1986. These were not on the *Black Enterprise* list, because they were not in the particular type of industries that *Black Enterprise* includes.

Black Enterprise also has a separate listing for savings and loan institutions, insurance companies, and commercial banks. In each of these three categories there was a Michigan firm. The First Independence National Bank of Detroit is particularly noteworthy for its growth in assets and profits.

Some state governmental policies will have a potentially positive impact on minority business enterprises. The state has pioneered a few creative venture and working capital mechanisms and has made modest funding available that would not otherwise have been within the reach of minority businesses in the state. Worthy of mention particularly are the minority business direct loan program, the Minority Business and Industrial Development Company program, and the minority venture capital company. How these programs operate is described in a newsletter by the Booker T. Washington Business Association (*Public Act 270,* 1984; Gregory, 1987).

New Detroit, Incorporated, has recently developed a new strategy for supporting minority business development. The New Detroit plan concentrates its resources on subcontracting with a minority business development firm as its implementation agency for developing a small number of large firms and for increasing minorities' access to financial institutions. Major corporations will also be encouraged to be more assertive in granting contracts and in doing business otherwise with minority firms. This brief description does not do justice to the program, but more information can be obtained from the Inner City Business Improvement Forum (ICBIF, 1987).

The composition of Michigan's black businesses that made the *Black Enterprise* listing is of great importance with regard to the largely unexploited potential impact of private policy. When the Reverend Leon Sullivan was appointed to the Board of Directors of General Motors, he began an effort to influence GM to promote the establishment of black motor vehicle dealerships. His effort was successful, and other automobile companies followed. It is therefore not surprising that nine of the eleven Michigan firms in the *Black Enterprise* list are automobile dealerships. This circumstance documents what can be done when an industry decides to confront the closed white business society by making a policy decision to do what it can to include minorities. American history awaits the next industry to follow the lead of the auto industry.

Although some fast-food franchisors have made a beginning, a major penetration of the fast-food industry and of the American business mainstream is not at hand. Much has to be done before this will be a fact. Many of the recommendations in the *State of Black Michigan* report of 1986 will have to be adopted if this is to take place (Gregory, 1986A). Indeed, avoiding retrogression will be a great challenge, as high rates of black unemployment continue, together with the previously discussed external shocks to Michigan's business system.

Among the *Black Enterprise* 100, the two black Michigan businesses that are not motor vehicle dealers are auto suppliers. Many other black firms not directly involved with the automobile industry have as their prime customers persons who work for the auto industry.

Occupational Participation

The analysis of the current economic trends affecting blacks would not be complete without a review of their employment participation by occupation and the changes in this participation in the post-1967 period. Data by state are not available showing a year close to 1966 and also a recent year, except from one source, the U.S. Equal Employment Opportunity Commission. This Commission enforces the antidiscrimination provisions of Title VII of the *Civil Rights Act of 1964.* It requires employers to complete an EEO-1 Form. This form identifies their total roster of employees, classified by minority group status, by sex, by occupation, and, in some recent years, by industry (for more detail, see footnote 1, Appendix A).

This data excludes small employers but includes large employers with at least 100 employees at one location. Those with a headquarters and separate locations with 50 or more employees must submit a report for each such location. A comparison in 1983 of national data from the EEO-1 reports with those from the more comprehensive U.S. Department of Labor studies shows that the EEO-1 reports covered in that year 33,681 employers with approximately 35 million workers, or 41.9 percent of the labor force covered by the U.S. Labor Department.

Coverage of employees by industry ranged from over 10 percent for construction to almost 70 percent for durable goods manufacturing. The latter is of great importance in Michigan. Hence, although the EEO-1 data are not comprehensive, their timing meets our needs uniquely, and they span a wide range of workers in Michigan by race, occupation, and industry.

In 1983, the Reagan Administration exempted employers having from 25 to 50 employees from completing the form. This change precludes comparing reliably over time the number of employees in occupations or industries. That change is not as likely to have as great a bias, however, if comparisons are limited to percentage changes in occupations and industries in each year, and if focus on the absolute numbers of employees through time is avoided. It is not likely that the smaller firms that were recently excluded would have a relatively larger proportion of blacks than the bigger firms that remained in the sample in all of the years shown. Any bias that might exist would be to overstate the penetration of blacks in the various occupations and industries in recent history.

As shown in Table 1-6, the percentage of blacks in such white-collar occupations as officials and managers, professionals, technicians, sales workers, and office and clerical workers was very small in 1966, and much below half of the percentage that blacks were of the surveyed labor force (10.6 percent). In 1966, the percentage of blacks in the blue-collar occupations (operatives, laborers, and service workers) was significantly above their percentage of the total population.

From 1966 to 1975 the proportion of blacks employed in all occupations increased by 2.6 percentage points to 13.2 percent, and also rose in each individual occupation shown in Table 1-6. Significant gains were made in each occupation other than laborers. Nevertheless, except for office and clerical workers, blacks in the white-collar occupations remained much below their percentage of the labor force.

In the next nine-year period, from 1975 to 1984, the gains in white-collar occupations were extremely modest. They were generally less than one-half of the gains made in the

Table 1-6. Participation of Blacks in Each Occupation in Michigan, EEO-1 Data, 1966, 1975, and 1984

	Blacks as a Percent of Each Occupation			Percentage Point Change in Participation	
Occupation	1966	1975	1984	1966 to 1975	1975 to 1984
Officials & mgrs.	1.0	4.1	5.6	3.1	1.5
Professionals	1.3	3.8	5.3	2.5	1.5
Technicians	3.9	8.0	9.6	4.1	1.6
Sales workers	3.7	6.1	7.9	2.4	1.8
Office/cler. wkrs.	4.5	12.8	14.1	8.3	1.3
Craft workers	3.3	6.1	6.3	2.8	0.2
Operatives	17.9	21.5	20.2	3.6	−1.3
Laborers	16.5	17.0	12.4	0.5	−4.6
Service workers	22.7	24.0	21.5	1.3	−2.5
Total	10.6	13.2	12.5	2.6	−0.7

SOURCE: Computed by the author from the EEO-1 Survey Data worksheets from the U.S. Equal Employment Opportunity Commission. (See Appendix A.)

earlier nine-year period from 1966 to 1975. This is empirical support for the view that the administration in Washington has had a deleterious effect through its undercutting of affirmative action programs (Swinton, 1987). Note, for example, in Table 1-6 that in the nine-year period from 1966 to 1975, the percentage of blacks among office and clerical workers rose by 8.3 percentage points, while in the following nine-year period ending in 1984, it only rose by 1.3 percentage points, or by less than one-sixth as much as in the former nine-year period. Similarly, the percentage of blacks in the blue-collar occupations (where it had previously risen) declined, and substantially so among laborers. Furthermore, even though the proportion of blacks among the total population rose between 1975 and 1984, the proportion of the employed blacks in Michigan among all occupations fell in the latter nine-year period, despite the larger outmigration of whites from the state. These findings support the view that the growth in jobs in the current recovery has been primarily in non-black areas in our state.

If the economic status of blacks is to improve significantly, the next nine-year period, from 1984 to 1993, must witness a return to at least the rates of increase blacks made between 1966 and 1975 in each of the white-collar occupations. Also, given the relative preponderance of unskilled persons among blacks, the proportion of the blue-collar workers who are black will also have to increase. A continuation of the trends from 1975 to 1984 in the next nine years would imply a locking-in of a larger proportion of blacks into the underclass and would widen the gap between the economic status of blacks and that of whites.

In contrast to Table 1-6, which reviews the participation of blacks in each occupation in Michigan, Table 1-7 shows the proportion of all employees and of black employees who are in each occupation. Instead of viewing shares of each occupation, as was done in Table 1-6, this study now shifts to viewing all employees and black employees in each occupation as a proportion of the totals for all occupations.

Table 1-7. The Participation of All Employees and Black Employees by Occupation in Michigan, 1966, 1975, and 1984

	Participation in Total Employment, in Percents[1]					
	All			Black		
Occupation	1966	1975	1984	1966	1975	1984
Officials & mgrs.	8.0	10.3	11.2	0.8	3.2	5.1
Professionals	5.9	8.0	12.1	0.7	2.3	5.2
Technicians	4.1	4.5	5.9	1.5	2.7	4.5
Sales workers	5.6	7.3	6.9	1.9	3.4	4.4
Office/cler. wkrs.	13.6	13.8	13.1	5.8	13.4	14.8
Craft workers	13.5	12.6	11.3	4.3	5.8	5.7
Operatives	34.4	28.4	23.9	58.2	46.2	38.8
Laborers	8.3	8.1	7.2	12.9	10.4	7.2
Service workers	6.5	7.0	8.3	13.8	12.7	14.4
Total[2]	100.0	100.0	100.0	100.0	100.0	100.0

SOURCE: Computed by the author from U.S. Equal Employment Opportunity Commission Survey Worksheets and U.S. EEOC Report No. 85-105, Washington D.C., 1985. For raw data, and a data base description, see Appendix A.

[1]Percent of the total employees in the occupation.

[2]Slight errors are due to rounding.

Relative gains have been made by blacks in each of the white-collar occupations. The ratio of black workers in the white-collar occupations to all black workers has increased significantly from 1966 to 1984. In 1966, black officials and managers were .8 of one percent of all black workers. Among all workers, without regard to minority status, officials and managers were 8 percent of all workers in Michigan that year. Hence, the ratio for blacks was 10 percent of the ratio for all workers. This ratio was increased, as shown in Table 1-7, to almost 46 percent in 1984, when black officials and managers were 5.1 percent of all black employees, compared to 11.2 percent for all officials and managers. It is clear that an increasing proportion of all black workers are joining the white-collar occupations, but the same is true for the entire work force. Racial differentials in occupational participation, however, are narrowing somewhat.

The greatest narrowing, indeed reversal, of differentials occurred among office and clerical workers. In 1966, the participation rate for blacks was 5.8 percent, which was less than half the participation rate for all workers at 13.6 percent. By 1984, however, this had reversed. The participation rate for black workers was 14.8 percent, as contrasted to a participation rate of 13.1 percent for all office and clerical workers. It appears that whites had moved out of this low-paid white-collar occupation into higher-paid white-collar occupations, and blacks assumed a large share of the employment opportunities in this area.

Among operators and laborers, there was a significant decrease in the share of employment accounted for by all workers, as well as by black workers. There was a disproportionately larger decline for black workers than for white workers. This is particularly regrettable in view of the lesser skills and lower educational levels of many blacks. Blacks

Table 1-8. Changes in Participation Rates by Occupation for All Employees and Black Employees in Michigan, 1966 to 1975 and 1975 TO 1984

	Percentage Point Change in Participation[1]			
	1966–1975		1975–1984	
Occupation	All	Black	All	Black
Officials & mgrs.	2.3	2.4	0.9	1.9
Professionals	2.1	1.6	4.1	2.9
Technicians	0.4	1.2	1.4	1.8
Sales workers	1.7	1.5	−0.4	1.0
Office/cler. wkrs.	0.2	7.6	−0.7	1.4
Craft workers	−0.9	1.5	−1.3	−0.1
Operatives	−6.0	−12.0	−4.5	−7.4
Laborers	−0.2	−2.5	−0.9	−3.2
Service workers	0.5	−1.1	1.3	1.7
Total	.0	.0	0.0	.0

SOURCE: Derived from the previous table and computed from the EEO-1 Survey Data worksheets provided by the U.S. Equal Opportunity Commission. (See Appendix A.)

[1]To illustrate the data, the 2.4 percentage point change in the black participation rate for officials and managers in 1966–1975 is computed from the last table. It is the difference between the 3.2 percent black participation in this occupation in 1975 and that in 1966 (0.8 percent). The other cells are computed similarly. The entries in some cells may appear to be in error by 0.1. This is due to rounding of the calculation from the original data.

need more of the jobs that are available at all levels for which they are qualified, if their disparately high unemployment rates are to be lowered. Among service workers, shares of total employment for blacks and for all workers remained relatively stable in the three years shown.

In Table 1-8, the changes in participation rates shown in Table 1-7 are presented in percentage points by subtracting the values in the former years from those in the latter years.

To narrow the gap between the participation by each occupation in total employment and black employment over time, the participation rates for blacks in the white-collar occupations and crafts must increase by a much larger number of percentage points than the increase in the participation by whites. In the lower occupations, achieving a reduced unemployment rate and a narrowing of the status between blacks and whites requires blacks to maintain their proportions until the total unemployment rates of the two groups have a greater degree of parity. Should parity in unemployment rates be reached, one would then expect increases in the proportion of black workers in the white-collar jobs to be offset by lower proportions in the blue-collar groups, as employment in manufacturing continues to give way to jobs in services and information processing.

The growth in black participation between 1966 and 1975 for the white-collar occupations was significantly larger than nonblack participation in only two occupations—the technical occupations and the office and clerical workers. In all of the other white-collar occupations, the growth in the participation of all workers equaled approximately or exceeded that of blacks.

The participation of all craft workers fell, but that for black workers rose by 1.5 percentage points. In the blue-collar occupations, other than for craft workers, black blue-collar workers had a substantially greater decline in their participation in their work force than did white blue-collar workers. This was particularly true for operators, where black participation fell by 11.9 percentage points—almost twice as much as the decline for white participation. Downsizing of autos, layoffs, and plant closings affected blacks more severely than whites.

The picture is more mixed for the changes between 1975 and 1984. In four of the five white-collar occupations, the increase in black participation was greater than that for all workers. However, the differences were quite small generally in comparison with the changes required in order to narrow the gaps significantly in occupational status by race.

With regard to the blue-collar occupations, black participation among service workers increased slightly more than that for all workers. Although both operators and laborers declined in their participation among the total employees, the reduction in the participation of blacks was much greater than that of all workers.

The conclusion from the analysis of these occupational data is that there has been slight progress for blacks among officials, managers, and technicians. There has been much retrogression for blacks relative to other workers among operatives and laborers, where blacks tend to be concentrated. In the few areas where there have been gains, the gains have been very slight compared with those that are required to close the gaps in participation between blacks and other workers.

Conclusion

This chapter continues the annual analysis of the economic status of blacks in Michigan. The focus this year on major economic trends since the uprising in Detroit in 1967 should not be interpreted as attributing the causation of these trends to that event. Other general forces were at play, including:

- the energy boycott in the 1970s
- an outmigration of businesses independent of the rebellion
- an overvalued U.S. dollar
- increased competition from abroad for U.S. firms
- shifts of political values nationally toward conservatism
- higher levels of residential segregation
- retrogression in enrolling blacks in higher education
- the flight of shopping centers to the suburban ring outside of central cities
- downsizing of cars, plant layoffs, and closings
- decision-making by the white power structure without involving authentic black leadership sufficiently until processes to determine outcomes are in place
- insufficient involvement in community betterment efforts by some of those who have benefited most from the civil rights movement

The analysis of post-1967 occurrences has led to the following conclusions:

The black population in the state expanded by 38 percent in the 1960s, but increased by only 21 percent in the 1970s. The white population rose by only 10 percent in the 1960s, but remained almost constant in the 1970s.

The gains made in the 1960s in the ratio of the median family income of blacks to that of whites were wiped out in the 1970s.

With regard to the distribution of income, nonwhites had twice as large a proportion of families in the income class below $5,000 as whites in both 1959 and 1969. By 1979, black status had worsened to tripling the proportion of whites in that income class. At the upper end of the income distribution, some blacks gained by moving into the lower middle-income classes, while whites were moving up into the upper-income classes on a scale much greater than blacks. Little or no progress has been made overall in narrowing income differentials by race for the masses in Michigan.

The gap between the poverty statuses of blacks and whites has worsened in the last two decades and may continue to worsen. The poverty rates for white families remained fairly constant at below 8 percent in both 1969 and 1979. For blacks, the poverty rate rose from 22.2 percent in 1969 to 25.8 percent in 1979.

The labor force participation rate of black males declined by 19 percent from 1970 to 1985, more than three times as much as the 6 percent decline in the rate for white males. White females increased their labor force participation rate by much more than black females, who have always had a high participation rate.

The labor force participation rates of blacks, regardless of gender, was lower in the Detroit Metropolitan Statistical Area in 1985 than it was in the state. For whites, the labor force participation rate was higher in the Detroit metropolitan area than it was in the state.

The unemployment rate for nonwhites in the state was 11 percent in 1967, more than three times the 3.3 percent rate for whites. By 1985, the rate for blacks in the state rose to 27.8 percent, in contrast to 7.6 for whites. The growth in unemployment for blacks in the City of Detroit was higher than for blacks statewide. Differentials in the unemployment rate racially narrowed between 1967 and 1976, but widened thereafter. Indeed, in the nine-year period ending in 1985, the unemployment rate for whites in the state fell by 1.2 percentage points. That for blacks rose by 13.6 percentage points, reflecting a one-sided recovery.

The unemployment rate for black teenagers has risen and was above 50 percent in 1985. Even this high level may be an understatement.

According to census data, the number of black-owned firms increased by an annual average of 4.5 percent from 1969 to 1982, and their sales in current dollars rose by 4.4 percent a year, less than the 7.6 percent annual average rise in the consumer price index. However, the larger black-owned businesses expanded substantially in number, employees, and sales, as reported in the *Black Enterprise* "Top 100." Most of the larger companies are auto dealers. This demonstrates what the policies of private companies can accomplish when black directors on their boards exert influence and are heard.

Significant gains were made by blacks in entering white collar occupations between 1966 and 1975. But the progress between 1975 and 1984 has been at rates much below those in the earlier period and have not been consistent with the changes needed to approach closing the gaps racially in participation among white-collar workers. This slowing or reversal of progress in recent years is a general theme in much of the data. Even in blue-collar occupations where blacks are disproportionately represented, there has been a relative reduction of blacks in the last nine years. Auto downsizings, layoffs, and plant closings have had a high toll.

A continuation of the trends of recent years would imply a locking-in of a larger number of blacks in the underclass.

The Kerner Commission Report Revisited

Some of the conclusions of the Kerner Commission Report after the events of 1967 are still cogent. For example, consider the following:

Segregation and poverty have created in the racial ghetto a destructive environment totally unknown to most white Americans.

What white Americans have never fully understood—but what the Negro can never forget—is that white society is deeply implicated in the ghetto. White institutions created it, white institutions maintain it, and white society condones it.

If is time now to turn with all the purpose at our command to the major unfinished business of this nation. It is time to adopt strategies for action that will produce quick and visible progress. It is time to make good the promises of American democracy to all citizens—urban and rural, white and black, Spanish-surname, American Indian, and every minority group (Kerner 1968, p. 2).

To continue present policies is to make permanent the division of our country into two societies: one, largely Negro and poor, located in the central cities; the other, predominantly white and affluent, located in the suburbs and in outlying areas (Kerner, 1968, p. 22).

Dr. Kenneth B. Clark, a distinguished and perceptive scholar, was one of the first witnesses to be invited to testify before the Kerner Commission. Perhaps Dr. Clark's skepticism is also still cogent, particularly under current public policies and inadequate private initiatives—nationally, statewide, and local. Referring to the reports of earlier riot commissions, he said:

I read that report . . . of the 1919 riot in Chicago, and it is as if I were reading the report of the investigating committee on the Harlem riot of '35, the report of the investigating committee on the Harlem riot of '43, the report of the McCone Commission on the Watts riot.

I must again in candor say to you members of this Commission—it is a kind of Alice in Wonderland—with the same moving picture re-shown over and over again, the same analysis, the same recommendations, and the same inaction (Kerner, 1968, p. 29).

There are no simple solutions to the problems that beset black Americans and white Americans twenty years after the Detroit rebellion of 1967. The task of building a just society can only be accomplished by committed, informed, determined, unceasing efforts on the part of concerned citizens from all racial groups. A sharing of power in decision-making is critical. Commission reports are not enough, as Kenneth Clark reminded us. Action is required.

It is time now to end the destruction and the violence, not only in the streets of the ghetto but in the lives of people (Kerner, 1968, p. 29).

REFERENCES

Bradford, Calvin P. and Rubinowitz, Leonard S. "The Urban-Suburban Investment-Disinvestment Process: Consequences for Older Neighborhoods." *The Annals of the American Academy of Political and Social Sciences*, V. 422, November 1975, pages 77–86.

Cross, Theodore. *Black Capitalism.* New York, N.Y.: Atheneum Press, 1969.

Cross, Theodore. *The Black Power Imperative.* New York, N.Y.: Faulkner Press, 1985, 907 pp.

Darden, Joe T. "The Housing Situation of Blacks in Metropolitan Areas of Michigan." *The State of Black Michigan: 1985.* East Lansing, Michigan: Urban Affairs Programs, Michigan State University, pages 11–22.

Gregory, Karl D. "The Economic Status of Blacks in Michigan." *The State of Black Michigan: 1984.* East Lansing, Michigan: Urban Affairs Programs, Michigan State University, pages 23–55.

Gregory, Karl D. "Toward a Strategy for Economic Development in the Black Community." *The State of Black Michigan: 1985.* East Lansing, Michigan: Urban Affairs Programs, Michigan State University, pages 47–57.

Gregory, Karl D. and McMurtry, Walter M. "Enhancing Michigan's Black Business Development." *The State of Black Michigan: 1986A.* East Lansing, Michigan: Urban Affairs Programs, Michigan State University, pages 3–25.

Gregory, Karl D. "Five Decades of Economic Trends in Black Detroit." The Fiftieth Anniversary Issue of *The Michigan Chronicle*, Vol. 50, No. 2, September 27, 1986B, page 13E.

Gregory, Karl D. "New Funding Sources for Businesses." *The Booker T. Washington Business Association Newsletter*, Vol. 5, No. 2, February 1987, pages 10 and 11.

Inner City Business Improvement Forum. "ICBIF Strategic and Operational Plan and the Implementation Plan for the Minority Business Development Partnership Plan." Mimeographed, 1987. 1553 Woodward Avenue, Suite 1535, Detroit, Michigan 48226.

Kerner, Otto. *The Report of the National Advisory Commission on Civil Disorders.* New York, N.Y.: A Bantam Book, March 1968, pages 2, 22, 29 and 107 ff.

Michigan Employment Security Commission, Research and Statistics Division, U.S. Department of Labor, Bureau of Labor Statistics, *Current Population Survey*, annually. 1967 and 1976 and unpublished data from the same source thereafter.

Public Act 270. Michigan Strategic Fund. State of Michigan, December 1984.

Swinton, David. "The Economic Status of Blacks, 1986." *The State of Black America, 1987.* New York, N.Y.: The National Urban League, 500 East 62nd Street, 10021, pages 49–64.

"Top Black 100 Businesses." *Black Enterprise.* New York, N.Y.: Earl G. Graves Publishing Co., Inc. Issues 1973–1987.

U.S. Department of Commerce, Bureau of the Census, Washington, D.C., *1970 Census of Population, General Social and Economic Characteristics*, 1970.

U.S. Department of Commerce, Bureau of the Census, Washington, D.C., *1980 Census of Population, General Population Characteristics*, 1980.

U.S. Department of Commerce, Bureau of the Census, Washington, D.C., *Statistical Abstract of the United States, 1970, 1979.*

U.S. Department of Commerce, Bureau of the Census, Washington, D.C., *1970 Census of Population, Characteristics of the Population*, 1970, Section 1 of 2, V. 24–108.

U.S. Department of Commerce, Bureau of the Census, Washington, D.C.: *U.S. Census of Population: 1960, Final Report PC (1)-248. General Population Characteristics, Michigan.*

U.S. Department of Commerce, Bureau of the Census, Washington, D.C.: *Minority Owned Enterprises—Black, 1969, 1972, 1977. 1982.*

U.S. Department of Commerce, Bureau of the Census, Washington, D.C.: "Money Income and Poverty, Status of Families and Persons in the United States: 1984." *Current Population Reports,* Series P-60, No. 149, August 1985.

U.S. Department of Commerce, Washington, D.C. *State and Metropolitan Area Data Book, 1986.* U.S. Government Printing Office, 1986.

U.S. Department of Commerce, Bureau of the Census. Washington, D.C.: *Characteristics of the Population, 1980.* Section 1 of 2, V. 24–108.

U.S. Equal Employment Opportunity Commission, Washington, D.C.: *EEO-1 Survey Data Worksheets, 1966, 1975 and 1984,* and Report No. 85–105, 1985.

Verway, David, ed., *Michigan Statistical Abstract,* 7th ed., 11th ed., and 18th ed., 1968, 1976, and 1984, published by Michigan State University Graduate School of Business Administration, and more recently by Wayne State University Bureau of Business Research.

APPENDIX A

EEEO-1 Data on All Employees and Black Employees in Michigan, 1966, 1975, and 1984[1]

	1966		1975		1984	
Occupation	All	Black	All	Black	All	Black
Officials & mgrs.	110,026	1,151	145,833	5,959	141,099	7,958
Professionals	81,369	1,041	114,156	4,309	152,238	8,112
Technicians	55,931	2,201	63,347	5,065	73,764	7,080
Sales workers	76,746	2,823	103,438	6,360	86,980	6,883
Office/cler. wkrs.	187,042	8,488	196,355	25,195	164,825	23,209
Craft workers	185,937	6,194	179,293	10,929	141,354	8,855
Operatives	472,627	84,671	404,108	87,027	300,655	60,792
Laborers	113,925	18,844	114,432	19,493	90,730	11,261
Service workers	88,944	20,156	99,483	23,855	104,626	22,535
Total	1,372,547	145,569	1,420,445	188,192	1,256,271	156,685

SOURCE: U.S. Equal Employment Opportunity Commission, EEO-1 Report Summary worksheets for Michigan 1966, 1975, 1984, made available to the author in January 1987, from the Office of Program Research, Survey Divisions, 2401 E. Street, N.W., Washington, D.C. 20507.

[1]EEO-1 data are collected by the U.S. Equal Employment Opportunity Commission under Title VII of the *U.S. Civil Rights Act of 1964*. Private employers have had to submit data since 1966 on employment by sex and for each of four minority groups: blacks, Hispanics, Asians or Pacific Islanders, and American Indians or Alaskan Natives. Such data have the advantage of being the only source of fairly comprehensive and recent data on the employment of minorities by industry and occupation. (The Census data give such information every ten years with at least a three-year lag to publication.)

In the years before 1983, employers with less than 50 employees did not have to file EEO-1 reports. After 1983, the limit for non-filing was increased, in a much protested move by the Reagan administration, to 100 employees, with certain exceptions, particularly federal contractors with 50 or more employees. "While each single-establishment employer submitted only one EEO-1 report, those employers with at least 100 employees whose business was conducted at more than one location were required to submit a company-wide consolidated report, a headquarters report and individual reports for each establishment having 50 or more workers ... In 1983, a total of 33,681 employers with approximately 35 million workers filed EEO-1 reports." In 1983, these surveys covered 41.9 percent of comparable data from the Bureau of Labor Statistics of the U.S. Department of Labor and had the advantage of being classified by race and state. U.S. Equal Employment Opportunity Commission, *Equal Employment Opportunity Report-1983*, Report No. 85-105, June 1985, pp. 1-6.

Unfortunately, the data do not permit analysis of the level of employment within industries and occupations. Blacks and women tend to be concentrated at entry and middle levels of white-collar occupations in most industries.

CHAPTER 2

Black-Owned Businesses in Michigan, 1982–1987, and the Top 31 in 1989

Karl D. Gregory

This chapter updates a previous report. In the annual *State of Black Michigan* series, the third report (released in 1986) contained a chapter entitled "Enhancing Michigan's Black Business Development." Using the most current data then available, the 1986 chapter analyzed the status of black-owned businesses, surveyed the major programs in Michigan to support black business development, and presented several recommendations for change. The earlier chapter rationalized the importance of black business development by stating:

> A people cannot survive and prosper with dignity in a capitalist country without capital. Capital (wealth) can be generated by business development. The creation and ownership of wealth increases jobs, enhances the tax base for supporting public services, and provides the owners of wealth with a basis for financing consumption. Wealth constitutes collateral against which one may borrow, gives pride and self-esteem that stems from being self-supporting, and lessens the incentive for illegal activities and the resulting victimization rates. Families with wealth are better able to stay together and face the future with confidence.
>
> Black families have much less wealth and income from wealth—profits, interest payments, rent, and dividends—than white families. Most of the wealth black families have is in home ownership. The major other form of wealth is in church property.

In July 1990, the Census Bureau updated to 1987 the previous 1982 data upon which the earlier study in this series was primarily based. The new edition of the *Survey of Minority-Owned Enterprises—Black 1987* presents recent statistics on the number of black-owned firms and their receipts; and for black-owned firms with paid employees, the same data plus the number of employees and payrolls.

The data enable a review of black business development in various geographic areas within Michigan in 1987 and a comparison of this development between 1982 and 1987 with that in the U.S. The data also permit an analysis of the number and sales of black-owned firms in the state of Michigan and contrasted to other states. Additional information from *Crain's Detroit Business* and from *Black Enterprise* magazine is employed in discussing the status of the largest 31 firms. Unfortunately, statistics on the profits of these firms are not available. This chapter summarizes the available data and adds to the recommendations made in the earlier study.

Terminology and Limitations of the Survey Data

The term "African-American" is used synonymously with the census term "black." Black-owned firms are defined by the Census Bureau as firms in which 50 percent or more of the ownership is by blacks.

The Census Bureau surveys blacks, other minorities, and women each five years, but the report is not published until three years after the survey. Hence, the next update will be for 1992 and will not be available until 1995.

The surveys have historically included partnerships and sole proprietorships, and have provided estimates for all corporations. In the 1987 survey, corporations other than subchapter S firms were excluded for the first time by the Bureau of the Census. (Subchapter S corporations are designated by the U.S. Internal Revenue Service; they are firms with 35 or fewer shareholders who choose for income tax purposes to be taxed as individual shareholders rather than as a corporation.)

The explanation given for the 1987 exclusion of corporations other than subchapter S firms is that the earlier reports used less-than-systematic methods to obtain data regarding the race of the owners of these firms. Race information was obtained more systematically for the firms included in the 1987 *Survey* by checking the Social Security number of the owner on tax returns and other records against the Social Security records that identify race. Records for other corporations, unlike those for subchapter S firms, have an employer identification number that is not recorded on Social Security files designating race. Therefore, the race of owners for earlier reports had to be obtained by improvised and not always reliable means.

The exclusion of corporations other than those in the subchapter S category may have resulted in an underestimate of the growth in the number, sales, employees, and payrolls of black-owned firms from 1982 to 1987. The underestimate may have been ameliorated, at least in part, by a tax change that promoted the use of the subchapter S form of organization—a change that resulted in a substantial growth in the number of these corporations. Some regular corporations, sole proprietorships, and partnerships undoubtedly shifted to subchapter S status.

The difference in the definition of firms limits the time period and number of comparisons that can be analyzed. For some analyses, the Census Bureau did offset the problem of a changed definition by recomputing and presenting the 1982 data, using the same definitions as those employed for 1987.

This adjustment was not made for years prior to 1982, however, nor for some data in the 1982 *Survey*. All comparisons in this study involve data without this limitation, since the author obtained special, previously unpublished retabulations from the Census Bureau for some 1982 data, using the definitions for 1987.

Another limitation of the data arises because 1982 was the low point of a national recession with a severe impact in Michigan. In contrast, 1987 represented a high level of business activity after five years of a sustained upswing in the national economy. This is expected to exaggerate in an unknown magnitude any apparent progress in black business development.

The exaggeration may be compounded by the unavoidable lag between the 1987 survey date and the preparation of this study during the recession in 1991. The ebullient conditions of 1987 in the national economy no longer exist. It is already apparent that the recession has had a deleterious impact on many firms (especially black-owned firms) in late 1990 and early 1991, as evidenced by tough times for auto dealers and auto suppliers and by a slowdown in the construction industry, among other similarly affected business enterprises.

Despite these limitations, analysis of the data does lead to useful and interesting findings.

Michigan Compared with the United States, 1987

In 1987, there were 13,695,000 U.S. firms, of which 3.1 percent (or 424,200) were owned by African-Americans. The total receipts for all U.S. firms were $1,995 billion; of this amount, $19.8 billion (1.0 percent) were received by the nation's black-owned firms (Table 2-1). Average receipts per firm nationally for all firms were more than three times as large as those for African-American firms ($145,670 compared with $46,589) (computed from data in Table 2-1).

Table 2-1. The Number and Receipts of All Firms and Black-Owned Firms* in Michigan and The U.S. and Firms with Paid Employees in 1987

	Michigan			United States		
		Black-Owned			Black-Owned	
Item	All	Number	Percent	All	Number	Percent
All Firms						
Number (000)	426.7	13.7	3.2	13,695	424.2	3.1
Receipts ($,000,000)	63,900	701.3	1.1	1,994,808	19,762.9	1.0
Firms With Paid Employees						
Number (000)	103.4	2.2	2.1	3,487	70.8	2.0
Percent	24.2	16.3	67.4	25.5	16.7	65.4
Receipts ($,000,000)	56,256	524.6	0.9	1,709,301	14,130.4	0.8
Percent	88.0	74.8	85.0	85.7	71.5	83.4

SOURCE: U.S. Department of Commerce, Bureau of the Census, *Survey of Minority-Owned Business Enterprises—Black, 1987*, July 1990, p. 11; and calculations by the author.

*Excludes corporations other than subchapter S (i.e., legally incorporated firms with 35 or fewer shareholders who elect under IRS rules to be taxed as individual shareholders rather than as corporations). Black-owned business firms are defined as firms in which 50 percent or more of the ownership is black. Data are obtained on a confidential basis using IRS, Census, and Social Security files. Comparability over time is affected by differences in definitions, business units covered, inability to obtain responses from all cases, reporting errors, mistakes in recording, and imputations.

Located in Michigan were 426.7 thousand firms, of which 13.7 thousand (or 3.2 percent) were black-owned firms. The black-owned firms accounted for $701.3 million in receipts, or 1.1 percent of the total ($63.9 billion) for all firms in the state. Average receipts per firm ($149.8 thousand) for all firms in the state were also about three times those for African-American businesses ($51.2 thousand) (computed from data in Table 2-1).

Only 24.2 percent of all firms in Michigan, and 16.3 percent of black-owned firms, had paid employees. Generally, these firms had a greater amount of receipts per firm than did firms without paid employees. The comparable data for the U.S. were 25.5 and 16.7 percent, respectively. The remainder were largely "ma and pa" establishments; among African-Americans, these were a larger proportion of all firms, in both the state and the U.S.

Michigan had 103.4 thousand firms with paid employees in 1987, only 2.2 thousand of which were owned by African-Americans. The receipts of all firms in Michigan with paid employees amounted to $56.3 billion, and of black-owned firms, $524.6 million, or 0.9 percent of that for all firms (Table 2-1). Clearly, with about 14 percent of the state's population, and only 2.1 percent of the firms and less than 1 percent of receipts, African-Americans have scarcely begun to penetrate business ownership.

All firms with paid employees in Michigan had average receipts per firm of $544.1 thousand, in contrast to $234.1 thousand for African-Americans (computed from data in Table 2-1). In this respect, both groups of firms were faring modestly better than their counterparts in the nation as a whole. Receipts per firm nationally averaged $490.2 thousand, compared with $202 thousand for black-owned firms alone. This no doubt reflects the greater industrialization of Michigan when compared with that of the nation as a whole.

An indication whether African-American firms are more frequently launched and sell better in Michigan than in other areas is provided by relating the number of firms to the size of the population. While blacks in 1990 were 13.9 percent of Michigan's population, and 11.1 percent of the nation's, according to census data, in 1987 they owned only 2.1 percent of the firms with paid employees in the state, compared with 2.0 in the nation (Table 2-2).

One might expect this slightly higher performance in the state to be associated with Michigan's edge in the proportion of the black population. Other related factors could include differences by geographic area in the distribution of entrepreneurial propensities, the level of government support, the quality of business education, the density of the black population, the degree of urbanization, the availability of capital, the observance of affirmative action guidelines by the private sector regarding minority business development, the patronage given to minority businesses within the minority community and by nonminorities, and the average income per capita, among other forces. The formal examination of these factors was beyond the scope of this study.

The penetration of the business sector in the nation and the state, holding population constant, can be gauged by comparing all firms and black-owned firms with paid employees in 1987 per 10,000 population in 1990. Michigan's level of business ownership lags behind that of the nation as a whole once population size is taken into account. The U.S. had a total of 140 firms (as defined in the census study) per 10,000 population, compared with 110 for the state; and 24 black-owned firms nationally, compared with 17 in Michigan (Table 2-2). The reasons for such differences require further study.

Table 2-2. Total Population and Black Population in 1990*, Firms in 1987 with Paid Employees, and Firms per 10,000 Population, in Michigan and The U.S.**

	Michigan			United States		
Item	All	Black	Percentage Black	All	Black	Percentage Black
Population, 1990 (000 except %)	9,295.3	1,291.7	13.9	248,709.9	29,986.1	11.1
Firms, 1987, with paid employees (000 except %)	103.4	2.2	2.1	3,487	70.8	2.0
Firms with paid employees per 10,000 population	110	17	—	140	24	—

SOURCE: U.S. Department of Commerce, Bureau of the Census, *Survey of Minority-Owned Business Enterprises—Black, 1987*, July 1990, p. 11; population data for 1990 from a Census pre-publication press release, "Census Bureau Completes Distribution of 1990 Redistricting Tabulations to States," Census Public Information Office, March 11, 1991, Table 1; and calculations by the author.

*Although admitting a 2 percent undercount nationally, affecting mainly minorities, the Department of Commerce has declined to make an adjustment in the population counts for 1990. Several governmental units, including the City of Detroit, are appealing the Department of Commerce decision in the courts.

**Excludes corporations other than subchapter S (i.e., legally incorporated firms with 35 or fewer shareholders who elect under IRS rules to be taxed as individual shareholders rather than as corporations). Black-owned business firms are defined as firms in which 50 percent or more of the ownership is black. Data are obtained on a confidential basis using IRS, Census, and Social Security files. Comparability over time is affected by differences in definitions, business units covered, inability to obtain responses from all cases, reporting errors, mistakes in recording, and imputations.

Michigan Compared with Other States

Among the 16 states with over 2,000 black-owned firms with paid employees in 1987, Michigan ranked 15th in the number of such firms. It was exceeded by California, which ranked 1st, followed by New York, Illinois, Ohio, and 10 Southern states. California had over three times as many black-owned firms as Michigan; and Texas, Florida, and New York had about twice as many. Even Mississippi and Alabama surpassed Michigan, but not by much (Table 2-3).

In terms of receipts obtained by African-American firms with paid employees in 1987, Michigan ranked 10th, with $525 million. This compares with $1.6 billion in California, $1.3 billion in New York, and over $800 million in Florida, Georgia, and Illinois. Also surpassing Michigan were Texas, North Carolina, Virginia, and New Jersey.

Michigan ranked 11th in the number of persons employed by black-owned firms with paid employees. Such Michigan firms employed 8,485 persons, compared with 22,631 in California and over 10,000 in 7 other states (Table 2-3).

Michigan ranked higher (4th) with respect to average receipts per firm ($234,000). New Jersey led all states with $337,000. Also exceeding Michigan were New York with $296,000 and Illinois with $271,000. This low level of average receipts suggests that, except for a few large firms, black-owned firms have tended to be small.

For example, the lowest ranking of the 1987 "Top 100" firms listed in *Black Enterprise* magazine, published in June 1988, was D.L. & J. Services, Inc. of Pennsylvania, which had

Table 2-3. Statistics for Black-Owned Firms* with Paid Employees in States with Over 2,000 Such Firms, 1987

	Firms with Paid Employees							
			Receipts				Receipts Per Firm	
State	Number	Rank	$(000,000)	Rank	Employees	Rank	($000)	Rank
California	7,614	1	1,619	1	22,631	1	213	6
Texas	5,570	2	679	7	12,374	4	122	15
Florida	4,919	3	830	4	13,583	3	169	10
New York	4,438	4	1,315	2	16,799	2	296	2
Georgia	4,079	5	916	3	12,306	5	225	5
North Carolina	3,843	6	529	9	10,930	7	138	12
Virginia	3,530	7	610	8	11,094	6	173	9
Illinois	3,014	8	816	5	10,655	8	271	3
Maryland	2,689	9	452	11	7,248	12	168	11
Louisiana	2,611	10	347	14	5,259	16	133	14
South Carolina	2,567	11	290	16	6,888	13	113	16
Ohio	2,548	12	440	12	8,888	10	173	8
Alabama	2,337	13	321	15	5,562	15	137	13
Mississippi	2,249	14	410	13	5,760	14	182	7
Michigan	2,241	15	525	10	8,485	11	234	4
New Jersey	2,169	16	731	6	8,969	9	337	1

SOURCE: U.S. Department of Commerce, Bureau of the Census, *Survey of Minority-Owned Business Enterprises—Black, 1987*, July 1990, p. 8; and calculations by the author.

*Excludes corporations other than subchapter S (i.e., legally incorporated firms with 35 or fewer shareholders who elect under IRS rules to be taxed as individual shareholders rather than as corporations). Black-owned business firms are defined as firms in which 50 percent or more of the ownership is black. Data are obtained on a confidential basis using IRS, Census, and Social Security files. Comparability over time is affected by differences in definitions, business units covered, inability to obtain responses from all cases, reporting errors, mistakes in recording, and imputations.

sales of $3.1 million. In contrast, the lowest ranking company in the 1987 "Top 500" listed in the April 25, 1988 issue of *Fortune* magazine was M.A. Hanna of Cleveland, a firm that had sales of $459 million. Indeed, the *Black Enterprise* "Top 100" had combined sales of $4.1 billion in 1987. According to the same issue of *Fortune*, the firm ranking 109th in 1987, Scott Paper of Philadelphia, had sales equal to all the *Black Enterprise* "Top 100" firms together.

Table 2-4 presents the same data by state on the number of firms (those with paid employees and located in states having over 2,000 black-owned firms in 1987) as in Table 2-3, but controls for the total and for the black population. The ranking of black firms per 10,000 of the population on both population bases differs considerably from the rankings of the total numbers of firms in the prior table.

When standardized against the African-American population, California still ranks 1st with 34 firms per 10,000; Florida, 3rd (28); and Michigan, 15th (17) among the 16 top states. The selected Southern states, except primarily for Louisiana, have higher rankings when the data are controlled by population.

The Midwestern and Eastern states, apart from New York, remain quite low in the rankings. New York ranked 4th without a relationship to population and last (16th) with 16 per

Table 2-4. Black-Owned Firms* in 1987 with Paid Employees, and Per 10,000 of the Total and Black Population in 1990 for States with Over 2,000 Such Firms in 1987**

	Black-Owned Firms in 1987 per 10,000 Population				Population in 1990			
	Black		Total					
State	Number	Rank	Number	Rank	Black (000)	Total (000)	Black-Owned Firms	Rank
California	34	1	.26	13	2,209	29,760	7,614	1
Virginia	30	2	.57	7	1,163	6,187	3,530	7
Florida	28	3	.38	9	1,760	12,938	4,919	3
Texas	28	4	.32	10	2,022	16,987	5,570	2
North Carolina	26	5	.58	5	1,456	6,629	3,843	6
South Carolina	25	6	.74	2	1,040	3,487	2,567	11
Mississippi	25	7	.87	1	915	2,573	2,249	14
Georgia	23	8	.63	3	1,747	6,478	4,079	5
Alabama	23	9	.58	6	1,021	4,041	2,337	13
Maryland	23	10	.56	8	1,190	4,781	2,689	9
Ohio	22	11	.23	16	1,155	10,847	2,548	12
New Jersey	21	12	.28	11	1,037	7,730	2,169	16
Louisiana	20	13	.62	4	1,299	4,220	2,611	10
Illinois	18	14	.26	12	1,694	11,431	3,014	8
Michigan	17	15	.24	15	1,292	9,295	2,241	15
New York	16	16	.25	14	2,859	17,990	4,438	4

SOURCE: U.S. Department of Commerce, Bureau of the Census, *Survey of Minority-Owned Business Enterprises—Black, 1987*, July 1990, p. 8; Bureau of the Census, Public Information Office Press Release, March 11, 1991, CB91-100, "Census Bureau Completes Distribution of 1990 Redistricting Tabulations to States," Table 2; and calculations by the author.

*Excludes corporations other than subchapter S (i.e., legally incorporated firms with 35 or fewer shareholders who elect under IRS rules to be taxed as individual shareholders rather than as corporations). Black-owned business firms are defined as firms in which 50 percent or more of the ownership is black. Data are obtained on a confidential basis using IRS, Census, and Social Security files. Comparability over time is affected by differences in definitions, business units covered, inability to obtain responses from all cases, reporting errors, mistakes in recording, and imputations.

**Although admitting a 2 percent undercount nationally, affecting mainly minorities, the Department of Commerce has declined to make an adjustment in the population counts for 1990. Several governmental units, including the City of Detroit, are appealing the Department of Commerce decision in the courts.

10,000 of population. It has a comparatively large number of black-owned firms, but does poorly in relationship to its black population. Although this study does not analyze the possible causative factors, population density, public transportation and residential mobility, and the cultural cohesion of the black population may be among the more important forces. Density and cultural cohesion are expected to relate positively with business formation and sustainability, while population mobility is expected to relate negatively.

When black-owned firms are standardized against the entire population for each of the selected states, the element of nonblacks buying from black-owned businesses enters into the analysis. This variable interacts with the proportion of blacks in the total population, among other variables, some of which have been noted in the preceding discussion. In this analysis, Mississippi rises to the top of the states with .87 black-owned firms per 10,000 of the total population, and California falls from first place to 13th, near the bottom, with .26 black-owned firms per 10,000 of the total population.

Michigan does not distinguish itself in this analysis either, for it ranks 15th among the 16 selected states. Except Texas, the Southern states (this time including Louisiana) tend to rank higher than the states in the other regions. The Midwestern and Eastern states continue to do poorly.

In absolute magnitudes, black-owned firms had a high of .87 firms per 10,000 of the total population, blacks and nonblacks together, in Mississippi, and a low of .23 in Ohio—just below Michigan's .24 per 10,000 of the total population.

Trends in Michigan and the U.S.

Between 1982 and 1987, the number of all African-American firms in the U.S. expanded by 37.5 percent, and those with paid employees by 87.1 percent. This growth was about 50 percent greater than Michigan's performance (computed from data in Table 2-5). All of these Michigan firms expanded in number by 25.2 percent, and those with paid employees by 58.3 percent to 2,241 such firms in 1987. In the same year, there were 11,467 firms in the state without any paid employees—83.7 percent of all black-owned firms (computed from data in Table 2-5).

In the same five-year period, the rate of expansion (based on receipts) was slightly greater for black-owned firms in Michigan than for their counterparts in the nation as a whole. The receipts of all African-American firms in this state expanded by 110.9 percent, compared with 105.4 percent for the U.S. The receipts of Michigan black-owned firms without paid employees grew by 34.0 percent-less than the rate for those in the U.S. as a whole (43.9 percent). For firms with paid employees, the rate of increase was greater in Michigan than in the U.S.—162.2 percent, compared with 147.7 percent.

The larger firms in Michigan outperformed the smaller ones—and by a wide margin. Of the $369 million increase in sales by black-owned companies in Michigan in the period, firms with paid employees accounted for $325 million, and other firms accounted for $44 million (computed from data in Table 2-5).

The size of firms grew substantially, as measured by receipts, in both Michigan and the U.S., even after adjusting for inflation, and particularly so for firms with paid employees. The Consumer Price Index increased in the period by 17.7 percent in the U.S. and by 15.4 percent in Michigan (Table 2-5)—much less than the change in receipts measured in current dollars.

The combination of a smaller growth in the number of black-owned firms (with paid employees) and a larger expansion of receipts in Michigan than in the U.S. as a whole produced a positive result—a larger increase in the state in the average receipts per firm. Viability requires the expansion of receipts per firm. In 1982, the average receipts for black-owned firms (with paid employees) in the U.S. ($151,000) were greater than the average receipts in Michigan ($141,000). This was reversed in 1987, when the average receipts per firm in the U.S. were $200,000, in contrast to $234,000 in Michigan, a gain of 32.4 percent in the U.S., compared with 66.0 in Michigan (computed from data in Table 2-5).

Table 2-5. Trends in the Number, Receipts, Employees, and Payroll of Black-Owned Firms* in Michigan and the United States, 1982–1987, with and without Paid Employees**

	Michigan				United States				Percent Change 1982–1987	
	1987		1982		1987		1982			
Item	Number	%	Number	%	Number	%	Number	%	Mich.	U.S.
All firms	13,708		10,947		424,165		308,260		25.2	37.5
W/out paid employees	11,467	83.7	9,531	87.1	353.350	83.3	270,419	87.7	20.3	30.7
With paid employees	2,241	16.3	1,416	12.9	70,815	16.7	37,841	12.3	58.3	87.1
Receipts ($)	(000,000)		(000,000)		(000,000)		(000,000)			
All firms	701		332		19,763		9,619		110.9	105.4
W/out paid employees	176	25.2	132	39.8	5,633	28.5	3,914	40.7	34.0	43.9
With paid employees	525	74.8	200	60.1	14,130	71.4	5,705	59.3	162.2	147.7
Avg. receipts per firm	.234		.141		.200		.151		66.0	32.4
	Number		**Number**		**Number**		**Number**		**%**	**%**
Employees in firms with paid employees	8,485		4,222		220,667		121,373		101.0	81.6
Avg. receipts per employee ($)	61,824		47,395		64,093		47,000		30.5	36.4
Avg. employees per firm	3.8		3.0		3.1		3.2		26.7	<0.3>
Annual payroll in firms with paid employees ($,000)	91,991		29,500		2,761,105		948,108		218.3	191.2
Avg. payroll per employee	10.8		7.0		12.4		7.8		54.3	59.0
Consumer Price Index, Detroit Metro Area, 1982–84 = 100	111.9		97.0		113.6		96.5		15.4	17.7

SOURCE: U.S. Department of Commerce, Bureau of the Census, *Survey of Minority-Owned Business Enterprises—Black, 1987,* July 1990, p. 8. Greater Detroit/Southeast Michigan Business Expansion and Attraction Council, *1989 Economic Fact Book,* September 1989, p. 35; and calculations by the author.

*Excludes corporations other than subchapter S (i.e., legally incorporated firms with 35 or fewer shareholders who elect under IRS rules to be taxed as individual shareholders rather than as corporations). Black-owned business firms are defined as firms in which 50 percent or more of the ownership is black. Data are obtained on a confidential basis using IRS, Census, and Social Security files. Comparability over time is affected by differences in definitions, business units covered, inability to obtain responses from all cases, reporting errors, mistakes in recording, and imputations.

**Includes 50 states and the District of Columbia.

In the same five-year period, the total employees in African-American firms doubled in Michigan to reach 8,485 in 1987, but only increased 81.6 percent in the nation. Reflecting this greater growth of employees in Michigan, average receipts per employee increased in Michigan by less than in the U.S. (30.5 vs. 36.4 percent); and average employees per firm rose in Michigan by more than in the U.S. (126.7 vs. <0.3> percent). It is not clear whether this was because of declining productivity, changing industry mix effects, or other reasons. Also, annual payroll increased more in Michigan than in the U.S. (218.3 vs. 191.2 percent), but not-payroll per employee (54.3 vs. 59.0 percent).

The small average payroll per employee at $10,000 in 1987, up from $7,000 in 1982, may be misleading. It represents an unknown combination of factors, perhaps including a relatively low average rate of compensation, part-time employment, a disproportionate presence of small service-oriented firms, an underrepresentation of black males, and other forces.

Trends by County in Michigan

The growth in the sales of black-owned firms in Michigan counties with 250 or more such firms in 1982 was reviewed. As shown in Table 2-6, only 6 of the 83 counties had at least 250 firms: Genesee, Ingham, Kent, Oakland, Washtenaw, and Wayne. Focusing only upon firms with paid employees, Wayne County led with two-thirds of these firms, with Oakland a distant second, trailed by Genesee. Each of these counties had at least one city with a population that included a relatively large proportion of African-Americans (Table 2-6).

Table 2-6. Statistical Trends, 1982–1987, for Counties in Michigan with 250 or More Black-Owned Firms* with Paid Employees in 1982

	1987		1982		% Change 1982–1987	
County (Major City)	Firms	Receipts ($,000)	Firms	Receipts ($,000)	Firms	Receipts ($,000)
Genesee (Flint)	141	23,396	76	(D)	86	—
Ingham (Lansing)	52	6,616	23	3,640	126	82
Kent (Grand Rapids)	68	26,791	38	(D)	79	—
Oakland (Southfield, Pontiac)	263	140,927	118	(D)	123	—
Washtenaw (Ann Arbor, Ypsilanti)	69	31,485	45	(D)	53	—
Wayne County (Detroit)	1,252	209,244	892	123,975	40	69

SOURCE: U.S. Department of Commerce, Bureau of the Census, *Survey of Minority-Owned Business Enterprises—Black, 1987*, July 1990, p. 46; and calculations by the author. Special tabulations from the Bureau of the Census sent to the author by Ms. Elaine Emanuel, 2/20/91.

*Excludes corporations other than subchapter S (i.e., legally incorporated firms with 35 or fewer shareholders who elect under IRS rules to be taxed as individual shareholders rather than as corporations). Black-owned business firms are defined as firms in which 50 percent or more of the ownership is black. Data are obtained on a confidential basis using IRS, Census, and Social Security files. Comparability over time is affected by differences in definitions, business units covered, inability to obtain responses from all cases, reporting errors, mistakes in recording, and imputations.

(D) Withheld to avoid disclosing data for individual companies; data are included in higher-level totals.

In the five-year period ending in 1987, the number of Wayne County black-owned firms with paid employees expanded by 40 percent, and sales by 69 percent. This was the smallest growth of any county for which there are data shown. Wayne County had 1,252 black-owned firms with paid employees in 1987. These firms had sales of $209 million and average receipts per firm of $167 thousand. Oakland County, with multiple African-American population concentrations (Southfield, Pontiac, and Oak Park), had 263 firms with paid employees in 1987, with receipts amounting to $141 million and receipts per firm of $536 thousand-over three times the amount for Wayne County (computed from data in Table 2-6).

Washtenaw County had only 69 firms with paid employees, but ranked just below Southfield with average receipts per firm of $456 thousand. Largely because of the city of Grand Rapids, Kent County had average receipts per firm of a respectable $394 thousand, but had only 68 African-American firms with paid employees (computed from Table 2-6).

Both Oakland and Ingham Counties led in the growth of the number of firms in the five-year period. According to a University of Michigan economic forecast, as reported on page 2B in the *Detroit Free Press* of April 4, 1991, 60 percent of the recent increase in jobs in the Detroit metropolitan area in the fields of computer programming, engineering services, and advertising occurred in Oakland County. The growth of service jobs in this county has involved high wages, stemming in part from a well educated workforce. Some of this growth apparently was stimulated by and spilled over to African-Americans.

Genesee, Kent, and Washtenaw Counties did less well, but surpassed Wayne County. Ingham County, the location of the State Capitol in Lansing and the site of Michigan State University, probably benefited from the proximity of these two institutions. Nonetheless, the growth in the number of firms in Ingham County surpassed the expansion in the average receipts of these firms, suggesting a declining trend in the receipts per firm during the period; new start-ups probably entered at a more rapid rate than the expansion and survival of older firms.

Given the relatively small number of the firms in some of these counties in 1982, a decline in sales per firm is an understandable occurrence—particularly in a period that commenced during a severe recession and ended during a sustained recovery in economic conditions. Firms tend to start at a faster rate during and after a downturn, as laid-off workers and their spouses try to maintain their incomes by starting a business.

When black-owned firms are ranked by county per 10,000 of the black population, Oakland County, with a large population concentration in Pontiac and between Eight- and Ten-Mile Roads in Southfield, ranks 1st with 33.9 firms in 1987. Oakland County is followed by Washtenaw with 21.7 firms. The remainder of the selected counties vary between a low of 14.7 in Wayne County to 18.7 per 10,000 in Ingham County, which ranks 3rd (Table 2-7).

In the rankings of black-owned firms per 10,000 of the total population, black and non-black together, the dominating factor seems to be the proportion of the total population that is black. Wayne County, ranking 1st, leads in this proportion (over 40 percent, computed from Table 2-7), followed by Genesee, with its black population being almost 20 percent. Washtenaw ranks 3rd; it had a black population of over 10 percent. All other counties bringing up the rear had black population percentages of below 10 percent.

Oakland County, which ranked 1st in the relationship of African-American firms to the black population, drops to 4th when related to the total population. This circumstance again

Table 2-7. Black-Owned Firms with Paid Employees in 1987, for Counties in Michigan with 250 or More Black-Owned Firms* with Paid Employees in 1982, and Per 10,000 of the Total and Black Population in 1990**

	Firms in 1987 per 10,000 Population					1990 Population (000)	
County (Major City)	Black	Rank	All	Rank	Firms 1987	Black	All
Genesee (Flint)	16.7	5	3.3	2	141	84.3	430.5
Ingham (Lansing)	18.7	3	1.8	6	52	27.8	281.9
Kent (Grand Rapids)	16.9	4	1.9	5	68	40.3	500.6
Oakland (Southfield, Pontiac)	33.9	1	2.4	4	263	77.5	1,083.6
Washtenaw (Ann Arbor, Ypsilanti)	21.7	2	2.4	3	69	31.7	282.9
Wayne (Detroit)	14.7	6	5.9	1	1,252	849.1	2,111.7

SOURCE: U.S. Department of Commerce, Bureau of the Census, *Survey of Minority-Owned Business Enterprises—Black, 1987*, July 1990, p. 46; and calculations by the author. Special tabulations from the Bureau of the Census sent to the author by Ms. Elaine Emanuel, 2/20/1991; Bureau of the Census "1990 MSA Press Release Alpha Sort," February 22, 1991, table entitled "Population of Metropolitan Areas: 1990 and 1980."

*Excludes corporations other than subchapter S (i.e., legally incorporated firms with 35 or fewer shareholders who elect under IRS rules to be taxed as individual shareholders rather than as corporations). Black-owned business firms are defined as firms in which 50 percent or more of the ownership is black. Data are obtained on a confidential basis using IRS, Census, and Social Security files. Comparability over time is affected by differences in definitions, business units covered, inability to obtain responses from all cases, reporting errors, mistakes in recording, and imputations.

**Although admitting a 2 percent undercount nationally, affecting mainly minorities, the Department of Commerce has declined to make an adjustment in the population counts for 1990. Several governmental units, including the City of Detroit, are appealing the Department of Commerce decision in the courts.

suggests the greater relevance of the black population than the total population. It also suggests consideration of strategies to increase the crossover of nonblack patronage, as well as greater minority patronage for minority firms.

Trends by City in Michigan

An analysis was also made by city for those jurisdictions that had 250 or more black-owned firms with or without paid employees in 1982, but focused only upon the firms with paid employees (Table 2-8). The City of Detroit in 1987 accounted for 78 percent of these firms, and only 68 percent of the receipts. In 1987, it had 1,091 firms and receipts of $168 million, or $154 thousand per firm on the average (computed from data in Table 2-8).

Detroit's black-owned firms increased in number from 1982 to 1987 by 38 percent; their receipts, by 70 percent; and average receipts per firm, by 23 percent. Given a 15 percent increase in the Consumer Price Index in the five-year period, average receipts per firm rose in Detroit by slightly above 1 percent per year in terms of dollars of constant purchasing power.

In the number of firms and receipts in 1987, Flint (with 107 firms and $14.6 million in receipts) and Southfield (with 101 firms and $49.6 million in receipts) were far below Detroit (with 1,091 firms and $168.4 million in receipts). Grand Rapids and Lansing trailed far behind, with 58 and 37 firms, and sales of $10.3 and $3.2 million, respectively.

Table 2-8. Statistical Trends, 1982–1987, for Cities in Michigan with 250 or More Black-Owned Firms* in 1982

	Firms with Paid Employees					
	1987		1982		Percentage Change, 1982–1987	
Cities	Firms	Receipts ($,000)	Firms	Receipts ($,000)	Firms	Receipts
Detroit	1,091	168,429	790	99,327	38	70
Flint	107	14,558	66	(D)	62	(D)
Grand Rapids	58	10,276	29	(D)	100	(D)
Lansing	37	3,245	17	902	118	260
Southfield	101	49,604	42	(D)	140	(D)

SOURCE: U.S. Department of Commerce, Bureau of the Census, *Survey of Minority-Owned Business Enterprises—Black, 1987*, July 1990, p. 55; and calculations by the author. Special tabulations from the Bureau of the Census sent to the author by Ms. Elaine Emanuel, 2/20/91.

*Excludes corporations other than subchapter S (i.e., legally incorporated firms with 35 or fewer shareholders who elect under IRS rules to be taxed as individual shareholders rather than as corporations). Black-owned business firms are defined as firms in which 50 percent or more of the ownership is black. Data are obtained on a confidential basis using IRS, Census, and Social Security files. Comparability over time is affected by differences in definitions, business units covered, inability to obtain responses from all cases, reporting errors, mistakes in recording, and imputations.

(D) Withheld to avoid disclosing data for individual companies; data are included in higher-level totals.

However, Southfield (140 percent) and Lansing (118 percent) led in the growth in the number of black-owned firms between 1982 and 1987. Grand Rapids followed closely with a growth rate of 100 percent, much above Flint (62 percent) and Detroit (38 percent).

Trends in receipts for the five-year period are unavailable, except for Lansing (260 percent) and Detroit (70 percent). For the other jurisdictions, the data in 1982 were omitted from the census results to decrease the possibility of disclosure of information on individual firms.

Southfield, uniquely among the cities of the state, had average sales per black firm approaching $500 thousand. It is hypothesized that, with the extraordinary growth of the economy in which Southfield is located (Oakland County), a few large black-owned firms, together with the small number of tiny businesses and of firms overall (101), increased the average. Grand Rapids ranked second among the cities with average receipts per firm in 1987 of $177 thousand. Lansing ranked last with nearly $88,000 per firm (computations based on data in Table 2-8).

An adequate annual sales volume for advancing the probability of viability for a firm varies with many factors. Among these factors are rents and location, exposure to crime, access to volume discounts and financing, and insurance costs and taxes. Other factors to be considered include the nature of the industry, depth of the market niche served by the firm, quality of management, number of employees and their productivity, quality of public services, and adequacy and cost of capitalization.

A crude, loose, and heroic rule of thumb, based on the author's experience in studying the performance of firms, is that the ranges in sales annually for a profitable, small, two-full-time-person service operation could vary from at least $250 to $500 thousand in sales; a fast-food franchise, $750 thousand to $1.3 million; a general contracting construction company, $3.0 to $7.0 million; an auto dealership, $12 to $80 million; and a manufacturing concern, upwards of $4.0 million, if the operations are not too capital intensive. The better the management and the more adequate the capitalization and other required attributes for success, the more a firm can tend toward the lower end of the range. The probability for success increases as a firm reaches and surpasses the upper part of the range.

If this rule of thumb is reasonably valid, the average receipts for other cities must more nearly approach Southfield's receipts in the future. Indeed, all firms on the average should do better, particularly if the mix by industries includes significant manufacturing and other capital-intensive firms, or locations in high-cost areas. Other policy options would include reducing the expenses in high-cost areas and promoting the possession of the attributes leading to successful operations. Various approaches should be used simultaneously to accelerate the survival and growth in the viability of these firms.

The State's Black-Owned Firms by Industry

Table 2-9 presents data that provided the basis for computations leading to the following findings: About 53 percent of the 13,708 black-owned firms in Michigan were in services in 1987. (Services include beauty, barber, and shoe repair shops; funeral homes; health providers; janitorial and amusement businesses; recreational services establishments, and other firms.) When retail trade is added to the 53 percent in services, the total reaches almost 70 percent; and when finance, insurance, and real estate are added, the total is 76.5 percent. Considering only firms with paid employees, the percentages were much the same as for all black-owned firms, except that the services component declined by 8 percentage points and retail trade rose by roughly the same proportion.

Relatively few firms with paid employees were in construction (233), manufacturing (46), or wholesale trade (32). These firms, like retail trade, generally have more jobs per establishment than most other industries.

Of receipts generated by black-owned firms with paid employees, retail trade accounted for 53.6 percent; services, 20.6 percent; and three groups—construction, wholesale trade, and manufacturing—about 6 percent each; summing to 92 percent of all receipts for these industries (computed from data in Table 2-9). Except services, these are the industries with the highest proportion of firms with paid employees; they also tend to exceed the other industries in receipts per firm. Very few receipts were generated by firms in agriculture, forestry, fishing, mining, finance, insurance, and real estate.

In contrast, among the receipts of *all firms in the U.S.* with paid employees, as shown in the 1987 *Survey of Minority-Owned Enterprises—Black*, retail trade accounted for 29.1 percent; services, 19.4 percent; and three groups—construction, wholesale trade, and manufacturing, 11.2, 16.3, and 12.9 percents, respectively. Retail trade receives much less emphasis in the U.S. overall than in the African-American community. Services are about the same, and most other industries have much more of a presence in the U.S.

This pattern reflects, among various other contributing factors, the African-American's lack of capital and low saving rate, the need for blacks to develop more entrepreneurial skills

Table 2-9. Michigan's Black-Owned Firms*, by Industry: Number, Receipts, and Average Receipts and Employees Per Firm, 1987

	Firms		Receipts (in $000,000)		Average per Firm with Paid Employees		Percentage of Firms
Item	All	With Paid Employees	All ($,000,000)	With Paid Employees	Receipts ($,000)	Employees	with Paid Employees
Entire State	13,708	2,241	701.3	524.6	234.1	3.8	16.3
Agricultural Services, Forestry, Fishing, and Mining	166	35	3.1	1.9	55.1	1.8	21.1
Construction	845	233	46.0	32.0	137.3	1.4	27.6
Manufacturing	146	46	32.6	31.2	677.3	8.3	31.5
Transportation and Public Utilities	936	142	38.7	20.2	142.6	2.5	15.2
Wholesale Trade	168	32	38.1	31.9	995.6	4.0	19.0
Retail Trade	2,289	561	313.2	281.4	501.6	6.5	24.5
Finance, Insurance, and Real Estate	934	91	24.7	11.9	130.9	1.3	9.7
Services	7,273	1,010	187.3	108.3	107.2	3.3	13.9
Unclassified	951	91	17.6	5.8	63.8	0.9	9.6

SOURCE: U.S. Department of Commerce, Bureau of the Census, *Survey of Minority-Owned Business Enterprises—Black, 1987*, July 1990, p. 11; and calculations by the author.

*Excludes corporations other than subchapter S (i.e., legally incorporated firms with 35 or fewer shareholders who elect under IRS rules to be taxed as individual shareholders rather than as corporations). Black-owned business firms are defined as firms in which 50 percent or more of the ownership is black. Data are obtained on a confidential basis using IRS, Census, and Social Security files. Comparability over time is affected by differences in definitions, business units covered, inability to obtain responses from all cases, reporting errors, mistakes in recording, and imputations.

and a taste for risk, the presence of barriers to entry into various industries where existing firms are already established (and highly protective and competitive), the inadequate number and variety of mentors available to blacks, and the comparative lack of access for blacks to many opportunities, including information and contacts in a substantially segregated society.

Black-Owned Firms by Metropolitan Area in 1987

Table 2-10 presents data that provided the basis for computations leading to the following findings: The Detroit Metropolitan Statistical Area (MSA) was first in the state in 1987 with 9,852 black-owned firms (71.9 percent of those in the state); these firms generated receipts of $514.3 million (73.3 percent of those in the state). This urban area had 1,581 black-owned firms with paid employees, which accounted for receipts of $379.4 million (computed from data in Tables 2-5 and 2-10).

Flint ranked second in the number of all black-owned firms (885), followed by Ann Arbor (538), and Lansing-East Lansing (428). In total receipts, however, Ann Arbor ranked second, and Flint was third, just ahead of Grand Rapids (Table 2-10).

Table 2-10. Selected Statistics for All Black-Owned Firms* and those Firms with Paid Employees in the Eleven Largest Metropolitan Statistical Areas in Michigan, 1987

Metropolitan Statistical Areas Large Cities	All Firms			Firms with Paid Employees				
	Number	Receipts ($,000)	Receipts per Firm ($,000)	Number	Receipts ($,000)	Receipts per Firm ($,000)	Employees Number	Employees per Firm
Ann Arbor	538	37,156	69.1	69	31,485	456.3	640	9.3
Ann Arbor City	249	4,645	18.6	26	2,304	88.6	69	2.7
Battle Creek	142	5,075	35.7	22	2,741	124.6	55	2.5
Benton Harbor	220	8,951	40.7	58	6,856	118.2	198	3.4
Detroit	9,852	514,324	52.2	1,581	379,433	240.0	5,912	3.7
Detroit City	7,116	258,375	36.3	1,091	168,429	154.4	3,861	3.5
Highland Park	118	10,197	86.4	26	9,240	355.4	87	3.3
Inkster	226	5,580	24.7	30	2,869	95.6	51	1.7
Oak Park	220	5,626	25.6	19	2,021	106.4	26	1.4
Pontiac	272	20,203	74.3	42	16,659	396.6	153	3.6
Southfield	729	64,167	88.0	101	49,604	491.1	414	4.1
Flint	885	32,756	37.0	141	23,396	165.9	390	2.8
Flint City	683	21,018	30.8	107	14,558	136.1	230	2.1
Grand Rapids	411	31,381	76.4	71	27,253	383.8	187	2.6
Grand Rapids City	312	13,719	44.0	58	10,276	177.2	107	1.8
Jackson	101	2,211	21.9	20	1,099	55.0	32	1.6
Kalamazoo	244	8,020	32.9	38	4,434	116.7	79	2.1
Kalamazoo City	146	3,615	24.8	22	1,952	88.7	43	2.0
Lansing-East Lansing	428	11,896	27.8	56	7,100	126.8	174	3.1
Lansing City	293	6,342	21.6	37	3,245	87.7	91	2.5
Muskegon	142	5,947	41.9	26	4,212	162.0	79	3.0
Saginaw-Bay City-Midland	347	9,884	28.5	73	6,771	92.8	109	1.5
Saginaw City	191	6,379	33.4	47	4,588	97.6	87	1.9

SOURCE: U.S. Department of Commerce, Bureau of the Census, *Survey of Minority-Owned Business Enterprises—Black, 1987*, July 1990, p. 16–37; and calculations by the author.

*Excludes corporations other than subchapter S (i.e., legally incorporated firms with 35 or fewer shareholders who elect under IRS rules to be taxed as individual shareholders rather than as corporations). Black-owned business firms are defined as firms in which 50 percent or more of the ownership is black. Data are obtained on a confidential basis using IRS, Census, and Social Security files. Comparability over time is affected by differences in definitions, business units covered, inability to obtain responses from all cases, reporting errors, mistakes in recording, and imputations.

Among the firms with paid employees, the City of Detroit had 69 percent (n=1,091) of the firms (n=1,581) in the metropolitan statistical area; 65.3 percent (n=3,861) of the employees (n=5,912), but only 44.3 percent (n=$168,429,000) of the sales (n=$379,433,000). Highland Park, Pontiac, and Southfield all experienced sales per firm of more than twice the amount for Detroit. The City of Detroit did exceed the average sales per firm of Inkster and Oak Park (based on data from Table 2-10).

In average receipts per firm having paid employees, the Ann Arbor and Grand Rapids MSAs topped the state, with $456.3 and $383.8 thousand, respectively. Detroit, with average receipts per firm of $240.0 thousand, was third among the eleven metro areas. Among the cities, Southfield ($491.1 thousand), Pontiac ($396.6 thousand), and Highland Park ($355.4 thousand) exceeded the others in average receipts per firm.

For the MSAs, Ann Arbor was far in front in average employees per firm (9.3). Detroit was next with 3.7. As with other averages in this study, these numbers conceal a wide variance between the firms. A few comparatively large ones or a sizable proportion of very small ones can swamp the average.

African-American firms in Battle Creek, Benton Harbor, Jackson, Kalamazoo, Muskegon, and Saginaw-Bay City-Midland generally experienced rates of business development lower than for the other metro areas.

The ranking of black-owned firms per 10,000 of the black population in the 11 largest MSAs is somewhat difficult to explain. A geographic area that is wider than by county or by city complicates the analysis and requires the study of factors that are beyond the scope of this study.

As shown in Table 2-11, Benton Harbor ranks 1st, Ann Arbor 2nd, and Kalamazoo 3rd. The Detroit MSA is 7th among the 11 MSAs. Bringing in the tail end of the rankings are Jackson, Battle Creek, and Muskegon.

Somewhat easier to explain are the rankings of the same 11 MSAs per 10,000 of the total population. Again, the proportion of the population that is African-American seems to be the driving factor in the probable absence of a large nonblack crossover in patronage. The Detroit SMA ranks 1st, Benton Harbor 2nd, and Flint 3rd. The top 8 MSAs have black population percentages of above 10 percent, except Kalamazoo and Saginaw-Bay City-Midland, and they are not too far below 10 percent. Ranking last are the Jackson, Lansing-East Lansing, and Battle Creek SMAs in that order. All but Battle Creek have black population percentages below 10 percent, and Battle Creek is just above that threshold.

The Larger Black-Owned Firms, 1982–1989

Great attention attaches to the largest firms, for they generate a major share of the jobs, sales, and capital investment provided by all African-American firms. Unfortunately, the census data do not reveal sales performance by size of firm within a state. Data on the larger black-owned firms are presented to fill this gap and to show more recent performance results. Table 2-12 shows sales data for the "Top 100 Black Business Firms" nationally that are located in Michigan, as published by *Black Enterprise* magazine for the years 1982, 1987, and 1990. Also, information for 1989 from *Black Enterprise* was combined with that in *The Book of Lists* from *Crain's Detroit Business* for the same year.

Firms are listed in Table 2-12 in the order of their receipts for 1989. For each firm, sales are also shown for 1982, 1987, and 1990, when such data appear in *Black Enterprise.* Only those firms that appear in the sources for 1989 are ranked. Listed after the last ranked firm (31), but not ranked, are other firms appearing in 1982 and 1987, but not in 1989 (or in 1990 for the first time). Some of the unranked firms are no longer in business. Others are in business, but perhaps did not respond to either survey or were too small to be included.

Table 2-11. Black-owned Firms* with Paid Employees in The Eleven Largest Metropolitan Statistical Areas in Michigan, 1987, and per 10,000 of The Black and Total Population, 1990**

Metropolitan Statistical Areas Large Cities	Firms in 1987 per 10,000 Population (1990 Census)					Population (000) 1990	
	Black	Rank	Total	Rank	Firms 1987	Black	All
Ann Arbor	21.8	2	2.4	4	69	31.7	282.9
Ann Arbor City	26.3		2.4		26	9.9	109.6
Battle Creek	15.3	10	1.6	8	22	14.4	136.0
Benton Harbor	23.3	1	3.6	2	58	24.9	161.4
Detroit	16.8	7	3.6	1	1,581	943.2	4,382.3
Detroit City	14.0		10.6		1,091	777.9	1,028.0
Highland Park	16.3		12.9		26	18.7	20.1
Inkster	15.6		9.7		30	19.2	30.8
Oak Park	18.3		6.2		19	10.4	30.5
Pontiac	14.0		5.9		42	30.0	71.2
Southfield	45.7		13.3		101	22.1	75.7
Flint	16.7	8	3.3	3	141	84.3	430.5
Flint City	15.9		7.6		107	67.5	140.8
Grand Rapids	17.2	6	1.0	11	71	41.3	688.4
Grand Rapids City	16.5		3.1		58	35.1	189.1
Jackson	16.7	9	1.3	9	20	12.0	149.8
Kalamazoo	19.1	3	1.7	6	38	19.9	223.4
Kalamazoo City	14.6		2.7		22	15.1	80.3
Lansing-East Lansing	17.9	5	1.3	10	56	31.3	432.7
Lansing City	15.7		2.9		37	23.6	127.3
Muskegon	12.0	11	1.6	7	26	21.6	159.0
Saginaw-Bay City-Midland	18.8	4	1.8	5	73	38.8	399.3
Saginaw City	16.8		6.8		47	28.0	69.5

SOURCE: U.S. Department of Commerce, Bureau of the Census, *Survey of Minority-Owned Business Enterprises—Black, 1987*, July 1990, p. 16–37; Bureau of the Census, "1990 MSA Press Release Alpha Sort," February 22, 1991, table entitled "Population of Metropolitan Areas: 1990 and 1980;" Bureau of the Census PL-94-171 population counts used for redistricting; and calculations by the author.

*Excludes corporations other than subchapter S (i.e., legally incorporated firms with 35 or fewer shareholders who elect under IRS rules to be taxed as individual shareholders rather than as corporations). Black-owned business firms are defined as firms in which 50 percent or more of the ownership is black. Data are obtained on a confidential basis using IRS, Census, and Social Security files. Comparability over time is affected by differences in definitions, business units covered, inability to obtain responses from all cases, reporting errors, mistakes in recording, and imputations.

**Although admitting a 2 percent undercount nationally, affecting mainly minorities, the Department of Commerce has declined to make an adjustment in the population counts for 1990. Several governmental units, including the City of Detroit, are appealing the Department of Commerce decision in the courts.

The 31 firms that are ranked had a combined sales total in 1989 of $814.7 million (in contrast to sales for all black-owned firms in Michigan of $701.3 million two years before, according to census data shown in Table 2-1). The smallest firm had $5.0 million in sales. In 1987, almost half as many firms as in 1989 are listed (16), and they sold $400.6 million of goods and services. Average receipts per firm were much the same in both years. The lowest ranking firm in 1987 had sales of $4.5 million.

Table 2-12. Michigan's Black-Owned Businesses Leading in Sales, 1982, 1987, 1989, and 1990; Employment, 1989*

Sales Rank in 1989	Firm and Location	Sales ($,000,000) 1982	1987	1989	1990	Percentage Increase 1982–1989	Employment 1989
1	Trans Jones, Inc./Jones Transfer Monroe		79.3	78.6	75.0		1,264
2	The Bing Group Detroit		42.9	73.9	61.0		170
3	Mel Farr Automotive Group Oak Park	10.6	36.5	54.2	84.3	411	146
4	Al Bennett, Inc. Flint	12.7	42.7	46.5		166	147
5	The Barfield Companies Ypsilanti	9.8	37.2	38.0		288	700
6	Barden Communications, Inc. Detroit			37.7	86.0		239
7	Wesley Industries, Inc. Flint			36.5	36.4		340
8	Northwestern Dodge Ferndale		27.3	34.9			68
9	Ponchelon Lincoln-Mercury Saginaw			34.4	11.6		36
10	Gilreath Manufacturing Howell			29.7			281
11	Trumark, Inc. Lansing		15.6	28.6	26.4		240
12	Regal Plastics Company Roseville			24.9	22.4		250
13	Allegan Ford-Mercury Sales, Inc. Allegan			24.9	18.0		18
14	Capital Chrysler-Plymouth Lansing			24.7			37
15	Southwest Hospital Detroit			24.2			617
16	Jim Bradley Pontiac, Cadillac, GM Truck Ann Arbor		19.3	22.6	25.1		59
17	Conyers Riverside Ford Detroit	8.4	22.1	21.2	24.2	152	68
18	Williams & Richardson Detroit		12.0	20.5	11.5		43
19	Ferndale Honda Ferndale		17.3	19.7	21.3		32
20	Campus Ford Okemos		19.0	19.4	18.5		70
21	Keys Group, Inc. Detroit	8.5	14.3	18.6	16.1	119	2,300

(*continued*)

Table 2-12. Michigan's Black-Owned Businesses Leading in Sales, 1982, 1987, 1989, and 1990; Employment, 1989* (*continued*)

Sales Rank in 1989	Firm and Location	Sales ($,000,000) 1982	1987	1989	1990	Percentage Increase 1982–1989	Employment 1989
22	Harrell Chevrolet-Oldsmobile Flat Rock		14.5	17.5	17.8		30
23	Engineered Plastic Products, Inc. Roseville			12.4			185
24	Davis Buick-Jeep Eagle, Inc. Battle Creek		10.6	12.3	12.1		36
25	Black River Manufacturing, Inc. Port Huron			10.4	11.4		87
26	First Independence Corp. Detroit			10.1			97
27	New Center Hospital Detroit			9.6			251
28	C.G. Enterprises Southfield			9.5	9.4		37
29	RAS Financial Corp. Detroit			7.2			12
30	WGPR, Inc. Detroit		4.5	6.4			78
31	Madison-Madison International Detroit			5.0			47
**	Prestige Pontiac-Oldsmobile Mt. Morris				18.8		
**	Saginaw Ford, Inc. DBA All American Ford Saginaw				16.1		
**	Superb Manufacturing Detroit				28.4		
**	Summa-Harrison Metal Products, Inc. Royal Oak				25.0		
**	Am-Tech Export Trading Co., Inc. Detroit				13.6		
**	Ellis Electronic, Inc. Detroit				11.4		
**	Universal Software Southfield				10.0		
**	Vicksburg Chrysler-Pontiac-Dodge, Inc. Vicksburg				13.0		

Table 2-12. Michigan's Black-Owned Businesses Leading in Sales, 1982, 1987, 1989, and 1990; Employment, 1989* (*continued*)

Sales Rank in 1989	Firm and Location	Sales ($,000,000) 1982	1987	1989	1990	Percentage Increase 1982–1989	Employment 1989
***	Clipper International Detroit		4.4				
***	Original Construction Detroit		3.2				
***	Porterfield Wilson, Pontiac, GMC-Truck, Mazda Detroit	12.4	42.7				
***	Woodruff Oldsmobile Detroit	14.2	13.0				
***	Plainfield Lincoln-Mercury-Merkur, Inc. Grand Rapids		11.6				
***	Dick Harris Cadillac, Inc. Detroit	14.4					
***	The Emanuel Co. Detroit	9.5					

SOURCE: "The Top 100 Black Businesses," *Black Enterprise*, June 1983, 1988, 1990, and 1991; "Leading Detroit-Area Black-Owned Businesses," *Crain's Detroit Business, Book of Lists*, 1991, p. 41.

**Black Enterprise* changed its procedure in 1987 to list auto dealers separately from "The Top 100 Industrial/Service Businesses" in the nation. *Crain's Detroit Business* lists only the black-owned firms in the Detroit area. The lists from both sources were merged for 1989 to include outstate firms identified in *Black Enterprise*. Although this merging presents the most complete list of large firms available, neither source is comprehensive, both for conceptual reasons and because of unintended omissions. Some Afro-American owners do not wish to be identified by race and, therefore, do not respond to surveys. Home Federal Savings and Wright Mutual Insurance Company, both of Detroit, were not listed, because no sales figures as such are available. Data on loans, total assets or insurance in force are available for these firms and institutions but do not lend themselves to comparison with the firms listed above.

**Listed in *Black Enterprise* in 1990 but not for the previous years shown above.

***Unranked. No data available for 1989. Clipper International is still in business. The Emanuel Company is restarting the business after the early retirement of its owner-manager. The following firms are no longer operating: Porterfield Wilson, Woodruff Oldsmobile, and Dick Harris Cadillac.

It is tempting to observe that these comparatively large black-owned firms accounted for 76 percent of the receipts of all such firms with paid employees in Michigan for 1987, regardless of size. However, the *Black Enterprise* survey of larger businesses may have included firms that were not covered by the Census Bureau, among other reasons because the census data exclude corporations other than subchapter S firms. Nonetheless, this rough estimate of the dominance of the larger firms also characterizes the U.S. as a whole. According to the census data for the nation in 1987, all firms with paid employees and receipts of $7.1 million or more generated almost 50 percent of the sales of all firms regardless of size.

In 1989, the 31 largest black-owned firms in Michigan employed a total of almost 8,000 persons, or an average of 257 jobs per firm. This represents a significant contribution to diversity and to the economic development of the areas in which these firms are located. Moreover, there is also an impact on lowering the unemployment rates of those who are hit hardest by unemployment, since blacks have higher unemployment rates than nonblacks, and these firms hire minorities disproportionately.

The distribution of the larger firms is quite different from that shown by the census data in that there is little representation of service companies which dominate the census profile. Of the 31 firms identified in 1989 with sales equal to or greater than $5.0 million, there were 12 motor vehicle dealerships; 9 suppliers to motor vehicle manufacturers; 2 each in construction, financial services, health care or hospitals; and one each for a TV and radio station combined, computer services, fast food franchising, and a cable television company.

Since the entire population of large firms has not been covered with certainty by these surveys, conclusions based on these data must be qualified. The identification of this composition of firms by industry cannot be said to represent the real distribution of firms if there were perfect knowledge (which there is not), given the nonresponse to surveys and the possible presence of other statistical biases. Still, the precariousness of the extremely limited penetration of the economic mainstream achieved by many of these larger black-owned businesses is apparent. This suggests the urgency of efforts for promoting their survival and growth, as well as the origination of other new businesses with growth potential.

The current recession and other factors have caused the closing of a few auto dealerships and have jeopardized others. Suppliers to the motor vehicle industry are similarly threatened. Hospitals, and particularly those serving low-income patients, are imperiled by the promised cutbacks in Medicaid and by other cuts in government programs affecting health care and drug abuse treatment. Such institutions do not wish to deny poor and uninsured patients needed treatment, yet these institutions frequently are unable to obtain proper reimbursement for health services rendered. This encourages health care organizations to reduce or close their operations in low-income areas and to move to affluent ones where all (or a much larger proportion of patients) are covered by private health insurance plans or have high incomes. Inadequate health care coverage and high health care costs are among the factors impacting minority firms adversely.

The recent decline in the construction industry has hit contractors with a fury. Of the large companies identified, only cable television, television combined with radio, fast foods, and financial firms appear to have some insulation, compared with the other industries identified. Fortunately, with good management and adequate access to capital, a few firms in a troubled industry can sometimes overcome the pressures on the industry as a whole.

The importance of a firm's survival is vividly demonstrated in Table 2-12 through analyzing the growth rate of those firms listed in both 1982 and 1989. The average growth rate in sales for these five firms (i.e., same firm sales) was 257 percent in the seven-year period, or 19.9 percent compounded annually—much higher than the rate of inflation. Further, this rate probably would have been even greater were the sales known for those firms that were too small in 1982 to have been listed then, but were large enough to have been listed in 1989. Increasing the survival and growth of such firms is clearly in the interest of the community at large and should obtain widespread support.

At least one organization, New Detroit, Inc., an urban coalition of industrial leaders, state and local elected officials, community organizational representatives, labor officials, and educators, has recognized the importance of supporting the growth and development of black-owned business firms. The coalition has designed a program called the New Detroit Business Partnership Plan, which matches larger successful majority-owned companies with 16 selected minority companies generally in the same or a related industry. This mentorship approach is expected to help expand and develop relatively large minority companies with growth potential into much larger and more viable firms. This study confirms the need and timeliness for such a program.

Another cogent new program attacks the limited access to capital faced by African-American and other minority firms. The Greater Detroit BIDCO (Business and Industrial Development Corporation), with funding from private investors, foundations, and the Michigan Strategic Fund of Michigan's Department of Commerce, has as its mission providing financing and management assistance primarily to minority companies in Michigan with good potential for growth in profits, sales, and jobs—companies that cannot obtain adequate financing through traditional sources.

This minority BIDCO, the first of its kind in the nation, seeks to complement and not to compete with either commercial banks or other very low risk-taking financial institutions. It was organized in 1990, one year before the announcement of New Detroit's Business Partnership Plan. Because of the newness of both programs, evaluation of performance is premature. The full impact of these programs has yet to be felt. Nonetheless, both programs appear to represent efforts that are consistent with the findings of this study.

The Larger Black-Owned Firms, 1990

Data for 1990 on the larger black-owned firms are not available at this time from *Crain's Detroit Business Book of Lists*. The June 1991 issue of *Black Enterprise*, however, provides information on these firms. Both the 1991 issue and the June 1990 issue listed separately four groups of black-owned firms: the top 100 industrial/service companies, the top 100 auto dealers, the top banks and savings and loan institutions, and the largest insurance companies. Listed from Michigan in 1990 were 15 industrial/service firms, 12 auto dealers, one commercial bank, and no savings and loan or life insurance companies.

The "B.E. 100s" refers to the combination of the largest 100 industrial/service companies and the largest 100 auto dealerships. Michigan led the U.S. in having the most companies (27) identified in the B.E. 100s. New York ranked a poor 2nd (19), Illinois 3rd (18), and California 4th (17).

Michigan was spotlighted positively in several other respects in the report in *Black Enterprise*. Barden Communications, Inc. received special attention. It had sales of $86.0 million in 1990 and ranked 6th nationally among the 100 industrial/service companies. It is in communications and real estate.

Barden Communications, Inc. also preserved Michigan's presence nationally among the highest ranking top 6 firms. Motown, Inc. had previously been high in the ranking for over a decade, but was not listed in 1990 for the first time since its entry in the Top 100. Motown is regarded nostalgically by many Michigan residents. Although it was relocated to California several years ago, it still maintains visibility in the state through the museum in its honor in Detroit and through events sponsored by the museum.

This state also had two of the five African-American companies with the largest employment in 1990. The Keys Group ranked 3rd with 1,400 workers. Trans Jones, Inc./Jones Transfer Co. ranked 5th with 1,189 workers.

Wesley Industries, Inc. in Flint received a special recognition as the "BE Company of the Year." The company produces metal coatings. The most rapidly growing company of the year in 1989, it was exemplary in 1990 for repositioning itself through diversifying its sales to reduce its dependence on the auto industry.

Five Michigan-based firms that were not listed in 1989 are identified in the 1990 list of the Top 100 industrial/service firms: Am-Tech Export Trading Co., Inc., in Vicksburg; Ellis Electronic, Inc., in Detroit; Summa-Harrison Metal Products, Inc., in Royal Oak; Superb Manufacturing in Detroit; and Universal Software in Southfield.

Eight industrial/service firms listed in 1989 were not reported in 1990: The Barfield Companies in Ypsilanti; Gilreath Manufacturing in Ferndale; Southwest Hospital in Detroit; RAS Financial Corporation in Detroit; WGPR-TV, Inc. in Detroit; Engineered Plastic Products, Inc., Rosedale; New Center Hospital in Detroit; and Madison-Madison International in Detroit.

Companies cease to be listed for many reasons, including the following: nonresponses to questionnaires; responses with sales below the cutoff point of $11.5 billion for industrial/service companies in 1990; sale of the business to non-black owners; and mergers, consolidations, and liquidations.

Two new firms listed, Am-Tech and Universal Software, had notable attributes. The specialization by Am-Tech exploits an opportunity for participating in the rapidly growing export industry. The U.S.-Canada free trade agreement and the probably forthcoming U.S.-Mexico agreement should present many opportunities for further growth.

Universal Software, the second of these two new firms, is partly woman-owned. The large proportion of female-headed families in the African-American community suggests that females should be represented to a greater extent than currently in business ownership. Among nonblacks, female-headed firms lead the way in the launching of new businesses. Computer software is also a growth industry with great potential in an increasingly information-based economy.

There was no net change in the 12 African-American auto dealers in Michigan who were included in the *Black Enterprise* Top 100 auto dealers in 1989 and 1990. Yet three new dealers were added in 1990 (Prestige Pontiac-Oldsmobile in Mt. Morris; Saginaw Ford, Inc., doing business as All American Ford; and Vicksburg Chrysler-Pontiac-Dodge, Inc.). Three were not repeated in the listings (Northwestern Dodge in Ferndale, Capitol Chrysler-Plymouth in Lansing, and Al Bennett Ford in Flint). As noted earlier, there are many reasons for unrepeated listings.

First Independence National Bank continued to be listed by *Black Enterprise* among the financial institutions in 1990. With this addition, the Top 31 in 1989 became the top 28 in Michigan in 1990. Reflecting the early stages of the current recession, most of the firms reported in both 1989 and 1990 had declines in sales. The toll taken by these large firms during the late stages of the recession will not be reported by our sources until 1992.

Summary and Recommendations

This chapter analyzed the census data for 1987 on black-owned businesses in Michigan, updating a study published in 1986, using data for 1982 and prior years. It also shows trends from 1982 to 1987 and the top 31 firms in Michigan in 1989, based on a combined list from two sources: *Black Enterprise* magazine and the *Crain's Detroit Business Book of Lists.*

Black business development is a method for producing wealth for one of the least wealthy groups in the U.S. population and for penetrating the economic mainstream.

The census data employed in this study have limitations, including the exclusion of some large companies—corporations other than subchapter S firms—in both 1982 and 1987. The five-year trend may be exaggerated by the starting point occurring in the depths of a severe recession and the ending point, at a high level of economic activity, fallowing five years of an upswing of the economy.

In 1987, there were 13,695,000 U.S. firms, of which 3.1 percent (or 424,200) were black-owned. The U.S. firms had total receipts of $1,995 billion; of this amount, $19.8 billion were received by black-owned firms in the U.S. The receipts for firms nationally averaged three times as much for all firms as for black-owned firms ($145,000 compared with $46,589).

In the same year, 426.7 thousand firms were located in Michigan, of which 13.7 thousand (or 3.2 percent) were black-owned firms. The black-owned firms accounted for $701.3 million in receipts, or 1.1 percent of the total ($63.9 billion) for all firms in the state.

Only 24.2 percent of all firms in Michigan (and 16.3 percent of black-owned firms) had paid employees. Generally, these firms had much greater receipts than the average for all firms. The comparable data for the U.S. was 25.5 percent for all firms and 16.7 percent for black-owned firms.

Michigan had 103.4 thousand firms with paid employees in 1987, only 2.2 thousand of which were owned by African-Americans.

All firms in Michigan with paid employees had receipts of $56.3 billion; and black-owned firms with paid employees had receipts of $524.6 million, or only 0.9 percent of the receipts for all firms in the state. Michigan blacks have only barely begun to penetrate business ownership; they accounted for almost 14 percent of Michigan's population, but only 2.1 percent of the state's firms, and less than 1 percent of business receipts.

All firms with paid employees in Michigan had average receipts of $544.1 thousand, in contrast to $234.1 thousand for black-owned firms.

Without regard to race, the U.S. had 140 firms with paid employees per 10,000 of population in 1987, compared with 110 for Michigan; and 24 black-owned firms nationally, compared with 17 in Michigan, a 41 percent greater edge for the nation than for the state.

Among the 16 states, each with over 2,000 black-owned firms, Michigan ranked 15th in the number of such firms. It ranked 10th in the receipts obtained by these firms—$525 million in 1987.

Michigan did best by ranking 4th with respect to the average receipts per firm ($234,000). Nonetheless, this low level of average receipts shows that, except for a few large firms, black-owned firms tend to be very small and below sales levels that are associated with viable levels of operations.

Michigan ranked 15th of the 16 selected states in black-owned firms (17) per 10,000 of the black population and 15th also per 10,000 of the total population. Compared with other states, particularly in the South, Michigan has a lesser proportion of blacks in its population—a factor that is not offset by the attraction of nonblack patronage to black-owned firms.

In the top 11 states, African-Americans owned a high of .87 firms per 10,000 of the total population, including blacks and nonblacks together, in Mississippi, compared with .24 in Michigan—just above the .23 of the lowest state, Ohio.

Between 1982 and 1987, the number of African-American firms in the U.S. expanded by 37.5 percent, and those with paid employees, by 87.1 percent. This growth was about 50 percent greater than Michigan's performance. Michigan's black-owned firms expanded in number by 25.2 percent, and those with paid employees by 59.3 percent—to 2,241 such firms in 1987.

The receipts of black-owned firms increased in Michigan by 110.9 percent from 1982 to 1987, compared with 105.4 in the U.S. For firms with paid employees, the rate of growth was greater in Michigan than in the U.S.—162.2 percent, compared with 147.7 percent. The larger Michigan firms outperformed the smaller ones. Of the $369 million of total sales increase in the period, the larger firms with paid employees accounted for $325 million, and other firms for $44 million. This was much greater than the rate of inflation, indicating gains in dollars of constant purchasing power.

In 1982, the average receipts for black-owned firms with paid employees in the U.S. ($151,000) was greater than the average receipts in Michigan ($141,000). This was reversed in 1987, when the average receipts per firm in the U.S. were $200,000, in contrast to $234,000 in Michigan. Gaining a viable level of operations requires growth in the level of average sales.

Only 6 of Michigan's 83 counties had 250 or more black-owned firms with paid employees in 1982: Genesee, Ingham, Kent, Oakland, Washtenaw, and Wayne. These tend to be counties with significant proportions of their populations being African-American and concentrated in certain areas. Wayne County has two-thirds of these firms, followed distantly by Genesee.

Ingham and Washtenaw Counties had the greatest growth in the number of black-owned firms with paid employees between 1982 and 1987. Both more than doubled. Wayne County had the least growth—40 percent.

Oakland County, with multiple concentrations of the black population in Pontiac, Southfield, and Oak Park, had 263 black-owned firms with paid employees in 1987. These firms had receipts of $141 million, and led in average receipts per firm, with $536,00—over three times that for Wayne County.

Among black-owned firms per 10,000 of the black population, Oakland County ranks first (33.9), followed by Washtenaw (21.7), and Ingham (18.7). Wayne County was last, with 14.7.

In terms of black-owned firms per 10,000 of the total population, Oakland County falls to 4th among the 6 counties shown in Table 2-6. Wayne County ranks 1st, and Ingham, last.

This is explained by the proportion of the total population that is black, in the absence of offsetting patronage of black-owned firms by nonblacks.

Of the cities in Michigan with 250 or more black-owned firms in 1982, with or without paid employees, the City of Detroit's firms with paid employees accounted in 1987 for 78 percent of the black-owned firms, but only 68 percent of the receipts. It had 1,091 firms with receipts amounting to $168 million. Its firms expanded from 1982 to 1987 by 38 percent, and their receipts by 23 percent—slightly more than the rate of inflation in the period.

In the number of firms and receipts in 1987, Flint (with 107 firms and $14.6 million in receipts) and Southfield (with 101 firms and $49.6 million in receipts) were distant followers to Detroit. Grand Rapids and Lansing trailed far behind.

Southfield (140 percent) and Lansing (118 percent) led in the growth in the number of black-owned firms with paid employees between 1982 and 1987. Grand Rapids followed closely with a growth rate of 100 percent, much above Flint (62 percent) and Detroit (38 percent).

Southfield was unique among the cities in Michigan by approaching $500,000 in average sales per black-owned firm with paid employees in 1987. Grand Rapids ranked a poor 2nd with $177,000.

Rules of thumb suggesting minimum levels of sales for increasing the probability for viable operations indicate that the average size of the firms must increase to Southfield's level and above, the amount of increase depending on various attributes.

About 53 percent of the state's black-owned firms were in the service industry in 1987. This percentage increases to 70 percent when retail trade is added. Another 6.5 percent is gained with the addition of finance, insurance, and real estate. The percentages are much the same for black-owned firms with paid employees, except that the services component declines by 8 percentage points, and retail trade increases by roughly the same amount.

For all firms in the U.S. with paid employees and without regard to race, the services category has much less of a presence, retail trade is about the same in percentage share by industry, and most other industries are more visible—particularly agriculture, forestry, fishing, mining, construction, wholesale trade, finance, insurance, real estate, and manufacturing—than are black-owned firms in Michigan.

The Detroit Metropolitan Statistical Area (MSA) was first in the state with 9,852 Afro-American-owned firms (71.9 percent of those in the state); these firms generated receipts of $514.3 million (73.3 percent of those in the state). The Flint MSA ranked 2nd in the number of black-owned firms (885), followed by Ann Arbor (538). Ann Arbor ranked second in receipts, with Flint next.

The top 31 black-owned firms in the state in 1989, compiled from lists in *Black Enterprise* and *Crain's Detroit Business Book of Lists*, had combined sales of $814.7 million. The smallest of these firms had $5.0 million in sales. The number of firms identified in 1989 was almost twice that in 1987, when there were 16 large firms with revenues of $400.6 million. Average receipts per firm were much the same in 1987 as in 1989.

These listings are not complete, for some firms do not respond to surveys and others prefer to remain anonymous. Also, *Black Enterprise* magazine shows a limited variety of industries, and *Crain's* lists only firms in the Detroit Metropolitan area, which it regards as its market.

These larger firms account for most of the sales and jobs in black-owned enterprises. They employed over 8,000 persons in the state in 1989, an average of 257 jobs per firm. Since black Americans have high unemployment rates and these firms hire blacks disproportionately, support for these enterprises has to be a component of all efforts to combat unemployment.

The top 31 firms in Michigan in 1989 included 12 motor vehicle dealers, 9 suppliers to motor vehicle manufacturers, 2 each in construction, financial services, health care or hospitals, and 1 each for a TV and radio station combined, computer services, fast food franchising, and a cable television company. The dominance of motor vehicle-related firms demonstrates the large dependence of the black business community on the auto industry, and its exposure to the many challenges confronting this industry. The black community may wish to rethink its purchases of cars from foreign producers and transplants unless it can be shown that these firms employ a significant number of blacks and use frequently African-American suppliers and service providers.

At least 25 of these 31 firms are extremely sensitive to the ups and downs of the economy, and particularly the downswings. Only two or three are in rapid growth industries. None in 1989 were in what stock market analysts call the emerging industries on the forefront of technological change.

Nevertheless, these 31 companies and the other large firms that were not listed offer hope for the future. The five firms listed in both 1982 and 1989 expanded by 257 percent in the seven-year period, or by 19.9 percent a year—much greater than the rate of inflation.

The top 31 Michigan black-owned companies in the BE's 100 in 1989 were reduced to 28 in 1990, according to a recent report in *Black Enterprise* magazine. Five new listings appeared for the industrial/service companies, and eight were not continued in the report. Most companies with continued listings had lower sales in 1990. The recession has taken its toll and may still be having an adverse effect.

The top Michigan 28 in 1990 included 15 industrial/service companies, 12 auto dealerships, and one bank.

Barden Communications, Inc., ranking 6th in the 1990 list of industrial/service companies, received special commentary, as did Wesley Industries, Inc. of Flint. Barden had the highest sales of Michigan-based black-owned firms ($86.0 million). Wesley restructured itself to reduce its dependence on the auto industry.

Two of the highest five U.S. black-owned companies in the number of persons employed were based in Michigan—the Keys Group and Trans Jones, Inc./Jones Transfer Company.

Programs like New Detroit's Business Partnership Plan, which matches experienced majority-owned firms in a mentor relationship with minority firms, deserve attention and support. Other promising efforts include support given by the Michigan Strategic Fund to the Greater Detroit BIDCO, Inc.—a minority-owned company providing capital to minority-owned firms that cannot obtain adequate financing through traditional sources. Both types of programmatic changes, had they existed a decade ago, might have had an impact that would have made the findings of this study more positive. Much remains to be done, if black-owned businesses are to enter the economic mainstream in Michigan. Recommended measures are given in the 1986 study which this chapter updates.

Recommendations for 1991

In addition, the following recommendations, consistent with the present findings, are offered:

(1) *Further research should be conducted by the Michigan Department of Commerce on the obstacles to launching, expanding, and sustaining black-owned businesses and on effective measures for surmounting those obstacles that can be overcome.*

(2) *Promising programs (such as the New Detroit Business Partnership and the Greater Detroit BIDCO) should be evaluated by the Michigan Department of Commerce and/or local Urban League chapters, and expanded if found to be effective.*

If judged to be successful, these efforts should be increased, along with other programs designed to accomplish the same or similar objectives. The priority of assisting relatively large minority-owned firms with growth potential and mitigatable risks is paramount. The advantages of economies of scale and leveraging existing institutions require that such expansion in these programs be carried out by existing successful institutions rather than by new duplicative ones. Chambers of Commerce or other organizations in areas outside the Detroit area should consider carrying out comparable business partnership plans.

(3) *New mechanisms for filling gaps in financing must be expanded or initiated by the Michigan Department of Commerce and by commercial banks.*

In addition to other programmatic thrusts, emphasis should be placed on means for providing equity and debt financing to firms needing amounts above and below the range of the Greater Detroit BIDCO, Inc.—that is, above, say, $1.0 million and below $100,000. There is also a large gap in financing available for both nonprofit and for-profit firms requiring small amounts of funds for short terms, such as for housing modernization before takeouts and construction contracts before the last draw, among other examples of needs with controllable risks.

(4) *A seed capital company for black entrepreneurs should be established by private investors in cooperation with the Michigan Department of Commerce.*

A seed capital firm provides funding for new start-ups where an entrepreneur has an idea that the seed capital company thinks is a good one in need of exploration. The funds may be used for developing a product prototype, marketing analysis, or other business launching purposes. This study has shown the need for new start-ups if there are to be new black-owned businesses to join the mainstream. Just expanding existing firms will not be enough, even though it is a priority. Through the Michigan Strategic Fund, several nonminority seed capital companies have come into existence, but there is not a single minority-owned one, although an application for a seed capital company was submitted by a group of black investors coordinated by the Inner City Business Improvement Forum. This application lost in the competition for limited funding from the Michigan Strategic Fund. Four nonminority seed capital companies were selected.

Further, since the problems confronted by minority entrepreneurs are so great, the incentives provided by the Michigan Strategic Fund should be stronger than those for existing companies. A major component of the program should be the search for potentially successful entrepreneurs with a good idea for a product or a service and good prospects for a reasonable business plan. This is essential for substantial growth in the proportion of firms in the state that are minority-owned and for a major reduction in the black-white unemployment rate differential.

(5) *The Department of Commerce should be encouraged to design and implement programs to provide low-cost management and technical assistance to emerging minority companies.*

Many small firms with employees and some "ma and pa" firms would be able to expand if they could obtain adequate management and technical assistance from experienced consultants. Frequently these firms could grow, increase their profitability, and employ more workers, if they were able to obtain such assistance. Often they cannot afford it, and existing financial institutions cannot provide such services at discounts from cost plus a normal return, despite the socially redeeming gains.

(6) *Supporters of business development should urge the Governor and the Legislature to rethink certain budget cuts that would weaken minority business development; and supporters should also inform appropriate parties of how helpful certain agencies have been.*

The two state agencies that are most relevant for supporting minority business development happen to be the ones that are under the greatest threat from Governor Engler's budget reduction thrust—the Department of Commerce, primarily, and the Social Services Department. The former had over 60 percent of its prior year's budget recommended for reduction. The latter has a program to help welfare clients establish small, largely home-based businesses for helping them graduate eventually from government assistance.

(7) *More resources should be directed by civil rights and church organizations and other community groups to promoting purchasing opportunities for consumers and other buyers in minority communities, particularly in central cities.*

Programs with this objective should be expanded and duplicated outstate—programs such as "Buy in Detroit," which is promoted by the Detroit Association of Black Organizations and by the Detroit branch of the National Association for the Advancement of Colored People. Some church groups have been helpful in this effort in the past. The effectiveness of these programs could be enhanced with the participation of more churches, NAACP branches, Urban League chapters, and other community organizations.

(8) *Public corporations should be encouraged to have a wider racial diversity of directors on their boards; and civil rights and other community groups should expose the racial composition of selected corporations in Michigan and consider boycotting those corporations that have all-white boards.*

(9) *Retail and other black-owned firms serving only blacks should explore reaching a wider market to take advantage of higher household incomes.*

This does not mean that lower-income markets should be abandoned, for there may be good market niches.

(10) *The positive outcomes from community reinvestment agreements with Detroit-based financial institutions should be strengthened, monitored closely, and progress verified by independent sources.*

The Ad Hoc Committee for Fair Banking Practices negotiated agreements with the largest Detroit area financial institutions for increasing their lending in the City of Detroit by about $3.0 billion over a recent three-year period. The institutions report that they have fulfilled this commitment. Since these agreements have expired, a mechanism must be developed for continuing the progress and monitoring it. Corroboration by a neutral outside source would give credibility to the externally unsubstantiated reports by these banking institutions that the agreed upon objectives have actually been attained.

(11) *Supporters of black economic development must give high priority to worker mobility and to enhancements in the education and training of black Americans and be conscious of the damage done to older and declining areas as well as to the metropolitan fringe as a result of urban sprawl.*

Two major constraining factors for the current and future competitiveness of business firms are (1) the mobility to get workers from where they live to where they work; and (2) the quality of the labor force. Black-owned firms, just like other businesses, have a self-interest in the success of current attempts to improve public transportation, to upgrade the quality of education in public schools and community colleges, and to provide relevant training programs in both the public and private sectors.

Addendum

After the submission of the above chapter to the typesetter, *Crain's Detroit Business* for August 4, 1991, became available. It listed the revenues and employment in 1990 and 1989 for 20 "Leading Detroit-Area Black-Owned Businesses." This Addendum presents updated information that did not appear in the chapter.

Crain's portrays data for 1990 for most of the Detroit-area firms shown in Table 2-12 and discussed in the chapter. Figures for two additional firms are listed:

	Sales ($,000,000)		Employment	
Firm and Location	1989	1990	1989	1990
Gilreath Manufacturing, Inc. Howell	29.7	17.0	281	175
T.A.S. Graphic Communications, Inc. Detroit	23.0	23.0	200	175

SOURCE: *Crain's Detroit Business,* July 29-Aug. 4, 1991, page E-27.

Gilreath does plastic-injection molding. T.A.S. is a printing company with binding and mailing facilities. With these two additions, the top 31 firms in 1989 were reduced to the top 30 in 1990, and not 28 as presented in the chapter.

Indicative of the severe impact of the recession, Gilreath's sales declined by 43 percent in 1990, and its employees by 38 percent. T.A.S. was able to maintain its sales, but reduced its employees by 12.5 percent in 1990.

New information given in *Crain's Detroit Business* includes some sales figures, for either 1989 or 1990. Shown below are the sales for both years, even though only one year contains new information.

Firm	Sales ($,000,000) 1989	Sales ($,000,000) 1990
Engineered Plastic Products, Inc.	12.4	14.2
First Independence Corporation	8.7*	9.8
New Center Hospital	9.6	11.0
R.A.S. Financial Corporation	7.2	10.2
Southwest Hospital	24.2	25.9
Summa-Harrison Metal Products, Inc.	18.8	25.0

SOURCE: *Crain's Detroit Business*, July 29-Aug. 4, 1991, page E-27.

Note: *Black Enterprise and Crain's Detroit Business* will differ, since they list firms according to different criteria. The former includes businesses throughout Michigan. The latter has a broader definition for included firms and is limited to the Detroit area.

**Crain's* shows in its 1990 issue $10.1 million for the First Independence Corp.'s 1989 revenues, but $8.7 million in its 1991 issue. This could be due to a revision by the bank holding company.

REFERENCES AND SOURCES

Crain's Detroit Business, Book of Lists, 1991: "Leading Detroit-Area Black-Owned Businesses." Detroit: Crain's Detroit Business, Subscriber Services, Department 77940.

Greater Detroit/Southeast Michigan Business Attraction and Expansion Council, *Economic Fact Book*, September 1989. Detroit: Greater Detroit Chamber of Commerce, Economic Development Group Research Department.

Gregory, Karl D. "The Economic Status of Blacks in Michigan." *The State of Black Michigan: 1984.* East Lansing, Michigan: Urban Affairs Programs, Michigan State University.

Gregory, Karl D. "Toward a Strategy for Economic Development in the Black Community." *The State of Black Michigan: 1985.* East Lansing, Michigan: Urban Affairs Programs, Michigan State University.

Gregory, Karl D. and McMurtry, Walter M. "Enhancing Michigan's Black Business Development." *The State of Black Michigan: 1986.* East Lansing, Michigan: Urban Affairs Programs, Michigan State University.

Gregory, Karl D. "Trends in the Economic Status of Michigan Blacks Since 1967." *The State of Black Michigan: 1987.* East Lansing, Michigan: Urban Affairs Programs, Michigan State University.

Gregory, Karl D. "Blacks in Michigan's Private Industry in the 1980s." *The State of Black Michigan: 1987.* East Lansing, Michigan: Urban Affairs Programs, Michigan State University.

"The Top 100 Black Businesses." *Black Enterprise.* New York, New York: Earl G. Graves Publishing Company, Inc. Issues for June 1983, 1988, 1990, and 1991.

U.S. Department of Commerce, Bureau of the Census, *Survey of Minority-Owned Business Enterprises—Black, 1987,* July 1990.

U.S. Department of Commerce, Bureau of the Census, "1990 MSA Press Release Alpha Sort," February 22, 1991, table entitled "Population of Metropolitan Areas: 1990 and 1980."

U.S. Department of Commerce, Bureau of the Census (pre-publication press release), "Census Bureau Completes Distribution of 1990 Redistricting Tabulations to States," Census Public Information Office, March 11, 1991.

CHAPTER 3

Black Business Development in Michigan, 1987–2002

Joe T. Darden

The Historical Legacy of Black-Owned Businesses

Business ownership has historically been a route of economic advancement for disadvantaged groups (Fairlie and Robb 2004). In the 1920s, black businesses were common in the United States. By 1930, an estimated 70,000 black-owned businesses were operating (Bates 1993). These businesses, however, were not run by the most educated blacks. Such businesses operated with limited capital and were usually very small firms concentrated in a few lines of service-oriented businesses (Bates 1993).

More recent research has shown that black-owned firms still suffer from limited market size. In other words, most black-owned businesses rely on black consumers to remain in business (Wilson 1975; Collins 1983). Such racially restrictive markets are due in part to racial residential segregation and discrimination. As Bates (1993) notes, white merchants have continued to open stores in black neighborhoods, but black merchants have historically been kept out of white areas. The typical black business has been characterized as a small business concentrated in the center of black neighborhoods where the customers are also poorer than customers in other neighborhoods (Young and Harding 1971).

Most black-owned businesses also continue to experience limited access to capital. Limited access to capital influences the size, location, and type of black-owned business. It is well documented that firms in construction, manufacturing, and wholesale trade usually require a larger amount of capital than small personal service businesses and retail establishments (Ong 1981). Thus, fewer blacks are represented in these types of firms.

The research suggests that the limited access of blacks to capital is related to the higher loan denial rates black business owners experience even after controlling for differences in credit worthiness and other factors (Cavalluzzo, Cavalluzzo, and Wolken 2002). Black business owners are also required to pay higher interest rates or put down more collateral than white business owners (Fairlie and Robb 2004; Meier 2006). The limited access to capital forces blacks into the types of businesses with higher turnover rates, such as small retail and services (Reynolds and White 1996). Fewer individual blacks can obtain the larger supply of capital to open manufacturing and wholesale businesses, which have lower turnover rates (Bates 1997). The data show that black-owned firms are more likely to be found in personal service-type operations, which usually have worse outcomes on average than other firms (Fairlie and Robb 2004). Thus, one cannot ignore the role that lending discrimination plays in reducing black business ownership (Meyer 1990).

Contrary to what the general public might believe, Fairlie and Robb (2004) found that, although black-owned businesses have a different regional distribution and are more likely to be located in urban areas than are white-owned businesses, racial differences in geographical locations do not appear to contribute substantially to the gap in small business outcomes.

Other researchers have noted that black business owners (compared to other owners) have a lower level of managerial skills, training, and experience (Bates 1985). A lower supply of human capital influences failure rates, reduces the amount of profits, and limits the access of black-owned businesses to black neighborhoods and black consumers.

Other researchers have attributed the low level of black business ownership to a lack of parental self-employment (Bates 1997; Fairlie 1999; Hout and Rosen 2000; Robb 2002). The lack of parental self-employment is related to the lack of a strong black tradition in owning businesses (Frazier 1957), which emerges through the inheritance of the family business and intergenerational transfer of business skills (Dunn and Holtz-Eakin 2000).

Fairlie and Robb (2003) examined data from the characteristics of business owners (CBO). The CBO data contain information on prior work experience in a managerial capacity and prior work experience in a business where goods and services were similar to those provided by the owner's business. The authors used data from the CBO to explore the role that intergenerational links in self-employment play in contributing to racial differences in such small business outcomes as size, profits, and sales. They concluded that the inability of blacks to acquire general and specific business human capital through exposure to businesses owned by family members may contribute to their limited success in business ownership (Fairlie and Robb 2004). However, because the CBO data do not contain information on a comparison group of wage/salary workers, the authors could not explore the actual causes of racial differences in rates of business ownership. Their focus instead was the determinants of racial patterns in business outcomes. Fairlie (1999) and other researchers (Hout and Rosen 2000) concluded that an individual who had a self-employed parent had a higher probability of becoming self-employed than an individual with a non-self-employed parent. Through the family business, an individual can get training and experience. Moreover, family businesses provide an opportunity for family members to acquire business human capital (Fairlie and Robb 2004).

Given the barriers and limitations faced by black business owners, the next section examines the present state of black business ownership in Michigan and the changes that have occurred since 1987.

Data

Most data for this chapter came from the U.S. Census Bureau's *2002 Survey of Business Owners*. The survey defined black-owned businesses as firms in which African Americans (blacks) own 51% or more of the stock or equity of the business. The data in the 2002 survey were collected as part of the 2002 Economic Census from a large sample of all nonfarm businesses filing 2002 tax forms, including individual proprietorships, partnerships, and any type of corporation with receipts of $1,000 or more (U.S. Census Bureau 2006).

Changes in Black-Owned Firms, 1987–2002

Table 3-1 reports the changes in the number and receipts of black-owned firms in Michigan from 1987 to 2002. The number of black-owned firms in Michigan increased from 13,700 in 1987 to 44,366 in 2002, or by 223%. The black percentage of total firms was 6%, almost doubling the 3.2% in 1987. However, underrepresentation in business ownership still existed since blacks constituted 14.2% of Michigan's population in 2000. The percentage of black-owned firms with paid employees increased from 2,241 in 1987 to 3,112 in 2002, or by 38.8% (Table 3-1). However, the percentage of black-owned firms with paid employees compared to all firms with paid employees in Michigan declined from 16.4% to 7.0% over the same time period.

Black Share of Various Kinds of Businesses in Michigan

The kinds of businesses owned by blacks varied. The extent of black ownership of business was highest in the health care and social assistance industries. Almost 18% of these kinds of businesses were owned by blacks. Service, excluding public administration, was another kind of business where blacks owned 10% or more. Black ownership of businesses was greater than 5% among transportation and warehousing firms (6.6%), administrative and support and waste management and remediation services (7.8%), and educational services (7.6%). Among all other kinds of businesses in Michigan except industries not classified, the black share of firms was 4% or less.

Kinds of Black-Owned Businesses Compared to All Businesses in Michigan

Table 3-2 shows that the kinds of black-owned businesses differed from the kinds of all-owned businesses in 2002. Compared to the kinds of all-owned businesses, black-owned

Table 3-1. Changes in the Number and Receipts of Black-Owned Firms in Michigan, 1987–2002 ($1,000)

Black-Owned Firms	1987	% of Total	2002	% of Total	% Changes, 1987–2002
Number	13,700	3.2	44,366	6.0	223
Receipts	$701,300	1.1	$4,293,679	5.4	5.1
Number with paid employees	2,241		3,112		38.8
% with paid employees		16.4		7.0	–9.4

SOURCE: Calculated by the author from data obtained from U.S. Census Bureau (2006).

Table 3-2. Differences in Kinds of Businesses Owned by Blacks Compared to All Kinds of Businesses in Michigan, 2002

Kind of Business	Total Number of Firms	% of Total Firms	Total Number of Black-Owned Firms	% of Total Black-Owned Firms	Difference
Forestry, fishing, and hunting	—[a]		—		
Mining	—		—		
Utilities	—		—		
Construction	96,543	13.8	1,585	3.7	−10.1
Manufacturing	24,348	3.5	344	0.9	−2.6
Wholesale trade	21,715	3.1	391	0.9	−2.2
Retail trade	87,758	12.6	3,378	7.9	−4.7
Transportation and warehousing	23,870	3.4	1,571	3.7	0.3
Information	8,243	1.2	401	0.9	−0.3
Finance and insurance	25,676	3.7	1,081	2.5	−1.2
Real estate, rental, and leasing	73,947	10.6	1,929	4.5	−6.1
Professional, scientific, and technical services	90,540	13.0	3,651	8.5	−4.5
Management of companies and enterprises	—		—		
Administrative & support and waste management & remediation services	47,323	6.8	3,689	8.6	1.8
Educational services	13,236	1.9	1,004	2.4	0.5
Health care and social assistance	78,576	11.3	13,912	32.5	21.2
Arts, entertainment, and recreation	—	—	—	—	—
Accommodation and food services	21,194	3.0	805	1.9	−1.1
Other services (except public administration)	87,091	12.5	8,887	20.8	8.3
Industries not classified	971	0.1	51	0.1	0.0
Total[b]	698,256	100	42,775	99.9	

[a](—) Comparisons with black-owned businesses could not be made.

[b]Total excludes forestry, fishing, and hunting; mining; utilities; management of companies and enterprises; and arts, entertainment, and recreation.

The index of dissimilarity between black-owned businesses and all businesses in Michigan was 32.5 in 2002.

SOURCE: Calculated by the author from data obtained from U.S. Census Bureau (2006).

businesses were underrepresented in construction; real estate, rental, and leasing; retail trade; and professional, scientific, and technical services. On the other hand, compared to all firms, black-owned businesses were overrepresented in health care and social assistance and other services except public administration. These two kinds of businesses accounted for 53% of all black-owned businesses.

The difference between the kinds of black-owned businesses and the kinds of all businesses was measured by the index of dissimilarity. The index determined the percentage of all black-owned businesses represented by each kind of black-owned business and the percentage of all businesses represented by each kind of business. The difference was then compared. If the representation of the kind of black-owned businesses and the representation of the kind of all businesses was the same, the index of dissimilarity would be 0. If the kinds of businesses represented were totally different, the index would be 100. The actual index of dissimilarity was 32.5. In order for the kinds of black-owned businesses to reflect the kinds of all businesses in Michigan, 32.5% of all black-owned businesses would have to change to another kind of business to eliminate the underrepresentation of black-owned businesses compared to all businesses (Table 3-2).

Black Share of Business Sales and Receipts

Although blacks constituted 14% of the total population in Michigan, black business owners' share of sales and receipts was much lower and therefore black owners were greatly underrepresented. Black owners generated a small part of $793 billion in sales and receipts for all firms in Michigan. The portion generated was only $4.2 billion, or 5.4% of the total profits. This was an increase from the 1.1% in 1987 (Gregory 1991).

Only 25.3% of the total firms in Michigan had paid employees in 2002, up from 24.2% in 1987. The percentage of black-owned firms with paid employees was 7.0% in 2002, a decrease from 16.4% in 1987 (Table 3-1). Generally, firms with paid employees are larger and generate higher sales and receipts. For example, of the total sales and receipts for black-owned firms, 84% were generated by firms with paid employees. These firms generated $3.5 billion in 2002.

Black business owners' share of sales and receipts varied depending on the type of business. The black percentage was highest in retail trade (7.6%), transportation and warehousing (3.6%), and manufacturing (2.5%) (Table 3-3). Ironically, the kinds of businesses where blacks are most represented (health care, social assistance, and other services except public administration) generate very little in sales and receipts compared to other kinds of businesses.

Black Business Participation Rate (BPR)

Table 3-4 presents the black BPR by county. The black BPR is measured as (the number of black-owned firms ÷ the number of blacks in the county or city) × 1,000. The black BPR was highest in Van Buren and Macomb counties, where it was 63.48 and 63.06, respectively. Oakland County ranked third, with a rate of 54.62. The black BPR was lowest in Jackson County, where the rate was only 16.50. The mean black BPR based on counties was 38.11 (Table 3-4).

Table 3-3. The Black Share of Businesses and Sales Receipts by Kind of Business, 2002

Kind of Business	% Black Owned	% Black Share of Sales and Receipts
Construction	1.6	1.3
Manufacturing	1.4	2.5
Wholesale trade	1.8	1.8
Retail trade	3.8	7.6
Transportation and warehousing	6.6	3.6
Information	0.01	0.3
Finance and insurance	4.2	0.03
Real estate, rental, and leasing	2.6	0.3
Professional, scientific, and technical services	4.0	0.5
Administrative % support and waste management % remediation services	7.8	0.7
Educational services	7.6	—
Health care and social assistance	17.7	1.1
Accommodation and food services	3.8	1.4
Other services (except public administration)	10.2	0.7
Industries not classified	5.3	—

SOURCE: Calculated by the author from data obtained from U.S. Census Bureau (2006).

Table 3-4. Black Business Participation Rates (BPRs) in Counties with 100 or More Black-Owned Firms, 2002

County	Number of Black-Owned Firms	Total Black Population	Black % of Total Population	Black BPR
Berrien	721	25,879	15.9	27.86
Calhoun	416	15,033	10.9	27.67
Genesee	3,015	88,843	20.4	33.93
Ingham	1,330	30,340	10.9	43.83
Jackson	207	12,543	7.9	16.50
Kalamazoo	908	23,217	9.7	39.10
Kent	1,739	51,287	8.9	33.90
Macomb	1,345	21,326	2.7	63.06
Monroe	104	2,766	1.9	37.59
Muskegon	716	24,166	14.2	29.62
Oakland	6,594	120,720	10.1	54.62
Van Buren	254	4,001	5.2	63.48
Washtenaw	1,420	39,697	12.3	35.77
Wayne	23,134	868,992	42.2	26.62
Mean				38.11

SOURCE: Calculated by the author from data obtained from U.S. Census Bureau (2006).

Table 3-5. Black Business Participation Rates (BPR) for Cities and Changes in Black-Owned Firms in Michigan, 1987–2002

City	Number of Firms	Sales and Receipts	% Change: Firms, 1987–2002	% Change: Sales and Receipts, 1987–2002	BPR[a]
Ann Arbor	270	22,205	8.4	378	26.81
Auburn Hills	152	17,737	—	—	57.94
Battle Creek	170	4,493	19.7	−11.5	17.89
Dearborn	139	29,604	—	—	111.38
Detroit[b]	19,530	1,583,591	174	513	25.17
Eastpointe	171	4,722	—	—	106.80
Farmington Hills	501	18,309	—	—	87.91
Ferndale	187	76,427	—	—	247.02
Flint[b]	1,731	63,469	153	202	26.01
Grand Rapids	1,141	53,348	266	288	28.26
Inkster[b]	773	14,793	242	165	38.02
Jackson	150	39,240	48.5	1674	20.97
Kalamazoo	607	32,520	315	799	38.12
Lansing	1,322	35,789	351	564	50.66
Muskegon	285	11,220	100	88.7	22.44
Oak Park	538	21,069	144	274	39.29
Pontiac	918	32,013	238	58.4	28.88
Southfield[b]	2,599	391,725	257	510	61.22
Troy	145	96,926	—	—	85.59
Warren	271	102,752	—	—	73.30
Mean					59.68

[a]Computed as: (number of black-owned firms ÷ number of blacks in population) × 1000.

[b]Majority-black municipality.

SOURCE: Calculated by the author from data obtained from U.S. Census Bureau (2006).

The black BPR for cities is presented in Table 3-5. The black BPR was highest in the suburban municipalities of Ferndale and Dearborn. The black BPR in those communities was 247.02 and 111.38, respectively. The suburban community of Eastpointe ranked third. These three suburban communities are located on the border of the city of Detroit. However, suburban communities not on Detroit's border also had on average higher black BPRs than central cities. Indeed, compared to all central cities in Michigan, the black BPR was higher on average in the suburbs. For example, the mean black BPR in Michigan's nine central cities was only 28.48, compared to 85.21 in the suburban communities. Thus, the representation of black business ownership in the suburbs was three times the representation in Michigan's central cities. The lowest black BPR was 17.84 in the city of Battle Creek (Table 3-5). The mean black BPR for all cities represented in Table 3-5 was 59.68.

Changes in Black-Owned Firms in Cities, 1987–2002

Table 3-5 also indicates the changes that occurred in black-owned firms from 1987 to 2002. The increase in the number of black-owned firms was lowest in Ann Arbor (8.4) and Battle

Creek (19.7), which probably impacted the low black BPR in Battle Creek compared to other cities. The increase in black-owned firms between 1987 and 2002 was greatest in Lansing and Kalamazoo, where the percentage change in black-owned firms was 351 and 315, respectively (Table 3-5).

Battle Creek was the only city that experienced a decline in sales and receipts among black-owned firms from 1987 to 2002. The increase in sales and receipts was highest in Jackson, followed by Kalamazoo, Lansing, Detroit, and Southfield (Table 3-5).

Do Majority-Black Cities Influence Black Business Ownership?

Traditionally, black businesses have been strongly dependent on the black population for success. What difference does a majority-black city make? Among the cities of Michigan examined are three majority black cities (Detroit, Flint, and Southfield, a suburban community). As indicated in the previous section, the majority-black cities of Detroit, Southfield, and Flint had the largest number of black-owned firms. Black-owned firms in Detroit and Southfield also generated the largest amount of sales and receipts ($1.5 billion in Detroit and $391 million in Southfield). Black firms in Flint, however, generated only $63 million, which was below the $102 million generated by firms in Warren and the $76 million generated by black-owned firms in Troy as well as the $76 million generated by firms in Ferndale. When majority-black cities in Table 3-5 are compared to other cities, the mean black BPR was 37.60 for majority-black municipalities and 65.20 for places with <50% black populations. Thus it appears that, while majority-black demographic situations may matter to a certain degree, they do not determine the black BPR. That it matters at all stems from the actions of black political figures in cities with black majorities. Studies have shown that black mayors (a product of black demographic dominance and political solidarity) were responsible for the initial opening of the government procurement market to black-owned businesses. Furthermore, many cities headed by black mayors with majority-black city councils aggressively sought to ensure equity in the distribution of city contracts by including minority- and women-owned businesses in the bidding process during the 1970s and 1980s as well as the provision for training programs for minorities and women (Bates 1997; Woodward 1997). Majority-black cities also more readily make provisions for loans and enhance black-owned businesses (Cohn and Fossett 1996; Gold and Light 2000).

Conclusions

This chapter has examined black business ownership in Michigan in 2002, as well as the changes since 1987. The data are based on the U.S. Census Bureau's (2006) *2002 Survey of Business Owners.*

Black-owned firms increased in number from 13,700 to 44,366, or by 223% from 1987 to 2002. Black-owned firms' sales and receipts increased from $701.3 million to $4.2 billion over the same time period. The number of black-owned firms was highest among health care and social assistance. Thus, the kinds of businesses owned by blacks differed from the kinds of businesses in the state as a whole. Blacks continued to lack representation in construction and real estate, rental, and leasing, businesses that require large capital investments.

Although blacks were 14% of the population in 2000, the black share of sales and receipts remained greatly underrepresented.

The black BPR was higher in suburban areas compared to central cities. The black BPR was also higher in cities and suburbs that were not majority black, which calls for a reassessment of the influence of black demographic dominance on black business ownership. This geographic (city vs. suburb) and demographic (majority black vs. non–majority black) finding is very significant because the same outcome applies whether the relationship is for the black BPR for all black-owned firms or the black BPR for black-owned firms with paid employees. Indeed, black-owned firms with paid employees located in the suburbs had an average black BPR of 6.21, compared to only 1.43 for black-owned firms with paid employees located in central cities. Thus, compared to central cities, the firms in the suburbs with paid employees had a black BPR that was 4.3 times the rate in central cities (Table 3-6).

Also, black-owned firms with paid employees that were not located in majority-black incorporated places had an average black BPR of 4.75, which was 1.70 times the 2.78 rate for black-owned businesses with paid employees located in majority-black incorporated places.

Employees and the Pattern of Location of Black-Owned Firms

Although blacks represent a small percentage of the suburban population compared to their representation in central cities, the percentage of black-owned firms with paid employees located in the suburbs was quite high. For example, black-owned firms with paid employees

Table 3-6. Business Participation Rate (BPR) for Black Firms with Paid Employees by City/Suburb and Number of Employees, 2002

City/Suburb[a]	Number of Firms	Number of Employees	Black Population	% Black	BPR[b]
Battle Creek	12	17	9,501	17.8	1.26
Dearborn[c]	18	92	1,248	1.3	14.42
Detroit	1,199	11,706	775,772	81.6	1.55
Flint	96	951	66,560	53.3	1.44
Grand Rapids	56	547	40,373	20.4	1.39
Inkster[c]	27	56	20,330	67.5	1.33
Kalamazoo	47	195	15,924	20.6	2.95
Pontiac[c]	38	190	31,791	47.9	1.19
Southfield[c]	290	3,189	42,454	54.2	6.83
Warren[c]	27	311	3,697	2.7	7.30
Total	1,810	17,254	1,007,650		1.79

[a]Includes incorporated places only.

[b]Computed as: (number of black-owned firms ÷ number of blacks in population) × 1000.

[c]Suburban incorporated place.

SOURCE: Calculated by the author from data obtained from U.S. Census Bureau (2006).

in the suburbs had 4,038, or 23.1%, of all employees in black-owned firms, yet these firms were located in suburban places where the total black population constituted only 9.8%. On the other hand, black-owned firms located in central cities employed 13,416 workers, or 76.8% of all workers in black-owned firms. However, these firms were located in incorporated places where 90.1% of the total black population resided (Table 3-6).

REFERENCES

Bates, T. 1993. Black businesses and the legacy of racism. *Focus* 21(6):5–6.

———. 1985. Entrepreneur human capital endowments and minority business viability. *Journal of Human Resources* 20(4):540–554.

———. 1997. *Race, self-employment and upward mobility: An illusive American dream.* Washington, DC: Johns Hopkins Univ. Press.

Cavalluzzo, K., L. Cavalluzzo, and J. Wolken. 2002. Competition, small business financing, and discrimination: Evidence from a new survey. *Journal of Business* 25(4):641–679.

Cohn, S., and M. Fossett. 1996. What spatial mismatch? The proximity of blacks to employment in Boston and Houston. *Social Forces* 75(2):557–572.

Collins, S. M. 1983. Making of the black middle class. *Social Problems* 30:369–381.

Dunn, T. A., and D. J. Holtz-Eakin. 2000. Financial capital, human capital, and the transition to self-employed: Evidence from intergenerational links. *Journal of Labor Economics* 18(2):282–305.

Fairlie, R. 1999. The absence of the African-American owned business: An analysis of the dynamics of self-employment. *Journal of Labor Economics* 17(1):80–108.

Fairlie, R., and A. Robb. 2003. Families, human capital, and small businesses: Evidence from the characteristics of business owners survey. Center Discussion Paper No. 871, Economic Growth Center, Yale Univ.

———. 2004. Why are black owned businesses less successful than white owned businesses? The role of families, inheritances, and business human capital. Discussion Paper Series 1ZADP No. 1292. http://www.IZA.org/publications/dps/.

Frazier, E. F. 1957. *The Negro in the United States.* New York: Macmillan.

Gold, S., and I. Light. 2000. Ethnic economies and social policy. *Research in Social Movements, Conflicts and Change* 22:165–191.

Gregory, K. 1991. Black-owned businesses in Michigan, 1982–1987, and the top 31 in 1989. In *The state of black Michigan, 1991,* ed. F. Thomas, 31–54. East Lansing: Urban Affairs Programs, Michigan State Univ.

Hout, M., and H. S. Rosen. 2000. Self-employment, family background, and race. *Journal of Human Resources* 35(4):670–692.

Meier, B. 2006. Quarterback turned politician calls own number as lobbyist. *New York Times* 1, B9. November 11.

Meyer, B. 1990. Why are there so few black entrepreneurs? Working Paper No. 3537, National Bureau of Economic Research, Cambridge, MA.

Ong, P. M. 1981. Factors influencing the size of the black business community. *Review of Black Political Economy* 11(3):313–319.

Reynolds, P., and S. Whites. 1996. *The entrepreneurial process: Economic growth, men, women, and minorities.* Westport, CT: Quorum Books.

Robb, A. 2002. Entrepreneurship: A path for economic advancement for women and minorities? *Journal of Developmental Entrepreneurship* 7(4):383–397.

U.S. Census Bureau. 2006. 2002 survey of business owners. Black owned firms, 2002. http://www.census.gov/csd/2bo/black2002.htm.

Wilson, F. D. 1975. The ecology of a black business district. *Review of Black Political Economy* 5(4):535–375.

Woodward, M. 1997. *Black entrepreneurs in America: Stories of struggle and success.* New Brunswick, NJ: Rutgers Univ. Press.

Young, H., and J. Harding. 1971. Negro entrepreneurship in southern economic development. In *Black Americans and white business*, ed. E. M. Epstein and D. R. Hampton, 240–264. Encino, CA: Dickerson.

CHAPTER 4

Black Self-Help in Michigan

Richard W. Thomas

Most research on the state of blacks in contemporary American society has justifiably focused on the range of problems still plaguing black communities. The worst and the most persistent of these problems are teenage pregnancies, high unemployment among black adults and teenagers, crime, socially and economically enforced welfare dependency, increasing numbers of black female-headed households, inadequate education, drug addiction, and related traditional and current forms of racism (*The Crisis*, 1984; *The State of Black America:* 1985, 1986; *The State of Black Michigan:* 1984, 1985).

Although this research has not deliberately ignored black self-help projects (or what Dr. W.E.B. DuBois entitled one of his books—*Efforts for Social Betterment Among Negro Americans*), it has tended to underestimate the significance of black self-help in the current struggles for black social, economic, and political equality (DuBois, 1909).

Recent developments, including cuts in social programs by the Reagan Administration, efforts by this same administration to dismantle a quarter of a century of hard-won protection in the field of equal rights, and the emergence of black conservatives emphasizing black self-help over the traditional focus on racism—these developments have necessitated the continuation and expansion of research that documents the larger society's responsibility for many of the problems facing black America.

Nowhere is this research more needed than in combating the philosophies and the ideologically motivated research of some contemporary black conservatives who have gotten much white press for their de-emphasis of racism and their emphasis on deficits within blacks as key factors in the current complex of problems still facing the black community (Lamar and White, 1985). This new research must do much more, however, than merely describe and reanalyze social problems and react to the nostrums of certain black conservatives. It must chart a new path and produce new visions and models for black survival and progress in the future. This is where contemporary black self-help must begin.

Building on the Tradition of Black Self-Help

In a 1985 article entitled "How to Stop the Mis-education of Black Children," M. Carl Holman, President of the National Urban Coalition, stressed the urgency of black self-help when he wrote, "As in the case of most of the painful breaking of ground and sowing of seeds in the 1950s and earlier, which led to the civil rights revolution of the '60s, much of the work to be done will have to be done by Blacks themselves" (Holman, 1985).

The 1985 report of *The State of Black America*, published by the National Urban League, pointed out that the current problems affecting black America "to a large degree reflect what America has done to black people in doling out to them, for so many years, the worst of jobs, housing, health care, education, and a host of other components that make up the human existence." Yet, the report continues, "at the same time, blacks must also share some of the responsibility for not acting before to address in a massive and coordinated way some of the social ills that sap the strength of their communities." Black institutions and organizations must rise to the occasion and "collaboratively and singularly . . . expand initiatives which enhance black families and communities." The report encourages these organizations and institutions to "sponsor youth groups [and] assist in preparing young people for competent and productive adulthood." In addition, black institutions should "provide services for children of working parents, particularly single female heads of households; and plan and implement programs which prevent crime in black communities" (*The State of Black America, 1985*).

The following year the report reemphasized the role of black self-help. "A massive effort must be undertaken by black America to increase the achievement level of all black students in the public schools." The black community should expand its efforts "to combat teen pregnancy" and "when possible, concentrate on prevention." Black parents have to play a leading role in solving the problem of teenage pregnancy. "Black parents must assume," the report urges, "a greater role in instilling responsible sexual standards in their children and must become more active in serving as a counterbalance to the sexually permissive messages that reach their children through the various media, including radio, records, and TV videos, and from the streets" (*The State of Black America: 1986*).

The message is purposely loud and clear. Blacks can not afford to ignore their own responsibility in changing the course of their history and guaranteeing their future survival and progress. Increasingly, black leaders and scholars, both conservative and liberal, are finding a meeting of the minds on the issue of black self-help (Wycliff, 1986). Blacks in Michigan, as well as throughout America, have always known what was necessary for their survival and progress. Self-help is the oldest and most cherished tradition in Afro-American history. The tradition goes back at least to the American Revolution. This is the time when independent black Baptist churches first emerged, followed by other independent black institutions wherever blacks settled, particularly in the North.

About 140 years ago, blacks in Detroit initiated the first in a long line of self-help projects by establishing schools in church basements. These schools were set up to educate black children barred from public schools, a practice common in other black communities. In 1843, Michigan blacks gathered in Detroit where they convened the Michigan State

Colored Convention. This convention was one of the first black self-help activities in Michigan. Among the issues discussed were education, temperance, the cultivation of good morals, and the development of habits of industry and thrift (Foner and Walker, 1979). This tradition continued as blacks in Michigan and the nation expanded the base of self-help. In 1895, black women formed the National Association of Colored Women, with the motto, "Lifting as We Climb." Working through its local branches, this great black organization established hospitals, homes for girls, and related self-help projects (Franklin, 1980).

Between 1896 and 1914, W.E.B. DuBois played a leading role in linking research to black self-help by holding the Conference on Negro Problems at Atlanta University. Each year blacks gathered together to discuss urgent problems and to publish a study of some pertinent area of black life. Booker T. Washington, notwithstanding his lack of vision in certain areas, implemented some of the best aspects of the tradition of black self-help by hosting the annual Negro Farmers' Conference at Tuskegee and by initiating the Negro Business League (Franklin, 1980). Furthermore, Washington also initiated a black self-help health campaign, the National Negro Health Week, aimed at lowering the high death rates among blacks. In the early 1920s, several black doctors and many black churches and organizations in Detroit participated in this effort (Thomas, 1976).

Marcus Garvey, influenced partly by Washington's self-help philosophy, organized the most impressive and widespread black self-help program in the history of blacks in the Western world. Barely five years after his arrival in America, Garvey's organization, The Universal Negro Improvement Association, had set up an array of businesses, including laundries, restaurants, grocery stores, small factories, and a printing establishment. Some of Garvey's self-help projects, such as his ship company (The Black Star Line), did not work out; but his self-help programs continued to grow and influence blacks even after his incarceration in the mid-1920s, and his death in 1940 (Martin, 1986).

Between the 1940s and the early 1970s, the Nation of Islam, under the leadership of Elijah Muhammad, initiated another form of black self-help. It was organized around an economic philosophy called "communalism" in which members volunteered to contribute part of their income for the establishment of businesses.

In 1947, the Chicago Temple of the Nation of Islam bought a 1400-acre farm in White Cloud, Michigan, because Muhammad wanted the organization to be able to "feed its own members" (Essien-Udom, 1962). Not only did the programs of the Nation of Islam embody the best self-help tradition of both Washington and Garvey, but they demonstrated an uncanny ability to transform the character of black criminals and to uplift layers of black society abandoned by traditional black self-help organizations. In a relatively short period of time, the Nation of Islam had established an economic empire, consisting of restaurants, snack bars, carry-out food shops, supermarkets (appropriately named "Your Supermarket"), canning factories, and 20,000 acres of farm land in Michigan, Georgia, and Alabama. Printing was among the largest of all the Nation of Islam's businesses. These activities continued throughout the 1950s, 1960s, and 1970s. In 1973, the organization's wealth was estimated to be around $70 million (Pinckney, 1976). A few years after the death of Elijah Muhammad, his son and successor, Warith Deem Muhammad, liquidated the organization's businesses as part of a larger strategy of reorganization (Ahmad and Nyang, 1985).

Two Detroit-based black newspapers, *The Detroit Tribune* and *The Michigan Chronicle*, founded in the 1930s, helped to promote a consciousness of black self-help throughout many black Michigan communities by publicizing such activities. The *Chronicle*, which has outlasted the *Tribune*, is still performing this function (See *The Detroit Tribune*, August 20, 1938; *The Michigan Chronicle*, January 21, 1939, and October 12, 1985).

The tradition of black self-help in Michigan has continued to operate primarily through black churches and fraternal, professional, and business organizations. Self-help has provided the foundation for every major black economic, social, and political advancement in the state. As the oldest tradition in the history of black struggle in this country, it behooves blacks to examine the more successful models in this tradition to determine to what extent they can be refined, modified, and applied to current problems.

The Status of Black Self-Help Projects and Activities in Michigan

Black self-help in Michigan is very much alive and thriving in black communities, even though some communities are still lacking in sophisticated organizational structures. Detroit has taken the lead in the development of black self-help projects, activities, and organizations, but has not monopolized the spirit of innovation and dedication reflected in black self-help efforts throughout the state. Black self-help projects can be found in Flint, Benton Harbor, Battle Creek, Muskegon, Pontiac, and other cities. Projects range from the very sophisticated, well-known, multifaceted programs of Detroit's Hartford Memorial Baptist Church, to the smaller and lesser-known self-help projects associated with smaller churches such as The Holy Trinity Church of God in Muskegon. Black churches, however, have not provided the only leadership in the field of black self-help. Blacks from many walks of life and associated with a variety of institutions and organizations have taken the initiative to help the black community pull itself up by its own bootstraps.

The black church in Michigan deserves to be discussed first because of its long and valiant history in the field of black self-help. Although there are still many black churches content to stress other-worldly concerns to the exclusion of the myriad pressing needs of this world, there are excellent examples of black churches in Michigan striving to meet the black community's needs in both worlds. Hartford Memorial Baptist Church is one of the best examples in the state and perhaps in the nation. It boasts a model urban ministry and represents black self-help at its historical and institutional best. Dr. Charles G. Adams, Hartford Memorial's pastor, is also president of the Detroit branch of the NAACP and writes a regular column in *The Michigan Chronicle.*

Among the many services offered by Hartford are: a medical clinic which provides free medical services to those who "have inadequate funds and no medical insurance"; a clothing mission where people in need are provided with new or cleaned and pressed used clothes and other items without charge; a hunger task force which feeds the hungry; a bookstore and boutique; a food co-op which reduces food cost for participants in the program; a print shop and school that not only trains people but also creates jobs; an auto school and shop that "provides automotive schooling, service and employment"; a legal consultation clinic where Hartford lawyers provide free legal consultation not only to members of the church but also to the larger community; the Hartford Social Services Department, which provides counseling for individuals and families; and a credit union boasting $2 million in assets, out of which a $500 college scholarship is awarded to every church member who graduates from high school ("Services for the Community," n.d.; *The Booster*, n.d.; *Detroit Free Press*, February 23, 1986).

Also impressive is the Hartford Economic Development Corporation, now in its seventh year, through which the church purchased between $1.5 and $2 million of commercial real estate. This commercial strip has already attracted Kentucky Fried Chicken and McDonald's restaurants. The church's future plans for the strip include a shopping center that will be called "Hartford Progress Plaza." According to a church member who is also a real estate consultant and who played a key role in Hartford's acquisition of the commercial strip, over the next two decades the church will earn several millions from leasing the property ("Services for the Community," n.d.; *The Booster*, n.d.; *Detroit Free Press*, February 23, 1986).

Few black churches in Michigan can match the range of black self-help activities at Hartford Memorial Baptist Church, but many black churches are busy doing what they can with whatever resources they have at their disposal. For example, according to Hugh Jackson, President of the Pontiac Area Urban League, most church-related black self-help efforts in Pontiac are concentrated on the problem of day care. Day-care services provide invaluable support for working mothers who are also heads of households. Among the Pontiac black churches that provide this service are the Antioch Baptist Church and the Macedonia Baptist Church (Jackson, letter, 1985).

Black churches in other Michigan cities provide similar services. In Grand Rapids, the New Hope Baptist Church provides emergency food and clothing for members in need and pays bills and rent for those without funds. The funds are donated by the members. The First AME Zion Church provides shoes for school children. The Franklin Street Church of Christ distributes food to the hungry (Grand Rapids Area Black Ministers, interviews, 1986).

The Hope United Methodist Church in Benton Harbor provides facilities for the monthly meetings of the Sickle Cell Support Group. Rev. Melvin Williams, the church's pastor, is the coordinator and facilitator of the group. The National Caucus for Black Aged also meets at the church. Pastor Williams and three other ministers have "adopted" Calvin Britain Elementary School for counseling services. Benton Harbor's Pilgrim Rest Baptist Church, pastored by Rev. Walter L. Brown, conducts tutorial classes for students from first through fourth grades and, in cooperation with their parents, monitors the students' academic progress. The church has also organized and hosted RAPP (young women's support group for single parents) (Williams, M., letter, 1986).

These selected church-related black self-help projects and activities are just a sample of work being conducted by black churches in Michigan. Although black churches cannot be expected to solve all the complex problems within Michigan's black communities, churches have continued to function as the primary "keepers of the fire" of black self-help in these communities.

Black Women and Black Self-Help

Black women and their organizations have long been among the leaders in the black self-help movement in both the nation and the state. Some of the most impressive black self-help projects and activities in the country have been initiated and are presently being conducted by black women in Michigan. Leading the list of organizations is one of America's major public service sororities, the Delta Sigma Theta Sorority, founded in 1913 at Howard University. This group of black college women pledged themselves "to serious endeavor and community service . . . demonstrating vital concern for social welfare, academic excellence and cultural enrichment." According to its Detroit Chapter fact sheet, "Today, Delta Sigma Theta is a public service sorority emphasizing scholarship, membership and organizational skills in the public interest" ("Fact Sheet," 1985).

Delta Sigma Theta Sorority was incorporated as a national organization in 1930. Its present national president, Mrs. Hortense Golden Canady, is Assistant Director of Student Financial Services, Lansing Community College, Lansing, Michigan. Among the Deltas' many achievements in the area of black self-help is the Delta Home for Girls, set up in 1947 by the Delta chapter in Detroit. Teenage girls placed in the Home by the Department of Social Services were provided with a "structured home environment other than with their natural parents or guardians." In 1983, the Chapter decided to terminate the Home and channel their energies and finances into building a senior citizens' apartment complex. The Chapter has recently received a $4.3 million H.U.D. 202 grant from the Federal Government to build this project ("Fact Sheet," 1985).

The Detroit Chapter also provides annual academic scholarships, given according to scholarship and financial need, to high school graduating seniors in Detroit. In the spring of each year, the Deltas conduct a workshop called "Delta Teen Lift" for the purpose of providing "educationally and culturally enriched experiences for middle and high school students." Students are provided with information in the areas of career awareness and college and vocational training. Community resource persons and Delta members conduct the workshop. In March 1984, the Deltas in Detroit planned and carried out a Pregnancy Prevention Workshop using resource persons from various social agencies. The workshop, titled "What's Happening Now," provided information for preteens, teens, and their parents ("Fact Sheet," 1985).

In the spring of 1985, the Deltas carried out drug and substance abuse programs for preteens, teens, and parents. These programs constituted part of the Deltas' "What's Happening Now" series. Both programs won a $500 award at the Deltas' 1985 National Convention in Dallas, Texas. The award is for the continuation of both programs in 1986 ("Fact Sheet," 1985).

The Delta Detroit Alumnae Chapter is presently leading the way for a major national Delta program called "Summit II—A Call to Action in Support of Black Single Mothers." The program was first made public in January 1984 by Mrs. Hortense G. Canady, the national president, at a news conference in Washington, D.C. Less than two years later, over 165 Summit II conferences have been held throughout the country under the auspices of local Delta chapters working with women's and community organizations, government agencies, and foundations (Summit II: A Call to Action, 1984).

The Delta Chapter in Detroit kicked off its Summit II conference on June 16, 1984, at King High School. Over 250 single mothers and fathers attended a workshop which addressed problems of single parenting. Mrs. Canady gave the keynote speech, segments of which were aired on the CBS television show, "Sunday Morning" ("Fact Sheet," 1985).

In October 1985, the Detroit chapter received a $98,000 grant from the state to fund a pilot program designed to help black single mothers in that city. Governor Blanchard commented, "This cooperative project between Delta Sigma Theta and state government is a pioneering effort with tremendous promise." He went on to remark, "I wholeheartedly support this project and congratulate Delta Sigma Theta's Detroit Alumnae for their leadership in addressing the problems of single black mothers through action." The program, called "Affecting Lifetime Income through Education/Employment," provides single mothers with six months of counseling as well as training three days a week. Facilities for the program are provided by the Detroit Public Schools, community colleges, and various social agencies in the area. The first phase will be followed by two years of vocational education training and job placement (*Delta Newsletter*, 1985–86).

Delta chapters in other cities in Michigan are organizing similar self-help projects. In 1985, the Grand Rapids Delta Sigma Theta Sorority started a series of public forums to provide blacks with "basic survival skills." The first forum, a financial symposium, was held at the Marriott Hotel and featured a tax attorney for the IRS, an investment counselor for Merrill Lynch, and a bank manager for Michigan National. An executive from Westinghouse acted as moderator. According to a Delta Sigma Theta representative, the symposium was "well received," and the participants "learned new ways of investing, budgeting, and finance, but most of all saving those tax dollars" (Perkin, letter, 1986).

In May 1986, the Grand Rapids Chapter held a parenting conference focusing on the problems of teen pregnancies and female heads of households. A range of workshops included such topics as financial planning, parent-child relations, planned parenthood, protecting children from sexual assault and abduction, choosing good child care, new ways of discipline, alternatives to spanking, wardrobe planning, food preparation, health, fitness, and stress management. The stated aim of the conference reflects the highest values of the tradition of black self-help. "Our aim here is to equip young mothers and fathers with coping skills and survival skills for providing good role models for their children and to help break this cycle of children raising children" (Perkin, letter, 1986).

In Muskegon Heights, the Deltas have an ongoing tutorial project for black children, starting at the beginning of the school year and working in cooperation with teachers. The Flint Delta Chapter held a Summit II Conference in May 1986. In Battle Creek, the Alumnae Chapter of the Deltas sponsored several black self-help projects in 1985, including a heritage and scholarship program and health fair ("Calendar of Events," 1985–86). These and other Michigan chapters of Delta Sigma Theta have engaged in black self-help projects and activities that have contributed to the continuation of the tradition of black self-help, both in the state and the nation.

Although the Deltas are one of the most active black women's organizations engaged in black self-help in Michigan, other black women's groups and organizations are also engaged in uplifting black communities in the state. One such organization is the Concerned Black

Women's Roundtable, founded in 1983 by Ms. Joyce Williams of Kalamazoo for the purpose of holding annual black women's conferences. According to the founder, the aim of the organization is to provide opportunities for black women to display their various skills and talents. The first conference was held in Kalamazoo and drew 500 participants. The second, in Battle Creek in September 1985, attracted 750 people, including a large group of black youth who had their own workshops. The third one will be held in Benton Harbor in the fall of 1986. The two preceding conferences included discussion of the role of music, arts and crafts, family relations, black churches, politics, economics, educators, social workers, and the role of social groups such as sororities and fraternities (Williams, J., letter, 1986).

Another black women's organization involved in black self-help in Michigan is the National Association of Negro Business and Professional Women's Clubs, Inc. The N.A.N.B.P.W., Inc. was founded in 1935 by black business and professional women to "encourage and develop opportunities for Negro women in business and the professions." The Battle Creek Club of the N.A.N.B.P.W., Inc., chartered in 1971, has been carrying on this organizational mandate for a decade and a half. Since 1971 the Club has hosted the Sojourner Truth Luncheon held annually in May. Awards are presented for outstanding community service. In addition, the Club helps to place minority women on community boards and sponsors the Champagne Sip for Scholarships for minority students attending predominantly black schools. The study of black history and culture is a key part of N.A.N.B.P.W.'s program. "There is a special commitment to help youth pursue and realize their formal education, to enroll in and graduate from college, and to enter the business and professional world," according to Ms. Deborah Brown, the present president of the Battle Creek Chapter (Perry, 1985).

There are other black women's self-help organizations working for the betterment of the black community in Michigan. Some are chapters of national black women's organizations while others are local and statewide. Some are well known to the public, in contrast to those known only to people who benefit from their services. Most black women's self-help projects and activities go unrecorded as they always have, healing and helping in a seemingly thankless and endless struggle to keep black communities from going under.

It should be noted that although black women have played a key role in the development of black self-help, both black men and women have participated in black self-help organizations, projects, and activities.

Building A Black Self-Help Network in Michigan

As more blacks become involved in the self-help movement in Michigan, a networking effect has been set into motion. Some of this networking has evolved from the conscious efforts of blacks with particular interests coming together to share experiences and compare strategies. In other cases, people have drifted together, carried along by the unpredictable undercurrents of shifting issues and popular controversies. Fortunately, the majority of the black self-help organizations in Michigan appear to be based on mutuality of interests.

This effort to network around key issues and problems reveals a new stage in the social consciousness of the black community in Michigan. Several black organizations in Michigan have contributed to the black self-help network by hosting conferences and distributing information about their activities. For example, the Michigan Association of Black Social Workers (MABSW) has been building a network of black self-help around black family and children issues for over fourteen years. This organization also has a broad range of other interests that contribute to the expansion and diversity of the network. Part of the organization's philosophy states that it regards as its "primary obligation the welfare of the Black individual, the Black family and the Black community, which includes action for improving social conditions. We recommend, therefore, that we adopt a combination of separation and coalition around all pertinent issues" (*Newsletter*, 1985). The concept of a "black extended family" is central to the philosophy of the MABSW.

Key aspects of MABSW's stated purpose relate directly to the process of black self-help networking: "to implement and establish the necessary groundwork to effect linkages between Black people; to provide a structure and forum through which Black practitioners and Black social workers in related fields of Health, Education, Social Services, and Social Welfare can exchange ideas, provide services, and develop programs in the interest of Black people; and to work in cooperation with Black people to develop and sponsor community projects and programs which will serve the interests of the Black community at large" (Constitution, MABSW, n.d.).

In October 1985, the Flint Association of Black Social Workers held a seminar on "Black Men Nurturing Black Boys." This seminar was the first in a series focusing on "Strengthening the Black Family" (*Newsletter*, Michigan Association of Black Social Workers, 1985).

The following month, the Grand Rapids chapter hosted MABSW's 14th annual State Conference. Workshops were conducted by members of the Grand Rapids black community. At the same time the members of the Grand Rapids Association of Black Social Workers were meeting, the Black Women's Health Project was having its official dedication ceremony in the same hotel. Some members of the MABSW attended the dedication ceremony, providing an example of ways in which black self-help organizations are becoming increasingly supportive of one another within the larger black self-help movement (*Newsletter*, MABSW, 1985).

In 1978, the Detroit Association of Black Social Workers (DABSW) created a private nonprofit agency, the Black Family Development, Inc. (BFDI), incorporated in May 1979. This initiative by the DABSW paved the way in consolidating and institutionalizing black community concern around black child and family care, and in providing a community base for networking around these issues. According to one of BFDI's documents, BFDI was created as "the social services project of the . . . DABSW . . . to promote and provide quality social work services to Detroit's Black Community . . . based on the assessed needs of Blacks by Blacks." This evolved into a "programmatic focus by BFDI on Black child abuse and neglect." One of DABSW's assessments pointed to the need of the black community to "target services to families of abused children to minimize the need for out-of-home placements." This view supports intervention programs to eliminate neglect and abuse of black children but argues that such intervention should at the same time strive to "preserve the family unit by introducing viable and stable alternatives to family dysfunctions" ("Abstract," BFDI, n.d.).

Since its founding, the BFDI has counseled clients within the home itself where presumably clients are more comfortable. Sessions involving groups and individuals have been conducted either at BFDI headquarters or other suitable places. A statement of BFDI philosophy explains: "It is the contention of Black Family Development, Inc. that the Black community, lay and professional, has the resources and the responsibility to be accountable for effecting enhanced interactions within the Black family. This can be done by emphasizing the strengths of Black families; and through the provision of services which are planned and implemented, staffed and controlled by Black helping professionals whose combined skills, cultural perspective, and experiential background give confirmation to the validity of the Black experience" ("Abstract," BFDI, n.d.).

The MABSW, DABSW, and the BFDI are all vital components in the statewide network of black self-help organizations raising the social consciousness of the black community about child and family care issues and a range of other related problems. More importantly, as stated in the BFDI document, they have also "learned the value of utilizing those support networks within the Black community which have been overlooked in recent years" (i.e., churches, block clubs, etc.).

The Albion Black Alumni Association (ABAA) is another black self-help organization with great potential for expanding the black self-help network in Michigan, especially in the area of black youth development. Established in October of 1982 as a non-profit organization, the ABAA has been involved in stimulating concern for career development among black youth, expanding the cultural and educational experiences of black youth through scholarships and special programs, and "networking with people that could have a positive influence on Black Youth." During the past two years, the ABAA has promoted and sponsored a variety of self-help projects and activities. These included: sponsoring 33 black Albion High School students to attend the National Scholarship Service for Negro Students (NSSFNS) held in Detroit in February 1984; sponsoring 10 black students to attend a Career Training workshop in Albion that same year; forming a youth branch of ABAA, called Educational Progress in the Community (EPIC), which uses "positive youth" who function as role models in the academic, social, and economic areas; presenting four scholarships to black youth; and sponsoring and organizing the 1985 Black History Month events. ABAA's plans for 1986 include giving increased attention to black youth in the areas of teenage pregnancy, options and opportunities in higher education, leadership training, networking, and the revival of the Clothe-A-Kid program (Lee, 1985).

Detroit has one of the best umbrella self-help organizations in the state and the nation. The Detroit Association of Black Organizations (DABO) has provided an excellent model for networking within a large urban community containing a black majority. The Detroit Association of Black Organizations was established on April 21, 1979, "as a non-profit, non-partisan federation of black organizations." The impetus for establishing DABO grew out of an increasing concern that the black community in Detroit "was suffering needlessly and at great cost by its senseless fragmentation—and a growing will to surmount it" (Brochure, DABO, n.d.).

DABO's goals are expressed in the preamble of its constitution: "We, the members of the Detroit Association of Black Organizations (DABO), solemnly commit ourselves and our organizations to uniting the black community to attain its greatest possible strength. Our joining together attests to: 1) our recognition that effective survival for black people in a frequently hostile environment will depend on our ability to make rational, studied and unemotional judgments on where the black community's intrinsic interests lie [on] each issue that arises; and 2) the imperative need for the black community to have a broadly based body through which emotional judgments [may be made] in matters affecting its intrinsic interests; and our firm support of the DABO as that body. Together, as one, we now move forward, confident we will overcome the division and discord among us that, for well over three centuries, have undermined and thwarted our struggle to secure the full measure of economic, political and social justice for black people that most every other American possesses and takes for granted. Ever mindful, therefore, that the costs of a fragmented black community are always oppressively high, and clearly destructive of the best interests and the well-being of black people, we, the members of DABO, under one banner to achieve common goals, shall set an irresistible example of unity for the black community to see. We shall overcome!" (Brochure, DABO, n.d.).

Any black organization is eligible for membership that has a predominantly black membership, is non-partisan, and is "constructively seeking to advance some aspect of the black community's well-being, with either a dues-paying or voting membership of twenty (20) or more members in good standing and . . . has been in existence for [at least] one year . . ." Some of DABO's objectives include empowering the black community to its maximum potential; supporting and encouraging the "dignity and integrity of the black community"; providing the foundation for a more "enlightened and responsible public opinion in the non-black community on the important problems and interests of black people"; advancing "the cultural, economic, political, and social interests of the black community at all levels—local, state, national, and international" ("Brochure," DABO, n.d.).

The two objectives which seem to be most relevant for building and maintaining a black self-help network are: "to be an effective bridge between non-black groups and institutions and the black community in the interest of achieving mutual understanding, the pursuit of shared goals, and the resolution of common concerns"; and "to provide, through the establishment of a voluntary mechanism for arbitration and conciliation, creative opportunities for the resolution of divisive conflicts and disputes between black organizations and individuals . . . that would otherwise erode the black community's unity and dissipate its strength" ("Brochure," DABO, n.d.).

In the last few years, DABO has developed networks of interests and concerns around issues of major importance to the black community. For example, in October 1983, DABO initiated an anti-crime program which involved helping the police department expand the base of citizen participation in its crime prevention programs (*The Urban Voice*, 1984).

In August 1984, DABO met with the Metropolitan Anti-Crime Coalition (MACC), a group of white northeast Detroiters. Both organizations agreed to combine their efforts in the struggle against crime. The name was changed to Detroit MACC. Its main objective is to build "a city-wide, broad-based, informed and effective anti-crime coalition." In a city known for its racial polarization, the significance of Detroit MACC goes even farther than being an anti-crime coalition. It is "a coming together of black and white Detroiters to fight crime" (*The Urban Voice*, 1984). This example of interracial unity around the issue of fighting crime is a good sign of future race relations in Detroit.

In March 1985, DMACC held an anti-crime conference that attracted over 1200 people. The "Let's Fight Back! Let's Save Our City" conference was a great success. Two reporters on the scene observed that "More than 1,000 people of all ages, ethnic backgrounds, and walks of life converged on Cobo Hall in a citizens' movement to fight crime in the street" (*The Urban Voice*, 1985).

In addition to DABO's crime-fighting programs and its participation in a number of other community projects, its weekly TV program on WJBK-TV Channel 2, expands the networking potential of black self-help organizations (*The Urban Voice*, 1984). DABO represents one of the best models of urban black self-help in the country, and other black organizations in the state and the nation would do well to study it.

Most of these examples of black self-help projects and activities have emerged as responses or reactions to local problems, with limited application to the development of a theory and strategy of social and economic development of black communities in Michigan and the nation. We need to develop a theoretical framework from which we can analyze the similarities and differences among individual black communities.

Furthermore, we need to know what aspects of black self-help projects and activities are replicable in other settings and situations. As a step in this direction, a concept paper called "A Process for Black Community Development" was presented by Dr. Karl D. Gregory, of Oakland University, to a gathering at the Detroit Urban League in October 1985. Gregory's idea is to come up with a process "for developing a strategy for black community development . . . to improve substantially the quality of life." This process could develop into a movement first within the state and then throughout the nation.

The mission would be to "launch a movement to promote community economic development and to narrow substantially the gaps in the economic station between blacks and whites by a united effort of community organization." Objectives would include "establishing specific, time-phased, and measurable targets for actions, short and long range, for review by an Executive Committee for presentation to a General Assembly of community leadership as selected by the Executive Committee."

Detroit would be the focus for coming up with a "well structured and replicable prototype" using organizations with statewide and national membership. Implementation would be accomplished through a Secretariat functioning as a technical support group carrying out such tasks as survey analyses of key concerns and priorities. An Executive Committee would, among other functions, "review and approve the operations of the Secretariat" and "schedule a convocation and determine which community leaders and organization representatives are to be invited." The primary aim of the convocations would be to marshal a range of "self-determined and change-oriented organizations." Those invited would comprise the initial membership (Gregory, 1985).

Gregory's proposal also includes other implementation strategies. His ideas are consistent with the best thinking in the black self-help tradition and reflect the level of sophistication that black self-help must attain if black communities are to break out of the cycle of poverty and dependency.

These are only samples of a wide range of black self-help projects and activities in Michigan. The ones presented here do not in any way exhaust the list of black self-help efforts in Michigan.

Establishing a Spiritual Foundation for Black Self-Help

Questions of spiritual and moral principles have often been deliberately left out of discussions of the state of blacks in contemporary society. One reason is that such discussions may seem inappropriate in scholarly discourses, where the presentation of statistical data is all too often given excessive importance. The black community has reached the point, however, where questions will have to be posed concerning the role of spiritual principles and values in programs for black social and economic development. For example, to what extent are such problems as black teenage pregnancy, black drug addiction, and black crime the result of social pathology born of poverty or the result of a lack of spiritual education? By spiritual education, I mean exposure to such values as: respect for one's body so as not to abuse it with drugs and alcohol; love and respect for young girls and women so as not to deliberately burden them with children that they cannot adequately care for by themselves; love and respect for work of any kind so long as it does not result in harm to others; a willingness to share one's good fortune with the less fortunate of the community rather than constantly indulging in the endless pursuit of material things; and a devotion to the building and nurturing of black family life. In addition, spiritual education should result in a willingness to apply spiritual principles and values to judgments about certain popular black movie and TV personalities who have made a virtue of vulgarity common among certain subgroups. These screen and TV personalities are influencing black youth in unproductive ways.

Black self-help, therefore, cannot be built upon a weak spiritual foundation or upon an agenda which reduces the problems of blacks to mere economic and political development. Although economics and politics are crucial building blocks, they are not sufficient by themselves. The black self-help tradition has always been at its best when it has embodied both material and spiritual goals. This spiritual education cannot be left only to black churches. Many black churches are still trapped in religious orthodoxy and require clarification of the role of spiritual education in the uplifting of a people.

As already mentioned, Hartford Memorial Baptist Church in Detroit is an excellent model of the application of spiritual teachings to urban problems. The Urban Leagues in Michigan have a slogan for black males, "Don't make a baby unless you can be a father." This slogan addresses a value lacking in many young black males—a lack that pervades American male popular culture. Young black females and males need more than the usual recommendation of birth control methods. These methods will not prevent AIDS or lay a solid foundation for building trusting, loving, and nurturing relationships. Neither will they address the fundamental feelings of inadequacy and hopelessness which pervade so many of these young people's lives, leading them into irresponsible and non-productive behavior. These feelings can only be addressed by helping young people to draw upon their spiritual heritage and to believe in themselves and their potential to overcome all barriers. This is the spiritual education which must form the foundation of all black self-help.

Conclusions

Black self-help is one of the most important traditions in Afro-American history. Black self-help in Michigan is part of this historical tradition. At the present time, blacks throughout

Michigan are involved in a range of black self-help projects and activities. The black church is still playing a leading role but not the only role. Other black organizations, both old and new, are endeavoring to address the many problems plaguing the black community in Michigan. As these organizations grow and develop around particular interest areas, they are evolving into a black self-help network. They must be certain, however, that such a network is based upon sound spiritual principles. In other words, black self-help must be both material and spiritual.

Recommendations

1. Black self-help of all kinds should be encouraged, especially among poor, black youth.
2. A statewide newsletter of black self-help organizations should be published.
3. Systematic research on the most successful past and current black self-help organizations, projects, and activities should be conducted from which models can be developed. A course on the history of black self-help organizations should be developed for community groups and adult education classes. Such a course should also be taught in public schools.
4. A national and international hookup of all black organizations engaged in any form of self-help should be established. There is a black self-help organization in Britain, The National Federation of Self-Help Organizations, which publishes a newsletter. (*Self-Help News*, 1985).
5. Black self-help must not be allowed to divert attention from the lingering effects of historical racism. Black self-help has always been part of the larger struggle against racism, and it has never been, nor is it now, a retreat from confronting racism.

REFERENCES

"Abstract," Black Family Development, Inc. Detroit, Michigan, n.d.

Ahmad, Mumtaz and Nyang, Sulayman. "A New Beginning for the Black Muslims." *Arabia*, July 1985, pages 50–51.

The Booster. Hartford Memorial Baptist Church, Detroit, Michigan, n.d.

"Brochure." Detroit Association of Black Organizations (DABO). Detroit, Michigan, n.d.

"Calendar of Events." Alumni Chapter, Delta Sigma Theta Sorority, Inc. Battle Creek, Michigan, 1985–86.

Constitution and Bylaws of the Michigan Association of Black Social Workers. Lansing. Michigan.

The Crisis. Vol. 91, No. 10, December 1984, pages 20–25.

Delta Newsletter. Delta Sigma Theta Sorority, Inc. Washington, D.C., Winter 1985–86, page 8.

Detroit Free Press. February 23, 1986.

The Detroit Tribune. August 20, 1938.

DuBois, W. E. B. *Efforts for Social Betterment Among Negro Americans.* Atlanta, Georgia: The Atlanta University Press, 1909.

Essien-Udom, E. U. *Black Nationalism.* New York: Del Publishing Company, Inc., 1962, pages 183 and 185.

"Fact Sheet." Delta Sigma Theta Sorority, Inc. Detroit, Michigan, 1985, pages 1, 2 and 5.

Foner, Philip S. and Walker, George E. *Proceedings of the Black State Conventions.* Philadelphia: Temple University Press, 1979, page 80.

Franklin, John Hope. *From Slavery to Freedom.* New York: Alfred A. Knopf, 1980, pages 285–290.

Grand Rapids Area Black Ministers. Interviews, January 31, 1986.

Gregory, Karl. "A Process for Black Community Development." Paper presented at the meeting of the Detroit Urban League, Detroit, Michigan, October 23, 1985.

Holman, M. Carl. "How to Stop the Miseducation of Black Children." *Ebony,* October 1985, pages 43 and 50.

Jackson, Hugh. Letter to Cleopatra Jones, November 20, 1985.

Lamar, Jacob, Jr. and White, Jack E. "Redefine the American Dilemma." *Time,* November 11, 1985, pages 33 and 36.

Lee, Tonya. "Albion Black Alumni Association Preparing Minority Youth for Tomorrow." *The Urban Advocate,* 1985. Battle Creek Urban League, Battle Creek, Michigan, page 6.

Martin, Tony. *Race First* Westport, Connecticut: Greenwood Press, 1986, pages 33, 34, and 284.

The Michigan Chronicle. January 21, 1939, and October 12, 1985.

Perkin, Girta R Letter to Cleopatra Jones, February 1, 1986.

Newsletter. Michigan Association of Black Social Workers. Lansing, Michigan, 1985, pages 1–3.

Perry, Patricia Patton. "National Association of Negro Business and Professional Women's Clubs, Inc. Promotes Education, Parity." *The Urban Advocate,* 1985, Vol. 1, No. 2, Battle Creek Urban League, Battle Creek, Michigan, page 9.

Pinkney, Alphonso. *Red, Black and Green: Black Nationalism in the United States.* Cambridge, Mass.; Cambridge University Press. 1976.

Self-Help News. London, England. No. 4, November/December 1985.

"Services for the Community." Hartford Memorial Baptist Church. Detroit, Michigan, n.d.

The State of Black America: 1985. New York, New York: National Urban League.

The State of Black America: 1986, New York, New York: National Urban League.

The State of Black Michigan: 1984. East Lansing, Michigan: Urban Affairs Programs, Michigan State University.

The State of Black Michigan: 1985. East Lansing, Michigan: Urban Affairs Programs, Michigan State University.

Summit II: A Call to Action in Support of Black Single Mothers. Proceedings of thirty-four of thirty-eight conferences sponsored by the Delta Sigma Theta Sorority, Inc., in cities throughout the United States, 1984, page 50.

Thomas, Richard. "The Black Urban Experience in Detroit; 1916–1967." In Homer Hawkins and Richard W. Thomas (eds.), *Blacks and Chicanos in Michigan Cities.* Lansing, Michigan: Michigan Historical Division, 1976, page 61.

The Urban Voice. Detroit, Michigan. Vol. 1, No. 4, August-December 1984, page 2.

The Urban Voice. Detroit, Michigan. Vol. 2, No. 5, January-July 1985. page 1.

Williams, Joyce. Letter to Joe T. Darden, Dean, Urban Affairs Programs, Michigan State University, January 13, 1986.

Williams, Melvin. Letter to Richard Thomas, January 22, 1986.

Wycliff, Don. "Blacks Joining Hands for Self-Help." *New York Times,* February 3, 1986.

CHAPTER 5

The Black Self-Help Tradition in Michigan, 1967–2007

Richard W. Thomas

The Post–Urban Disorder Period

The urban disorders in several Michigan cities during July of 1967, particularly the worst of them, in Detroit, which claimed the lives of 43 people and destroyed close to $20 million worth of property (National Advisory Commission on Civil Disorders 1968), shocked the state and nation. Riots also occurred in Flint, Muskegon, Saginaw, Pontiac, Grand Rapids, Kalamazoo, and Albion (e.g., *Flint Journal* 1967; *Grand Rapids Press* 1967a, 1967b; *Saginaw News* 1967). Through it all, African Americans never ceased their self-help efforts.

In the aftermath of the urban disorder in Detroit during that fateful and bloody July, African American leaders, organizations, groups, and ordinary individuals began picking up the pieces and rebuilding what they could out of the ashes. Between 1967 and the present many black self-help organizations in Michigan—some predating the 1967 riots—have dedicated themselves to addressing the problems of poverty and racism that gave rise to the riots (Thomas 2004). They set up youth programs in storefronts, organized programs to teach life skills to black teenagers, strengthened the black family, encouraged single parents to better their lives, taught "Black Pride" to children and youth, healed the hurt and pain of families of slain kids, reconciled these families with the families of kids who had murdered their kids, and much more.

In addition, since the 1967 riots these black self-help organizations in Michigan developed statewide and nationwide networks that greatly enhanced their effectiveness. This chapter is a short story of some of them.

The Inner City Sub-Center

The Inner City Sub-Center (ICSC) and Operation Get Down (OGD) were among the most impressive creations of the black self-help tradition in Michigan during this period. Both emerged soon after the 1967 "riot" and were innovative community-based organizations reflecting the core values of the black self-help tradition. The ICSC, one of several African American community-based organizations that arose in response to the needs of African American youth, was established in a store front on Detroit's east side the same year as the riot, or what many would call " The Black Rebellion" (Inner City Sub-Center Project, Inc. 1986; Taylor 1987). It was established by the Education Committee of the Association of Black Studies at Wayne State University to serve the needs of residents in poor black neighborhoods.

The ICSC was called "The Center" and it had a big picture of Malcolm X on the front of the building. Black youth in the neighborhood were immediately drawn to The Center. There, in the wake of the worst urban disorder in the nation's history, in desolate neighborhoods, African American youth had a haven in which they could learn African American history and culture taught by the staff of The Center and speakers brought in to raise their social consciousness (Inner City Sub-Center Project, Inc. 1986; Taylor 1987).

In 1968 the ICSC incorporated as a nonprofit organization which greatly enhanced its resources without comprising the core values of its self-help mission. A year later it received a grant from the Youth Opportunity Program that enabled it to expand its programs. In 1972, five years after the riot, New Detroit Inc. funded the ICSC for a three-year developmental program. With these additional funds The Center moved to a larger building and expanded its services to include preschool, senior citizens, adult education programs, and a food co-op. As a result, The Center's program expansion enabled it to serve more than 2,000 people a year (Inner City Sub-Center Project, Inc. 1986; Taylor 1987).

Twenty years later, in 1987, the ICSC's youth program formed the centerpiece of the organization's programs. Throughout its history the ICSC has focused on the problems of African-American youth, guiding them away from "the street" to more socially responsible roles in the community. In 1987 Paul Taylor explained to an interviewer: "When it comes down to the most significant thing we do, the main program has always been and always will be the youth program, because it's our contention that consciousness raising for the young folk is the key to the struggle." If "resources get so tight that we have to scrap everything, we would scrap everything but the youth program."

Operation Get Down

A few short miles away in another poor and distressed African American neighborhood, OGD was founded in September 1971 as a nonprofit organization. Both the ICSC and OGD were founded by young African American radicals inspired by the life of Malcolm X and the Black Power movement of the 1960s. Both sought solutions to the plight of the black urban poor in the postriot period. In addition, both organizations accessed white resources to develop some of their most important community-based programs (Operation Get Down 1986).

Notwithstanding what some purists might consider to be a contradiction of the philosophy of the black self-help tradition, neither organization compromised its commitment to the philosophy and practice of black self-help as a practical strategy of community building. In fact, this postdisorder period witnessed the marriage of the best of the interfaith and black self-help traditions in healing the wounds of the 1967 riot. For example, in 1970, the United Methodist Church hired Barry L. Hankerson to work in Detroit as a community developer. He became part of a working group that included Bernard Parker, Jr., senior citizens, a group of young African Americans, college students, and families from the community (Operation Get Down 1986; Parker 1986).

These meetings fostered the growth and development of leadership skills, problem-solving techniques, conflict management, and group motivation. Hankerson played a major role in conducting these classes. A local white minister also contributed to this process of skill-building by teaching Parker and some African American youth problem-solving techniques, long-range planning, and self-development (Parker 1986). All of these proved useful in applying the principles of the black self-help tradition.

White involvement did not distract OGD from viewing itself as a black self-help organization. According to one source, "Their guiding principle was self-help, the motivating forces and motto was [*sic*] adopted from Malcolm X," who said, "I believe that when you give the people a through understanding of what confronts them and the basic causes, they will create their own programs; and when the people create a program you get ACTION!" (Operation Get Down 1986).

Alternative Funding and the Black Self-Help Tradition: The Black United Fund of Michigan

Three years after the riots in Michigan cities, a statewide African American network organization was founded: the Black United Fund (BUF) of Michigan. It was "established as a community resources center to enhance self-help empowerment efforts through grass roots activities and organizations" (BUF of Michigan 2006). In 1972 the BUF of Michigan was chartered as a nonprofit corporation, and in August of 1974 it became affiliated with the national BUF. Three decades later, the BUF of Michigan (2006) could make the following claim: "For over 30 years, the Black United Fund of Michigan, Inc., has stood firm on the principle of community enrichment, self-help and education. The Black United Fund of Michigan, Inc., serves as a non-competitive Fund of Choice that assists community efforts through referrals, funding, consultation and/or technical assistance."

The black self-help tradition is reflected in all aspects of the BUF of Michigan's mission, vision, and philosophy. The mission statement says that the organization is "committed to impact and support positive social and economic changes in the African American community, as well as the community at large serving as a funding institution which provides quality resources" (BUF of Michigan 2006). The "vision" statement follows with the bold claim that it "funds ideas, needs and dreams!" Aspects of the vision include advancing community awareness and development, providing job training support, and promoting self-help and economic empowerment. Finally, the philosophy of the BUF of Michigan (2006) builds and expands on the above: "The community is our ultimate concern . . . we believe in and are committed to the principle of self-help, a circle of help that takes people from a point of need . . . to a point of helping someone else . . . giving back what has been given to us."

In addition to the above, BUF could boast that since its founding, it had established "a rich heritage of redistributing wealth in the community providing for development and growth." In short, according to one of its Web site themes, Focus 2000 & Beyond, "Building BUF means strategically building and strengthening the future" (BUF of Michigan 2006).

Contrary to what many observers might think, the BUF of Michigan has not duplicated the United Way. Instead, over the years it has served those community organizations and social and economic needs that are "outside the traditional institutional objectives, such as "small start-up and emerging programs" seeking "alternative funding sources." Alternative funding represents those funds and resources accessible through nontraditional organizations. The BUF of Michigan was among the first self-help organizations in the forefront of the alternative funding movement in 1970.

Organizations supported by the BUF of Michigan reflect the range of needs within the African American community, from at-risk children, to the elderly, to the displaced homeless. As the need for self-help community organizations and programs increased, they were often faced with fewer and fewer "support opportunities." As a result, the BUF of Michigan has been called the "Fund of Choice" or "Charity of Choice," because for many of these emerging black self-help organizations, BUF has become the first choice, "The Charity of Choice" (BUF of Michigan 2006).

Allocating resources to self-help organizations is not the only service provided by BUF. In keeping with the tradition of black self-help, BUF also provides "referrals, consultative services to individuals and groups who desire to initiate community programs," and "professional assistance in proposal development" (BUF of Michigan 2006).

The support structure for BUF consists of membership, annual employee campaigns, corporate gifts, direct contributions, special events, a developmental commission, a committee of 100, volunteer corps, ministerial advisory board, and a Board of Directors. On the Web page "Support the BUF," BUF explains the importance of support: "You are a resource. Your membership, along with direct contributions, support of special events, payroll deductions and service on various committees, are [*sic*] the means through which BUF gains support." A member, therefore, "is an individual or a group that contributes funds to the BUF. Annual gifts of $25 or more entitles [*sic*] the contributor voting rights in selection of the BUF Board of Directors" (BUF of Michigan 2006).

Annual employee campaigns make for more convenient donations at the place of employment. Donors who give more than $100 in these campaigns are acknowledged as BUF "alliance members." One of the most effective strategies developed by BUF is the "diversified donor opportunities in the workplace." Donations from employees give them a feeling of community involvement while providing more resources for the community. In turn, the company's image as an employer is enhanced within the company (BUF of Michigan 2006).

Corporate and business contributions in various amounts are essential to BUF. A direct contribution to BUF is at the "donor's discretion and is a non-structured donation." There are three special events "designed to enhance BUF's public image and raise additional resources": BUF Sunday, when on a particular Sunday churches rally in support of BUF; an annual puppet show, used as a form of "educational entertainment to promote positive self-awareness among young people"; and BUF's major benefit celebration, the annual benefit dinner, "designed to promote, inspire and encourage the community's continued support" (BUF of Michigan 2006).

To access larger sources of funding BUF set up a Developmental Commission to "identify and cultivate annual major gifts of $500 to $10,000, or more, from private sources throughout the community." Still another funding source, called the Committee of 100, is a coalition of 100 individuals who pledge to contribute $100 or more annually. Over the years additional support has come from the Volunteer Corps, individuals who "affirm the BUF vision and objectives by contributing their time and energy"; the Ministerial Advisory Board, composed of ministers who "encourage positive growth by serving as the link between BUF, the church and the community we serve"; and a diverse Board of Directors representing business, civic, clergy, and other community leaders who review all written proposals requesting funds and resources and make their decisions based on BUF guidelines and policies (BUF of Michigan 2006).

Unreasonably high administrative costs can hamper the effectiveness of nonprofit organizations, particularly self-help ones. "Although Federal Law allows 25% for administrative overhead," it is to the credit of the BUF of Michigan that it "spends approximately 9–12% with little or no 'in kind services' support for operational costs" (BUF of Michigan 2006).

Throughout its history the BUF of Michigan has supported a diverse group of organizations throughout the state, making it one of the best models of the black self-help tradition in Michigan since the urban disorder in the 1960s. These organizations include Inkster Christians in Action, Grace Episcopal Church, Michigan Associations for Leadership Development, Planned Parenthood, Latin Americans for Social and Economic Development, Greater Detroit Area Health Council, Marygrove Community Interfaith Volunteer Caregivers, and Kabaz Cultural Centers, among many others (BUF of Michigan 2006).

Black Family Development Inc.

Black Family Development Inc. (BFDI) is another African American self-help organization in Michigan that has flourished during the post–urban disorder era. BFDI was founded in 1978 by the Detroit Chapter of the National Association of Black Social workers (DABSW) (Thomas 1986). The DABSW grew out of the National Association of Black Social Workers (NABSW), established in San Francisco in 1968 "when a group of African American social workers attending a meeting of an established national social work organization disengaged from those meetings to form what would become the foremost advocacy group established to address social issues of concern in the African American community" (NABSW 2004).

By far one of the most viable black self-help organizations to emerge during this era, the NABSW was "designed to promote the welfare, survival and liberation of the African American community and advocates at a national, state and local level for social change. Headquartered in Detroit, Michigan, the organization is made up of over 100 member chapters throughout the continental United States and the Caribbean, with affiliate Groups in West and South Africa." BFDI, therefore, is the offspring of this history (NABSW 2004).

BFDI's mission is to "set the framework for the provision of culturally competent, family focused and advocacy services to meet the needs of African American families." The well-being of the African American family is a core concern of the organization. "The recognition of family as a pivotal change agent of neighborhoods was recognized then, and continues now." In 1993 the international accrediting agency, Commission on Accreditation of Rehabilitation Facilities (CARF), confirmed DABSW's "sound management, fiscal accountability and integrity, and quality services." This confirmation extends to the year 2008 (Black Family Development 2005).

Since its founding, BFDI has instituted a "comprehensive array of programs and services." These include child abuse and neglect services, juvenile justice programs, substance abuse programs, prevention programs, family preservation programs, and homeless prevention services. In its 2005 annual report it could boast of having "two nationally recognized best practices model programs, and a replication model." According to the report, "the agency's services and programs reflect the ever changing needs of the community and support the growth and development of children, youth and families. BFDI has continued to mobilize in the interest of families. . . . Black Family Development Inc. remains committed to the needs of neighborhoods and families, staying true to the mission of 'strengthening and preserving African American families'" (Black Family Development 2005).

Not unlike other black self-help organizations, over the years BFDI has of necessity developed many funding sources. Among these are the Southeast Michigan Community Alliance (SEMCA); State of Michigan Department of Human Services; Bureau of Substance Abuse, Prevention, Treatment and Recovery (DHWP-BSAPIR); Detroit Public Schools; State of Michigan Department of Human Health; Wayne County Department of Children and Family Services; and United Way for Southeastern Michigan (Black Family Development 2005).

Along with funding sources, black self-help organizations have greatly benefited from affiliation with organizations and groups sharing similar missions, such as the Inner City Sub-Center, New Detroit, Inc., the Wayne County Council Against Family Violence, the New Vision Foundation, the NAACP, the Detroit Schools of Arts, Hope Academy, and Eastern Michigan University (Black Family Development 2005)

African American Women and the Black Self-Help Tradition in Michigan: The Delta Sigma Theta Sorority

African American women have founded and led some of the oldest and most effective self-help organizations and groups in Michigan. Long before the urban disorders of the late 1960s and throughout the postdisorder period, they have stayed the course, focusing on each and every problem affecting the African American community. The Delta Sigma Theta Sorority, founded in 1913 at Howard University, pledged themselves "to serious endeavor and community service, demonstrating vital concern for social welfare, academic excellence and cultural enrichment." In its 1985 Fact Sheet, the Detroit Chapter reported that "today, Delta Sigma Theta is a public service sorority emphasizing scholarship, membership and organizational skills in the public interests" (Delta Sigma Theta Sorority, Inc. Fact Sheet 1985).

Throughout the 1980s, when African American communities in Michigan were experiencing devastating economic and social stresses, the Delta chapters provided scholarships to high school students, carried out Pregnancy Prevention Workshops, and set up programs for single mothers and workshops on financial planning and parent-child relationships, along with many other efforts aimed at addressing the needs of the most vulnerable segments of the African American community (Delta Sigma Theta Sorority, Inc. 1984, 1986).

Twenty years later, the Deltas in Michigan were still engaged in self-help community efforts. With chapters in most Michigan cities, they have continued to remain in the vanguard of the black self-help tradition in the state. In April 2005, the Delta Southfield Alumni Chapter (SAC), along with members of their families and supporters, "volunteered their time in Pontiac, Michigan . . . to help a local family in their time of need. . . . We climbed ladders, worked electric saws, cleared away land and hammered soffit to the exterior of the home." Donating their time and effort to this project was not enough, however. The Southfield Alumnae then "donated a whopping $1,000 to support the local Habitat chapter" (Delta Theta Sigma SAC 2005).

Beginning in the late 1980s, the SAC has sponsored a tutorial program in Southfield, Michigan. From November through June of 2005 the SAC program tutored more than 30 students at Southfield's Adler Elementary School. The majority of the students were fifth graders and "the most requested subjects were math and reading, although SAC chapter members and other community volunteers offered tutoring in a variety of subjects." Twenty tutors participated in the program and represented an impressive array of professions that included teachers, medical doctors, engineers, directors, counselors, community leaders, and pharmaceutical representatives (Delta Theta Sigma SAC 2005).

The SAC's tutorial program created a desire for learning among the students and increased their "enthusiasm during the school year." As one student commented, "Now I fully read all my assignments to get the correct answer rather than guessing. Before coming to tutoring I would skim through chapters and turn in answers to the teachers without fully completing the assignment" (Delta Theta Sigma SAC 2005).

Concerned about the plight of African American teenage girls, the national organization created the Delta GEMS: Growing and Empowering Myself Successfully. This program was "a natural outgrowth and expansion for the continuation of the highly successful 'Dr. Betty Shabazz Delta Academy: Catching the Dreams of Tomorrow.'" The GEMS, therefore, would "catch the dreams" of African American at-risk, adolescent girls aged 14–18 (Delta Sigma Theta Sorority, Inc. 1986).

Since special tasks were required to "catch the dreams" of these young African American women, the Delta GEMS provided a framework to "actualize those dreams through the performance of specific tasks designed to develop a 'CAN DO' attitude" (Delta Sigma Theta Sorority, Inc. 1986). The following goals developed by the Delta GEMS were essential elements of this self-help program:

> To instill the need to excel academically; to provide tools that enable girls to sharpen and enhance their skills to achieve levels of academic success; to assist girls in proper goal setting and planning for their future—high school and beyond; and to create compassionate, caring and community minded young women by actively involving them in service learning and community service opportunities. (Delta Sigma Theta Sorority, Inc. 1986)

While all of these goals are geared to empower at-risk African American girls, the goals related to the creation of "compassion, caring, community-minded . . . community service" are organically and historically linked to the core principles of the black self-help tradition. It is a way of "lifting as we climb."

The framework, as explained by the Delta GEMS, is made up of five major components: "Scholarship, Sisterhood, Show Me the Money, Service, and Infinitely Complete." These five components are part of a roadmap for "college and career planning." The five major components are divided into topics designed to "provide interactive lessons and activities that provide opportunities for self-reflections and individual growth. Delta Sigma Theta chapters throughout the country, including those in Michigan, have implemented Delta GEMS" (Delta Sigma Theta Sorority, Inc. 1986).

Throughout the years, the self-help work of the Deltas has attracted the attention and praise of public officials and private citizens. For example, on April 29, 2004, the Michigan Senate passed a resolution in recognition of the Flint Alumni Chapter's years of service to the black community (*Journal of the Senate* 2004).

Like its sister chapters, the Inkster Michigan Alumni Chapter of Delta Sigma Theta has been involved in providing educational opportunities for African American youth throughout the state. For the past 45 years it has been "distributing scholarships to hundreds of deserving high school seniors" as well as students bound for college and vocational schools. According to its 2005 newsletter, the chapter has also been involved in working with middle school students. Similarly to other chapters' Dr. Betty Shabazz Delta Academies, the Inkster chapter is "helping young women make the sometime-difficult transition from childhood to young adulthood" by providing etiquette training and a money management workshop (Delta Sigma Theta Sorority, Inc. 2005).

In addition, the Inkster chapter engaged in an "impressive development program designed to help students from elementary school to college." It collaborated with local chapters of other African American sororities—Alpha Kappa Alpha, Top Ladies of Distinction, and Zeta Phi Beta—for what they called a "Super Saturday," a weekend program devoted to tutoring students at Inkster's Baylor-Woodson Elementary School. The Deltas offered "creative programming to engage students in math and science." As a result of their efforts, "the program has reaped tangible results for the students whose standardized test scores have dramatically increased, lifting the school from a state of takeover." In recognition of their service, the Western Wayne County Branch of the YWCA awarded the Inkster Alumni Chapter a Women of Achievement Award (Delta Sigma Theta Sorority, Inc. 2005).

Black Self-Help and Youth Violence: Save Our Sons and Daughters

While the Delta Sigma Theta sorority chapters in Michigan were carrying out their historic role in uplifting generations of African American girls and young women, many African American young males were killing each other in poor and drug-infested neighborhoods throughout Michigan cities. This would become the major challenge to the black self-help tradition in Michigan after the urban disorders of the late 1960s and would be concentrated in Detroit.

In the mid-1980s African American teenage male violence in Detroit rocked the African American community. Notwithstanding great strides in black political empowerment, culminating in the election of Coleman Young as Detroit's first African American mayor (Darden et al. 1987; Rich 1989), the African American community was losing the struggle for the lives of its youth. Black youth were declaring war on themselves, maiming and killing each other with little regard for their future (Taylor 1990).

Through no fault of their own, the black youth of the 1980s had inherited a legacy of institutional racism, deindustrialization, and high levels of poverty and unemployment. In 1980, 25% of the black households in metropolitan Detroit were living below the defined level of poverty, compared to 7% of whites (Darden et al. 1987).

This generation could but look on helplessly as the seeds of black tomorrows were destroyed. In one year alone, 1986, more than 300 black youth were shot in Detroit by other black youth. Of the 300, 41 died. At the end of this bloody year, the black youth death toll had jumped 32% over the 1985 death toll, with 32 black youths dying. By April 1987, 99 black youths had been shot that year. Ten died (*Detroit Free Press* 28 December 1986, 18 July 1987, 19 July 1987, 7 September 1987, 9 September 1987, 17 November 1987, 22 November 1987).

Nothing in the black self-help tradition in Michigan could have prepared African American communities for this groundswell of black youth self-destruction. Fortunately, in the midst of this self-afflicted carnage of black youth, an African American mother, Clementine Barfield, whose 16-year-old son was killed in the summer of 1986, founded an organization appropriately named Save Our Sons and Daughters (SOSAD 13 November 1997). Ms. Barfield, along with other black parents, "decided to go beyond mourning and began working together to create positive alternatives to violence throughout the community." A little over a year later, SOSAD emerged as the major self-help organization in the Detroit African American community devoted to stemming the tide of black youth violence. During this period in the 1980s when black youth violence was destabilizing many black neighborhoods, SOSAD moved onto the center stage to save them.

SOSAD's approach to black youth violence focused on counseling and training in violence prevention, crisis intervention, multicultural conflict resolution, gang redirection, and peer and bereavement support. The organization's Crisis Intervention Program won praise not only in Detroit but across the country as "the model grassroots initiative used to address the issues of trauma, grief and conflict." This included counseling for survivors and their extended families and friends and a 24-hour crisis hotline for survivors of homicide and others who had been traumatized by violence (SOSAD 13 November 1997).

SOSAD responded to school violence by providing Crisis Response Teams "throughout the community to respond swiftly and meaningfully to crises, as they arise." The increase in black youth violence in Detroit during the 1980s in Detroit created a demand for these teams to "perform critical incident debriefing and follow-up responses after a tragedy." For example, after children witnessed a homicide or had people close to them killed, SOSAD teams went to the schools and conducted eight weeks of crisis counseling (SOSAD, 13 November 1997)

In July 1987, SOSAD's first year, it sponsored a march described by its founder as "historic for some and a resurrection of hope for others." The mobilization for the march began several weeks earlier with a premarch youth rally at the state fair grounds. The premarch notices preached to the public: "Kids Killing Kids" and "Getting to the Root of the Problem." The premarch youth rally was a success. Much of the success was due to the participation of some recording artists from Motown (SOSAD 12 July 1987).

The buildup to the march galvanized a network of other black self-help organizations in Detroit as they rallied to lend their support to SOSAD's efforts. These included the Inner City Sub-Center, Association of Black Social Workers, Nation of Islam, Detroit Urban League, and Community Action Program (formerly Operation Get Down) along with "countless churches and block clubs all over the city" (SOSAD 12 July 1987).

On a deeper personal and emotional level, organizing the march provided a healing effect for those youth volunteers who had had close relatives killed. In the Special Pre-March Issue of the SOSAD *Newsletter* (12 July 1987), a writer explained the importance of the march for the entire community: "Now we have organized the July 18 march so that we can bring thousands of Detroiters together to say that Kids Killing Kids must stop. This is not just SOSAD's march: it is a march to preserve our future, which is in our children."

SOSAD's practice of reaching out provided comfort to families of children who had been killed. Just as important, Barfield saw the need to make a healing connection between parents of murdered kids and parents whose kids murdered kids:

> We all have to reach the point where we reach out and touch [each other] with love. We have to teach them love. Society is only showing them the negative aspect. We must show them the positive aspect. If we are going to do real healing, children have to see us coming together. (SOSAD 7 June 1987)

The message of healing between families of murdered kids and familes of the kids who murdered them infused new meaning in the black self-help tradition, transforming it into a powerful spiritual force. As Barfield explained, "The perpetrator is a victim too. Anybody who does these things has no self-esteem. The first thing kids say is that 'My life isn't worth much.'" In an encouraging note to both set of parents, she said, "We need to make changes in how we view ourselves and know that we can make changes. Once you feel that, we can do anything. Children will stop killing one another . . . if we mothers can do it [make changes in how we view ourselves] we feel that everybody can do it (SOSAD 7 June 1987).

For the next 10 years SOSAD gradually emerged as the leading community organization in Detroit working to prevent youth violence in the black community and to offer comfort to families of slain children. In 1988, SOSAD's programs included prayer breakfasts for families of slain children, conflict resolution, a 24-hour poetry reading called "Words Against Weapons," and "alternatives to violence" exhibits by local artists, among others. In September 1988, Barfield and SOSAD appeared on *20/20*, the television news magazine program. Sadly, at the year's end, as Barfield pleaded for no shooting on New Year's Day, 52 children younger than 17 years old had been killed (SOSAD February 5, 1988; March 10, 1988; April 11, 1988; May 11, 1988; June 17, 1988; September 13, 1988; *Detroit Free Press* 30 December 1988).

Year by year SOSAD continued the struggle against youth violence. In early 1989, SOSAD hosted still another breakfast for families of slain youth, along with a "workshop for bereaved persons and those who care for them." The next year the organization sponsored the film *Stop the Madness*, a documentary about youth violence. In April of that year, the area chapter of Women's Actions for Nuclear Disarmament awarded Clementine Barfield the Annual Peace Day Award (*Detroit Free Press* 28 April 1990).

By 1997 SOSAD was known around the world for its work in preventing violence. Reporters representing televisions, magazines, newspapers, and radio from around the United States and Europe visited SOSAD offices. Mothers from SOSAD appeared on *The Oprah Winfrey Show* (Boggs 1998). At the Tenth Anniversary Breakfast Celebration on November 13, 1997 (SOSAD 13 November 1997), the author witnessed parents crying and carrying pictures of their slain children. I realized that I was also the parent of black youth, now grown, fortunate enough to have been spared the violence that gave birth to SOSAD.

On January 31, 2001, Democratic Senator Carl Levin (2001) put in the *Congressional Record* a message to President Bush relating to the concealed gun law and the work of SOSAD:

> Mr. President, on New Year's Day, the Governor of Michigan signed into law a bill to take discretion away from local gun boards in issuing concealed gun licenses. The new law, scheduled to take effect on July 1st of this year, would increase the number of concealed handgun licenses in our state by 200,000 to 300,000—a ten-fold increase. The concealed weapons law is being challenged by a coalition of law enforcement community groups across our state called the People Who Care About Kids. This coalition is working to obtain 151,000 signatures needed to suspend the implementation of the law and put the issues before voters in 2002.
>
> Other groups in our state are also working along side the coalition to keep our streets and our communities safe. One such group is the Detroit-based Save Our Sons and Daughters (SOSAD). I would like to insert an article in the Record from the *Detroit News* about SOSAD to show what they are doing to fight the concealed weapons bill and to keep our children safe from gun violence.

The Detroit News articles Senator Levin referred to pointed out that after 14 years of "helping hundreds of grieving families, who've lost a loved one as a result of homicide, suicide, disease and natural death . . . Save Our Sons and Daughters . . . is facing a new challenge. Michigan's latest concealed gun legislation, which limits the power of county gun boards to deny gun permits, has moved the group to turn up the heat in their efforts to promote peace." The article quoted Clementine Barfield's response to the law:

> Homicide is real and the effects on children in our community is immeasurable. People should not believe that they are immune to this type of tragedy. Many children already have a false sense of confidence in weapons, as evidenced by reports of their use of guns and violence in the news. If ever there was a right time to promote peace in our community, the time is now. (Rudd-Bates 2001)

A year later, in January 2002, Bishop Thomas J. Gumbleton, Auxiliary Bishop of the Archdiocese of Detroit Michigan, mentioned SOSAD in his weekly Sunday homily at Saint Leo Church in Detroit:

> I was thinking about our own city of Detroit. It wasn't many years ago that we had a city that was known throughout the country as the murder capital of the world. I'm sure many of us remember

> that. We had set record numbers of murders. And I remember one special event. It was maybe twenty years ago now, there was a special service held at Saint Paul Episcopal Cathedral on Woodward Avenue. The place was packed with people and religious leaders from every religious denomination. Do you remember what that was all about? It was a memorial service for 43 youngsters under the age of 16 who had been murdered by other children under the age of 16.
>
> We were living in a city of horrific violence and it seemed as if there was no way out of it. But out of that service something happened and you may remember this too. Some of the parents, led by Clementine Barfield, started an organization which they named SAVE Out Sons and Daughters.
>
> It was "so sad" what was happening in our city. But Clementine, who had one of her children murdered during that previous year and another critically injured, said, 'The only way to end this is through forgiveness and reconciliation.' And so she formed that organization, SOSAD. It's still going on in our city. They reached out to those who were doing the violence and doing the killing and they forgave. And reconciliation began to happen.
>
> Our city is not a totally, peaceful city now. But certainly, it is not the violent place that it once was. No, we were able to be reconciled. Forgiveness and love brought a deeper sense of peace. Our city is better for the fact that Clementine Barfield and SOSAD continue to do their work of helping children to understand ways to settle conflict without violence. They are carrying on programs all the times and it is making a difference. (Gumbleton, 2002)

For over three decades SOSAD has been struggling to save inner-city youth. At the present time it is still in the trenches, curbing violence and healing souls.

Conclusion

The black self-help tradition in Michigan can still be found pulsating within the heart of every African American community, whether large or small, economically depressed, socially isolated, or upwardly mobile. It is the oldest tradition in African-American history. It is that collective urge, as we are climbing up, to look down to lift up someone else. Thus we have the glorious and wonderful Deltas, the caring Black United Fund, the long-struggling Inner City Sub-Center and Operation Get Down, the loving Black Family Development Inc., and the forgiving and healing Save Our Sons and Daughters, as well as many other black organizations and institutions, dedicated to the mission of empowering African Americans.

Even in the worst of conditions the black self-help tradition has been that crucial spark of hope that has burst into a flame guiding the community. Deeply imbedded in this tradition is the spoken and unspoken mission that we, as African Americans, are first and foremost responsible for each other.

REFERENCES

Black Family Development. 2005. Annual report. http://www.blackfamilydevelopment.org.

Black United Fund of Michigan. 2006. http://www.bufmi.org/history.htm.

Boggs, G. L. 1998. *Living for change: An autobiography*. Minneapolis: University of Minnesota Press.

Darden, J. T., R. C. Hill, J. Thomas, and R. Thomas. 1987. *Detroit: Race and uneven development*. Philadelphia: Temple University Press.

Delta Sigma Theta Sorority, Inc. 1985. *Fact Sheet.*

Delta Sigma Theta Sorority, Inc. 1986. Delta Gems: Growing and empowering myself successfully. *Delta News Letter 1985–1986.* http://199.236.89.103.

———. 2005. Inkster Alumnae offers stronger educational programs. *Midwest Missile: The Official Newsletter of the "Mighty."* Midwest Region, Spring. http://www.dstmidwestregion.org/newsletter/spring.

———. 1984. *Summit 11: A call to action in support of black single mothers.* Proceedings of 34 of 38 conferences sponsored by the Delta Sigma Theta Sorority Inc., in cities throughout the United States.

Delta Sigma Theta Southfield Alumni Chapter. 2005. Community report. *Delta Digest* 21(2), June. http://www.deltasac.org.

Flint Journal. 1967. Disorder hits Flints but abates near daybreak. July 25.

Grand Rapids Press. 1967a. City declares emergency, imposes curfew after gangs threaten riots, S. Division beset by young mob. July 25.

———. 1967b. City rioting brought under control. July 27.

Gumbleton, T. J. 2002. The peace pulpit. *National Catholic Reporter,* January 13. www.nationalcatholicreporter.org/pe.

Journal of the Michigan Senate, April 29, 2004.

Inner City Sub-Center Project, Inc. 1986. *Inner City Sub-Center, Inc., is about helping people.* 17th anniversary souvenir brochure.

Levin, C. 2001. Safeguarding children. News release. 107th Cong., 1st sess., *Congressional Record* (January 31). http://www.Senate.gov/-levin/newsroom./r.

National Advisory Commission on Civil Disorders. 1968. *Report of the National Advisory Commission on Civil Disorders.* New York: Bantam Books.

National Association of Black Social Workers. 2004. Capital District records 1970–1991. http://library.albany.edu/speccoll/findaids/apap096.htm.

National Association of Black Social Workers. History. http://www.nabsw.org.

Operation Get Down. 1986. *History of Operation Get Down.* Brochure.

Parker, B. 1987. Personal Interview. February 24.

Rich, W. C. 1989. *Coleman Young and Detroit politics.* Detroit: Wayne State Univ. Press.

Rudd-Bates, R. 2001. New state gun law alarms SOSAD. Group redoubles efforts to safeguard children. *Detroit News,* January 31.

Saginaw News. 1967. Uprisings spread to Flint, Pontiac and Grand Rapids. July 26.

Save Our Sons and Daughters. 1987. *Newsletter 1,* June 7.

———. 1987. *Newsletter 2,* June 21.

———. 1987. Special Pre-March Issue. *Newsletter,* July 12.

———. 1987. *Newsletter 4,* August 18.

———. 1988. *Newsletter 9,* February 5.

———. 1988. *Newsletter 10,* March 10.

———. 1988. *Newsletter 11,* April 11.

———. 1988. *Newsletter 12,* May 11.

———. 1988. *Newsletter 13,* June 17.

———. 1988. *Newsletter 16,* September 13.

———. 1997. SOSAD Tenth Anniversary Breakfast Celebration. November 13.

Taylor, C. 1990. *Dangerous society*. East Lansing: Michigan State University Press.

Taylor, Paul. 1987. Co-Director, Inner-City Sub-Center, Inc. Interview. March 26.

Thomas, R. 1986. Black self-help in Michigan. In *The state of black Michigan: 1986*. Lansing: Urban Affairs Programs, Michigan State University, and Council of Michigan Urban League Executives.

———. 2004. The black community building process in post-urban disorder Detroit, 1967–1997. In *The African American urban experience: Perspectives from the colonial period to the present*, ed. J. W. Trotter, E. Lewis, and T. W. Hunter, 209–240. New York: Palgrave.

PART 3

Social Conditions

CHAPTER 6

The Housing Situation of Blacks in Metropolitan Areas of Michigan

Joe T. Darden

Introduction

Blacks in metropolitan areas of Michigan face critical housing problems. In this chapter four areas of concern will be discussed, all involving the question of accessibility for blacks: (1) non-segregated housing, (2) mortgage and home improvement loans, (3) quality housing, and (4) home ownership.

Following a discussion of the conclusions reached in this examination, recommendations will be offered for possible ameliorative actions in all four areas.

The Accessibility for Blacks to Non-Segregated Housing

Despite passage of the Federal Fair Housing Act of 1968[1] and of Michigan's Elliott-Larsen Civil Rights Act of 1977,[2] most blacks in Michigan continue to live in racially segregated housing. In Michigan's Standard Metropolitan Statistical Areas (SMSAs), central cities, and suburbs, the majority of blacks are residentially segregated. As used here, residential segregation is defined as the overall unevenness in the spatial distribution of blacks and whites over census tracts of each metropolitan area. The degree of residential segregation was measured by the *index of dissimilarity.* This index, considered the standard measure of residential segregation, is simple to compute and easy to understand. It can be stated mathematically as:

$$D = 100\left(\frac{1}{2}\sum_{i=1}^{k}|x_i - y_i|\right)$$

Where x_i = the percentage of a Standard Metropolitan Statistical Area's white population living in a given census tract;

y_i = the percentage of a Standard Metropolitan Statistical Area's black population living in the same census tract;

D = the index of dissimilarity, or one-half the sum of the absolute differences (positive and negative) between the percentage distribution of the white and black populations in each Standard Metropolitan Statistical Area.[3]

The index value may range from "0" indicating no segregation to "100" indicating total segregation. Whatever the value of the index, it reflects the minimum percentage of either group that would have to move from one tract to another to achieve an even spatial distribution throughout a Standard Metropolitan Statistical Area (SMSA).

In 1980, 1,167,728 blacks, representing 97.4 percent of the state's total black population, lived in Michigan's 12 SMSAs. As indicated in Table 6-1, residential segregation was high (i.e., above 50 percent) between blacks and whites in each SMSA except Ann Arbor (44.5 percent) and Lansing (44.7 percent). The mean level of segregation for the 12 SMSAs was 66.8 percent. However, the level of black segregation was above 80 percent in metropolitan Detroit (85.8 percent), Flint (83.3 percent), Saginaw (83.0 percent), and Benton Harbor (82.1 percent). These four SMSAs were the most segregated in the state.

Although black residential segregation in Michigan's metropolitan areas remains very high, a slight declining trend can be observed over the last two decades. In 1960, the mean

Table 6-1. Changes in Black Residential Segregation in Metropolitan Areas of Michigan, 1960–1980

	Index of Dissimilarity*			Percentage Point
SMSA	1960	1970	1980	Change 1960–1980
Detroit	87.1	88.9	85.8	−1.3
Flint	83.0	86.4	83.3	0.3
Saginaw	81.6	83.7	83.0	1.4
Benton Harbor	**	**	82.1	**
Grand Rapids	83.9	84.6	71.9	−12.0
Jackson	80.2	80.9	71.5	−8.7
Muskegon	74.5	80.5	63.0	−11.5
Battle Creek	**	**	61.5	**
Kalamazoo	76.2	71.3	59.1	−17.1
Bay City	**	76.4	52.2	**
Lansing	83.3	64.8	44.7	−38.6
Ann Arbor	72.6	51.9	44.5	−28.1
Mean	80.3	76.9	66.8	−13.5

SOURCE: Computed by the author from data obtained from U.S. Department of Commerce. Bureau of the Census, 1960. *Census of Population: Characteristics of the Population Census Tracts*, Washington, D.C. U.S. Government Printing Office, 1962; *1970 Census of Population and Housing: Census Tracts, Final Reports*. Washington, D.C. U.S. Government Printing Office, 1972; *Population and Housing Summary Tape File 1–A*, Michigan, 1982.

*For computation of the index, see formula stated in text and/or Darden, Joe T. and Arthur A. Tabachneck, "Algorithm 8: Graphic and Mathematical Descriptions of Inequality, Dissimilarity, Segregation, or Concentration." *Environment and Planning A*, Vol. 12, (1980): 227–234.

**Data not available by tract.

Table 6-2. Black Population and Housing Segregation in Central Cities of Michigan, 1980

Central Cities	Black Population	Percent of Total Population	Index of Dissimilarity
Ann Arbor	9,957	9.2	41.1
Battle Creek	8,087	22.6	60.6
Bay City	737	1.8	45.8
Benton Harbor	12,581	85.5	33.6
Detroit	754,274	62.7	67.4
Flint	65,596	41.1	77.2
Grand Rapids	28,233	15.5	69.5
Jackson	6,053	15.2	61.4
Kalamazoo	12,327	15.5	57.4
Lansing	16,919	13.4	38.7
Muskegon	8,671	21.2	42.3
Saginaw	27,339	35.3	77.6
Mean			56.1

SOURCE: Computed by the author from U.S. Bureau of the Census, *Population and Housing Summary Tape File 1–A*, Michigan, 1982.

level of black segregation for all of Michigan's metropolitan areas was 80.3 percent. From 1960 to 1970, segregation declined to 76.9 percent. From 1970 to 1980, black segregation dropped to 66.8 percent, reflecting a −13.5 percentage point change from 1960 to 1980 (Table 6-1).

Clearly, most blacks are not evenly distributed within Standard Metropolitan Statistical Areas. Instead, most blacks are residentially segregated within central cities. In 1980, 950,774 blacks, representing 79.3 percent of the state's black population, lived in Michigan's 12 central cities.

Residential segregation was above 50 percent in 7 of the 12 central cities. The most residentially segregated central cities were Saginaw (77.6 percent) and Flint (77.2 percent). Blacks were least segregated in Benton Harbor (33.6 percent) and Lansing (38.7 percent). The mean level of segregation for the 12 central cities was 56.1 percent (Table 6-2).

Although black suburbanization has been increasing, relatively few blacks compared to whites lived in the suburbs in 1980. The 214,424 surburban blacks represented only 17.8 percent of the state's black population, whereas 64.7 percent of the state's white population lived in the suburbs. Ann Arbor had the highest percentage (11.6 percent) of blacks living in the suburbs. The suburban areas with the least percentage of blacks were Bay City (0.4 percent) and Grand Rapids (0.8 percent) (Table 6-3).

The percentage increase in the suburban population of Michigan's SMSAs was greater for blacks than for whites between 1960 and 1980 (Table 6-4), but black suburbanization in Michigan has not generally been synonymous with black residential desegregation. Blacks living in the suburbs of Benton Harbor, Detroit, Jackson, and Muskegon were more residentially segregated in 1980 than blacks living in the central cities of those areas (Tables 6-2 and 6-5). Blacks in the suburbs of Detroit were the most residentially segregated (83.9 percent) of all suburban blacks in Michigan SMSAs. The least segregated blacks in suburban areas were in Kalamazoo (20.9 percent). The mean level of segregation for the 12 suburban areas

Table 6-3. Population and Percent Distribution in Suburban Areas of Michigan's SMSAs by Race, 1960–1980

Suburban Area		Population			Percent Distribution		
		1960	1970	1980	1960	1970	1980
Ann Arbor	Totals:	105,100	134,369	157,432			
White		96,358	122,570	135,766	91.7	91.2	86.2
Black		8,597	11,139	18,318	8.2	8.3	11.6
Other Races		145	660	3,248	0.1	0.5	2.1
Battle Creek	Totals:	*	*	151,614			
White		*	*	144,081	*	*	95.0
Black		*	*	5,500	*	*	3.6
Other Races		*	*	2,033	*	*	1.3
Bay City	Totals:	53,438	67,890	78,288			
White		53,346	67,638	76,789	99.8	99.6	98.1
Black		16	50	278	0.1	0.1	0.4
Other Races		76	202	1,221	0.1	0.3	1.6
Benton Harbor	Totals:	*	*	156,569			
White		*	*	142,069	*	*	90.7
Black		*	*	12,124	*	*	7.7
Other Races		*	*	2,376	*	*	1.5
Detroit	Totals:	2,092,216	2,688,449	3,149,423			
White		2,012,402	2,580,843	2,962,565	96.2	96.0	94.1
Black		76,647	96,655	131,478	3.7	3.6	4.2
Other Races		3,167	10,951	55,380	0.1	0.4	1.8
Flint	Totals:	219,299	303,341	361,978			
White		216,605	295,989	343,450	98.8	97.6	94.9
Black		2,501	6,440	12,747	1.1	2.1	3.5
Other Races		193	912	5,781	0.1	0.3	1.6
Grand Rapids	Totals:	284,583	341,576	419,837			
White		283,662	339,273	409,130	99.7	99.3	97.4
Black		581	1,133	3,490	0.2	0.3	0.8
Other Races		350	1,170	7,217	0.1	0.3	1.7
Jackson	Totals:	81,274	97,790	111,756			
White		78,525	95,011	105,766	96.6	97.2	94.6
Black		2,694	2,547	4,707	3.3	2.6	4.2
Other Races		55	232	1,283	0.1	0.2	1.1
Kalamazoo	Totals:	87,623	115,995	199,470			
White		87,047	114,461	187,578	99.3	98.7	94.0
Black		479	1,045	8,449	0.5	0.9	4.2
Other Races		97	489	3,443	0.2	0.4	1.7
Lansing	Totals:	191,142	256,877	342,508			
White		189,700	242,790	327,306	99.2	98.3	95.6
Black		836	2,465	7,728	0.4	1.0	2.5
Other Races		606	1,622	7,474	0.4	0.7	2.2
Muskegon-Muskegon Hts.	Totals:	83,906	95,491	124,157			
White		82,220	93,752	120,121	98.0	98.2	96.7
Black		1,450	1,303	1,385	1.7	1.4	1.1
Other Races		236	436	2,651	0.3	0.5	2.1
Saginaw	Totals:	92,487	127,894	150,551			
White		90,165	122,749	138,004	97.5	96.0	91.7
Black		2,227	4,568	8,286	2.4	3.6	5.5
Other Races		95	577	4,261	0.1	0.5	2.8

SOURCE: U.S. Department of Commerce. Bureau of the Census. *1980 Census of Population and Housing,* Advance Reports, Michigan PHC80-V-24; 1970 *Census of Population and Housing: General Demographic Trends for Metropolitan Areas, 1960–1970, Final Report,* PHC (2)-24, 1971.

*SMSA data not available prior to 1980.

Table 6-4. Percent Change in Population in Suburban Areas of Michigan's SMSAs by Race, 1960–1980

Suburban Area		Percent Change 1960–1970	1970–1980	1960–1980
Ann Arbor	Totals Population:	27.8	17.2	49.8
White		27.2	10.8	40.9
Black		29.6	64.4	113.1
Other Races		355.2	407.3	220.9
Battle Creek	Totals Population:	*	*	*
White		*	*	*
Black		*	*	*
Other Races		*	*	*
Bay City	Totals Population:	27.0	15.3	46.5
White		26.8	13.5	43.9
Black		212.5	456.0	1,637.5
Other Races		165.8	54.5	1,506.6
Benton Harbor	Totals Population:	*	*	*
White		*	*	*
Black		*	*	*
Other Races		*	*	*
Detroit	Totals Population:	28.5	17.1	50.5
White		28.2	14.8	47.2
Black		26.1	36.0	71.5
Other Races		245.8	405.7	164.9
Flint	Totals Population:	38.3	19.3	65.1
White		36.6	16.0	58.0
Black		157.5	97.9	409.7
Other Races		372.5	533.9	2,893.3
Grand Rapids	Totals Population:	20.0	22.9	47.5
White		19.6	20.6	44.2
Black		95.0	208.0	590.7
Other Races		234.3	516.8	1,962.0
Jackson	Totals Population:	20.5	14.3	37.7
White		21.0	11.3	34.7
Black		–5.5	84.8	74.7
Other Races		321.8	453.0	2,232.7
Kalamazoo	Totals Population:	32.4	72.0	127.6
White		31.5	63.9	115.5
Black		118.2	708.5	1,663.9
Other Races		404.1	604.1	3,449.5
Lansing	Totals Population:	29.2	38.7	79.2
White		28.0	34.8	72.5
Black		194.9	213.5	824.4
Other Races		167.7	360.8	1,133.3
Muskegon-Muskegon Hts.	Totals Population:	13.8	30.0	48.0
White		14.0	28.1	46.1
Black		–10.1	6.3	4.5
Other Races		84.7	508.0	1,023.3
Saginaw	Totals Population:	38.3	17.7	62.8
White		36.1	12.4	53.1
Black		105.1	81.4	272.1
Other Races		507.4	638.5	4,285.3

SOURCE: Computed by the author from data obtained from U.S. Department of Commerce. Bureau of the Census. *1980 Census of Population and Housing,* Advance Reports, Michigan PHC80-V-24; *1970 Census of Population and Housing: General Demographic Trends for Metropolitan Areas, 1960–1970, Final Report,* PHC (2)-24, 1971.

*Percent change could not be computed since no SMSA data were available prior to 1980.

Table 6-5. Black Population and Housing Segregation in The Suburbs of Michigan's SMSAs, 1980

Suburban Area	Black Population	Percent of Total	Index of Dissimilarity
Ann Arbor	18,318	11.6	45.7
Battle Creek	5,500	3.6	56.9
Bay City	278	0.4	27.8
Benton Harbor	12,124	7.7	48.8
Detroit	131,478	4.2	83.9
Flint	12,747	3.5	54.6
Grand Rapids	3,490	0.8	42.0
Jackson	4,707	4.2	82.4
Kalamazoo	8,449	4.2	20.9
Lansing	7,728	2.5	31.6
Muskegon	1,385	1.1	78.1
Saginaw	4,261	5.5	32.4
Mean			58.9

SOURCE: Computed by the author from U.S. Bureau of the Census, *Population and Housing Summary Tape File 1-A*, Michigan, 1982.

was 58.9 percent (Table 6-5). In accounting for the high degree of black segregation in Michigan SMSAs, central cities, and suburbs, the question arises as to the importance of economic factors—i.e., the cost of housing in non-segregated areas.

According to theorists[4] of human ecology, a critical factor affecting the residential segregation of a population group in an open market economy is the cost of housing. The cost of housing can vary by census tracts and by neighborhoods. Thus, if the black population is disproportionately located in census tracts or neighborhoods where housing values and rents are low, it would be logical to conclude that the segregation of the black population may be related to the cost of housing. If, on the other hand, little or no relationship exists, it would be logical to conclude that housing cost is probably not a strong variable in explaining black residential segregation. In other words, the question of whether most blacks in Michigan live in segregated housing because of the high cost of housing in non-segregated areas is one that can be subjected to scientific test.

Using U.S. Bureau of Census population and housing data by census tracts, Pearson correlation coefficients[5] were computed between the percentage distribution of blacks and median housing value and median rent for all census tracts in the 12 Standard Metropolitan Statistical Areas (SMSAs) of Michigan. The results revealed that the relationship between the spatial distribution of blacks and the median value of owner-occupied housing was weak in 7, or 58.3 percent of the 12 SMSAs. The correlations ranged from −.23 for metropolitan Lansing to −.69 for metropolitan Benton Harbor. Housing cost had its strongest influence on the spatial distribution of blacks in metropolitan Benton Harbor. Even there, however, housing cost could explain only 47 percent of the spatial variation of the black population, leaving 53 percent unexplained (Table 6-6). The importance of housing cost was negligible in explaining the spatial distribution of the black population in metropolitan Ann Arbor and

Table 6-6. Correlation Coefficients between Percent Black and Median Housing Value and between Percent Black and Median Rent in Michigan's SMSAs, 1980

	Correlation Coefficients					
	Median Value			Median Rent		
SMSA	r	r^2	N	r	r^2	N
Ann Arbor	−.24**	−.05	83	−.19**	−.03	84
Battle Creek	−.45*	−.20	62	−.14	−.02	62
Bay City	−.50*	−.25	34	−.22	−.04	34
Benton Harbor	−.69*	−.47	66	−.27**	−.07	67
Detroit	−.52*	−.27	903	−.53*	−.28	910
Flint	−.48	−.23	127	−.25*	−.06	126
Grand Rapids	−.38*	−.14	149	−.18*	−.03	150
Jackson	−.41*	−.16	43	−.21	−.04	43
Kalamazoo	−.44*	−.19	94	−.23**	−.05	15
Lansing	−.23*	−.05	134	−.08	−.00	138
Muskegon	−.52*	−.27	65	−.22**	−.04	65
Saginaw	−.62*	−.38	56	−.39*	−.15	56

*Significant at the .01 level.

**Significant at the .05 level.

N = the number of census tracts on which the analysis was based.

Lansing. In both metropolitan areas, only 5 percent of the spatial variation of the black population could be attributed to housing cost, leaving 95 percent unexplained or attributed to other factors. The data indicate, then, that housing cost is not the major reason most blacks in owner-occupied housing in metropolitan areas of Michigan live in racially segregated housing.

The relationships between the spatial distribution of blacks and median housing rent were even weaker than those of median owner-occupied housing value. Housing rent had its strongest influence on the spatial distribution of the black population in metropolitan Detroit. Even there, however, the cost of rental housing could explain only 28 percent of the spatial variation of the black population, leaving 72 percent unexplained (Table 6-6). The cost of rental housing is clearly not an important factor in explaining the spatial distribution of blacks in 10 (83 percent) of the 12 metropolitan areas. Although this analysis was performed on the 12 Standard Metropolitan Statistical Areas, it is likely that the results would be essentially the same if the analysis were performed on central cities and/or suburbs.

In summary, most blacks in Michigan live in racially segregated housing, and the cost of home ownership or renting is not the primary reason for such segregation. The pattern of segregated living, however, does have certain negative economic consequences. One such consequence is related to the differential accessibility to mortgage and home improvement loans.

The Accessibility for Blacks to Mortgage and Home Improvement Loans

Although Michigan's Anti-Redlining Act prohibits geographic discrimination in the making of mortgage and home improvement loans,[6] the number, percent, and type of loan are not

Table 6-7. Numbers of 3 Types of Loans Made by Financial Institutions in Michigan's 12 SMSAs, 1982 and 1983

	FHA/FmHA/VA Loans		Conventional Mortgage Loans		Home Improvement Loans	
SMSA	1982	1983	1982	1983	1982	1983
Ann Arbor	28	118	593	1,887	708	1,090
Battle Creek	54	200	577	1,199	771	1,056
Bay City	182	74	185	536	290	377
Benton Harbor	154	32	311	1,139	789	951
Detroit	1,744	3,196	7,745	26,312	20,362	25,220
Flint	708	1,375	669	1,743	3,149	4,968
Grand Rapids	844	1,920	1,786	4,877	2,155	4,435
Jackson	84	176	163	591	553	485
Kalamazoo	180	437	859	1,948	519	490
Lansing	398	1,124	1,284	3,420	2,858	5,579
Muskegon	106	285	496	822	1,449	2,034
Saginaw	321	296	480	1,399	962	1,502
Total	4,803	9,955	15,158	45,873	34,565	48,187
Percentage Increase	107.0%		202.6%		39.4%	

SOURCE: Michigan Department of Commerce. Financial Institutions Bureau. *Mortgage and Home Improvement Lending in Michigan Pursuant to the Anti-Redlining Act* Annual Report, 1983, Lansing: A Report of the Financial Institutions Bureau, January 1985.

evenly distributed in Michigan's SMSAs. Instead, the racial composition of census tracts or neighborhoods is related to the pattern of lending.

In 1983, the number and total volume of mortgage loans in Michigan's 12 SMSAs increased above 1982 levels. Table 6-7 shows that the total number of FHA/FmHA/VA loans increased an average 107 percent above the 1982 level; the number of conventional loans rose 202.6 percent, and the number of home improvement loans advanced 39.4 percent.

However, the percentage of loans made between 1982 and 1983 in moderate-to-high minority tracts decreased for two of the three loan categories reported. (Moderate-to-high minority tracts are defined as tracts with more than 5 percent minority population.[7]) Table 6-8 shows that between 1982 and 1983, the percentage of FHA/FmHA/VA loans made in moderate-to-high minority tracts decreased in 9 (75 percent) of the 12 SMSAs listed. During the period, the percent of conventional mortgage loans made decreased in 5 (41.6 percent) of the 12 SMSAs listed. The percent of home improvement loans made in moderate-to-high minority tracts decreased in 8 (66.6 percent) of the SMSAs.

Additionally, Table 6-8 shows that the percentages of FHA/FmHA/VA loans made in 1983 in moderate-to-high minority tracts were greater than the percentages of single-family structures in those tracts for 8 (66.6 percent) of the 12 SMSAs. Conversely, in 1983, the percentages of conventional mortgage loans made were less than the percentages of single-family structures in those tracts for 11 (91.6 percent) of the SMSAs. Clearly, residents of moderate-to-high minority tracts are receiving less than their fair share of conventional mortgage loans.

Table 6-8. Percentage of Loans in Moderate-to-High Minority (MHM) Tracts as a Percentage of SMSA/City Total, 1982 and 1983

	Percent of SMSA *S/F Structures in MHM Tracts	Percent of FHA/FmHA/VA Loans		Percent of Conventional Loans		Percent of Improvement Loans	
SMSA	1980	1982	1983	1982	1983	1982	1983
Ann Arbor	63.9	60.7	80.5	59.6	65.2	61.5	59.9
Battle Creek	24.7	34.6	28.8	17.0	16.4	21.6	21.8
Bay City	11.1	12.8	19.4	11.9	8.2	12.8	8.5
Benton Harbor	41.3	36.6	34.4	33.5	34.2	38.7	40.9
Detroit	13.9	14.4	11.5	15.7	12.8	14.1	13.9
Flint	18.5	28.6	28.2	16.4	15.7	19.3	20.1
Grand Rapids	27.1	31.2	30.1	14.7	17.6	23.6	21.7
Jackson	23.2	37.0	21.2	14.1	15.3	25.3	20.8
Kalamazoo	43.6	55.9	43.9	30.2	31.5	40.4	39.6
Lansing	34.4	55.6	44.2	21.9	28.2	33.9	31.6
Muskegon	42.9	44.2	38.8	26.0	27.6	37.4	42.8
Saginaw	42.7	37.8	43.4	36.5	30.7	60.3	50.1

SOURCE: Michigan Department of Commerce. Financial Institutions Bureau. *Mortgage and Home Improvement Lending in Michigan Pursuant to the Anti-Redlining Act* Annual Report, 1983, Lansing: A Report of the Financial Institutions Bureau, January 1985.

*S/F = Single family.

Between 1979 and 1983, for nearly all of the SMSAs, the percentages of loan applications denied for both conventional mortgage loans and home improvement loans were higher in moderate-to-high minority tracts or neighborhoods than the percentages of loan applications denied in low-minority tracts.[8] It appears that in moderate-to-high minority tracts, lenders are applying lending standards that are different from those applied in low-minority tracts.

Furthermore, based on foreclosure data from Michigan's Department of Commerce, such differential lending patterns cannot be economically justified. For more than half of the SMSAs analyzed, the foreclosure rates in moderate-to-high minority tracts were lower than the foreclosure rates in low-minority tracts during four of the five years from 1979 to 1983.[9] The results refute a frequent assumption that lending in moderate-to-high minority tracts constitutes higher economic risk. In sum, one probable consequence of living in racially segregated or moderate-to-high minority neighborhoods is differential treatment by lenders in the allocation of conventional and home-improvement loans. When lending practices and policies are differentially applied on the basis of location and race, such practices and policies may affect the quality of housing and the quantity of home-ownership.

The Accessibility for Blacks to Quality Housing

Because blacks in Michigan are disproportionately located in central cities, a higher percentage of blacks (compared to whites) are more likely to live in older, overcrowded housing. Table 6-9 shows the number and percent, in the 12 SMSAs, of housing units built in 1939 or earlier and occupied by each racial group in 1980.

Table 6-9. Racial Differences in the Age of Housing in Standard Metropolitan Statistical Areas of Michigan, 1980

	Housing Units Built in 1939 or Earlier		Housing Units Built in 1939 or Earlier		
SMSA	Black No.	Black Percent	White No.	White Percent	Racial Difference Gap
Ann Arbor	954	10.6	17,942	22.0	+11.4
Battle Creek	1,982	43.2	22,845	37.3	−5.9
Bay City	93	31.7	13,682	33.8	+2.1
Benton Harbor	2,156	29.5	15,656	29.8	+0.3
Detroit	119,491	40.8	225,475	18.8	−22.0
Flint	5,435	22.5	36,478	24.1	+1.6
Grand Rapids	5,035	50.8	53,325	27.6	−23.2
Jackson	1,215	51.1	17,997	37.4	−13.7
Kalamazoo	2,326	35.1	25,944	28.6	−6.5
Lansing	1,537	20.7	43,748	29.4	+8.7
Muskegon	2,170	38.3	15,782	28.5	−9.8
Saginaw	2,945	27.0	17,726	28.1	+8.1
Mean		40.5		28.7	−11.7

SOURCE: Computed by the author from data obtained from U.S. Department of Commerce. U.S. Bureau of the Census. *1980 Census of Housing — General Housing Characteristics for Michigan,* Volume 1, part 24.

+ = older housing for whites.

− = older housing for blacks.

On the average, 40 percent of the housing units occupied by blacks in 1980 were built in 1939 or earlier, compared to 28.7 percent of the housing units occupied by whites. Racial differences as related to the age of housing varied within individual metropolitan areas. Indeed, within 6 of the 12 SMSAs, a higher percentage of whites (compared to blacks) lived in housing built in 1939 or earlier (Table 6-9). Where this occurred, however, the percentage of older housing compared to newer housing was relatively low, ranging from 22.1 percent in Ann Arbor to 33.8 percent in Bay City. On the other hand, within the 6 SMSAs where blacks occupied a higher percentage of housing built in 1939 or earlier, the percentage of older housing compared to newer housing was relatively high, ranging from 35.1 percent in Kalamazoo to 51.1 percent in Jackson. As Table 6-9 shows, over 50 percent of the housing units occupied by blacks in metropolitan Jackson and Grand Rapids and over 40 percent of the housing occupied by blacks in metropolitan Battle Creek and Detroit were built in 1939 or earlier. In none of the SMSAs does the percentage of housing occupied by whites reach this level. Finally, the racial difference gap in the age of housing ranged from 23.2 percentage points (more older housing for blacks) in metropolitan Grand Rapids to 0.3 percentage point (more older housing for whites) in the Benton Harbor SMSA.

Since most older housing is disproportionately located in areas of high population density, there is often a relationship between older housing and overcrowded living conditions. Tables 6-10 and 6-11 present data on the extent of overcrowding among blacks and whites in owner-occupied and renter-occupied housing units.

Table 6-10. Overcrowding Among Blacks and Whites in Owner-Occupied Housing in SMSAs in Michigan, 1980

SMSA	Number of Overcrowded Units*		Total Owner-occupied Units Black	Total Owner-Occupied Units White	Black Percentage	White Percentage	Black/White Ratio
	Black-Occupied	White-Occupied					
Ann Arbor	252	675	3,245	45,482	7.8	1.5	5.2
Battle Creek	113	849	2,497	47,502	4.5	1.8	2.5
Bay City	9	927	186	32,184	4.8	2.9	1.6
Benton Harbor	395	658	3,359	38,787	11.8	1.7	6.9
Detroit	9,993	21,533	154,765	905,898	6.5	2.4	2.7
Flint	1,206	2,757	14,252	118,494	8.5	2.3	3.6
Grand Rapids	246	2,560	4,753	146,876	5.2	1.7	3.0
Jackson	70	760	1,249	36,846	5.6	2.1	2.6
Kalamazoo	201	1,071	3,154	63,445	6.4	1.7	3.7
Lansing	191	1,874	2,920	100,960	6.5	1.9	3.4
Muskegon	304	1,076	3,302	43,527	9.2	2.5	3.6
Saginaw	538	1,168	5,868	49,031	9.2	2.4	3.8
Mean Percentage					7.1	2.0	3.5

SOURCE: U.S. Department of Commerce. Bureau of the Census. *1980 Census of Housing: General Housing Characteristics for Michigan*, Volume I, part 24.

*Units with 1.01 or more persons per room

NOTE: A black/white ratio of 1.0 = racial equality
a ratio greater than 1.0 = black disadvantage
a ratio less than 1.0 = white disadvantage

On the average, in 1980, blacks in owner-occupied housing in metropolitan areas of Michigan were 3.5 times more likely than whites to live in overcrowded housing. The problem of overcrowding among blacks was greatest in metropolitan Benton Harbor, where 11.8 percent of the blacks in owner-occupied housing lived in units with 1.01 or more persons per room—6.9 times the rate for whites. Overcrowding was less of a problem for blacks in owner-occupied housing in metropolitan Bay City and Battle Creek.

On the average, blacks in renter-occupied housing in metropolitan areas of Michigan in 1980 were 2.7 times more likely than whites to live in overcrowded housing. The problem of overcrowding among blacks was greatest in metropolitan Benton Harbor, where 12.9 percent of the blacks in renter-occupied housing lived in units with 1.01 or more persons per room—2.6 times the rate for whites (Table 6-11).

The Accessibility for Blacks to Homeownership

As stated previously, mortgage loans are not distributed evenly throughout metropolitan areas of Michigan. It is more difficult to secure a mortgage loan in moderate-to-high minority tracts. This differential accessibility to mortgage loans can be a significant factor in

Table 6-11. Overcrowding Among Blacks and Whites in Renter-Occupied Housing in SMSAs in Michigan, 1980

SMSA	Number of Overcrowded Units* Black-Occupied	White-Occupied	Total Renter-occupied Units Black	Total Renter-Occupied Units White	Black Percentage	White Percentage	Black/White Ratio
Ann Arbor	465	911	5,723	35,745	8.1	2.5	3.2
Battle Creek	112	377	2,180	13,637	5.2	2.8	1.8
Bay City	9	927	173	8,109	5.2	1.4	3.7
Benton Harbor	513	658	3,987	13,480	12.9	4.9	2.6
Detroit	8,269	7,076	138,499	284,822	6.0	2.5	2.4
Flint	797	931	9,866	32,819	8.1	2.8	2.8
Grand Rapids	324	981	5,161	95,853	6.3	2.1	3.0
Jackson	63	312	1,103	11,277	5.7	2.8	2.0
Kalamazoo	247	724	3,548	26,827	7.0	2.7	2.5
Lansing	331	1,352	4,528	47,061	7.3	2.9	2.5
Muskegon	235	377	2,329	11,835	10.1	3.2	3.1
Saginaw	387	261	4,996	13,716	7.7	1.9	4.0
Mean Percentage					7.4	2.7	2.8

SOURCE: U.S. Department of Commerce. Bureau of the Census. *1980 Census of Housing: General Housing Characteristics for Michigan*, Volume 1, part 24.

*Units with 1.01 or more persons per room

NOTE: A black/white ratio of 1.0 = racial equality
a ratio greater than 1.0 = black disadvantage
a ratio less than 1.0 = white disadvantage

explaining the differential rates of homeownership between blacks and whites in metropolitan areas of the state.

On the average, 49.8 percent of the black-occupied units in Michigan's SMSAs were owned in 1980, compared to 72.8 percent of the white-occupied units (Table 6-12). In each of the 12 SMSAs, the homeownership rate for blacks was lower than the rate for whites. Indeed, over 70 percent of the white-occupied housing units were owned in 10 of the 12 SMSAs in Michigan in 1980. On the other hand, over 50 percent of the black-occupied housing units were owned in only 7 of the 12 SMSAs. Furthermore, the racial difference gap remained wide in each of the SMSAs. The racial difference gap ranged from 12.6 percentage points in metropolitan Grand Rapids to 29 percentage points in metropolitan Lansing. Metropolitan Lansing and Ann Arbor have the lowest rates of black homeownership, due in part to the fact that both areas have large universities where rental units are in greater demand. As indicated in Table 6-12, the white homeownership rate is also low in these two areas compared to the other metropolitan areas (except for Grand Rapids).

The economic impact of the differential rates of black and white homeownership in the 12 metropolitan areas should not be underestimated. Restrictions on homeownership opportunities have far-reaching implications, since homeownership is related to wealth

Table 6-12. Racial Differences in Homeownership in Standard Metropolitan Statistical Areas of Michigan, 1980

SMSA	Total Units Black Owner-occupied	Total Units White Owner-occupied	Percentage of Home Ownership: Black	Percentage of Home Ownership: White	Racial Difference Gap
Ann Arbor	3,245	45,482	36.2	56.0	19.7
Battle Creek	2,497	47,502	53.3	77.6	24.3
Bay City	186	32,184	51.8	79.8	28.0
Benton Harbor	3,359	38,787	45.7	74.2	28.5
Detroit	154,765	905,898	52.7	76.0	23.3
Flint	14,252	118,494	59.0	78.3	19.3
Grand Rapids	4,753	146,876	47.9	68.2	12.6
Jackson	1,249	36,846	53.1	76.5	23.4
Kalamazoo	3,154	63,445	47.0	70.2	23.2
Lansing	2,920	100,960	39.2	60.5	29.0
Muskegon	3,302	43,527	58.6	78.6	20.0
Saginaw	5,868	49,031	54.0	78.1	24.1
Mean			49.8	72.8	23.0

SOURCE: Computed by the author from data obtained from U.S. Department of Commerce. Bureau of the Census. *1980 Census of Housing—General Housing Characteristics for Michigan,* Volume 1, part 24.

accumulation. For example, the average house purchased with an FHA 203 mortgage in 1949 (a time when few FHA mortgages were issued to blacks) had a value of $8,286 and a mortgage of $7,101. If a thirty-year-old household head had purchased this house with a 20-year mortgage, and assuming no appreciation or depreciation, the savings would have amounted to more than $7,000 and the purchaser would have owned the house by age 50. Assuming that the value increased by a conservative 2.5 percent per year, the purchaser would have accumulated assets worth at least $16,000, a considerable accumulation that could be used to borrow against for children's college education or simply to hold until retirement.[10]

Since homeownership is subsidized by the Federal Government through tax deductibility of mortgage interest and property taxes, the Federal and State Governments must take the responsibility to assure that racial restrictions are eliminated. During each fiscal year the Federal Government foregoes revenues of several billion dollars as a result of federal income tax provisions enabling homeowners to take itemized deductions for mortgage interest and property taxes paid on their owner-occupied homes. In fiscal year 1980, for example, the amount lost to the Federal Treasury was $14.6 billion.[11]

Conclusions

This chapter has examined some of the most critical housing problems facing blacks in metropolitan areas of Michigan. The conclusions are as follows:

1. Blacks in metropolitan areas of Michigan do not have equal accessibility to housing. Despite passage of the Federal Fair Housing Act of 1968 and Michigan's Elliott-Larsen Civil Rights Act

of 1977, most blacks in Michigan continued to live in racially segregated housing in 1980. This situation is not due primarily to the high cost of housing in non-segregated areas.

2. Blacks in metropolitan areas of Michigan do not receive an equal share of the conventional mortgage loans and home improvement loans. Despite passage of Michigan's Anti-Redlining Act of 1977, the number and percent of loans made to moderate-to-high minority neighborhoods are decreasing at a time when the number and percent of total mortgage loans are increasing. Additionally, the percentages of loan applications denied for both conventional mortgages and home improvement loans were higher in moderate-to-high minority neighborhoods than the percentages of loan applications denied in low-minority neighborhoods. Such disparity occurs by racial composition of neighborhoods, although the foreclosure rates in moderate-to-high minority neighborhoods were lower during four of the five years from 1979 to 1983 than the foreclosure rates in low-minority neighborhoods. Clearly, the differential lending pattern in metropolitan areas of Michigan cannot be economically justified.
3. Inasmuch as blacks in Michigan are disproportionately located in central cities, a higher percentage (compared to whites) are more likely to live in older, overcrowded housing. On the average, 40 percent of the SMSA housing units occupied by blacks in 1980 were built in 1939 or earlier, compared to 29 percent of the housing units occupied by whites. On the average, blacks in owner-occupied housing in metropolitan areas of Michigan were 3.5 times more likely than whites to live in overcrowded housing in 1980. In renter-occupied housing, the ratio was 2.3 times.
4. Inequality exists in black and white homeownership rates. In 1980, an average of 50 percent of the black-occupied units in Michigan's SMSAs were owned, compared to 73 percent of the white-occupied units.

Recommendations

1. The enforcement of fair housing laws must be strengthened through closer monitoring of the flow, accuracy, and completeness of information real estate brokers pass on to black and white home seekers about housing availability throughout the metropolitan areas of Michigan. This will help to reduce segregation and the disproportionate concentration of blacks in central cities.
2. Lending institutions should be required by the Federal and/or State Governments to insure that equity in the distribution of mortgage loans occurs. One approach would be to increase the number of minority loan officers.
3. Efforts should be made to increase the rate of black homeownership. One approach is to pressure Congress to modify present housing legislation to permit the option of a 30-year, no-down-payment mortgage for single-family home purchases.

Footnotes

1. Civil Rights Act of 1968, 42 U.S.C., sec. 3613, 1970.
2. Michigan, Elliott-Larsen Civil Rights Act, Public Acts of 1976, No. 453; Public Acts of 1977, No. 162; Public Acts of 1982, No. 45.

3. Joe T. Darden and Arthur A. Tabachneck, "Algorithm 8: Graphic and Mathematical Descriptions of Inequality, Dissimilarity, Segregation, or Concentration." *Environment and Planning A*, Vol. 12, (1980): 227–234.
4. Ernest W. Burgess, "The Growth of the City: An Introduction to a Research Project." *Proceedings of the American Sociological Society* 18 (1923): 57–85.
   Douglas Massey, "Hispanic Residential Segregation: A Comparison of Mexicans, Cubans and Puerto Ricans." *Sociology and Social Research* 65 (April 1981): 311–322.
5. The Pearson correlation coefficient assesses the degree of relationship between two variables. A coefficient near +1.00 reflects a strong positive relationship, a coefficient near −1.00 reflects a strong negative relationship, and a coefficient near zero reflects little or no relationship. See W. James Popham, *Educational Statistics* (New York: Harper and Row Publishers, 1967), pp. 313–315.
6. Michigan, The Anti-Redlining Act, Public Acts of 1977, No. 135, Sec. 8.
7. Michigan Department of Commerce. Financial Institutions Bureau. *Mortgage and Home Improvement Lending in Michigan Pursuant to the Anti-Redlining Act* Annual Report, 1983, Lansing: A Report of the Financial Institutions Bureau, January, 1985.
8. Ibid., p. 32.
9. Ibid., p. 32.
10. John F. Kain, "Racial Discrimination in Urban Housing Markets and Goals for Public Policy." Paper prepared for the Conference on Blacks, Presidential Politics and Public Policy. Howard University, Washington, D.C., October 25–27, 1979, p. 18.
11. Congressional Budget Office, *The Budget of the United States, Fiscal Year 1980* (Washington, D.C.: U.S. Government Printing Office, January, 1979), p. 17.

REFERENCES

Bell, Duran, Jr. "Indebtedness of Black and White Families." *Journal of Urban Economics 1* (1974): 48–60.

Burgess, Ernest W. "The Growth of the City: An Introduction to a Research Project." *Proceedings of the American Sociological Society* 18 (1923): 57–85.

Civil Rights Act of 1968, 42 U.S.C., sec. 3613, 1970.

Darden, Joe T. and Arthur A. Tabachneck. "Algorithm 8: Graphic and Mathematical Descriptions of Inequality. Dissimilarity, Segregation, or Concentration." *Environment and Planning A*, Vol. 12, 1980, 227–234.

Kain, John F. "Racial Discrimination in Urban Housing Markets and Goals for Public Policy." Paper prepared for the Conference on Blacks, Presidential Politics and Public Policy. Howard University, Washington, D.C. October 25–27, 1979.

Massey, Douglas. "Hispanic Residential Segregation: A Comparison of Mexicans, Cubans and Puerto Ricans." *Sociology and Social Research* 65 (April 1981): 311–322.

Michigan, The Anti-Redlining Act, Public Acts of 1977, No. 135, sec. 8.

Michigan Department of Commerce, Financial Institutions Bureau. *Mortgage and Home Improvement Lending in Michigan Pursuant to the Anti-Redlining* Act, Annual Report, 1983, Lansing: A Report of the Financial Institutions Bureau, January 1985.

Michigan, Elliott-Larsen Civil Rights Act, Public Acts of 1976, No. 453; Public Acts of 1977, No. 162; Public Acts of 1982, No. 45.

Popham, W. James. *Educational Statistics.* (New York: Harper and Row, Publishers, 1967.)

U.S. Bureau of the Census. *Population and Housing Summary Tape File 4-A,* 1982.

U.S. Department of Commerce. Bureau of the Census. *1970 Census of Population and Housing: General Demographic Trends for Metropolitan Areas, 1960–1970.* Final Report PHC (2) – 24, 1971.

U.S. Department of Commerce. Bureau of the Census. *1980 Census of Population and Housing.* Advance Reports, Michigan PHC 80-V-24.

CHAPTER 7

Residential Segregation of Blacks in Metropolitan Areas of Michigan, 1960–1990

Joe T. Darden

Federal housing policies have been in existence since the 1930s. Prior to the 1960s, however, virtually all federal housing policies had a racially segregative effect. For example, the Federal Housing Administration (FHA) established and implemented a mortgage insurance policy in the 1930s which subsidized the growth of suburban areas and benefited primarily middle-income, working-class white residents. Blacks did not benefit because the FHA adopted a racially segregationist policy and refused to insure projects that did not comply (Darden, 1984; Orfield, 1969; U.S. Commission on Civil Rights, 1973; Federal Housing Administration, 1938).

The common belief of white appraisers was that racial integration of the suburbs would lower property values. Although there was no supportive evidence, official FHA policy was based on this assumption until 1948. White appraisers were told to look for physical barriers between racial groups, or to find and honor racially restrictive covenants. Race was officially listed as a valid reason for rejecting a mortgage. Thus, although the FHA provided an important service for young white families, blacks were viewed as a liability and denied equal access to the suburbs.

By promoting racially restrictive covenants, the Federal Housing Administration helped to create a movement that was to make "white residential areas" in general, and white suburban residential areas in particular, unavailable to blacks. Thus, the Federal Housing Administration's discriminatory policies widened the social and spatial gap between the living conditions of whites and blacks and increased the concentration of blacks in the older, more deteriorated neighborhoods. It did this by aiding the supply of new housing, particularly in the suburbs, while denying blacks access to such housing. As a result, communities tended to retain their existing segregated racial composition, and the expected integration that might have occurred because of increasing black economic gains failed to materialize (Weaver, 1948).

It was not until the 1960s that the federal government's housing policies reflected a non-discrimination posture. In November of 1962, Executive Order 11063 was issued, prohibiting discrimination in federally assisted housing. Following the Executive Order was Title VI of the Civil Rights Act of 1964, which prohibited discrimination in all federally assisted housing programs. Title VIII of the Civil Rights Act of 1968 prohibited discrimination in most of the nation's housing and made discrimination by institutions financing housing illegal (Civil Rights Act of 1968, 1970). Finally, such legislation was bolstered by the Supreme Court decision, prohibiting all racial discrimination in any housing, public as well as private (*Jones* v. *Mayor*, 1968).

In 1977 the State of Michigan passed the Elliott-Larsen Civil Rights Act which prohibits racial discrimination in the sale and rental of housing in Michigan (Michigan Elliott-Larsen Civil Rights Act, 1977).

What has been the pattern of reductions, if any, that have occurred in black residential segregation since antidiscrimination provisions in housing policies were introduced? What has been the nature of the commitment of the federal government and the State of Michigan to equality of opportunity in the effort to undo the deeply entrenched segregated housing patterns which have long been characteristic of America's metropolitan areas including those in Michigan? If black residential segregation remains high, what new strategies can be used to substantially reduce it?

The purpose of this chapter is to assess the extent of residential segregation of blacks in metropolitan areas of Michigan over a thirty-year period (1960 to 1990)—i.e., before and after passage of the Federal Fair Housing Act in 1968 and Michigan's Elliott-Larsen Civil Rights Act of 1977. Twelve Standard Metropolitan Statistical Areas (SMSAs) of Michigan constitute the study areas: Ann Arbor, Battle Creek, Bay City, Benton Harbor, Detroit, Flint, Grand Rapids, Jackson, Kalamazoo, Lansing, Muskegon, and Saginaw (Figure 7-1).

Data and Methodology

Data for this paper were obtained from the U.S. Bureau of the Census (U.S. Bureau of the Census, 1962, 1971, 1981, 1982, 1991). The method employed to measure residential segregation, which is defined as the overall unevenness in the spatial distribution of blacks and whites, is the *index of dissimilarity* (Darden & Tabachneck, 1980). It can be stated mathematically as:

$$D = 100\left(\frac{1}{2}\sum_{i=1}^{k}|x_i - y_i|\right)$$

Where x_i = the percentage of a Standard Metropolitan Statistical Area's black population living in a given census tract;

y_i = the percentage of a Standard Metropolitan Statistical Area's white population living in the same census tract;

D = the index of dissimilarity, or one-half the sum of the absolute differences (positive and negative) between the percentage distribution of the blacks and whites in a Standard Metropolitan Statistical Area.

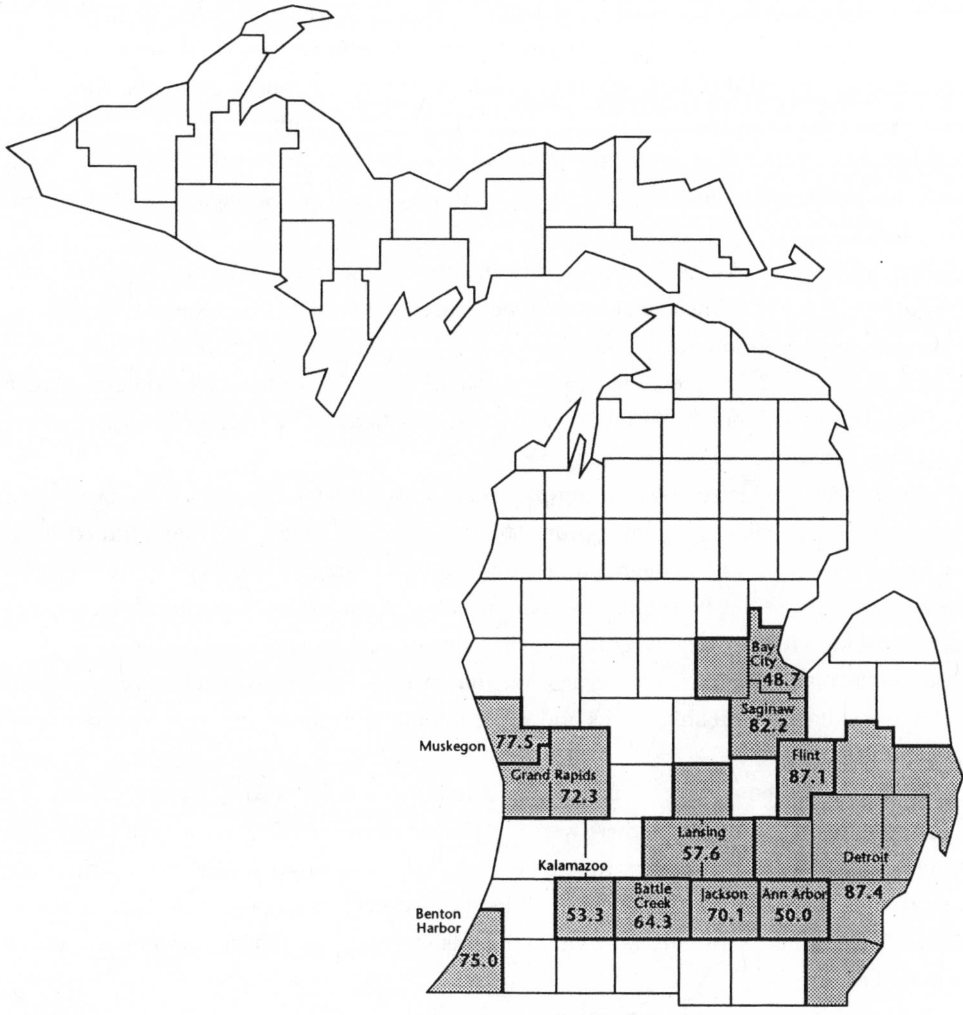

FIGURE 7-1
Location of Standard Metropolitan Areas in Michigan and Their Indexes of Dissimilarity, 1990

The index value may range from "0" indicating no segregation to "100" indicating total segregation. Whatever the value of the index, it reflects the minimum percentage of either group that would have to move from one tract to another to achieve an even spatial distribution throughout the SMSA.

A Standard Metropolitan Statistical Area consists of a central city and the area outside the central city—i.e., the suburbs. Indices of dissimilarity were computed separately for central cities and their suburbs.

Technical Limitations of the Method of Measuring Residential Segregation

Although the *index of dissimilarity* is considered the standard measure of residential segregation, it has some limitations that merit discussion. It should be noted that the index is sensitive to the size of the spatial units used. The smaller the subareas, the greater the degree of identifiable residential segregation and the larger the values that will be obtained on any given index (Taeuber & Taeuber, 1965). For example, let us assume that a segregation index value based on census tracts is 50.0. A segregation index value based on wards would not be greater than 50.0, and would probably be less. On the other hand, a segregation index value based on blocks would not be less than 50.0 and would probably be greater (Darden, 1973).

Although city blocks are the smallest readily identifiable spatial units for which data can be obtained, they have their limitations. Block-based data do not allow useful comparisons of segregation levels among central cities, suburbs, and entire Standard Metropolitan Statistical Areas. In other words, the choice of spatial unit to measure segregation must be a function of the problem under investigation and of data availability; there is no such thing in measurement procedures as "the best spatial unit."

For this study, which involved a comparison of segregation in central cities, suburbs, and SMSAs, census tracts were more appropriate than wards or blocks. The major limitation of census tracts was that the degree and magnitude of segregation by block could not be determined. The segregation index used in this study takes into account only differences in the percentage of the two racial groups in each census tract and reveals nothing about intratract spatial distributions. Thus, it is possible that in a tract classified as nonsegregated, with equal percentages of an area's black and white populations, there could still be total segregation by block.

It should also be noted that the index value may be influenced by boundary changes such as annexations. Although there were annexations in some of the areas in the study, the populations of the annexed areas were small. Previous studies have indicated that where the annexed population is small, the effect of the index value is negligible (Taeuber & Taeuber, 1965). Thus, no adjustments were made in this study for boundary revision and tracts annexed during the decades.

Once the patterns in black residential segregation were determined, the second objective was to suggest new strategies for reducing the level of segregation that continues to exist.

Blacks in Michigan's Suburban Areas in 1960

In 1960, prior to the passage of the Federal Fair Housing Act in 1968 and Michigan's Elliott-Larsen Civil Rights Act in 1977, blacks were unevenly distributed within Michigan's metropolitan areas. The representation of blacks in the suburbs was small. Only 16 blacks lived in suburban Bay City compared with more than 53,000 whites. Only 581 blacks lived in suburban Grand Rapids compared with more than 283,000 whites. Blacks were also grossly underrepresented in suburban Kalamazoo (479 compared with 87,047) and Lansing (836 compared with 189,700) (Table 7-1). Only suburban Detroit and suburban Ann Arbor had more than 8,000 blacks. In fact, suburban Ann Arbor was the only area where the suburban black population was greater than 4 percent. The mean suburban black population in 1960 was 2.1 percent.

Table 7-1. Number and Percentage of Population in Suburban Areas of Michigan's SMSAs by Race, 1960–1990

	Population				Percentage			
Suburban Area	1960	1970	1980	1990	1960	1970	1980	1990
Ann Arbor	105,100	134,369	157,432	175,258				
White	96,358	122,570	135,766	146,549	91.7	91.2	86.2	83.6
Black	8,597	11,139	18,318	21,815	8.2	8.3	11.6	12.4
Other Races	145	660	3,248	6,894	0.1	0.5	2.1	3.9
Battle Creek	**	**	105,833	83,397				
White	**	**	98,822	75,511	**	**	93.4	90.5
Black	**	**	5,434	5,529	**	**	5.1	6.6
Other Races	**	**	1,577	2,357	**	**	1.5	2.8
Bay City	53,438	67,890	78,288	73,562				
White	53,346	67,638	76,789	71,301	99.8	99.6	98.1	96.9
Black	16	50	278	289	0.1	0.1	0.4	0.3
Other Races	76	202	1,211	1,972	0.1	0.3	1.6	2.7
Benton Harbor	**	**	156,569	150,093				
White	**	**	142,069	132,329	**	**	90.7	88.1
Black	**	**	12,124	13,355	**	**	7.7	8.9
Other Races	**	**	2,376	4,709	**	**	1.5	3.1
Detroit	2,092,216	2,688,449	3,149,423	3,260,294				
White	2,012,402	2,580,843	2,962,565	2,980,960	96.2	96.0	94.1	91.4
Black	76,647	96,655	131,476	163,224	3.7	3.6	4.2	5.0
Other Races	3,167	10,951	53,380	116,110	0.1	0.4	1.8	3.6
Flint	219,299	303,341	361,976	292,797				
White	216,605	295,989	343,450	266,863	98.8	97.6	94.9	91.1
Black	2,501	6,440	12,747	16,772	1.1	2.1	3.5	5.7
Other Races	193	912	5,781	9,162	0.1	0.3	1.6	3.1
Grand Rapids	284,593	341,576	419,837	506,286				
White	283,662	339,273	409,130	479,323	99.7	99.3	97.4	94.7
Black	581	1,133	3,490	6,238	0.2	0.3	0.8	1.2
Other Races	350	1,170	7,217	20,725	0.1	0.3	1.7	4.1
Jackson	81,274	97,790	111,756	113,190				
White	78,525	95,011	105,766	105,537	96.6	97.2	94.6	93.2
Black	2,694	2,547	4,707	5,368	3.3	2.6	4.2	4.7
Other Races	55	232	1,283	2,289	0.1	0.2	1.1	2.0
Kalamazoo	87,623	115,955	199,470	144,241				
White	87,047	114,461	187,578	135,388	99.3	98.7	94.0	93.9
Black	479	1,045	8,449	4,826	0.5	0.9	4.2	3.4
Other Races	97	489	3,443	4,027	0.2	0.4	1.7	2.8
Lansing	191,142	256,877	342,508	313,968				
White	189,700	242,790	327,306	289,826	99.2	98.3	95.6	92.3
Black	836	2,465	7,728	9,460	0.4	1.0	2.5	3.0
Other Races	606	1,622	7,474	14,682	0.4	0.7	2.2	4.7
Muskegon	83,906	95,491	124,457	120,055				
White	82,220	93,752	120,121	105,783	98.0	98.2	96.7	88.1
Black	1,450	1,303	1,385	10,701	1.7	1.4	1.1	8.9
Other Races	236	436	2,651	3,571	0.3	0.5	2.1	3.0
Saginaw	92,487	127,894	150,551	145,301				
White	90,165	122,749	138,004	129,106	97.5	96.0	91.7	88.9
Black	2,227	4,568	8,286	8,803	2.4	3.6	5.5	6.0
Other Races	95	577	4,261	7,392	0.1	0.5	2.8	5.0

SOURCE: U.S. Bureau of the Census, Population and Housing Summary Tape File 1-A, Michigan 1992; U.S. Department of Commerce. Bureau of the Census. 1980 Census of Population and Housing, Advance Reports, Michigan PHC80-V-24; 1970 Census of Population and Housing: General Demographic Trends for Metropolitan Areas, 1960–1970, Final Report, PHC (2)-24, 1971.

**SMSA data not available prior to 1980.

Black Suburbanization, 1960–1990

Between 1960 and 1990, black suburbanization greatly increased, varying from an increase of 99 percent in Jackson to an increase of 1,706 percent in Bay City. In seven of the suburban areas, the rate of black suburbanization exceeded 200 percent. In addition to Bay City, the suburbs experiencing the highest rates of change in black suburbanization between 1960 and 1990 were Lansing (1,031 percent), Grand Rapids (973), Kalamazoo (740), Muskegon (638), and Flint (570) (Table 7-2).

Thus, the black suburban population increased after passage of the 1968 Fair Housing Act, although black representation in suburban populations remained small (Table 7-1). The percentage of blacks in 1990 was highest in suburban Ann Arbor with 12.4 percent. Other suburban areas with at least 5 percent black population in 1990 were Muskegon (8.9), Benton Harbor (8.9), Battle Creek (6.6), Saginaw (6.0), Flint (5.7), and Detroit (5.0) (Table 7-1).

Changes in Black Residential Segregation, 1960–1990

More important questions, however, are whether black suburbanization is synonymous with black residential desegregation, and whether blacks in the suburbs are more segregated or less segregated residentially than blacks in the central cities. Finally, what changes have occurred in black residential segregation in central cities, suburbs, and the entire Standard Metropolitan Statistical Areas of Michigan since 1960?

As shown in Table 7-3, residential segregation declined between 1960 and 1990 in the suburbs of Ann Arbor, Detroit, Flint, Grand Rapids, Jackson, Kalamazoo, Muskegon, and Saginaw. On the other hand, segregation slightly increased in suburban Lansing by 1.4 percentage points. Data were not available at that time for Battle Creek, Bay City, and Benton Harbor. The results showed an overall mean decline in suburban segregation of −8.1 percentage points over the 30-year period.

The greatest decline occurred in suburban Jackson (−16.2 percentage points), whereas suburban Kalamazoo experienced the least decline (−1.5 percentage points).

In 1960, blacks in every suburban area examined were highly segregated residentially with the exception of suburban Kalamazoo where blacks were moderately segregated (Table 7-3). The mean level of residential segregation for all suburbs examined was 71.3 percent. Blacks in the central cities were only slightly more segregated (mean = 73.9 percent) than blacks in the suburbs (Table 7-4). Thus, black residence in the suburbs was not synonymous with black residential desegregation in 1960.

Blacks were even more segregated when examined throughout the Standard Metropolitan Statistical Areas. Blacks were highly segregated in all of the SMSAs in 1960. The mean level of segregation was 80.3 percent (Table 7-5).

Between 1960 and 1990, the mean level of the index of black residential segregation declined in the suburban areas, central cities, and Standard Metropolitan Statistical Areas examined. The greatest average decline occurred in the central cities (−24.1 percentage points) (Table 7-4). The least average decline occurred in the suburbs (−8.1 percentage points) (Table 7-3). Thus, between 1960 and 1990, blacks in central cities became less residentially segregated than blacks in the suburbs. In 1990, the mean level of the index of

Table 7-2. Percentage Changes in Population in Suburban Areas of Michigan's SMSAs by Race, 1960–1990

Suburban Area	Percentage Changes			
	1960–1970	1970–1980	1980–1990	1960–1990
Ann Arbor	27.8	17.2	11.3	66.6
White	27.2	10.8	7.9	52.1
Black	29.6	64.4	19.1	153.8
Other Races	355.2	407.3	112.3	4,654.5
Battle Creek	**	**	−21.2	**
White	**	**	−23.6	**
Black	**	**	1.8	**
Other Races	**	**	49.5	**
Bay City	27.0	15.3	−6.0	37.7
White	26.8	13.5	−7.1	33.7
Black	212.5	456.0	4.0	1,706.2
Other Races	165.8	504.5	62.8	2,494.7
Benton Harbor	**	**	−4.1	**
White	**	**	−6.9	**
Black	**	**	10.1	**
Other Races	**	**	98.2	**
Detroit	28.5	17.1	3.5	55.8
White	28.2	14.8	0.6	48.1
Black	26.1	36.0	24.1	113.0
Other Races	245.8	405.7	117.5	3,566.3
Flint	38.3	19.3	−19.1	33.5
White	36.6	16.0	−22.3	23.2
Black	157.5	97.9	31.6	570.6
Other Races	372.5	533.9	58.5	4,647.1
Grand Rapids	20.0	22.9	20.6	77.9
White	19.6	20.6	17.1	69.0
Black	95.0	208.0	78.7	973.7
Other Races			187.1	5,821.4
Jackson	20.5	14.3	1.3	39.3
White	21.0	11.3	−0.2	34.4
Black	−5.5	84.8	14.0	99.3
Other Races	321.8	453.0	78.4	4,061.8
Kalamazoo	32.4	72.0	−27.7	64.6
White	31.5	63.9	−27.8	55.5
Black	118.2	708.5	−42.9	740.7
Other Races	404.1	604.1	17.0	4,051.6
Lansing	29.2	38.7	−90.8	64.3
White	28.0	34.8	−11.5	52.8
Black	194.9	213.5	22.4	1,031.6
Other Races	167.7	360.8	96.4	2,322.8
Muskegon	13.8	30.0	−3.1	43.1
White	14.0	28.1	−11.9	28.7
Black	−10.1	6.3	672.6	638.0
Other Races	84.7	508.0	34.7	1,413.1
Saginaw	38.3	17.7	−3.5	57.1
White	36.1	12.4	−6.5	43.2
Black	105.1	81.4	6.2	295.3
Other Races	507.4	638.5	73.5	7,681.0

SOURCE: Computed by the author from U.S. Bureau of the Census, Population and Housing Summary Tape File 1-A, Michigan, 1992; U.S. Department of Commerce. Bureau of the Census. 1980 Census of Population and Housing, Advance Reports, Michigan PHC80-V-24; 1970 Census of Population and Housing: General Demographic Trends for Metropolitan Areas, 1960–1970, Final Report, PHC (2)24, 1971.

**Percentage change could not be computed since no SMSA data were available prior to 1980.

Table 7-3. Housing Segregation in the Suburbs of Michigan's SMSAs, 1960–1990 (Based on Census Tracts)

	Index of Dissimilarity*				
Suburban Area	1960	1970	1980	1990	Percentage Point Change 1960–1990
Ann Arbor	77.1	58.3	45.7	67.0	−10.1
Battle Creek	**	**	56.9	67.0	**
Bay City	**	56.0	27.8	49.3	**
Benton Harbor	**	**	48.8	65.0	**
Detroit	89.8	92.2	83.9	78.1	−11.7
Flint	72.9	82.8	54.6	67.2	−5.7
Grand Rapids	59.8	51.6	42.0	47.8	−12.0
Jackson***	87.4	81.0	82.4	71.2	−16.2
Kalamazoo	44.0	42.8	20.9	42.5	−1.5
Lansing	55.2	58.2	31.6	56.6	+1.4
Muskegon	82.2	87.7	78.1	77.5	−4.7
Saginaw	73.7	79.7	32.4	69.7	−4.0
Mean	71.3	69.0	58.9	63.2	−8.1

SOURCE: Computed by the author from U.S. Bureau of the Census, Population and Housing Summary Tape File 1-A, Michigan, 1982 and 1992.

*For computation of the index, see formula stated in text and/or Darden, Joe T. and Arthur A. Tabachneck, "Algorithm 8: Graphic and Mathematical Descriptions of Inequality, Dissimilarity, Segregation or Concentration." Environment and Planning A, Vol. 12, (1980): 227–234.

**Data not available by tract.

***The indexes for the Jackson area may be affected by the circumstance that a large percentage of the population consists of inmates of a penal institution.

Table 7-4. Housing Segregation in Central Cities of Michigan, 1960–1990 (Based on Census Tracts)

	Index of Dissimilarity*				
Suburban Area	1960	1970	1980	1990	Percentage Point Change 1960–1990
Ann Arbor	62.8	41.1	41.1	33.4	−29.4
Battle Creek	**	**	60.6	55.7	**
Bay City	**	67.8	45.8	19.8	**
Benton Harbor	**	**	33.6	27.2	**
Detroit	80.4	78.2	67.4	64.8	−15.6
Flint	82.9	77.7	77.2	75.9	−7.0
Grand Rapids	81.5	80.0	69.5	63.1	−18.4
Jackson	65.0	67.1	61.4	54.4	−10.6
Kalamazoo	70.6	72.9	57.4	48.2	−22.4
Lansing	78.7	59.2	38.7	35.6	−43.1
Muskegon	64.5	70.8	42.3	39.5	−25.0
Saginaw	78.8	78.4	77.6	80.3	+1.5
Mean	73.9	69.3	56.1	49.8	−24.1

SOURCE: Computed by the author from U.S. Bureau of the Census, Population and Housing Summary Tape File 1-A, Michigan, 1982 and 1992.

*For computation of the index, see formula stated in text and/or Darden, Joe T. and Arthur A. Tabachneck, "Algorithm 8: Graphic and Mathematical Descriptions of Inequality, Dissimilarity, Segregation or Concentration." Environment and Planning A, Vol. 12, (1980): 227–234.

**Data not available by tract.

Table 7-5. Patterns of Black-White Residential Segregation in Metropolitan Areas of Michigan, 1960–1990

	Index of Dissimilarity*				Percentage Point Change	
SMSA	1960	1970	1980	1990	1980–1990	1960–1990
Ann Arbor	72.6 (9)***	51.9 (10)***	44.5 (12)***	50.0 (11)***	5.5	−22.6
Battle Creek	**	**	61.5 (8)	64.3 (8)	2.8	**
Bay City	**	76.4 (7)	52.2 (10)	48.7 (12)	−3.5	**
Benton Harbor	**	**	82.1 (5)	75.0 (5)	−7.1	**
Detroit	87.1 (1)	88.9 (1)	85.8 (1)	87.4 (1)	1.6	0.3
Flint	83.0 (4)	86.4 (2)	83.3 (2)	87.1 (2)	3.8	4.1
Grand Rapids	83.9 (2)	84.6 (3)	83.0 (3)	72.3 (6)	−10.7	−11.6
Jackson	80.2 (6)	80.9 (5)	71.5 (6)	70.1 (7)	−1.4	−10.1
Kalamazoo	76.2 (7)	71.3 (8)	59.1 (9)	53.3 (10)	−5.8	−12.9
Lansing	83.3 (3)	64.8 (9)	44.7 (11)	57.6 (9)	12.7	−25.7
Muskegon	74.5 (8)	80.5 (6)	63.0 (7)	77.5 (4)	14.5	3.0
Saginaw	81.6 (5)	83.7 (4)	83.0 (3)	82.2 (3)	−0.8	0.6
Mean	80.3	76.9	66.8	68.8	2.0	−11.5

SOURCE: Computed by the author from data obtained from U.S. Department of Commerce, Bureau of the Census, 1960. Census of Population: Characteristics of the Population Census Tracts, Washington, D.C.: U.S. Government Printing Office, 1962; 1970 Census of Population and Housing: Census Tracts, Final Reports. Washington D.C.: U.S. Government Printing Office, 1972; Population and Housing Summary Tape File 1-A, Michigan 1982 and 1992.

*For computation of the index, see formula stated in text and/or Darden, Joe T. and Arthur A. Tabachneck, "Algorithm 8: Graphic and Mathematical Descriptions of Inequality, Dissimilarity, Segregation or Concentration." Environment and Planning A, Vol. 12, (1980): 227–234.

**Data not available by tract.

***( ) Numbers in parentheses indicate ranks for each SMSA.

dissimilarity in central cities was 49.8 percent compared with 63.2 percent in the suburbs. In 1990, blacks in the suburbs of Detroit, Muskegon, and Jackson were the most segregated, with dissimilarity indexes of 78.1, 77.5, and 71.2, respectively.

In 1990, the mean level of the index of dissimilarity in the various metropolitan areas investigated was 68.8 percent (Table 7-5). No metropolitan area had an index below 40 percent—the rate that would indicate much sharing of residential space. The least segregated metropolitan area in 1990 was Bay City, with an index of 48.7 percent. Detroit remained the most racially segregated metropolitan area in Michigan with an index of 87.4 percent (Figure 7-1).

Racial Steering as a Factor in Residential Segregation: The Case of Detroit

It is not surprising that the Detroit Standard Metropolitan Statistical Area was found to be the most segregated SMSA in Michigan. Studies conducted since 1968 suggest that discriminatory tactics persist in the form of racial steering by white real estate brokers. In a study of 97 randomly selected real estate agents in the Detroit Standard Metropolitan Statistical Area between 1974 and 1975, it was found that blacks, more often than whites, were shown houses not located in the suburb where the sales agent's office was located; that is, they were steered out of town.

In addition, where and whether houses were shown to blacks depended upon the location of the sales office within the suburban municipality. The chances were significantly greater for whites than for blacks to be shown houses in the same municipality as the real estate office's location (56 percent vs. 33 percent, p. <.05). Moreover, when whites were steered out, about four-fifths of the municipalities where they were shown houses were nearby white suburbs. In contrast, when blacks were steered out, two-thirds of the houses shown were in the predominantly black municipalities of Inkster and Detroit (Pearce, 1979).

Detroit alone accounted for almost a third of the homes shown to blacks, although only 13 percent of the real estate firms were located in Detroit. Not only did blacks see a disproportionate number of houses in Inkster and Detroit, but they were steered there disproportionately by firms located in the western, southern, and eastern shore suburbs. Clearly then, the study revealed a consistent pattern of racially differentiated treatment of home seekers. The data showed that these were not isolated instances of individual racism. Instead, there was a high level of consistency across the entire metropolitan area. There was a clear existence of practices that excluded three-fourths of black families from ever seeing homes and steered out many of the few that did see homes.

The existence of racial steering and/or racial discriminatory treatment was also revealed by a national study conducted by the U.S. Department of Housing and Urban Development (1979). Of the 40 nationwide Standard Metropolitan Statistical Areas studied, Detroit ranked first in discriminatory treatment of blacks in the rental housing market and third behind Cincinnati and Columbus, Ohio, in discrimination in housing sales. In the rental market in Detroit, whites were favored 67 percent of the time and blacks only 10 percent—a statistically significant difference of 57 percentage points. In the housing sales market, whites were favored 64 percent of the time and blacks 22 percent—a statistically significant difference of 42 percentage points.

In 1990, a discriminatory housing market producing intense racial residential segregation remained a characteristic feature of metropolitan Detroit (Wayne, Oakland, and Macomb Counties). Census figures for 1990 reveal that most of the region's whites are living in the suburbs, while most of the region's blacks resided in the City of Detroit.

Of the 413,730 whites who resided in the city in 1980, 46 percent had left by 1990, thus increasing the black proportion of the city to 76 percent. The suburbanization process also involved a substantial number of blacks who moved—primarily to Oakland County. During the decade, Oakland County's black population increased from 47,962 to 77,488, or by 61.6 percent, compared with an increase of only 13.8 percent for Macomb County and 2.3 percent for Wayne County. Between 1980 and 1990, the percentage increase in Oakland County's black population (61.6 percent) was 20 times greater than the percentage increase in the white population (3.0 percent).

Black suburbanization was likewise characterized by black residential segregation. In 1990, 80.7 percent of the 77,488 blacks in Oakland County were concentrated primarily in three suburban municipalities—Pontiac, Southfield, and Oak Park. On the other hand, only 11 percent of Oakland County's white population lived in these same three municipalities.

It appears that the housing market in metropolitan Detroit has not been allowed to operate without intervention. Race-conscious intervention to segregate the races, by means of racial steering and other forms of racial discrimination in housing, has been pervasive (Darden, 1990). This intervention denies equal access to housing, in violation of the 1968 U.S. Fair Housing Act and Michigan's 1977 Elliott-Larsen Civil Rights Act. As a result, considering a black and a white of equal socioeconomic status, it is likely that the white will reside in a better neighborhood, with better schools, services, and cultural advantages.

Discrimination results in lower-, middle-, and upper-class blacks living in closer proximity on the average than do lower-, middle-, and upper-class whites. Such clustering of blacks, regardless of class, is often mistakenly attributed (by most whites) to black preference for segregated living. Most whites have a tendency to comfort themselves with the idea that most blacks want to live in black neighborhoods. Yet the evidence is overwhelming that *discrimination in housing has been the major factor in black residential segregation* (Darden, 1987).

In 1979, the *Detroit Free Press* assigned four reporters (two black and two white) to pose as married couples who wanted to buy homes in Oakland County. The two couples sought to buy homes in affluent suburbs north of Detroit but were directed by real estate agents to different areas. Such practices perpetuate segregated housing patterns. For example, the white couple received 31 recommendations for houses within the mostly white suburb of Birmingham. Going to the same firms, the black couple was given only six recommendations for houses in Birmingham (*Detroit Free Press*, 1979). Some real estate agents described Birmingham as overpriced, and said that it had "snob appeal." For the white couple, agents described Birmingham as a charming, older community with great investment values. Most real estate agents suggested that the black couple look at houses near Pontiac or Southfield, two of the three suburban municipalities where blacks in Oakland County were already concentrated.

In 1984, two teams of *Detroit News* reporters posed as apartment seekers, randomly visiting buildings in Detroit and 24 suburbs. In 21 of the 51 apartments tested, blacks received different treatment from what whites received. At 5 of 8 buildings visited in Detroit, reporters found evidence of discrimination. In suburban Wayne County, agents or owners at 9 of 19 buildings tested treated the black reporters differently. In Oakland County, reporters found evidence of discriminatory practices at 5 of 14 apartments tested. In Macomb County, black reporters were treated differently in 2 of the 10 buildings visited *(Detroit News*, 1984a).

In the *Detroit News* investigation, a white reporter and a black reporter of the same sex visited the same apartment buildings within a few minutes of each other. Each asked for a one-or two-bedroom apartment. Black reporters visited apartment buildings in Detroit suburbs such as Warren, Dearborn Heights, and Farmington Hills and were told that there were no vacancies, or that the waiting lists were long, or that nothing was available for up to a year. White reporters visiting the same buildings were offered an apartment by the next month—and at one apartment, as soon as that weekend. In the Detroit suburbs of Westland and Oak Park, apartments tested were immediately available to white reporters, while none were available to the black reporters.

This differential treatment of black and white reporters is consistent with other testing studies. The Fair Housing Center in Detroit, a private nonprofit agency which investigates cases of discrimination, found that 70 percent of the landlords tested in the Detroit area

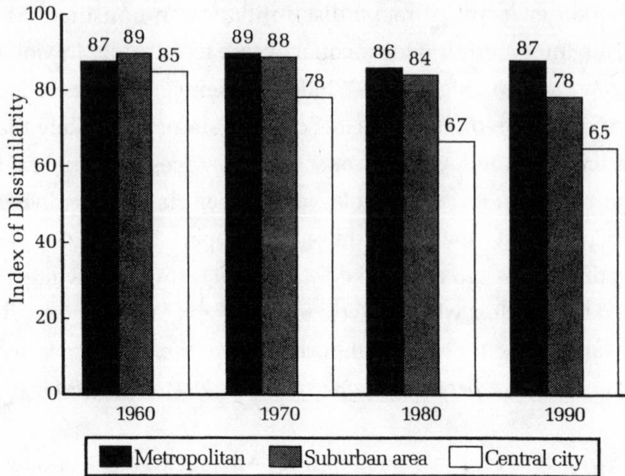

FIGURE 7-2
Levels of Black Residential Segregation in Metropolitan Area of Detroit 1960, 1970, 1980, 1990

treated black apartment seekers differently from white seekers. The center used tests in which black and white investigators visited the same building posing as apartment seekers. The conclusion was based on 600 tests of housing availability, taken throughout the Detroit metropolitan area over a period of five years (*Detroit News*, 1984b).

Finally, a 1991-released National Housing Discrimination Study, which included metropolitan Detroit among its 25 metro areas, revealed that black home seekers were still experiencing some form of discrimination in at least half of their encounters with sales and rental agents. The estimated overall incidence of discrimination was 56 percent for black renters and 59 percent for black home seekers (Turner, Struyk, & Yinger, 1991). Such discrimination occurred despite passage of the 1988 Fair Housing Act Amendments. As a consequence of these and other factors, residential segregation in metropolitan Detroit has remained virtually unchanged over a 30-year period. In 1960, the index of dissimilarity in black-white housing stood at 87 percent. By 1990, the level was still 87 percent (Figure 7-2).

SOURCE: Based on computations by the author using U.S. census data.

Conclusions

The objective of this chapter was to assess the patterns of black residential segregation in Michigan over a thirty-year period—i.e., before and after passage of the 1968 Federal Fair Housing Act and the Elliott-Larsen Civil Rights Act of 1977.

The study area consisted of 12 Standard Metropolitan Statistical Areas in Michigan. An analysis of U.S. census data by race revealed the following:

1. Michigan's black suburban population increased between 1960 and 1990, although blacks as a percentage of the total suburban population remained small.
2. Between 1960 and 1990, the mean level of the index of dissimilarity of black and white residential patterns declined in the suburban areas, central cities, and Standard Metropolitan Statistical Areas in the study.

3. The greatest average decline in residential segregation over the thirty-year period occurred in central cities, while the least decline occurred in the suburban areas, resulting in blacks in central cities becoming less residentially segregated than blacks in suburban areas.
4. Detroit remained the most residentially segregated metropolitan area in the state before and after passage of the 1968 Federal Fair Housing Act and Michigan's 1977 Elliott-Larsen Civil Rights Act.

Recommendations

Background and Rationale

Most empirical evidence points to discrimination, not income or preferences, as the major barrier to fair housing. Economic factors are of minor importance. Since blacks are not an ethnic group in the way in which foreign-born families once were, voluntary segregation is unlikely except as a response to intimidation. Thus, black segregation is largely compelled (Wolfe, 1981). As a result, it remains severe, widespread, unresponsive to black economic improvement, and impervious to the assimilative processes that dispersed ethnic groups.

Recent research suggests that the most effective way to remove barriers to fair housing is through a combination of economic incentives and economic disincentives. There should be economic incentives for those who take action to remove the barriers and economic disincentives through penalties for those who act to maintain barriers (Darden, Duleep, & Galster, 1992).

The removal of the barriers to fair housing will result in an expansion of the housing options for blacks and other racial minorities throughout cities and suburbs so that the housing options of racial minorities equal the options of the white majority. To achieve this goal requires bold, creative leadership on the part of the federal government, state government, local government, public school systems, and the private sector. Such a plan must go beyond affirmative marketing to include "integration incentives." Affirmative marketing is an effort to promote integration or prevent segregation by taking special steps to provide information about available housing to persons or racial groups who, without such efforts, would not be likely to know of the availability of, or to express an interest in, the homes or apartments being offered (U.S. Department of Housing and Urban Development, 1983). An "integration incentive" plan not only promotes integration by providing information about available housing to both whites and nonwhites where they are underrepresented, but provides an incentive that makes it economically advantageous to purchase or rent such housing.[1]

The recommendations that follow are divided into two parts: (1) incentives to desegregate; and (2) disincentives to discriminate.

Incentives to Desegregate

1. The federal government (or some other agency or private source) should subsidize a percentage of the down payment for any family that moves into an area where members of its racial group are underrepresented.

2. The federal and state governments should provide substantial tax deductions to any family that purchases a home in an area where members of its racial group are under-represented.
3. The state and local governments should provide low (i.e., below-market-rate) interest loans to any family that purchases a home in an area where members of its racial group are under-represented.
4. The state and local governments should provide loans at even lower interest rates to families who send their children to public schools, since the quality and racial composition of the public schools are important factors influencing young families' choice of neighborhoods.
5. The federal, state, and local governments should provide tax deductions to real estate firms according to the proportion of sales made to families in areas of racial underrepresentation.

In order for such an "integration incentive" plan to work, it must be metropolitan in scope and must involve effective partnerships between representatives of the federal government, state government, local government, real estate and banking industry, and fair housing centers or other community or neighborhood-based organizations. Such partnerships, however, will not be sufficient as long as there is racial steering and/or racial discrimination.

Disincentives to Discriminate

A vigorous attack on racial steering and/or discrimination must occur if the integration incentive plan is to work. A successful attack on racial steering and discrimination will require the use of the most effective tools to date: (1) testing, and (2) lawsuits resulting in substantial economic penalties in order to serve as economic disincentives.

Following are specific recommendations with respect to disincentives to discriminate and/or steer to segregate.

1. Concerned citizens of Michigan should establish fair housing centers in sufficient numbers and in strategic areas in order to monitor discrimination problems in housing and to provide effective remedies.
2. The federal, state, and local governments should provide sufficient financial support to fair housing centers so that they may be able to employ full-time professional testers or inspectors to detect violators in the housing industry.
3. Fair housing centers, in cooperation with attorneys and plaintiffs (i.e., victims of discrimination), should file a sufficient number of lawsuits, using the data gathered through testing, so that the suits will serve as a deterrent against acts of unlawful discrimination.
4. The State of Michigan's Department of Licensing and Regulation should vigorously enforce regulations that would lead to *revoking* licenses of real estate brokers found guilty of discrimination.

To date, testing remains the most effective tool to assess the extent of discrimination in housing. The processing of complaints alone will never solve the discrimination problem since complaints far underrepresent the actual extent of discrimination.

Testing must be expanded to become a full-time occupation in which individuals are trained and employed to detect discrimination. Just as the city, state, and federal governments employ inspectors to detect unlawful acts in other areas of life, the government must employ testers or inspectors to detect violators in the housing industry.

A positive step was made in this direction in 1987 when HUD received statutory authority under the Housing and Community Development Act to fund private agencies, civil rights organizations, and local fair housing groups to enable them to conduct tests of rental and real estate sales offices to uncover discrimination (Housing and Community Development Act, 1987).

Testing by private groups can supply evidence of discrimination to HUD and to state and local fair housing agencies. It can also produce evidence that testers themselves can use in private fair housing suits. The Supreme Court ruled in *Havens Realty Company* v. *Coleman* in 1982 that a black tester who has been denied information about the availability of housing is a bona fide complainant with standing to sue in court under Title VIII.

As a result of the *Havens* case, private civil rights groups that conduct testing could possibly become a more effective force in combating housing discrimination, thereby removing a major barrier to fair housing (Downing & Gladstone, 1989). However, they need more resources.

In the final analysis, if the Fair Housing Act is to be a deterrent, it must convince a potential violator that illegal acts will be detected and punished with a high degree of certainty (Galster, 1989).

The use of both "incentives to desegregate" and "disincentives to discriminate," with a strong attack on racial steering and racial discrimination, may provide the best approach for Michigan metropolitan areas to substantially reduce their persistent patterns of racial residential segregation. What is at stake is a future of permanent apartheid with continuous racial conflict or a future holding the prospect of increased racial harmony.

Notes

[1]The closest approximation of an integration incentive plan at the state level is the Ohio Bonus for Integrative Moves. This program was created in 1985 and was conducted by the Ohio Housing Finance Agency. The Agency agreed in 1985 to set aside 10 percent of its $20 million state mortgage revenue bond program for first-time buyers making integrative moves (Saltman, 1990).

An evaluation of pro-integrative mortgage incentives provided by four fair housing agencies in suburban Cleveland was released in 1992. A survey was made of program participants who purchased homes in suburban Cleveland. One hundred eighty-eight (52.5 percent of all participants) responded. The study found that almost all participants had a positive experience. Most were satisfied with their choices of neighborhoods and neighbors. Almost all were supportive of pro-integrative mortgage incentive programs. Just over half considered the pro-integrative mortgage incentive as very important to their home purchase decision (Keating, 1992).

A second survey questioned 385 residents of suburban Cleveland about pro-integrative mortgage incentives. Overall, 55 percent of all residents surveyed were supportive. Black support was higher than white support by a margin of 71 percent to 49 percent. Generally, the higher the educational level and the greater the income of the residents interviewed, the more supportive they were of pro-integrative mortgage incentives. Overall, 57 percent of all suburban residents surveyed were supportive of someone of another race with a pro-integrative mortgage incentive moving into their neighborhood, with only 9 percent opposed. Fifty-four percent of white residents were supportive, although the rates of white support varied among suburbs (Keating, 1992; see also Cromwell, 1990).

REFERENCES

Civil Rights Act of 1968, 42 U.S.C. Sec. 3601, Sec. 3605 (1970).

Cromwell, B.A. (1990). "Pro-Integrative Subsidies and Their Effects on Housing Markets: Do Race Based Loans Work?" *Working Paper 9018*. Cleveland: Federal Reserve Bank of Cleveland.

Darden, J.T. (1973). *Afro-Americans in Pittsburgh: The Residential Segregation of a People* (p. 5). Lexington: D.C. Heath.

Darden, J.T. (1984). Metropolitan Detroit. In L. Sommers (Ed.), *Michigan: A Geography* (Chapter 10). Boulder, CO: West view Press.

Darden, J.T. (1987). "Choosing Neighbors and Neighborhoods: The Role of Race in Housing Preference." In G.A. Tobin (Ed.), *Divided Neighborhoods Vol. 32, Urban Affairs Annual Reviews* (pp. 15–42). Newbury Park: Sage Publications.

Darden, J.T. (1990). "Racial Residential Segregation and Discrimination in Housing: The Evidence from Municipalities in Three Michigan Counties (Oakland, Wayne, and Macomb Counties), 1970–1990." Unpublished paper.

Darden, J.T., Duleep, H.O., & Galster, G. (1992). "Civil Rights in Metropolitan America." *Journal of Urban Affairs*, (Special Issue).

Darden, J.T., & Tabachneck, A. (1980). "Algorithm 8: Graphic and Mathematical Descriptions of Inequality, Dissimilarity, Segregation, or Concentration." *Environment and Planning A, 12*, 227–234.

Detroit Free Press, July 1, 1979.

Detroit News, April 1, 1984a.

Detroit News, April 8, 1984b.

Downing, P.M. & Gladstone, L. (1989, May 25). *Segregation and Discrimination in Housing: A Review of Selected Studies and Legislation*. Washington, D.C.: Congressional Research Service, The Library of Congress.

Federal Housing Administration (1938). *Underwriting Manual*.

Galster, George. (1989, April-May). "Audits Show Racial Discrimination Still Severe in 1980s." *Trends in Housing*, 27(6), pgs. 3,12.

Havens Realty Co. v. *Coleman* (1982). 455 U.S. 363.

Housing and Community Development Act of 1987, P.L. 100–242, Title V, Subtitle C, Section 561.

Jones v. *Alfred H. Mayor Co.* (1968). 392 U.S. 409.

Keating, D. (1992, May). "Racial Integration in Housing Programs and Neighborhoods: Pro-Integrative Housing Policies and Programs in Cleveland, Ohio." Paper presented at the 22nd annual conference of the Urban Affairs Association, Cleveland, Ohio.

Michigan Elliott-Larsen Civil Rights Act. MCLA 37.2501; MCLA 37.2502(1)(b); Public Acts of 1977, No. 162, Public Acts of 1982, No. 45.

Orfield, G. (1969). *Must We Bus? Practices of Real Estate Brokers* (p. 202). Minneapolis: University of Minnesota Press.

Pearce, D. (1979, February). "Gatekeepers and Home Seekers: Institutional Patterns in Racial Steering." *Social Problems*, 26(3), p. 335.

Saltman, J. (1990). *A Fragile Movement: The Struggle for Neighborhood Stabilization*. New York, NY: Greenwood Press.

Taeuber, K., & Taeuber, A. (1965). *Negroes in Cities* (p. 239). Chicago: Aldine Publishing Co.

Thomas, S.A. (1991, June). "Efforts to Integrate Housing: The Legality of Mortgage-Incentive Programs." *New York Law Review*, 66(3), pp. 940–978.

Turner, M., Struyk, R.J., & Yinger, J. (1991). *Housing Discrimination Study: Synthesis*. Washington, D.C.: U.S. Department of Housing and Urban Development, Office of Policy Development and Research.

U.S. Bureau of the Census. (1962). *1960 Census of Population. Characteristics of the Population: Census Tracts* (Vol. 1). Washington, D.C.: U.S. Government Printing Office.

U.S. Bureau of the Census. (1972). *1970 Census of Population and Housing: Census Tracts* (Final Reports). Washington, D.C.: U.S. Government Printing Office. 1972.

U.S. Bureau of the Census. (1981). *1980 Census of Population and Housing* (Advance Reports, Michigan PHC 80-V-24). Washington, D.C.: U.S. Government Printing Office.

U.S. Bureau of the Census. (1982). *Population and Housing Summary Tape File 1-A*. Michigan.

U.S. Bureau of the Census. (1991). *Population and Housing Summary Tape File 1-A*. Michigan.

U.S. Commission on Civil Rights. (1973). *Understanding Fair Housing* (A Report of the Commission). Washington, D.C.: U.S. Government Printing Office.

U.S. Department of Housing and Urban Development. (1979). *Measuring Racial Discrimination in American Housing Markets*. Washington, D.C.: Office of Policy Development and Research.

Weaver, R. (1948). *The Negro Ghetto*. New York: University Press.

Wolfe, E.P. (1981). *Trial and Error: The Detroit School Segregation Case*. Detroit: Wayne State University Press.

CHAPTER 8

Changes in Black Residential Segregation in Metropolitan Areas of Michigan, 1990–2000

Joe T. Darden

Background

The State of Michigan passed the Elliot-Larsen Civil Rights Act in 1977 and the U.S. Congress passed the Fair Housing Act in 1968, yet most blacks in Michigan continue to live in highly segregated residential areas. This chapter updates Chapter 7.

Geographically, a metropolitan area includes a county or contiguous counties with at least one central city of 50,000 people or more. The city and all of the suburbs in the county are part of the metropolitan area. Here I analyze metropolitan areas for the rate of residential segregation, which is defined as the overall unevenness in the *spatial* distribution of two racial groups over subunits within metropolitan areas. Such units may include census tracts, block groups, or city blocks. The degree of residential segregation presented here was measured by the index of dissimilarity. The index value ranges from 0, indicating no segregation, to 100, indicating total segregation. The higher the index, the greater the degree of residential segregation. Whatever the value of the index, it reflects the minimum percentage of either group that would have to move from one subunit to another to achieve an even spatial distribution throughout the metropolitan area, county, or city (Darden 1992).

Residential Segregation by Metropolitan Area

Table 8-1 shows the level of residential segregation by race for the nine metropolitan areas in Michigan. These are the areas where the majority of the state's black residents live. The levels of segregation for blacks, based on the 2000 census, range from an index score of 53 in metropolitan Kalamazoo-Battle Creek to 84.7 in metropolitan Detroit.

Table 8-1. Residential Segregation in Metropolitan Areas of Michigan, 1990–2000

Metropolitan Area	Population, 2000	Percentage by Race: Whites	Blacks	Hispanics	Asians
Ann Arbor	578,736	83.7	7.9	3.0	4.2

	Dissimilarity Index: 1990	2000	Percentage Point Change
Whites vs. blacks	61.5	63.2	1.7
Whites vs. Hispanics	39.3	37.9	−1.4
Whites vs. Asians	56.1	58.7	2.6

Metropolitan Area	Population, 2000	Percentage by Race: Whites	Blacks	Hispanics	Asians
Benton Harbor	162,453	78.1	16.5	3.0	1.4

	Dissimilarity Index: 1990	2000	Percentage Point Change
Whites vs. blacks	75.2	73.7	−1.5
Whites vs. Hispanics	35.9	40.1	4.2
Whites vs. Asians	51.3	44.3	−7.0

Metropolitan Area	Population, 2000	Percentage by Race: Whites	Blacks	Hispanics	Asians
Detroit	4,441,551	69.7	23.3	2.9	2.7

	Dissimilarity Index: 1990	2000	Percentage Point Change
Whites vs. blacks	87.5	84.7	−2.8
Whites vs. Hispanics	39.8	45.7	5.9
Whites vs. Asians	42.9	45.9	3.0

Metropolitan Area	Population, 2000	Percentage by Race: Whites	Blacks	Hispanics	Asians
Flint	436,141	74.1	21.1	2.3	1.0

	Dissimilarity Index: 1990	2000	Percentage Point Change
Whites vs. blacks	81.3	76.7	−4.6
Whites vs. Hispanics	31.9	27.3	−4.6
Whites vs. Asians	38.1	35.2	−2.9

Metropolitan Area	Population, 2000	Percentage by Race: Whites	Blacks	Hispanics	Asians
Grand Rapids-Muskegon-Holland	1,088,540	83.0	7.7	6.3	1.8

Table 8-1. Residential Segregation in Metropolitan Areas of Michigan, 1990–2000 (*continued*)

	Dissimilarity Index		
	1990	2000	Percentage Point Change
Whites vs. blacks	75.0	67.2	−7.8
Whites vs. Hispanics	44.8	51.6	6.8
Whites vs. Asians	35.5	41.4	5.9

		Percentage by Race			
Metropolitan Area	Population, 2000	Whites	Blacks	Hispanics	Asians
Jackson	158,422	87.4	8.6	2.2	0.7

	Dissimilarity Index		
	1990	2000	Percentage Point Change
Whites vs. blacks	70.3	65.2	−5.1
Whites vs. Hispanics	29.8	30.8	1.0
Whites vs. Asians	40.5	35.6	−4.9

		Percentage by Race			
Metropolitan Area	Population, 2000	Whites	Blacks	Hispanics	Asians
Kalamazoo-Battle Creek	452,851	57.7	53.0	3.6	1.6

	Dissimilarity Index		
	1990	2000	Percentage Point Change
Whites vs. blacks	57.7	53.0	−4.7
Whites vs. Hispanics	31.9	38.9	7.0
Whites vs. Asians	41.4	40.3	−1.1

		Percentage by Race			
Metropolitan Area	Population, 2000	Whites	Blacks	Hispanics	Asians
Lansing-East Lansing	447,728	82.2	8.8	4.7	3.0

	Dissimilarity Index		
	1990	2000	Percentage Point Change
Whites vs. blacks	57.9	57.1	−0.8
Whites vs. Hispanics	38.8	39.1	0.3
Whites vs. Asians	51.9	48.4	−3.5

		Percentage by Race			
Metropolitan Area	Population, 2000	Whites	Blacks	Hispanics	Asians
Saginaw-Bay City-Midland	403,070	82.3	10.6	4.9	1.0

	Dissimilarity Index		
	1990	2000	Percentage Point Change
Whites vs. blacks	82.3	74.5	−7.8
Whites vs. Hispanics	46.3	44.3	−2.0
Whites vs. Asians	43.3	42.0	−1.3

SOURCE: Lewis Mumford Center for Comparative Urban and Regional Research, State University of New York at Albany.

Table 8-2. Mean Levels of Residential Segregation by Race in Nine Michigan Metropolitan Areas, 1990–2000 (*N* = 9)

Groups	Year	Mean Index
White vs. black	1990	72.0
	2000	68.4
White vs. Hispanic	1990	37.6
	2000	39.5
White vs. Asian	1990	44.5
	2000	43.5

SOURCE: Computed from indexes obtained from Lewis Mumford Center for Comparative Urban and Regional Research, State University of New York at Albany.

Blacks were more segregated on average than Hispanics and Asians. The levels of segregation between Hispanics and non-Hispanic whites were substantially lower than the levels between whites and blacks. Segregation between whites and Hispanics ranged from an index score of 27.3 in metropolitan Flint to 51.6 in metropolitan Grand Rapids-Muskegon-Holland. Levels of segregation between Asians and whites were higher on average than between Hispanics and whites. Asian-white residential segregation ranged from 35.2 in metropolitan Flint to 58.7 in metropolitan Ann Arbor.

Table 8-2 shows the average changes in residential segregation between 1990 and 2000. Blacks, the only minority group with levels of segregation above 50, saw a slight average decline in segregation (−3.6 percentage points) over this 10-year period. Specifically, the index score for average segregation dropped from 72.0 to 68.4 overall. At this slow rate of decline in residential segregation, the majority of blacks in metropolitan areas of Detroit would still be residentially segregated in the year 2060.

Residential segregation of Hispanics, the least segregated group, increased from 37.6 to 39.5 over the 10-year period 1990–2000. Asian segregation levels remained slightly higher than those of Hispanics but decreased slightly, from 44.5 to 43.5, or by 1.0 percentage points, over the decade.

Blacks in all metropolitan areas were highly segregated in 2000, but the most segregated metropolitan area was Detroit, with an index of dissimilarity of 84.7. The least segregated metropolitan area was Kalamazoo-Battle Creek, which had an index of 53.0, a difference of 31.7 percentage points. Given its very high level of residential segregation (the highest level not only in Michigan but in the entire nation), a detailed assessment of Metropolitan Detroit will be made later.

Black Residential Segregation by County

The previous section measured the extent of black-white residential segregation by metropolitan area. This section measures the extent of black-white residential segregation in the 10 largest counties. The analysis is also extended to include blacks and whites sharing residential space at three geographic subunits of decreasing size—the census tract (the level at which metropolitan segregation was based), block groups, and city blocks.

Table 8-3. Black Residential Segregation in the 10 Largest Counties in Michigan, 2000

	Population			Index of Dissimilarity		
County	White	Black	% black	Tract	Block Group	Blocks
Wayne	1,028,984	864,627	42	86.3	87.1	88.7
Oakland	988,194	120,720	10.0	72.6	73.1	77.1
Macomb	721,882	21,151	2.7	51.4	57.8	72.3
Kent	461,162	49,994	8.7	63.1	64.9	71.8
Genesee	323,136	88,356	20.3	77.7	80.6	84.1
Washtenaw	249,916	39,697	12.2	52.5	54.8	61.1
Ingham	214,685	29,712	10.6	50.5	51.2	59.2
Kalamazoo	201,784	23,217	9.6	48.6	54.6	62.2
Ottawa	211,058	2,380	1.0	44.9	51.0	75.5
Saginaw	151,979	38,675	18.4	73.2	75.8	80.5
Mean			16.6	62.1	65.1	73.2

NOTE. The higher the index, the greater the amount of black vs. white residential segregation. Since tracts are larger than block groups, black segregation is higher, and since blocks are the smallest subunits, segregation is highest.

SOURCE: http://enceladus.isr.umich.edu/race/links.html.

Table 8-3 shows that in Wayne County, where 864,627 blacks, or 61.2% of all blacks in Michigan, resided in 2000, blacks experienced the highest level of residential segregation. The index of dissimilarity was 86.3 at the census tract level and reached 88.7 at the city block level. Blacks were least segregated by tract in Ottawa County. The index of dissimilarity at the census tract level was 44.9. However, only 2,380 blacks lived there in 2000, representing only 1% of the total county population. The mean level of residential segregation for the 10 largest counties in Michigan was 62.1 in 2000 at the census tract level and 73.2 at the block level (Table 8-3).

Residential Segregation in Michigan's Central Cities in 2000

A central city is the largest city in a metropolitan area, also often called a core city. There are 12 central cities in the state. Most blacks in the state are concentrated in these 12 cities: Ann Arbor, Battle Creek, Bay City, Detroit, Flint, Grand Rapids, Benton Harbor, Jackson, Kalamazoo, Lansing, Muskegon, and Saginaw. In 2000, 995,717 blacks, constituting 70% of all blacks in the state, resided in these areas. Table 8-4 reveals the extent to which blacks were residentially segregated from whites in these areas. Blacks in the cities of Flint and Saginaw were the most residentially segregated. These were the only two cities where the index of dissimilarity exceeded 75. Although the Detroit metropolitan area as a whole was the most residentially segregated area in the state (87.4; see Table 8-1), the city of Detroit itself had a slightly lower level (63.3), but this is still a high level of residential segregation. Other cities with high levels of segregation, i.e., above 50 but not as high as 75, were Grand Rapids (58.6), Jackson (54.8), Battle Creek (53.3), and Kalamazoo (51.3). Muskegon, Ann Arbor, Lansing, and Benton Harbor had levels of segregation below 50. The mean level of residential segregation in 2000 was 52, which was a decline of 11.2 percentage points from the mean level of segregation in 1990. Five of the cities, specifically Saginaw, Detroit, Grand Rapids,

Table 8-4. Black Residential Segregation in Michigan's Central Cities, 2000

City	Total Black	Total White	% black	Index of Dissimilarity	Change, 1990–2000
Flint	66,231	50,020	53.0	76.8	0.9
Saginaw	26,440	26,372	43.0	76.4	−3.9
Detroit	771,966	99,921	81.2	63.3	−1.5
Grand Rapids	39,401	123,537	19.9	58.6	−4.5
Jackson	7,069	26,204	19.5	54.8	0.4
Battle Creek	9,440	38,761	17.7	53.3	−2.4
Kalamazoo	15,757	53,589	20.4	51.3	3.1
Bay City[a]	972	32,333	2.6	47.0	27.2
Muskegon	12,582	23,231	31.3	46.7	7.2
Ann Arbor	9,906	82,975	8.7	38.7	5.3
Lansing	25,498	73,105	21.4	38.1	2.5
Benton Harbor	10,457	600	93.5	19.6	−7.6
Mean			34.4	52.0	

[a] Caution is advised in interpreting the index due to the small size of the black population, which may influence the evenness in the spatial distribution of the population.

SOURCES: (1) Frey, W., and D. Myers. *Racial segregation in the U.S. metropolitan areas and cities, 1990–2000: Patterns, trends, and explanations report 05-573.* Ann Arbor: Population Studies Center, University of Michigan, Institute for Social Research. (2) Darden, J. Residential segregation of blacks in metropolitan areas of Michigan, 1960–1990. In *The state of black Michigan, 1992,* 13–24. East Lansing: Michigan State University Urban Affairs Programs. Used with permission.

Battle Creek, and Benton Harbor, experienced a decline over the decade. Seven of the cities, Flint, Jackson, Kalamazoo, Muskegon, Ann Arbor, and Lansing, experienced an increase. While Bay City reflects an increase in segregation, caution is advised in interpreting the index due to the small size of the black population (972).

Explaining Racial Residential Segregation: The Case of Metropolitan Detroit

Prior research on blacks in metropolitan Detroit has revealed extreme inequality in the neighborhoods occupied by blacks and those occupied by whites (Darden et al. 1987). However, the residential location of blacks in the central city could not be explained by differences in the housing values and rents between blacks and whites. Other studies using 1990 census data have found similar results. Indeed, Darden and Kamel (2000a) specifically examined the questions of whether socioeconomic status matters in the level of residential segregation and isolation between blacks and whites in the city and suburbs of Detroit and whether blacks in the city of Detroit were more segregated and isolated than blacks in the suburbs (as commonly believed) when socioeconomic status was controlled. The authors used data from the U.S. Census Bureau's (1993) *Summary Tape File 4*. The methods employed consisted of the index of dissimilarity and the isolation index P*. The spatial units included census tracts within the city and suburbs, with controls on income, education, and occupation. The results revealed that socioeconomic status had little influence on the high level of black residential segregation and isolation in the city of Detroit or its suburbs. Blacks remained highly segregated and isolated from whites at all socioeconomic levels. Furthermore, blacks in the suburbs were more segregated and isolated from whites than blacks in the city of Detroit at each educational, occupational, and income level (Darden and Kamel 2000a).

In another approach, the significance of class in residential segregation was further assessed (Darden and Kamel 2000b). The authors determined whether or not blacks with higher socioeconomic status than whites were living in suburban municipalities that were less residentially segregated than blacks with lower socioeconomic status living in other suburban municipalities. The study area consisted of suburban municipalities located within the Detroit tricounty metropolitan area (Wayne, Oakland, and Macomb). The data were obtained from the U.S. Census Bureau's (1992) *1990 Census Summary File 3A* and were analyzed on the census tract level. The results revealed that the socioeconomic status of blacks mattered little in explaining suburban residential segregation of blacks.

In a recent book by Farley, Danziger, and Holzer (2000), the authors concluded that blacks and whites in Detroit differ greatly in both their economic status and their neighborhoods. However, differences in income, occupational achievement, and educational attainment account for only a small fraction of residential segregation in Detroit. The authors came to this conclusion after examining census data on the incomes of all households living in a block group and the incomes of all blacks and whites throughout metropolitan Detroit. The method used involved assigning households to block groups on the basis of their income and the average incomes of the households in each block in 1990. That is, in this model, everyone was assigned to a neighborhood on the basis of household income, not on the basis of skin color. The results revealed that if household income alone determined where people lived, the index of dissimilarity would have been 15 instead of what it actually was—88—in 1990. If households were assigned based on occupation, the index of dissimilarity would have been 5, and if they were assigned based on education, the index of dissimilarity would have been 6. Thus, the authors concluded that residential segregation is a matter of skin color, not income, occupation, or education (Farley, Danziger, and Holzer 2000). In Detroit, income, education, and occupation did not explain why blacks and whites were so highly segregated in 1990.

However, several socioeconomic and demographic changes have occurred in the Detroit metropolitan area since 1990. Whatever changes occurred, the outcome was that blacks in the Detroit metropolitan area became the most racially segregated minority group in the United States. Since a continual debate exists over whether or not class is more important than race in explaining residential segregation (Clark and Ware 1997), this chapter examines the socioeconomic and demographic changes in metropolitan Detroit over the last decade and analyzes 2000 census data to determine whether or not class, rather than race, was the primary reason for the high level of residential segregation of blacks in metropolitan Detroit in 2000.

Socioeconomic and Demographic Changes in Metropolitan Detroit, 1990–2000

The metropolitan Detroit area experienced slow growth over the last decade. In 2000, the metropolitan Detroit area (Wayne, Oakland, and Macomb counties) consisted of 4,043,467 people. Of this total, 2,720,689, or 67.2%, were white, while 1,000,853, or 25%, were black. Of these, 96% of all whites lived in the suburbs and only 4.3% resided in the city, as whites continued to move out of the city of Detroit to the suburbs over the decade. This made an already predominantly black city even blacker. By 2000, the city of Detroit had declined in population from 1 million people in 1990 to 951,270. It had also become 81.3% black, which was up from 75% in 1990 (U.S. Census Bureau 2002). Indeed, over the decade, Detroit lost 44.5% of its white population. On the other hand, the decline of the black population was less than 1%. In 2000, at least 77% of all blacks in the metropolitan area lived in the city of Detroit.

The metropolitan Detroit area's socioeconomic condition improved sharply between 1990 and 2000. Indeed, improvements in per capita income and median household income and a reduction in poverty improved Detroit's ratings among the 50 largest metropolitan areas from 36 to 21 (Logan 2002). Much of the improvement in Detroit's socioeconomic condition may be related to the decline in high-poverty neighborhoods, that is neighborhoods where the poverty rate is 40% or higher. Most are disproportionately black. Metropolitan Detroit's decline in high-poverty neighborhoods was substantially larger than in any other metropolitan area (Jargowsky 2003). As a result, the concentrated poverty rate among blacks in metropolitan Detroit declined from 53.9% in 1990 to 16.4% in 2000, a drop of 37.5 percentage points. According to Jargowsky (2003), this reduction in the concentrated poverty rate between 1990 and 2000 changed metropolitan Detroit's ranking from the number one metropolitan area in 1990 for blacks in concentrated poverty to a rank lower than that of Chicago, St. Louis, Baltimore, Tampa, Houston, New York, Philadelphia, Atlanta, and Los Angeles.

The city of Detroit also improved over the decade, although it still suffers from high poverty and unemployment. The poverty rate dropped from 32.4% in 1990 to 26.0% in 2000, a difference of 6.4 percentage points. The unemployment rate declined slightly, from 14.3% in 1990 to 13.8% in 2000 (U.S. Census Bureau 1992, 2002). In addition, the median household income of blacks increased from $17,767 to $29,647, and the median household income of whites increased from $21,120 to $29,402 over the 1990s decade. Thus, the racial inequality income ratio increased from 0.84 in 1990 to 1.00 in 2000. Equally important is the fact that the percentage of middle-class blacks (that is, blacks earning $75,000 or more) who were living in Detroit increased from 4% in 1990 to 14% in 2000 (U.S. Census Bureau 1993, 2002).

Given these demographic and socioeconomic changes over the 1990s, blacks and whites in metropolitan Detroit continued to live in separate neighborhoods, resulting in an index of dissimilarity for the metropolitan area of 85. This index for blacks and whites was higher than the index for any other group in America's large metropolitan areas.

The following section of this chapter analyzes 2000 census data on race, residential location, income, and education to determine whether or not differences in the class status of blacks and whites can be considered the primary factor for the low representation of blacks in the suburbs and the high level of black-white residential segregation in metropolitan Detroit.

Black Suburban Representation

Analysis of the spatial distribution of blacks and whites in the metropolitan Detroit area over the city and its suburbs revealed that blacks and whites live disproportionately in separate parts of the metropolitan area. Indeed, 95.7% of whites reside in the suburbs, and only 4.3%

Table 8-5. Residential Segregation between Blacks and Whites with the Same Levels of Household Income for the City of Detroit, 2000

Income Level	Number of Whites	% of Total Whites	Number of Blacks	% of Total Blacks	Dissimilarity Index
<$14,999	13,288	26.91	74,121	27.42	63.01
$15,000 to $34,999	14,961	30.30	79,108	29.27	63.02
$35,000 to $74,999	15,001	30.38	80,351	29.73	64.10
≥$75,000	6,121	12.40	36,712	13.58	64.16
Total house-holds	49,371	100.00	270,292	100.00	
Mean					63.57

SOURCE: Computed by the author from data obtained from U.S. Census Bureau (2002).

of whites reside in the city. On the other hand, 77% of blacks reside in the city of Detroit and only 23% live in the suburbs. Thus, the city-suburb dissimilarity index in 2000 was 72.7, indicating that 72.7% of all blacks in the Detroit metropolitan area would have to relocate to the suburbs for blacks to be spatially distributed the same as whites. This was the second-highest city-suburb dissimilarity index among metropolitan areas of 500,000 or more people. Only metropolitan Gary, Indiana, had a higher index: 76 (Frey 2001).

Residential Segregation between Blacks and Whites with Comparable Incomes

The following analysis is designed to answer the question of whether blacks and whites with the same incomes are residentially integrated in the same neighborhoods. Table 8-5 examines blacks and whites in the city of Detroit at comparable income levels ranging from less than $14,999 to $75,000 or more. The results reveal that blacks and whites earning less than $14,999 had an index of dissimilarity of 63. These groups can be considered "poor" blacks and whites. The results also revealed that blacks and whites earning $75,000 or more (that is, middle-class blacks and whites) were no less segregated. In fact, these groups had an index of dissimilarity of 64.2. When blacks and whites at each income level are examined, the results suggest that blacks and whites in the city of Detroit are residentially segregated when the two groups have the same incomes. Regardless of comparable incomes, blacks and whites have, on average, an index of dissimilarity of more than 60. Poor blacks and poor whites are as residentially segregated as middle-class blacks and whites (Table 8-5). On average, 63.5% of black households would have to move to another neighborhood within the city in order to achieve even spatial distribution with white households at the same income level.

According to the ecological theory and the spatial assimilation process, when a minority group moves to the suburbs, there is an expectation of a lower level of residential segregation than what was experienced in the city, yet Table 8-6 shows that blacks in the suburbs of Detroit with the same incomes as whites are even more segregated than blacks in the city. The average level of segregation is 70.9, which was 7.4 percentage points higher than the average segregation experienced by blacks in the city. Poor suburban blacks and whites were slightly more segregated, with an index of dissimilarity of 73.2, while affluent blacks and

Table 8-6. Residential Segregation between Blacks and Whites with the Same Levels of Household Income for the Suburban Area of Detroit, 2000

Income Level	Number of Whites	% of Total Whites	Number of Blacks	% of Total Blacks	Dissimilarity Index
<$14,999	95,620	8.97	15,766	18.02	73.26
$15,000 to $34,999	213,097	19.99	20,397	23.32	72.05
$35,000 to $74,999	392,788	36.85	29,622	3.86	69.93
$75,000 or more	364,339	34.18	21,695	24.80	68.53
Total house-holds	1,065,844	100.0	87,480	100.00	
Mean					70.94

SOURCE: Computed by the author from data obtained from U.S. Census Bureau (2002).

whites had an index of dissimilarity of 68.5. At each comparable income level, blacks and whites in the suburbs of Detroit were more residentially segregated from each other than were blacks and whites in the city of Detroit.

Residential Segregation between Blacks and Whites with Comparable Educational Levels

Table 8-7 shows that most blacks and whites with the same level of education do not share residential neighborhoods in the city of Detroit. The average index of dissimilarity for blacks and whites at all educational levels was 59. However, the indexes of dissimilarity declined from a score of 66.5 among blacks and whites with no high school to 54.1 among blacks and whites with graduate or professional degrees.

More importantly, blacks in the suburbs with levels of education comparable to that of suburban whites experienced higher levels of residential segregation than blacks in the city of Detroit at each comparable educational level (Table 8-8). Similar to the patterns in the city, suburban blacks experienced a decline in the level of segregation as the level of education increased. For example, the index of dissimilarity among blacks and whites with no high

Table 8-7. Residential Segregation between Blacks and Whites with the Same Levels of Education for the City of Detroit, 2000

Education Level	Number of Whites	% of Total Whites	Number of Blacks	% of Total Blacks	Dissimilarity Index
No high school	29,847	35.27	128,512	28.58	66.57
High school	42,759	50.53	278,364	61.90	60.40
College degree	6,739	7.96	29,321	6.52	55.26
Professional degree	5,275	6.23	15,918	3.50	54.11
Total house-holds	84,620	100.00	452,115	100.5	
Mean					59.09

SOURCE: Computed by the author from data obtained from U.S. Census Bureau (2002).

Table 8-8. Residential Segregation between Blacks and Whites with the Same Levels of Education for the Suburban Area of Detroit, 2000

Education Level	Number of Whites	% of Total Whites	Number of Blacks	% of Total Blacks	Dissimilarity Index
No high school	259,718	14.19	25,812	18.21	72.49
High school	1,084,640	59.25	84,99-	59.96	70.87
College degree	310,035	16.94	19,180	13.53	66.70
Professional degree	176,319	9.63	11,763	8.30	65.93
Total house-holds	1,830,712	100.00	141,745	100.00	
Mean					69.00

SOURCE: Computed by the author from data obtained from U.S. Census Bureau (2002).

school diploma was 72.4. On the other hand, blacks and whites with graduate or professional degrees had an index of dissimilarity of 65.9, which is 6.5 percentage points lower. Overall, however, the average level of residential segregation between blacks and whites of comparable incomes in the suburbs was 69, compared to 59 among blacks and whites in the city, a difference of 10 percentage points.

In sum, this section has examined the residential segregation between blacks and whites with comparable incomes and educational attainment in the city of Detroit and the area outside the city, that is, the suburbs. The results reveal that most blacks and whites with comparable incomes and education do not live in the same neighborhoods in the city or in the suburbs. Poor blacks and poor whites are segregated; so are middle-class blacks and whites. In fact, blacks in the suburbs of Detroit with the same income and education as whites are even more segregated than blacks in the city of Detroit.

Thus, contrary to ecological theory and spatial assimilation, black residential segregation seems to occur independently of socioeconomic status. These findings, based on 2000 census data, present further evidence that ecological theory and spatial assimilation are insufficient to explain the high level of black residential segregation in America's most racially segregated metropolitan area. Instead, these findings reconfirm the importance of place stratification as defined by Alba and Logan (1993). In this model, it is argued that regardless of socioeconomic status, blacks, because of *racial steering* and/or *discrimination*, are not able to fully convert their socioeconomic status into the same neighborhoods as whites.

The next section examines racial housing discrimination and racial steering in 20 metropolitan areas, including metropolitan Detroit.

Discrimination in Housing and/or Racial Steering, 1989–2000

In 1989 a study of racial discrimination in housing and racial steering revealed that black home seekers in Detroit and 25 other metropolitan areas were experiencing some form of discrimination in at least half of their encounters with sales and rental agents (Turner, Struyk, and Yinger 1991).

A more recent 2000 study conducted by the Department of Housing and Urban Development that included metropolitan Detroit revealed that discrimination *still persists* in both rental and sales in metropolitan Detroit and other large metropolitan areas (Turner et al. 2002). However, the incidence of discrimination has generally declined since 1989. The results, based on 4,600 paired tests nationwide (including metropolitan Detroit), showed that in 21.6% of paired tests, whites were consistently favored over blacks in the rental market. In particular, whites were more likely to receive information about available housing units and to make an appointment to inspect available units. However, the overall incidence of consistent white-favored treatment dropped by 4.8 percentage points, from 26.4 % in 1989 to 21.6% in 2000 (Turner et al. 2002).

Although the incidence of discrimination against blacks was a problem in 2000, the incidence of consistent adverse treatment against black renters in metropolitan Detroit was actually below the national average. According to Turner and coworkers (2002), black home buyers, like renters, continued to face discrimination in metropolitan Detroit in 2000. It was found in paired tests that the overall incidence of consistent white-favored treatment dropped by 12 percentage points, from 29.0% in 1989 to 17.0% in 2000 (Turner et al. 2002). Thus, discrimination against black homebuyers declined between 1989 and 2000; however, it was not eliminated. More importantly, *geographic racial steering* rose. Specifically, white home buyers were more likely to be shown and be able to inspect available homes in more predominantly white neighborhoods than comparable blacks. Whites also received more information, assistance with financing, and encouragement than comparable black homebuyers. These results suggest that whites and blacks are increasingly likely to be recommended and shown homes in different neighborhoods.

Racial Differences in Financing Assistance

In 2000, black and white testers frequently received different levels of information and assistance with mortgage financing from real estate agents they visited. The overall incidence for financing assistance showed that nationwide whites were favored 36.6% of the time, while blacks were favored 31.7% of the time, with a statistically significant net measure of 4.9% (Turner et al. 2002).

Such differential assistance may impact the differential rejection rates for conventional mortgages for black and white applicants. In 2001, 84,830 applications were made for conventional home purchase loans in metropolitan Detroit: 69,493 white applications and 11,534 black applications. Whereas the white denial rate was 16.3%, the black denial rate was 31.5%, meaning a 1.93 black/white denial ratio. In other words, black applicants for conventional loans in metropolitan Detroit were almost twice as likely as white applicants to be denied a conventional loan in 2001 (Darden 2003).

Conclusions

This chapter has examined changes in black residential segregation in Michigan between 1990 and 2000 and examined whether the level of black residential segregation in metropolitan Detroit (the most segregated area in the United States) could be explained by differential socioeconomic status between blacks and whites or by discrimination in housing and racial steering in the market.

The results revealed that an average level of black-white residential segregation for Michigan's nine metropolitan areas declined from 72.0 in 1990 to 68.4 in 2000, a difference of −3.6 percentage points.

Further examination revealed that differential socioeconomic status (defined by income and education) was not the primary reason for the very high level of residential segregation in metropolitan Detroit in 2000. Regardless of equal income and equal educational attainment, blacks and whites were highly segregated residentially in the city of Detroit and in the suburbs.

A national study that included metropolitan Detroit concluded that blacks were less likely to experience outright racial discrimination in housing in 2000 compared to 1989. However, blacks were more likely in 2000 to experience racial steering by neighborhood racial composition compared to 1989. Thus, racial steering remains a barrier to equal access to housing in metropolitan Detroit 40 years after the civil disorders of 1967.

REFERENCES

Alba, R., and J. R. Logan. 1993. Minority proximity to whites in suburbs: An individual level analysis of segregation. *American Journal of Sociology* 98(6):1388–1427.

Clark, W. A. V., and J. Ware. 1997. Trends in residential integration by socioeconomic status in southern California. *Urban Affairs Review* 32(6):825–843.

Darden, J. T. 1992. Residential segregation of blacks in metropolitan areas of Michigan, 1960-1990. In *The state of black Michigan, 1992,* ed. F. Thomas, 13–24. East Lansing: Michigan State Univ. Urban Affairs Programs.

———. 2003. The plight of African Americans in Michigan: Residential segregation and predictable outcomes in mortgage lending and educational achievement. In *Multicultural geographies: The changing racial/ethnic patterns of the United States,* ed. J. Frazier and F. Margoi, 41–54. Binghamton, NY: Gobal Academic.

Darden, J. T., R. Hill, J. Thomas, and R. Thomas. 1987. *Detroit: Race and uneven development.* Philadelphia: Temple University Press.

Darden, J. T., and S. M. Kamel. 2000a. Black residential segregation in the city and suburbs of Detroit: Does socioeconomic status matter? *Journal of Urban Affairs* 22:1–13.

———. 2000b. Black residential segregation in suburban Detroit: Empirical testing of the ecological theory. *Review of Black Political Economy* 27(3):103–123.

Farley, R., S. Danzinger, and H. Holzer. 2000. *Detroit divided.* New York: Russell Sage Foundation.

Frey, W. 2001. *Melting pot suburbs: A census 2000 study of suburban diversity.* Washington, DC: The Brookings Institution.

Jargowsky, P. A. 2003. *Stunning progress, hidden problems: The dramatic decline of concentrated poverty in the 1990s.* Washington, DC: The Brookings Institution.

Logan, J. 2002. *Separate and unequal: The neighborhood gap for blacks and Hispanics in metropolitan America.* Albany, NY: Lewis Mumford Center for Comparative Urban and Regional Research.

Turner, M., S. Ross, G. Galster, and J. Yinger. 2002. *Discrimination in metropolitan housing markets: National results from Phase 1 HDS 2000.* Washington, DC: The Urban Institute.

Turner, M., R. J. Struyk, and J. Yinger. 1991. *Housing discrimination study: Synthesis*. Washington, DC: U.S. Department of Housing and Urban Development, Office of Policy Development and Research.

U.S. Census Bureau. 1992. *1990 census summary file 3 (SF3). State of Michigan*. Washington, DC: Data User Services Division.

———. 1993. *Summary tape file 4*. Washington, DC: Data User Services Division.

———. 2002. *2002 census summary file 3 (SF3). State of Michigan*. Washington, DC: Data User Services Division.

CHAPTER 9

The Health of Black Michigan

Clifford L. Broman

The goal of this chapter is to examine the health status of black Michigan since the civil disorders of 1967. We begin this chapter by sketching out some general patterns of black health status in the United States. We then move to an examination of the data for Michigan, and end with presenting major conclusions and recommendations.

Although it is true that the health status of Americans is generally improving, the disparity in health status between black and white Americans persists. Statistics for the American population as a whole show that average life expectancy for blacks in 1983 was 69.6 years, a figure reached by whites in the 1950s. Life expectancy for whites in 1983 was 75.2 years (Secretary's Task Force, 1985, volume 1, page 2). In 1984, the black infant mortality rate was approximately twice that of whites, and death rates for all other major causes of death—heart disease, cancer, cerebrovascular disease, homicide, accidents, and diabetes—exceeded the rate for whites (Secretary's Task Force, 1985, volume 1, page 67).

The causes for this disparity in health status are varied, but the evidence suggests strongly that socioeconomic factors play an important role (Haan and Kaplan, 1985). It is well known that in the United States the socioeconomic status of blacks is lower than that of whites. With respect to health, this fact serves to disadvantage blacks in two ways. First, it increases the likelihood that blacks are exposed to hazardous living environments. This, in turn, increases the likelihood that the health of blacks will suffer from accidents, fires, cancer, and violent confrontations that lead to injury or death. Living in hazardous environments is also known to be associated with increased levels of anger, anxiety, and stress—factors which contribute to coronary heart disease (Johnson and Broman, 1987; Poussaint, 1983). A second way in which socioeconomic status adversely affects black health is through its influence on treatment. Low socioeconomic position increases the likelihood that people will not seek treatment even when their need for medical care is urgent (Aday, Andersen, and Fleming, 1980). Generally speaking, the level of income does not account for this pattern. Rather, socioeconomic position is likely related to health perceptions which function as barriers to seeking needed health care (Aday, Fleming, and Andersen, 1984).

Data and Methodology

The data used in this chapter come generally from Michigan Health Statistics Annuals. These data are for mortality only, as no morbidity data are given. The general method used compares the mortality rate for racial groups (non-white and white) by the cause of death. Figures are given across years by sex and age group. The years examined will be 1965, 1975, and 1985.

The data used for these analyses are extremely limited and problematic. One major limitation is that data are for nonwhites, and not specific to blacks. Even though blacks in Michigan make up the majority of the nonwhite population for these years (from 97 percent in 1960 to 86 percent in 1980), one cannot assume that figures for the nonwhite group necessarily reflect figures for blacks. The key reason for this is that the nonwhite category merges together several minority groups which have very different health profiles from blacks.

In the nonwhite category are included Native Americans and Hispanics, whose health profiles are significantly worse than those of blacks, and Asian-Americans, whose health profiles are significantly better than those of blacks (Secretary's Task Force, 1985, Volume 1). For this reason, the nonwhite data should be interpreted with caution.

A second major limitation of the data is that for 1975 and 1985, figures are given only for the leading causes of death. This leads to difficulty in comparing race and sex groups for causes of death that are not leading causes of death for all sets of population groups. This is particularly the case for diabetes and homicide. Also, changes over time in the presentation of the data hinder comparisons over time.

The 1965 data do not suffer from these limitations, but they have two other important limitations. The first is that there are no 1965 data by race-sex groupings. This means that the data presented for this year are limited, since the cause of death is presented for the entire race group, not separately for males and females. The second major limitation is that the cause of death is not listed by age for the different race-sex groups. Because of this, only overall death rates by cause for all ages can be compared. This may lead to problems in comparing across race because the age distribution across race is not identical. More will be said about this later.

The limitations of these data proscribe the type of analysis that can be performed. We are limited to comparing the rate of death for whites and nonwhites for leading causes of death. This methodology cannot be used to discuss one racial group's leading cause of death when it is not a leading cause of death for another. Another limitation of the methodology is that there is no control for the possibility that the health-related characteristics of nonwhites and whites may have changed in different ways across race groups over time. Important factors related to health are socioeconomic position, the age and sex distribution of the two groups, and behavioral risk factors such as smoking, drinking, and the use of seat belts. The data used here are unadjusted for any of these and other associated factors, and thus must be interpreted with caution when comparisons are made over time across race-sex groups. The 1985 data are age adjusted, but not for gender. These limitations result from deficiencies in the presentation of health statistics in the Michigan Health Statistics reports. In spite of the many limitations of the data, some persistent patterns emerge as the data are examined.

Findings

A useful summary indicator of comparative health status is life expectancy. Table 9-1 presents data on life expectancy and life expectancy ratios by race (nonwhite/white), sex, and year. Among males, the gap in life expectancy has actually increased (from a ratio of .94 to .90), while there has been a slight improvement among females (.92 to .94).

This finding suggests that the gap in health status between races has persisted over the past twenty-five years. The data from Tables 9-2, 9-3, and 9-4 bear more directly on this. The Table 9-2 data show that the leading causes of death in 1965 were cardiovascular disease, cancer, and cere-brovascular disease (stroke). When compared to nonwhites, whites were more or equally likely to die from these diseases. The nonwhite causes of death were slightly greater for accidents, greater for diabetes and cirrhosis, and much greater for homicide. These figures are not adjusted for the differing age distribution of the white and nonwhite population, however, and this fact may make the comparison of the 1965 data somewhat misleading.

Since these figures are not age-adjusted, they do not account for the fact that whites are more likely to die from heart disease because they live longer than nonwhites, and heart disease is predominantly a disease of the old. Nonwhites are less likely to die from heart disease because they are less likely than whites to live long enough to develop the disease. These figures also do not adjust for sex differences. These limitations of the 1965 data are more clearly seen in the figures for 1975 and 1985 (see Tables 9-3 and 9-4, respectively). These tables show the ratio (nonwhite/white) of the mortality rate due to a particular cause

Table 9-1. Life Expectancy by Race (Nonwhite/White), Sex, and Year; and Life Expectancy Ratios (Nonwhite/White) by Sex and Year, Michigan, 1960, 1970, 1980, 1985

	Life Expectancy					Life Expectancy Ratio* (Nonwhite/White)			
	1960	1970	1980	1985		1960	1970	1980	1985
White Male	67.5	68.2	71.0	71.2	Male	.942	.894	.906	.897
Nonwhite Male	63.6	61.0	64.3	63.9					
White Female	74.0	75.3	77.6	78.0	Female	.915	.922	.937	.937
Nonwhite Female	67.7	69.4	72.7	73.1					

SOURCE: Data User's Services Unit, Statistical Services Section. Office of the State Registrar and Center for Health Statistics, Michigan Department of Public Health (Advance data from 1985 *Health Statistics Annual*).

*Life expectancy ratio computed by dividing life expectancy figure for nonwhites by life expectancy figure for whites. A ratio of 1.00 would indicate equality.

Table 9-2. Percentage of Deaths by Cause and Race; and Ratio (Nonwhite/White), Michigan, 1965

	White	Nonwhite	Ratio* (Nonwhite/White)
Cardiovascular disease	39.3	28.2	.718
Cancer	17.0	15.8	.929
Cerebrovascular disease	10.5	10.6	1.01
Accidents	6.1	6.4	1.05
Homicide	.25	2.9	11.6
Diabetes	2.8	3.6	1.29
Cirrhosis of the liver	1.4	2.0	1.43
Other causes	22.65	30.5	1.35

SOURCE: Computed by the author from *Michigan Health Statistics Annual Report 1964-65*, Table 7A.

*Ratio computed by dividing percentage for nonwhites by percentage for whites. A ratio of 1.00 would indicate equality.

Table 9-3. Mortality Rate Ratio (Nonwhite/White) for Leading Causes of Death by Sex and by Age Group: Michigan, 1975

		Ratio*	
Age Group at Death	Cause of Death	Male	Female
All Ages	Cardiovascular disease	.649	.672
	Cancer	1.01	.769
	Cerebrovascular disease	.869	.674
	Accidents	.993	.927
	All causes	1.05	.863
15–24 Years	Accidents	.516	.431
	Suicide	.970	NA
	Homicide	12.70	9.63
	Cancer	NA	.887
	All causes	1.86	1.86
35–49 Years	Cardiovascular disease	1.19	1.61
	Cancer	1.63	2.65
	Accidents	1.55	NA
	Cirrhosis of the liver	4.66	4.74
	All causes	2.37	2.46
65 and Over	Cardiovascular disease	.677	.804
	Cancer	1.05	.892
	Cerebrovascular disease	.864	.806
	Influenza & Pneumonia	.856	NA
	Diabetes	NA	1.07
	All causes	.799	.827

SOURCE: Computed by the author from *Michigan Health Statistics*, Annual Statistical Report 1975, Table 2.5

NA—Data not available for both racial groups.

*These ratios are computed by dividing the nonwhite mortality rate by the white mortality rate. A ratio of 1.00 would indicate equality.

Table 9-4. Mortality Rate Ratio (Nonwhite/White) for Leading Causes of Death, by Sex and by Age Group: Michigan, 1985

		Ratio*	
Age Group at Death	Cause of Death	Male	Female
All Ages	Cardiovascular disease	.790	.702
	Cancer	.951	.763
	Cerebrovascular disease	.901	.767
	Accidents	1.06	.706
	All causes	1.04	.815
15–24 Years	Accidents	.789	.755
	Suicide	.885	NA
	Cancer	1.05	.778
	All causes	2.43	1.76
35–44 Years	Cardiovascular disease	1.81	2.15
	Cancer	1.02	1.53
	Accidents	1.92	1.53
	All causes	3.19	2.50
65–74 Years	Cardiovascular disease	1.16	1.31
	Cancer	1.41	1.05
	Cerebrovascular disease	1.28	1.80
	Chronic lung disease	.863	.476
	Influenza & Pneumonia	1.28	.710
	All causes	1.25	1.29

SOURCE: Computed by the author from data provided by Data Users Services Unit, Statistical Services Section, Office of the State Registrar and Center for Health Statistics, Michigan Department of Public Health (Advance data from 1985 *Health Statistics Annual*).

NA—Data not available for both racial groups.

*These ratios are computed by dividing the nonwhite mortality rate by the white mortality rate. A ratio of 1.00 would indicate equality.

by sex and by age groups. Table 9-3 shows that in the group category "all ages," whites are more likely than nonwhites to die from cardiovascular disease. Yet such a pattern does not hold in the 35–49 age group, in which nonwhites are more likely to die from cardiovascular disease than whites.

Table 9-3 shows that in 1975 the nonwhite death rate from all causes for both sexes was much greater than the white death rate for the younger ages of 15–24 and 35–49 years. Nonwhites were about twice as likely to die in these age ranges as whites. Major contributors to this pattern were homicide for the young adults, and cirrhosis of the liver for the middle-aged. For young nonwhites, the death rate due to homicide was ten to thirteen times greater than that for whites. When this is compared to the data for 1965, we can see that there is not much change. Deaths due to cirrhosis among the 35–49 age group were approximately five times greater for nonwhites than for whites. This represents a major change from 1965.

In Table 9-4, for 1985, the presentation of the data has changed such that the age ranges are now 35–44 years and 65–74 years. Despite this change, these data can still be compared with the 1975 data for most age ranges, even though caution is necessary. There is little change for both sexes from 1975 in the group category "all ages." Among females, whites are more likely than nonwhites to die from cardiovascular disease, cancer, cerebrovascular disease, and accidents. Among males, whites are more likely to die from cardiovascular disease, cancer, and cerebrovascular disease. Nonwhite males are slightly more likely to die from accidents than white males.

Comparing nonwhite and white females in the age group of 15–24 years, we see that the health of nonwhite females compared to white females did not improve substantially from 1975 to 1985. The ratio in 1975 was 1.86 for all causes; in 1985, it was 1.76. The health of nonwhite males compared to white males, aged 15–24, was worse in 1985 than in 1975. The ratio in 1975 was 1.86 for all causes; in 1985, it was 2.43. The data for the 15–24 age group do not indicate the homicide death rate by race. This is because homicide was not a leading cause of death in 1985 for the total Michigan population. It was a leading cause of death for young nonwhites, but no comparison is possible. This illustrates the problem with presenting only data for leading causes of death. In this case, a leading cause of death for one population group, nonwhites, is not presented in the data, leaving the reader with no information for 1985.

For the middle-aged group of 35-44 years, it again must be noted that caution is required in comparing these data, since the age groups have changed from 35–49 years in 1975 to 35–44 years in 1985. We can still see, however, that for males, the mortality rate due to all causes was much worse in 1985. Nonwhite males in this age group were more likely than white males to die from cardiovascular disease and accidents than was the case in 1975. The mortality rate ratio for all causes for females in this age range remained similar to the 1975 figure; nonwhite females in the middle-age range were about 2 1/2 times more likely to die from all causes than were white females in 1975 and in 1985.

The presentation of the data has also changed for the older age group. This very likely affects the comparison by racial group in 1985, since the older adults (aged 75 and older) are excluded. These people are more likely to be white than nonwhite, and excluding them increases the mortality rate ratio.

Another indicator of the health of nonwhites in Michigan is the infant mortality rate. Table 9-5 shows the rate of infant mortality for 1974 and 1985 for blacks and whites. No information by race could be obtained for 1965. The rate of infant mortality of blacks actually got worse relative to whites in this time period. In 1974, the rate of black infant mortality was

Table 9-5. Michigan Infant Mortality Rate and Ratio by Race (Black/White) (Per 1,000 Live Births)

			Ratio* (Black/White)	
	1974	1985	1974	1985
White	14.9	9.3	2.03	2.42
Black	30.2	22.5		

SOURCE: Data User's Services Unit, Statistical Services Section. Office of the State Registrar and Center for Health Statistics, Michigan Department of Public Health (Advance data from 1985 *Health Statistics Annual*).

*Ratio computed by dividing the black infant mortality rate by the white infant mortality rate. A ratio of 1.00 would indicate equality.

twice as great as the rate for white infants. In 1985, the rate of infant mortality was lower for both races, but the white rate decreased more than the black rate. In 1985, the black infant mortality rate was almost two-and-a-half times as great as the rate for whites.

A general conclusion to be drawn from these data is that since the civil disorders of 1967, the health of Michigan blacks has not improved relative to that of whites. There may be several reasons for this, but we will focus on two of critical importance: socioeconomic status and behavioral risk factors.

Table 9-6 presents data on selected social and economic characteristics by race for 1960, 1970, and 1980. These data are striking in that they mirror the health data of Tables 9-1 through 9-4. The gap is growing between whites and nonwhites in social and economic characteristics (except for education); and nonwhites, compared to whites, are generally worse off now than they were in the 1960s. In short, there has been little or no change in the gap in socioeconomic characteristics for nonwhites and whites in Michigan from 1960 to 1980. Where there has been change, it is for the worse: the ratio of people in poverty, median family income ratio, and the ratio of percentage of children who live with both parents. Only for education has the gap been greatly reduced, but this positive change is not reflected in either health status or the socioeconomic status of nonwhites relative to whites in Michigan.

A second important class of factors related to health status are health-related behaviors that increase the risk of injury or death. Important health behaviors in this regard are smoking, drinking, using drugs, being overweight, failing to use seat belts, and having high levels of stress (a cause of hypertension and other diseases). Little data are available on these factors over time, but a 1982 statewide telephone survey provided information on health-related behavior by race (Holmes, Harding, and Lafkas, 1983). Blacks were more likely to have behavior-related health problems than were whites. Blacks were more likely to have hypertension, to not use seat belts, to have greater levels of stress, and to be overweight. Whites were more likely to be current smokers and drinkers than were blacks. While no data over time are available, this 1982 telephone survey established an important baseline for future studies of behavioral risk factors for the control and prevention of morbidity and premature death among the Michigan population.

AIDS: A Growing Concern

Acquired Immune Deficiency Syndrome (AIDS) is a relatively recent medical concern. In less than five years, AIDS has grown from a virtually unknown disease with a small impact to one of the leading medical concerns in the United States. Although AIDS is primarily a disease of gay/bisexual men and intravenous drug users, recent figures have shown that a growing proportion of the population who have neither of these characteristics are developing AIDS. Of major concern is that, while the number of deaths due to AIDS grows, there is no known cure for the usually fatal disease.

In Michigan, the concern is much the same as in the nation; the incidence of AIDS is growing, and the disease is affecting people from all walks of life. More germane to this report is that AIDS is a disease that is disproportionately affecting blacks and other minorities. While blacks are 12 percent of Michigan's population, they represent 43.2 percent of the

Table 9-6. Selected Social and Economic Characteristics by Race (Nonwhite/White) and Year, State of Michigan

Group	1960		1970		1980	
			Median Years of School			
Persons 25 and over	No. of Years	Ratio*	No. of Years	Ratio*	No. of Years	Ratio*
white	11.0		12.1		12.5	
		.827		.876		.976
nonwhite	9.1		10.6		12.2	
			Living with Both Parents			
Persons Under 18	Percent	Ratio*	Percent	Ratio*	Percent	Ratio*
white	92.0		88.6		83.3	
		.755		.665		.497
nonwhite	69.5		58.9		41.4	
			Unemployed			
Males 14 and over	Percent	Ratio*	Percent	Ratio*	Percent	Ratio*
white	4.6		3.7		9.5	
		2.70		1.78		2.26
nonwhite	12.4		6.6		21.5	
			Median Income			
Families	Annual $	Ratio*	Annual $	Ratio*	Annual $	Ratio*
white	$6,442		$11,303		$22,841	
		.684		.755		.692
nonwhite	4,407		8,536		15,817	
			In Poverty			
Families	Percent	Ratio*	Percent	Ratio*	Percent	Ratio*
white	NA**		6.0		6.1	
		NA**		3.20		3.85
nonwhite	NA**		19.2		23.5	

SOURCE: Computed by the author from the following sources:

1960: U.S. Bureau of the Census, *U.S. Census of Population: 1960*, part 24, Michigan, U.S. Government Printing Office 1963. Tables: #16—Population Figures; #47—Education; #51—Living Arrangements.

1970: U.S. Bureau of the Census, *U.S. Census of Population: 1970*, part 24, Michigan, volume 1, Characteristics of the Population, U.S. Government Printing Office 1973. Tables: #46—Education and Unemployment; #47—Income; #52—Living Arrangements; #58—Poverty.

1980: U.S. Bureau of the Census, *U.S. Census of Population: 1980*, part 24, Michigan, General Social & Economic Characteristics, Chapter C, U.S. Government Printing Office 1983. Tables: #74—Living Arrangements; #76—Education; #77—Employment; #81—Income; #82—Poverty (1980 figures are for black, not nonwhite).

Figures for 1980 Social and Economic Characteristics are for blacks.

*Ratios computed by dividing nonwhite figure by white figure. A ratio of 1.00 would indicate equality.

**Not Available

AIDS cases in Michigan (Michigan Department of Public Health, 1987). This pattern is consistent with nationwide trends.

The major reason for this is intravenous (IV) drug abuse. The proportion of IV drug abusers is greater in nonwhite communities than in the white community. Medical authorities believe that AIDS can be spread only by means of bodily fluids such as semen or blood. It is thought that the practice of needle-sharing by IV drug abusers encourages the spread of the disease among this population. The fact that AIDS is also spread through some forms of sexual intercourse, however, has negative implications for the heterosexual, non-drug-using population. To the extent that AIDS is spread from bisexual men or IV drug abusers to the heterosexual population through sexual intercourse, AIDS will continue to be a major threat to the health of everyone. It has been estimated that AIDS among the heterosexual population will have increased ten times by 1992 in Michigan (Michigan Department of Public Health, 1986).

Summary and Recommendations

The limitations of the available data necessitate caution in interpreting these findings. It seems apparent, however, that the health of nonwhite Michigan residents is generally poorer than that of white residents, and that the gap in health status between white and nonwhite Michigan residents is unchanged or has been growing since 1967.

From this analysis, several recommendations can be made:

1. The Michigan Department of Public Health must collect more comprehensive and detailed data on the health of the minority population of Michigan.
2. The presentation of data in the Michigan Health Statistics Annuals should include figures for both unadjusted and adjusted epidemiological risk factors for mortality.
3. Morbidity data should also be presented in the Health Statistics Annuals, as mortality data usually do not fully capture the health profile of a population.
4. Intensive studies of health-related behaviors and epidemiological risk factors among the black population of Michigan are needed to adequately assess their impact on health status.
5. The lack of improvement in the health status of nonwhites relative to whites demands further investigation and policies designed to address the problem.
6. Aggressive action should be taken to educate the Michigan population (especially the black population) about the potentially fatal impact of intravenous drug use that may cause the spread of AIDS and premature death.

REFERENCES

Aday, L., Andersen, R., and Fleming, G. *Health Care in the United States: Equitable for Whom?* New York: Sage Publications, 1980.

Aday, L., Fleming, G., and Andersen, R. *Access to Medical Care in the United States: Who Has It, Who Doesn't.* Chicago: Pluribus Press, 1984.

Haan, M. N., and Kaplan, G. A. "The Contribution of Socioeconomic Position to Minority Health." Pages 67–103 in Secretary's Task Force on Black and Minority Health, Volume II: *Crosscutting Issues in Minority Health.* Washington, D.C.: U.S. Department of Health and Human Services, 1985.

Holmes, R. E., Harding, S. H., and Lafkas, G. A. *Michigan Opinion: Behavioral Risk Factors.* Lansing: Michigan Department of Public Health, 1983.

Johnson, E. H., and Broman, C. L. "The Relationship of Anger Expression to Health Problems among Black Americans in a National Survey." *Journal of Behavioral Medicine,* 1987, Volume 10, pp. 103–116.

Michigan Department of Health. *AIDS Update.* Volume 2, no. 2, January 13, 1987. Lansing, MI 1987.

Michigan Department of Health. *Health Update: AIDS. November*, 1986. Lansing, MI 1986.

Poussaint, A. F. "The Mental Health Status of Blacks—1983." *The State of Black America 1983.* New York: National Urban League.

Secretary's Task Force on Black and Minority Health. Volume I: *Executive Summary.* Washington, D.C.: U.S. Department of Health and Human Services, 1985.

CHAPTER 10

The Health of Black Michigan, 2006

Clifford L. Broman and Renee B. Canady

Introduction

By several indicators, the health of the American population continues to improve. Life expectancy continues to increase for all populations. Additionally, rates of survival after the incidence of diseases such as heart disease, cancer, and human immunodeficiency virus (HIV)/acquired immune deficiency syndrome (AIDS) have also improved greatly in the past 20 years. Yet while this is true, there remain persistent health disparities between blacks and whites in the United States (Smedley, Stith, and Nelson 2003). In this chapter we discuss these health disparities for the State of Michigan.

A series of reports on the issue of health disparities in Michigan was published several years ago (Broman 1987; Bouknight 1990, 1993; Davis 1992; Ross-Lee 1993). These reports discussed the overall findings, some factors that contribute to health disparities, and implications for policy, as we seek to close the gap in health disparities and eventually eliminate them. These early reports highlighted three key facts. First, for every leading cause of death for both the U.S. and the Michigan population, death rates for blacks exceed those of whites. Health disparities were present for all major causes of deaths, such as cancer, cardiovascular disease and stroke, HIV/AIDS, diabetes, homicides, accidents (unintentional injuries), and infant mortality. Second, Federal and State policies have had little effect in addressing these health disparities. Third, there seemed to be very little change in health disparities in Michigan, as far back as reliable data could be obtained.

Overall Patterns for the United States

Blacks have the highest overall age-adjusted cancer rates for both incidence and mortality of any U.S. population group (National Center for Health Statistics [NCHS] 2004). Blacks experience higher age-adjusted incidence rates than whites for cancers of all types. In addition, the mortality rate for blacks is significantly higher for many cancers. There are also disparities in cancer survival rates, with fewer blacks surviving a diagnosis of cancer. Similar patterns are observed for cardiovascular and cerebrovascular diseases. Rates of death from cardiovascular and cerebrovascular diseases are higher for black men and women than for whites and other racial-ethnic minorities of comparable ages (NCHS 2004). Diabetes mellitus is a major contributor to years of potential life lost for blacks, especially black females (NCHS 2004). The prevalence of diabetes is significantly higher in the black population than in the white population. Of course, the significance of diabetes as a health problem is increased because it is a risk factor for other major diseases such as coronary heart disease and peripheral vascular disease. Further, complications of diabetes are more frequent among the black population of diabetics compared with their white counterparts. For example, the prevalence of large-vessel disease, causing heart disease and stroke, and small vessel disease, which leads to kidney failure and blindness, appear to be more frequent among blacks with diabetes than in whites with diabetes (for more details see Braithwaite and Taylor 1992; NCHS 2004).

Some of the largest health disparities concern drug use and its negative impact on health and HIV/AIDS. HIV/AIDS is discussed more extensively later. Data also reveal higher rates of mortality among blacks compared to whites due to both the use of legal drugs, such as alcohol and tobacco, and illicit drug use (NCHS 2004). Among adults, black men, in particular, have more health problems due to alcohol use. Some of these are cirrhosis, alcoholic fatty liver, hepatitis, heart disease, and cancers of the mouth, larynx, tongue, esophagus, and lung (U.S. Public Health Service 1990). Drug use is also a factor in unintentional injuries, homicide, and HIV/AIDS.

Patterns for the State of Michigan

Here we present data on health patterns in Michigan. The data used come primarily from health data compiled by Federal or State agencies. The data used in this chapter are from the most up-to-date sources that could be obtained at the time of writing.

A useful summary indicator of health is life expectancy. Table 10-1 reports this pattern. The data show the gap in life expectancy. The highest life expectancy is for white females, followed by white males. Black males have the lowest life expectancy. The ratio statistic reveals that black men live, on average, only 90% as long as do white men, while the gap is narrower among women.

Table 10-2 presents data on death rates by cause. These data allow us to see the differences in major causes of death for blacks and whites in Michigan. Table 10-2 is generally organized to present causes of death by the frequency at which they occur. The major cause of death is cardiovascular disease, followed by cancer and cerebrovascular disease, or stroke. The disparity in health is clear from these data. Blacks are more likely to die from these leading causes in every case. The biggest disparity is for HIV/AIDS; blacks are 11 times more likely to die from this cause.

Table 10-1. Life Expectancy by Race and Gender: Michigan, 2005

	Life Expectancy (Yr)	Black:White Ratio
Men		
White	75.8	
Black	68.0	0.897
Women		
White	80.1	
Black	75.1	0.938

SOURCE: 1950–2005 Michigan resident death files. Vital Records & Health Data Development Section, Michigan Department of Community Health.

Table 10-3 reports data on death rates by age for black males and black females. The last column provides the ratio of black to white, even though the table does not give figures for whites. Homicide is the leading cause of death for young black males in Michigan, who are 29 times more likely to die of homicide than are young white males. Disparities are also seen for older black males. The leading cause of death for these ages is heart disease. Black men aged 35 to 49 are more than twice as likely to die from heart disease as white men of the same age, and slightly more likely than whites to die from heart disease at ages 65 and older. However, note that heart disease death rates at older ages reflect longevity; one must live long enough to die from cardiovascular disease. Because white men live much longer, on average, than black men, we would expect heart disease death rates to converge somewhat.

The data for females show very different causes of death at older ages. The leading cause for young black women is accidents, and they are less likely than white women to die from this cause. A likely factor in this lower rate of death due to accidents is the lower propensity

Table 10-2. Age-Adjusted Death Rate (Per 100,000 Population) by Cause and Race: Michigan, 2005

Disease	White	Black	Black:White Ratio
Cardiovascular disease	219.0	322.8	1.47
Cancer	186.3	225.7	1.21
Cerebrovascular disease	44.2	61.6	1.39
Diabetes	24.7	40.0	1.62
Accidents	32.7	33.4	1.02
HIV/AIDS	0.9	10.0	11.1

SOURCE: 2005 Michigan resident death file. Vital Records & Health Data Section, Michigan Department of Community Health.

Table 10-3. Leading Cause of Death for Black Men and Women by Age: Michigan, 2005

	Leading Cause of Death	Black:White Ratio
Black men		
Ages 15–24	Homicide	29.01
Ages 35–49	Heart disease	2.26
Ages ≥65	Heart disease	1.24
Black women		
Ages 15–24	Accidents	0.634
Ages 35–49	Cancer	1.69
Ages ≥65	Heart disease	1.10

SOURCE: 2005 Michigan resident death file. Vital Records & Health Data Development Section, Michigan Department of Community Health.

to use alcohol and other drugs among black adolescents and young adults than is the case for white adolescents and young adults (Johnston, O'Malley, and Bachman, 2000; Vega et al. 1993). Drug and alcohol use is a major factor in death due to automobile and other accidents (U.S. Public Health Service 1990). For black women at the older ages, the leading causes of death are cancer and heart disease, and black women are more likely to die from these diseases than are white women. However, as is the case for men, at older ages heart disease death rates for blacks and whites begin to converge.

Table 10-4 presents data on infant morbidity, in the form of low birth weight, and infant mortality. The rate of low birth weight is more than two times higher for blacks than for whites. Even more disparate are the mortality rates. The rates of infant and neonatal mortality are more than two and a half times higher for blacks than for whites.

Overall, the data presented show clear health disparities between blacks and whites in Michigan. These disparities are in life expectancy, death rates by cause, and infant mortality. How might this be different than in the recent past?

Table 10-4. Infant Morbidity and Mortality, per 1,000 Births: Michigan, 2000–2003

	White	Black	Black:White Ratio
Low birth weight (2001–2003)	6.76	14.08	2.08
Infant mortality (2000–2002)	6.00	16.9	2.82
Neonatal mortality (2000–2002)	4.2	11.4	2.71

SOURCE: Birth File and Linked Birth/Infant Death Data Set, 2005. Centers for Disease Control and Prevention, National Center for Health Statistics, National Vital Statistics System.

Current versus Past Health Disparities

As noted earlier, there has been a series of reports on the health of black Michigan published over the past 20 years. A comparison of data from those reports with the present data demands the unfortunate conclusion that health disparities in Michigan are very little changed. For example, disparities in life expectancy are virtually identical to those in 1985; then, as now, black men lived, on average, only 90% as long as white men, and black women only 94% as long as white women (Broman 1987). Infant mortality rates remain more than twice as high as the rates 20–30 years ago (Broman 1987; Bouknight 1990). In some cases, the black population is healthier than in the past, but the gap in health status between blacks and whites in Michigan persists.

A Focus on HIV/AIDS

More than 1 million people in the United States are estimated to be living with HIV (MMWR 2006). Since 1996, treatment for AIDS and HIV infection has improved to the extent that individuals infected with HIV are living longer and progression to AIDS has slowed significantly (MMWR 2005). HIV/AIDS was once thought to have peaked in the late 1980s (Valleroy et al. 2000), but it has continued to present with increasing incidence in many vulnerable populations, including women and youth. The "face" of AIDS is now consistently described as darker and increasingly female (Andriote 2001; Centers for Disease Control [CDC] Women 2002). After more than two decades of experience with HIV/AIDS in the United States, our failure to make greater inroads in prevention of this disease is clear. Despite many public health interventions, new cases continue to appear, and HIV/AIDS disproportionately affects minority individuals and their communities (MMWR 2006).

Current racial trends in the epidemiology of HIV underscore these points. Blacks comprise more than half of the current cases of HIV/AIDS diagnosed, with rates of diagnosis 8.5 times higher among blacks than among whites. People of color in the United States experience significantly higher rates of HIV-associated mortality than whites. While Hispanic Americans experience a notably greater risk of HIV-related death than whites (7 per 100,000 and 3 per 100,000, respectively), blacks die at the astounding rate of 29 per 100,000 (Anderson 2002).

Data from 2001 report African Americans as comprising 50% of those infected by HIV, while they comprised approximately 12% of the U.S. population. The leading cause of infection among African American women remains heterosexual contact; for African American men, the leading causes are sexual contact with other men and injection drug use (CDC 2001). This disproportionate risk persists among youth, with young black women seven times as likely as young white women to be infected with HIV (MMWR 2006). The CDC describes the following hierarchy of transmission: (1) male-to-male sexual contact, (2) injection drug use, (3) both male-to-male sexual contact and injection drug use, and (4) high-risk heterosexual contact (sex with someone of the opposite sex who is known have HIV or involvement in the above-mentioned risk factors) (MMWR 2005).

The data for Michigan are presented in Table 10-5. The data are clear: blacks are 11 times more likely to die from HIV/AIDS than are whites.

Table 10-5. Age-Adjusted Death Rates (Per 100,000 Population) Due to HIV/AIDS, by Race: Michigan, 2005

White	Black	Black:White Ratio
0.9	10.0	11.1

SOURCE: 2005 Michigan resident death file. Vital Records & Health Data Section, Michigan Department of Community Health.

Causes of Health Disparities

Social factors and treatment access are important issues in health disparities. Social and economic characteristics play a critical role in health status all across the United States, and differences between blacks and whites influence their risk of disease. Social and economic factors are critical determinants of residence in areas of high social stress and instability and environmental pollutants. These are all circumstances that increase the risk of disease in the African American population. Social and economic factors are also important in treatment. Disparities in access to treatment are also a consequence of lower socioeconomic status. Table 10-6 reports the differences in a variety of socioeconomic factors for blacks and whites in Michigan.

The data show the important differences: the median income of blacks is 66 cents per dollar of white median income. Blacks are almost two and a half times more likely to be unemployed and less likely to have graduated from high school. The poverty rate for blacks in Michigan is more than three times higher than the rate for whites. Health status and access to treatment are critically affected by these socioeconomic disparities. Because most Americans gain access to health insurance through employment, the higher unemployment rate of blacks means reduced access to treatment. Poorer access to treatment for blacks in the United States has been clearly established. Despite clearly documented health disparities for a number of diseases, blacks often lag in the receipt of critical surgical and clinical procedures (Schulman et al. 1999; Weisse et al. 2001).

Table 10-6. Selected Social and Economic Characteristics: Michigan, 2000

	White	Black	Black:White Ratio
Median income	$46,907	$31,061	0.662
Unemployed (2004)	5.8%	14.4%	2.48
High school graduate or more	85.6%	74.3%	0.868
In poverty	7.2%	23.9%	3.32

SOURCE: U.S. Census Bureau, summary files 2 and 4. U.S. Department of Labor, Bureau of Labor Statistics, Local Area Unemployment Statistics.

Conclusions

When considering health, America is not one country but several. Patterns of health are so disparate that in reality we have eight Americas (Murray et al. 2006). In some of these Americas, patterns of health are consistent with those of a wealthy industrialized nation, but in others health patterns are more similar to those of a 19th-century agrarian nation. In these eight Americas, there is a gap in life expectancy of more than 20 years, with Asian American women having the highest life expectancy and urban black men having the lowest (Murray et al. 2006). These eight Americas vary substantially in exposure and vulnerability to conditions leading to poor health outcomes and early mortality. Access to treatment differs greatly in these eight Americas, varying across routine checkups and more expensive diagnostic and surgical procedures. The lack of health insurance coverage and the location of treatment facilities are major factors in this. Murray et al. (2006, 0008) note: ". . . Mortality disparities in the eight Americas are largest for young (ages 15–44) and middle-aged adults (ages 45–64). In these age groups, blacks living in high-risk urban areas have mortality risks more similar to ones in the Russian Federation and sub-Saharan Africa."

REFERENCES

Andriote, J. 2001. Black women, gay and bisexual men face high HIV risks in US, Canada. Population Reference Bureau. www.prb.org.

Anderson, R. N. 2002. Deaths: Leading causes for 2000. *National Vital Statistics Reports* 50(16): Table 1.

Bouknight, L. Michigan's black–white mortality gap: the impact of AIDS. In *The state of black Michigan, 1990,* ed. F. Thomas, 29–36. East Lansing: Urban Affairs Programs, Michigan State University.

——. 1993. The first decade of AIDS in Michigan: The impact on blacks and whites. In *The state of black Michigan, 1993,* ed. F. Thomas, 21–29. East Lansing: Urban Affairs Programs, Michigan State University.

Braithwaite, R. L., and S. E. Taylor. 1992.. *Health issues in the black community.* San Francisco: Jossey-Bass.

Broman, C. 1987. The health of black Michigan. In *The state of black Michigan, 1987,* ed. F. Thomas, 45–52. East Lansing: Urban Affairs Programs, Michigan State University.

Centers for Disease Control. 2001. *HIV/AIDS surveillance report.* Vol. 13, 2. Atlanta, GA: CDC.

Centers for Disease Control Women. 2002. HIV/AIDS among U.S. women: minority and young women at continuing risk. http://www.cdc.gov/hiv/pubs/facts/women.pdf.

Johnston, L. D., P. M. O'Malley, and J. G. Bachman. 2000. Monitoring the future: national results in adolescent drug use: overview of key findings, 1999. NIH Publication No. 00-4690. Bethesda, MD: Department of Health and Human Services.

MMWR. 2005. Trends in HIV/AIDS diagnosis—33 states, 2001–2004. http://www.cdc.gov/mmwr/preview/mmwrhtml/mm5445.html.

———. 2006. Racial/ethnic disparities in diagnosis of HIV/AIDS—33 states, 2001–2004. http://www.cdc.gov/mmwr/preview/mmwrhtml/mm5505a1.htm.

Murray, C. J. L. et al. 2006. Eight Americas: Investigating mortality disparities across races, counties, and race-counties in the United States. *PLOS Medicine* 3(9):e260. doi:10.1371/journal.pmed.0030260.

National Center for Health Statistics. 2004. *Health, United States, 2004.* Hyattsville, MD: NCHS.

Roos, B. L. 1993 Black – white health disparity in Michigan: A commentary on issues of equity. In *The state of black Michigan, 1993,* ed. F. Thomas, 11–20. East Lansing: Urban Affairs Programs, Michigan State University.

Schulman, K. A., J. A. Berlin, W. Harless, J. F. Kerner, S. Sistrunk, B. J. Gersh, R. Dube, and C. K. Taleghani. 1999. The effect of race and sex on physicians' recommendations for cardiac catheterization. *New England Journal of Medicine* 340:618–626.

Smedley, B. D, A. Y. Stith, and A. R. Nelson. 2003. *Unequal treatment: confronting racial and ethnic disparities in health care.* Washington, DC: National Academies Press.

U.S. Public Health Service. 1990. *Alcohol and health.* Seventh special report to the U.S. Congress. Publication No. ADM. 90-1656, Washington, DC: U.S. Government Printing Office.

Vega, W. A., R. S. Zimmerman, G. J. Warheit, E. Apospori, and A. Gil. 1993. Risk factors for early adolescent drug use in four ethnic and racial groups. *American Journal of Public Health* 83:185–189.

Velleroy, L. A., et al. 2000. HIV prevalence and associated risks in young men who have sex with men. *Journal of the American Medical Association* 284(2):198–204.

Weisse, C. S., P. C. Sorum, K. N. Sanders, and B. L. Syat. 2001. Do gender and race affect decisions about pain management? *Journal of General Internal Medicine* 16:211–217.

CHAPTER 11

The Young Black Offender in Michigan

Homer C. Hawkins

The problem of the young black offender deserves attention on the part of researchers, criminal justice professionals, lawmakers, and others. Information regarding juvenile arrests can contribute to greater understanding of the nature and dimension of the problem.

In this chapter, the 1978–1987 data relevant to arrests of juveniles for crimes against the person (homicide, rape, robbery, and aggravated assault) and for narcotics laws violations will be examined. The data, which will be drawn from the five largest urban areas in the state (Detroit, Flint, Grand Rapids, Lansing, and Warren) will be viewed from a racial perspective.

Questions to be addressed include the following: What changes, if any, have occurred over the period of time from 1978 to 1987 in the number and percentage of arrests of young black offenders for violent crimes and for drug laws violations? What does the evidence indicate about the relationship between arrests of juveniles for narcotics laws offenses and arrests of juveniles for violent crimes? How do the five largest cities in Michigan compare with each other in terms of juvenile arrests for various crimes, including narcotics laws violations?

Researchers have investigated various factors that may be related to crime—factors such as the family, education, economic status, and drugs. In this chapter, a review will be presented of literature on the possible relationship between the general development of delinquency and such factors as unstable family environment, poor educational opportunities, poverty, and the usage and selling of drugs.

Factors Related to the Development of Delinquency

Family

Evidence From Past Research

Many articles have been written over the years concerning the relationship of the family to delinquency. Various factors, such as family size and family structure, have been examined.

With respect to family size, some of the data suggest that large family size is related to delinquency. There tends to be more delinquency emanating from families where there are a large number of children. Fischer (1984) notes that a review of the literature shows that:

> . . . large family size is related to greater delinquency. The relationship remains when a number of variables, i.e., income, socioeconomic status, parental criminality, and family composition, have been controlled.

Glueck and Glueck (1950) also observed that delinquent boys came from larger families than did non-delinquent boys. Robins, West, and Herjanic (1975) in a study of delinquency over two generations of black urban families with low-income status in St. Louis, Missouri, found that there was a relationship between large families and delinquency, even when parental criminality was controlled. Shanock and Lewis (1977) found a relationship between family size and delinquency when socioeconomic status was controlled.

Another issue related to large family size is that it is often more difficult for parents to supervise their children. Fischer (1983) suggests that a possible hypothesis for explaining the relationship between family size and delinquency is that in large families it may be more difficult for parents to provide adequate supervision than is the case with smaller families. Fischer (1984) also posits another hypothesis that could explain the relationship between large families and delinquency—namely, that the presence of delinquent siblings can lead to delinquency by infectious example. Fischer also notes that large families often seem to be associated with a number of undesirable family conditions (e.g., poor parental behavior, parental criminality, sibling delinquency), poor child-rearing practices (e.g., inadequate parental supervision and discipline), and competition for physical resources (e.g., space, money) and psychological resources (e.g., attention, affection, family interaction).

The structure of the family is another factor that is often suggested as being related to delinquency. There is a frequently mentioned premise in criminology that links broken homes to juvenile delinquency. In discussions of the life-style of families which produce juveniles who become delinquent, the broken home is an often mentioned factor. Juveniles from poor, minority families headed by a female tend to show an increase of delinquency. Miller (1959) and Moynihan (1959) suggest that the absence of the father in the household is related to juvenile delinquency. Johnson (1979) notes:

> A father's role in reducing delinquency appears to be somewhat greater than the mother's role. For both boys and girls, distance from father is more predictive of theft, vandalism, and assault than is distance from mother. Even though a youth's relationship with mother is generally more emotionally satisfying, there seem to be aspects of father's role that supersede affection in influencing delinquency.

Stern et al. (1984) point out that the father seems to provide the prime teaching and deterrent force in the family through his role of value transmitter and disciplinarian. The authors go on to note that a father who is geographically removed from the family setting would be less effective in fulfilling these functions.

Cernkovich and Giordano (1987) focus on the factors that led to the broken home rather than on the effect of living in the situation after it has occurred. They note:

> . . . far more important than the effects of the actual parental separation and/or living in a broken home, are the familial problems and conflicts that brought about the separation in the first place. It seems as though it is generally accepted that harmonious, yet physically broken, homes are far less detrimental to the development and mental health of the child than are physically intact but psychologically broken homes.

Farnworth (1984), in considering this same issue, raises questions with the thesis that the broken home is related in any meaningful way to juvenile delinquency. In her study she points out:

> The results from this analysis suggest that the importance of family structure for delinquency has been highly exaggerated in the popular thesis linking broken homes to delinquency. The failure of broken homes to explain most delinquency within the present sample for either males or females is especially provocative since the broken-home thesis gained popularity in the context of observations of low-income black families in Moynihan's influential report. These results argue for an alternative explanation for high rates of official delinquency among lower-class black juveniles. It is interesting to note, for example, that when family structure is implicated in delinquency within this sample of young, low-income families, an integral feature of structure is parental employment: when both parents are employed and the father is present, delinquency is reduced. This suggests that a fruitful research focus in the future may be the economic dimensions of black families rather than their structure.
>
> Recent critiques suggest a modification of the broken-home thesis, proposing that it is not family structure in itself that affects delinquency but the personal relationships within the family unit which result from family disorganization in single-parent families.

Roberts (1987), in viewing the mother as a social agent, notes that when children get into trouble, people are quick to place the blame on the mother who is raising her children alone. What seems to be overlooked is that most of these women are trying to be effective parents. It is very difficult, however, because their efforts to do so are undermined by the social conditions that envelope their lives and are beyond their control. Their lives are based on a number of insecurities, both financial and emotional.

Education

Evidence From Past Research

The level of educational attainment through childhood and youth is linked to quality of life as an adult. It also appears to be linked to involvement in criminal activity. Success at the high school level is a critically important step toward a lifetime of achievement.

Garbarino and Asp (1981) suggest that one of the most powerful influences on educational achievement is the socioeconomic level of the adolescent's family. Middle-class adolescents score higher on basic tests of academic skills, earn higher grades in school, and complete more years of schooling than their working-class and lower-class peers. Featherman (1980) supports this premise and suggests that even though the gap between middle-class and working-class/lower-class adolescents is closing, many of the disparities between social classes remain strong and are important factors in determining educational achievement.

With the changing times, it is becoming even more critical that individuals receive an education. Our society is becoming more technically oriented. No longer can young men and women graduate from high school and move into high-paying jobs. Entry-level jobs in factories, for example, are requiring higher technical skills than was true twenty years ago. Instead of hiring high school graduates, managers are using low-seniority individuals who have been laid off. These adults are being retrained to fill the sparse number of jobs that are available. This means that the high school dropout has little or no chance of getting the kind of job that was available to his counterpart of twenty years ago. Steinberg (1985) addresses this issue:

> There was a time when leaving high school before graduating did not have the dire consequences that it does today. With changes in the labor force, however, have come changes in the educational prerequisites for entry into the world of work. Today educational attainment is a powerful predictor of adult occupational success and earnings. Not surprisingly, high school dropouts are far more likely than graduates to live at or near the poverty level, experience unemployment, depend on the government-subsidized income maintenance programs, and be involved in delinquent and criminal activity.

Thornberry et al. (1985) observed that a direct spin-off of dropping out of high school is the increased probability of later criminal activity. Their research suggests that because of a lack of educational attainment the probability of being involved in criminal activity is greatly enhanced.

Beverly (1988) commented on 1985–86 data on black and white high school dropouts and black and white arrests rates:

> . . . in composite terms, blacks represented 76 percent of the dropout totals and 74 percent of the arrests. Whites represent 18 percent of the dropout totals and 24 percent of those arrested. Unavailability of data makes it impossible to ascertain to what extent those who dropped out of school are also among those arrested. Nevertheless, the equivalency factor between the percentages is sufficiently strong to suggest a reasonable association between dropouts and arrests, given the fact that nationally, 71 percent of prison inmates never completed high school.

A study by Figueira-McDonough (1986) focuses on two different kinds of high schools and suggests that the probability of delinquency is either increased or diminished as a function of the way the school relates to the student. She notes that a school strongly devoted to its academic reputation, maintaining a highly competitive environment, handling student problems in a standardized way, and providing weak supervision has students who are less attached to the school and have a greater access to illegitimate opportunities. She also notes that a school having diversified goals, dealing with problems in a differentiating but predictable fashion, and offering tight supervision shows a closer relationship to students and clearly serves as a restraint to delinquent involvement. A school with diversified goals and with consistent discipline in varying situations takes a greater interest in the students' nonacademic needs and diverse vocational desires. This type of school also appears to have a more positive general effect on the student population.

At the postsecondary level of education, a distressing trend is the decline in the number of black males on our college campuses. This decline is in the face of increased numbers of black women attending college. Daniels (1989) points out:

> A dramatic decline in the number of black men in college is raising concern that a gap in social and economic status is opening between black men and black women.
>
> Sixty percent of black students in higher education are women, the highest female-to-male ratio of any racial group. The American Council on Education reported that the number of black male undergraduates continued a decade-long decline in 1986 even as enrollments were increasing for whites, black women and members of other minority groups.
>
> The American Council on Education said black enrollment in higher education peaked in 1980 at 1.1 million out of a total of 11.8 million undergraduate and graduate students. By 1986 total enrollment in higher education increased to 12.5 million students, but the total number of black students had fallen by 30,000 from its 1980 high.
>
> The slippage was in black male students. In 1976, they numbered 470,000; by 1986 that figure had fallen 7.2%, to 436,000. In the same period, the number of black women in college increased to 645,000 from 563,000.
>
> Educators and social policy experts say the decline in black men in college has accelerated as a result of the severe social and economic problems that tend to beset black boys, even more than black girls, from an early age. These can include inferior schools, drugs, crime, gangs, lower expectations by parents and harsher or biased treatment by teachers in the early grades.

This trend portends a dismal future for many young black males. Not only are high school dropout rates high, but the chance to go to college is diminishing. As we move to the year 2000, the positive opportunities for young black males appear to be lessening. How this is related to the probability of increased criminal activity deserves further study.

Poverty

Evidence From Past Research

Many studies have found that there appears to be a relationship between poverty and violent crime in America. Studies of police records show that homicide offenders are disproportionately drawn from the poor segments of the population (Schmid and Schmid, 1972; Wolfgang, 1958). In addition, there have been comparative studies showing that homicide rates are positively related to indicators of deprivation such as low education, substandard housing, high infant mortality rates, and low income (Benson and Schroeder, 1960; Ventura, 1975; Smith and Parker, 1980).

Other researchers argue that poverty is not linked to violent crime. Messner (1982) and Judith and Peter Blau (1982), for example, suggest that poverty is not related to homicide rates. One criticism of these studies has been that the single variable of income was used as an indicator of poverty. Loftin and Parker (1985) conclude that studies that use multiple indicators of poverty (e.g., high infant mortality, substandard housing, and low income) generally find significant positive effects, while those which rely on a single variable of income find weak and inconsistent effects.

Good et al. (1986) argue that there is a link between employment and delinquency. They suggest that improving the employability of youths will have a positive immediate payoff by reducing juvenile criminality. They also suggest that young repeat offenders are less employable, and that successful efforts to reduce their criminal tendencies will increase the probability of their taking part in legal forms of employment. Krohn (1976) also focuses on the issue of employment as it relates to homicide. He notes that the results from correlation analyses indicated a moderate positive relationship between the rate of unemployment and homicide rates.

Darnell Hawkins (1983) notes that "to the extent that criminal violence is caused by economic deprivation and powerlessness, homicide rates will occur at a higher rate among the black underclass than among the black middle class." This suggests that poverty and powerlessness are related; and, as such, in this type of environment the probability of violence is higher.

Drugs

Evidence From Past Research

The strength of the relationship between drug usage and crime is open for discussion, but the literature suggests that the usage of drugs can reduce one's inhibitions and make the individual freer to commit crimes. In addition, it is suggested that individuals may commit crimes in a revenue-producing effort in order to purchase drugs. Gandossy et al. (1980) found that a selective review of the literature on criminal behavior patterns of addicts revealed that addicts frequently take part in income-generating crimes. This becomes apparent when an analysis is made of the charges against drug users, convictions of addicts in prison, arrest records of penal populations, and observations of street addicts. Although addicts appear to commit fewer violent crimes than non-addict offenders, there is evidence that they will commit violent offenses. Some researchers have suggested that the tendency to commit violent crimes has become more prevalent among contemporary addicts, compared with addicts of the 1950s (Chambers, 1974; Stevens and Ellis, 1975).

Innes (1988) noted that there appears to be a relationship between drugs and crime. His findings include the following:

1. In 1986, 35 percent of state prison inmates reported that they were under the influence of drugs at the time they committed their current offense, compared with 32 percent in a 1979 survey.
2. Inmates were more likely to report that they were under the influence of cocaine but less likely to report using heroin at the time of the offense than in earlier surveys.
3. Of state prisoners who were sentenced for robbery, burglary, larceny, or a drug offense, half were daily drug users and about 40 percent were under the influence of an illegal drug at the time they committed the crime.
4. The greater the offender's use of major drugs (heroin, methadone, cocaine, PCP, or LSD) the more prior convictions the inmate reported.
5. Users of major drugs were substantially more likely than non-users to report that they received income from illegal activities during the time they were last free (48 percent versus 10 percent).

An area that needs greater attention is the trafficking of drugs in American society. Billions of dollars are made each year in profits due to the selling of drugs. In addition, there is a tremendous amount of violence involved in the drug traffic process. Drug-related murders that stem from the entrepreneurial side of drugs are daily occurrences in most large urban areas. Much of the literature describes the fears that residents of urban areas have because of crimes committed by drug users who are "high and irrational." In addition, the literature focuses on drug users' attempts to gain revenue to support their addictive habits.

A greater fear held by urban residents involves the violence related to drug traffickers. Nadelmann (1988) notes:

> The drug/crime link is the violent, intimidating and corrupting behavior of the drug traffickers. Illegal markets tend to breed violence—not only because they attract criminal-minded individuals, but also because participants in the market have no resort to legal institutions to resolve their disputes. During prohibition, violent struggles between bootlegging gangs and highjackings of booze-laden trucks and sea vessels were frequent and notorious occurrences. Today's equivalents are the boobytraps that surround some marijuana fields, the pirates of the Caribbean looking to highjack drug-laden vessels enroute to the shores of the United States, and the machine-gun battles and executions carried out by drug lords—all of which occasionally kill innocent people. Most law enforcement officials agree that the dramatic increase in urban murder rates during the past few years can be explained almost entirely by the rise in drug-dealer killings.

In this environment, we have the juvenile offenders who follow suit and interact in urban areas just as their adult counterparts. The juvenile offender has become part of the drug violence that permeates urban areas. In Detroit there were 258 cocaine-related juvenile arrests in 1980 and 647 in 1987. In New York City the arrests increased from 349 to 1,052; in Washington the figures were 315 and 1,894; and in Los Angeles there were 41 cocaine-related juvenile arrests in 1980 and 1,719 in 1987 (Ward, 1989). Selling crack cocaine is extremely lucrative, and when individuals feel that their territory is being invaded, they respond with violence.

The involvement of the young in drug trafficking was described in an Associated Press article (1989):

> As the crack problem grows ever larger, its victims have become ever younger. The latest two in New York—an 11-year-old alleged to be a drug courier and a 10-year-old crack dealer—left officials wondering whether they're losing the drug fight.
>
> "Crack and drugs are so pervasive that of course it trickles down into the lower grades," said Paul Berczeller, a spokesman for the United Federation of Teachers. "You have young kids used every day as drug runners."
>
> On Tuesday, Mark Birmingham, 11, arrived at his Bronx elementary school carrying what looked like a lunch bag. Inside, school officials said they found 411 vials of crack. Most of them were in 10-packs worth $50 apiece.
>
> The special education student told police his 17-year-old brother had given him the drugs. Police searched Wednesday for the brother.
>
> The 10-year-old was arrested January 15 after police watched him and a 14-year-old partner make a half-dozen crack sales in Wyandanch, Long Island. The 5-footer had three $20 vials of crack and $226 cash on him when arrested.

The involvement of juveniles in drug-related violence is becoming more prevalent each day. A Gannett News Service (1989) article notes:

> In the past week, a 16-year-old was shot at a suburban Maryland high school, thirteen people were shot and three killed on Valentine's Day, and a 15-year-old was arrested with a sawed-off shotgun.

> As of Sunday, 75 people have been killed in Washington since January 1st. At that rate the city will log more than 600 murders in 1989. The Washington murder rate in 1988—372 homicides or 59.4 for each 100,000 residents—netted the city the distinction of murder capital of the United States that had previously belonged to Detroit.

Drug-related violence is escalating in Detroit and in other large urban areas. Drug arrests have soared in the last few years. Drug-related arrests in most of the USA's top 50 cities increased from 1983 to 1987. During this period, Atlanta showed an increase of +40.3 percent; Cleveland, +54.6 percent; Los Angeles, +47.4 percent; Miami, +147.7 percent; New York, +68 percent; and Detroit, +54.8 percent (Greenberg et al. 1989).

Incidence of Arrests in Selected Michigan Cities

This section will focus on arrests for violent crimes as well as for narcotics laws violations in the five largest urban areas in Michigan: Detroit, Flint, Grand Rapids, Lansing, and Warren. With regard to arrests for violent crimes, the focus will be on homicide, rape, robbery, and aggravated assault. Arrests for violations of narcotics laws will encompass all forms of violations, such as possession or selling of heroin, marijuana, or cocaine.

For the most part, this discussion will view narcotics laws violations as a joining together of sales and usage, rather than breaking the violations down into separate categories. There is no breakdown in reporting arrests for the various forms of drug laws violations in Detroit; instead, everything is lumped under the framework of narcotics laws violations. In keeping with the pattern in Detroit (the locus of a large segment of the data), no breakdown is given for the other four cities in reporting arrests for narcotics laws violations. A correlation was made between narcotics laws violations arrests and arrests for violent crimes. This analysis was done for each of the five cities separately, for all five cities as a group, and for all of the cities except Detroit.

In order to put the data in perspective, the percentage black and the percentage white in the population, as well as the racial breakdown of the juvenile population of each city, are reported. These figures, based on 1980 census data, are displayed in Table 11-1.

Tables 11-2–11-6 show the number and percentage of arrests for violent crimes by race and by sex for each of the five designated cities for 1978 to 1987. Table 11-7 shows the number and percentage of arrests for narcotics laws violations by race (black and white) and by sex for each of the five designated cities from 1978 to 1987.

Detroit

Murder—(Detroit)

The total number of arrests for murder in Detroit increased from 430 in 1978 to 1,520 in 1987 (or by 253.5 percent). Of those arrested in 1978 for murder, 56 (or 13 percent) were juveniles. Although the number of juveniles arrested for murder also increased over the ten-year period—from 56 to 183 (or by 226.8 percent)—the juvenile percentage of total arrests remained relatively constant: from 13 percent of the total in 1978 to 12 percent of the total in 1987. Thus, the increase in the number of arrests for murder in Detroit occurred primarily among the adult population.

Table 11-1. Number and Percentage by Race* and Sex of Population in the Five Designated Cities of Michigan: 1980

City	Grand Total (GT)	Juvenile Grand Total (JGT)	White Total	White Male	White Female	White Juveniles Total (1)	White Juveniles Male (2)	White Juveniles Female (3)	Black Total	Black Male	Black Female	Black Juveniles Total (4)	Black Juveniles Male (5)	Black Juveniles Female (6)
DETROIT	1,203,339	364,618	413,730	198,174	215,556	83,861	43,199	40,662	758,939	355,676	403,263	269,922	135,659	134,263
			(34.4%)	(16.5%)	(17.9%)	(23.0%)	(11.9%)	(11.2%)	(63.1%)	(29.6%)	(33.5%)	(74.0%)	(37.2%)	(36.8%)
FLINT	159,611	50,870	89,647	42,367	47,280	22,591	11,651	10,940	66,124	31,180	34,944	26,650	13,341	13,309
			(56.2%)	(26.5%)	(29.6%)	(44.4%)	(22.9%)	(21.5%)	(41.4%)	(19.5%)	(21.9%)	(52.4%)	(26.2%)	(26.2%)
GRAND RAPIDS	181,843	49,844	147,171	68,976	78,195	35,023	17,996	17,027	28,602	13,402	15,200	12,090	6,028	6,062
			(80.9%)	(37.9%)	(43.0%)	(70.3%)	(36.1%)	(34.2%)	(15.7%)	(7.4%)	(8.4%)	(24.3%)	(12.1%)	(12.2%)
LANSING	130,414	38,127	104,880	49,877	55,003	27,305	13,856	13,449	18,179	8,670	9,509	7,492	3,731	3,761
			(80.4%)	(38.2%)	(42.1%)	(71.6%)	(36.3%)	(35.3%)	(13.9%)	(6.6%)	(7.3%)	(19.7%)	(9.8%)	(9.9%)
WARREN	161,134	44,771	158,283	77,622	80,661	43,823	22,316	21,507	297	158	139	76	37	39
			(98.2%)	(48.2%)	(50.1%)	(97.9%)	(49.8%)	(48.0%)	(.2%)	(.1%)	(.1%)	(.2%)	(.1%)	(.1%)

SOURCE: 1980 Census of Population, General Population Characteristics, Michigan, U.S. Department of Commerce, Bureau of Census, Vol. 1, Part 24, Table 25.

*This includes white and black only.

(1) This is the total white juvenile population as a proportion of the total juvenile population.

(2) This is the total white male juvenile population as a proportion of the total juvenile popuation.

(3) This is the total white female juvenile population as a proportion of the total juvenile population.

(4) This is the total black juvenile population as a proportion of the total juvenile population.

(5) This is the total black male juvenile population as a proportion of the total juvenile population.

(6) This is the total black female juvenile population as a proportion of the total juvenile population.

Table 11-2. Number and Percentage of Violent Crime Arrests by Race* and Sex for Detroit, 1978–1987

		Grand	Juvenile	Percent of	White Juveniles				Black Juveniles			
Year	Crime	Total	Total	Total	Male	Percent	Female	Percent	Male	Percent	Female	Percent
1978	Murder	430	56	13.0	3	5.4	1	1.8	50	89.3	2	3.6
	Rape	565	181	32.0	15	8.3	1	.6	163	90.0	2	1.1
	Robbery	1,692	720	42.5	49	6.8	2	.3	649	90.2	20	2.8
	Agg. Assault	1,449	565	39.0	80	14.2	11	2.0	409	72.4	65	11.5
1979	Murder	314	58	18.5	7	12.1	0	.0	47	81.1	4	6.9
	Rape	577	237	41.1	11	4.7	0	.0	224	94.5	2	.9
	Robbery	1,263	606	48.0	31	5.1	3	.5	548	90.4	24	4.0
	Agg. Assault	1,194	609	51.0	79	13.0	10	1.7	461	75.7	70	9.7
1980	Murder	509	39	7.7	4	10.3	0	.0	32	82.1	3	7.7
	Rape	711	48	6.8	4	8.3	0	.0	41	85.5	3	6.2
	Robbery	1,484	280	18.9	19	6.8	3	1.1	234	82.1	24	8.6
	Agg. Assault	1,606	523	32.6	41	7.8	17	3.3	395	75.4	70	13.4
1981	Murder	597	46	7.7	1	2.2	0	.0	45	97.8	0	.0
	Rape	981	192	68	17	8.8	0	.0	173	90.1	2	1.0
	Robbery	2,817	601	18.9	30	5.0	3	.5	559	93.0	9	1.5
	Agg. Assault	3,025	472	32.6	57	12.0	10	2.1	348	73.7	54	11.5
1982	Murder	787	48	6.1	1	2.1	1	2.1	41	85.4	5	10.5
	Rape	1,033	191	18.5	20	10.5	1	.5	169	88.5	1	.5
	Robbery	3,549	795	22.4	34	4.3	4	.5	736	92.6	21	2.6
	Agg. Assault	3,756	467	12.4	50	10.7	11	2.3	352	75.4	54	11.6

1983	Murder	806	57	7.1	5	8.8	0	.0	50	87.7	2	3.5
	Rape	1,163	209	18.0	17	8.1	0	.0	190	91.0	2	1.0
	Robbery	3,323	775	23.3	38	4.9	3	.4	716	92.4	18	2.3
	Agg. Assault	3,576	481	13.4	64	13.3	8	1.6	339	70.5	70	14.6
1984	Murder	764	76	10.0	2	2.6	1	1.3	71	93.4	2	2.6
	Rape	1,328	221	16.6	19	8.6	0	.0	200	90.5	2	1.0
	Robbery	3,385	828	24.5	35	4.2	1	.1	772	93.3	20	2.4
	Agg. Assault	3,162	514	16.3	50	9.7	6	1.2	392	76.3	66	12.9
1985	Murder	998	89	8.9	3	3.4	0	.0	84	94.4	2	2.2
	Rape	1,343	187	13.9	20	10.7	0	.0	165	88.3	2	1.1
	Robbery	3,187	817	25.6	33	4.1	4	.5	751	91.9	29	3.5
	Agg. Assault	3,358	514	16.3	58	11.1	6	1.2	403	76.6	59	11.2
1986	Murder	1,078	98	9.1	3	3.1	1	1.0	86	87.8	8	8.1
	Rape	1,216	228	18.8	13	5.7	0	.0	213	93.4	2	.9
	Robbery	3,169	737	23.3	24	3.3	5	.7	681	92.4	27	3.7
	Agg. Assault	4,262	683	16.0	76	11.1	6	.9	520	76.1	81	11.9
1987	Murder	1,520	183	12.0	8	4.4	1	.6	162	88.5	12	6.6
	Rape	1,278	199	15.6	15	7.5	1	.5	178	89.5	5	2.5
	Robbery	2,957	502	17.0	24	4.8	1	.2	456	90.8	21	4.2
	Agg. Assault	4,725	810	17.1	57	7.1	14	1.8	657	81.1	82	10.2

SOURCE: Central Records Division of the Crime Reporting Section, Michigan Department of State Police.

*This includes black and white only.

Table 11-3. Number and Percentage of Violent Crime Arrests by Race* and Sex for Flint, 1978–1987

					White Juveniles				Black Juveniles			
Year	Crime	Grand Total	Juvenile Total	Percent of Total	Male	Percent	Female	Percent	Male	Percent	Female	Percent
1978	Murder	45	3	6.7	0	.0	0	.0	3	100.0	0	.0
	Rape	57	9	15.5	1	11.1	0	.0	8	89.0	0	.0
	Robbery	248	48	19.4	14	29.2	0	.0	34	70.9	0	.0
	Agg. Assault	501	73	14.6	19	26.0	0	.0	44	60.5	9	12.4
1979	Murder	50	2	4.0	0	.0	0	.0	2	100.0	0	.0
	Rape	62	16	25.8	4	25.0	0	.0	12	75.0	0	.0
	Robbery	249	74	29.7	11	14.9	0	.0	63	85.1	0	.0
	Agg. Assault	571	95	16.6	25	26.3	4	4.2	54	56.9	12	12.6
1980	Murder	37	0	.0	0	.0	0	.0	0	.0	0	.0
	Rape	72	12	16.7	7	58.3	0	.0	5	41.6	0	.0
	Robbery	215	28	13.0	2	7.1	1	3.6	25	89.3	0	.0
	Agg. Assault	394	53	13.5	12	22.7	3	22.7	34	64.2	12	7.6
1981	Murder	36	2	5.6	0	.0	0	.0	2	100.0	0	.0
	Rape	73	7	9.6	3	10.2	0	.0	4	57.1	0	.0
	Robbery	210	49	23.3	5	10.2	0	.0	43	87.8	1	2.1
	Agg. Assault	337	75	22.3	15	20.0	3	4.0	45	60.0	12	15.0
1982	Murder	33	2	6.1	0	.0	0	.0	2	100.0	0	.0
	Rape	86	17	19.8	4	23.5	0	.0	12	70.6	0	.0
	Robbery	309	49	15.9	10	20.4	0	.0	36	73.5	3	6.1
	Agg. Assault	384	64	16.7	16	25.0	4	6.2	38	59.4	5	7.8

1983	Murder	34	7	20.6	0	.0	0	.0	5	71.4	2	28.6
	Rape	53	18	34.0	2	11.1	0	.0	16	89.0	0	.0
	Robbery	268	56	20.9	6	10.7	3	5.4	45	80.3	2	3.6
	Agg. Assault	378	69	18.3	11	16.0	4	5.8	42	60.9	12	17.4
1984	Murder	41	0	.0	0	.0	0	.0	0	.0	0	.0
	Rape	68	24	35.3	8	33.3	0	.0	15	62.5	0	.0
	Robbery	235	41	17.5	9	22.0	2	4.9	30	73.2	0	.0
	Agg. Assault	438	64	14.6	21	32.8	0	0.0	37	57.8	4	6.2
1985	Murder	43	4	9.3	0	.0	0	.0	3	75.1	1	25.1
	Rape	88	14	15.9	3	21.4	0	.0	11	78.6	0	.0
	Robbery	191	54	28.3	7	13.0	4	7.4	36	66.7	7	13.0
	Agg. Assault	494	76	15.4	21	27.6	2	2.6	44	58.0	9	11.8
1986	Murder	52	11	21.2	1	9.1	0	.0	9	81.8	1	.9
	Rape	95	15	15.8	5	33.3	0	.0	10	66.7	0	.0
	Robbery	260	67	25.8	6	9.0	0	.0	59	88.1	1	1.3
	Agg. Assault	544	60	11.0	13	21.7	2	3.4	36	60.0	8	13.3
1987	Murder	50	8	16.0	3	37.5	0	.0	5	62.5	0	.0
	Rape	71	8	11.3	1	12.5	0	.0	6	75.0	0	.0
	Robbery	211	67	31.8	14	20.9	0	.0	52	77.6	1	1.5
	Agg. Assault	467	84	18.0	18	21.4	0	.0	53	63.1	13	15.5

SOURCE: Central Records Division of the Crime Reporting Section, Michigan Department of State Police.

*This includes black and white only.

Table 11-4. Number and Percentage of Violent Crime Arrests by Race* and Sex for Grand Rapids, 1978–1987

					White Juveniles				Black Juveniles			
Year	Crime	Grand Total	Juvenile Total	Percent of Total	Male	Percent	Female	Percent	Male	Percent	Female	Percent
1978	Murder	11	1	9.1	1	100.0	0	.0	0	.0	0	.0
	Rape	74	19	25.7	6	31.6	1	5.3	12	63.2	0	.0
	Robbery	114	36	31.6	11	30.6	0	.0	22	61.1	3	8.3
	Agg. Assault	274	53	19.3	25	52.8	2	3.8	21	39.6	1	1.9
1979	Murder	7	0	.0	0	.0	0	.0	0	.0	0	.0
	Rape	71	12	16.9	5	41.7	0	.0	7	58.3	0	.0
	Robbery	127	29	22.8	10	34.5	0	.0	18	62.1	0	.0
	Agg. Assault	285	66	23.2	27	40.9	7	10.6	26	39.4	4	6.0
1980	Murder	28	1	3.6	1	100.0	0	.0	0	.0	0	.0
	Rape	93	21	22.6	13	61.9	0	.0	8	38.1	0	.0
	Robbery	165	48	29.1	8	14.6	0	.0	40	66.7	0	.0
	Agg. Assault	316	56	17.7	24	41.1	4	8.9	28	39.3	0	.0
1981	Murder	17	2	11.8	2	100.0	0	.0	0	.0	0	.0
	Rape	112	21	18.8	5	23.8	0	.0	16	76.2	0	.0
	Robbery	108	10	9.3	3	30.0	0	.0	7	70.0	0	.0
	Agg. Assault	288	38	13.2	16	42.2	2	5.2	16	42.1	4	10.5
1982	Murder	23	2	8.7	1	50.0	0	.0	1	50.0	0	.0
	Rape	80	21	26.3	9	42.9	0	.0	10	47.6	2	9.5
	Robbery	138	31	22.5	8	25.8	1	3.2	21	67.8	0	.0
	Agg. Assault	363	75	20.7	18	24.0	6	8.0	41	54.7	7	9.3

1983	Murder	11	0	.0	0	.0	0	.0	0	.0	0	.0
	Rape	92	17	18.5	10	58.8	1	5.9	5	29.4	1	5.9
	Robbery	114	39	34.2	5	12.8	0	.0	30	76.9	0	.0
	Agg. Assault	312	58	18.6	24	41.4	1	1.7	23	39.6	9	15.5
1984	Murder	18	1	5.6	0	.0	0	.0	0	.0	1	100.0
	Rape	92	26	28.3	14	53.9	0	.0	12	46.1	0	.0
	Robbery	98	19	19.4	7	36.8	1	5.3	11	57.9	0	.0
	Agg. Assault	330	60	18.2	20	33.3	7	11.7	22	36.7	10	16.7
1985	Murder	15	2	13.3	0	.0	1	50.0	1	50.0	0	.0
	Rape	78	18	23.1	7	38.9	4	22.2	7	38.9	0	.0
	Robbery	185	72	38.9	13	18.0	0	.0	57	79.2	0	.0
	Agg. Assault	350	75	20.9	28	32.3	0	.0	44	53.7	0	.0
1986	Murder	15	1	6.7	0	.0	0	.0	1	100.0	0	.0
	Rape	101	27	26.7	17	63.0	0	.0	10	37.0	0	.0
	Robbery	111	28	25.2	4	14.3	1	3.6	20	71.4	0	.0
	Agg. Assault	379	73	19.3	27	37.0	1	1.4	38	52.1	6	8.2
1987	Murder	13	2	15.4	1	50.0	0	.0	0	.0	1	50.0
	Rape	81	16	19.8	10	62.5	0	.0	6	37.5	0	.0
	Robbery	109	38	34.9	9	23.7	2	5.3	24	63.2	3	7.9
	Agg. Assault	371	98	26.4	44	44.9	2	2.0	35	35.7	11	11.2

SOURCE: Central Records Division of the Crime Reporting Section, Michigan Department of State Police.

*This includes black and white only.

Table 11-5. Number and Percentage of Violent Crime Arrests by Race* and Sex for Lansing, 1978–1987

					White Juveniles				Black Juveniles			
Year	Crime	Grand Total	Juvenile Total	Percent of Total	Male	Percent	Female	Percent	Male	Percent	Female	Percent
1978	Murder	6	0	.0	0	.0	0	.0	0	.0	0	.0
	Rape	7	0	.0	0	.0	0	.0	0	.0	0	.0
	Robbery	44	13	29.6	6	46.2	0	.0	7	53.8	0	.0
	Agg. Assault	129	15	11.6	10	66.6	1	6.7	4	26.7	0	.0
1979	Murder	6	0	.0	0	.0	0	.0	0	.0	0	.0
	Rape	14	0	.0	0	.0	0	.0	0	.0	0	.0
	Robbery	41	7	17.1	3	42.9	0	.0	4	57.2	0	.0
	Agg. Assault	113	10	8.9	6	60.0	1	9.9	2	19.9	1	9.9
1980	Murder	4	1	25.0	1	100.0	0	.0	0	.0	0	.0
	Rape	13	0	.0	0	.0	0	.0	0	.0	0	.0
	Robbery	42	13	31.0	6	46.0	0	.0	7	53.8	0	.0
	Agg. Assault	205	33	16.1	10	30.3	3	9.1	20	60.6	0	.0
1981	Murder	5	1	20.0	0	.0	0	.0	1	100.0	0	.0
	Rape	15	2	13.3	1	50.0	0	.0	1	50.0	0	.0
	Robbery	34	12	35.3	5	41.7	0	.0	7	58.4	0	.0
	Agg. Assault	177	22	12.4	16	72.7	1	4.5	3	13.6	2	9.0
1982	Murder	7	0	.0	0	.0	0	.0	0	.0	0	.0
	Rape	27	1	3.7	0	.0	0	.0	1	100.0	0	.0
	Robbery	26	1	3.9	1	100.0	0	.0	0	.0	0	.0
	Agg. Assault	108	6	5.6	5	83.3	1	16.7	0	.0	0	.0

1983	Murder	1	0	.0	0	.0	0	.0	0	.0	0	.0
	Rape	26	5	19.2	3	60.0	0	.0	2	40.0	0	.0
	Robbery	50	15	30.0	6	40.0	0	.0	5	33.3	1	6.7
	Agg. Assault	142	18	12.7	7	38.9	4	22.2	5	27.8	2	11.1
1984	Murder	3	0	.0	0	.0	0	.0	0	.0	0	.0
	Rape	18	2	11.1	1	50.0	0	.0	1	50.0	0	.0
	Robbery	52	1	1.9	0	.0	0	.0	1	100.0	0	.0
	Agg. Assault	221	14	6.3	4	18.6	0	.0	8	57.2	2	14.2
1985	Murder	4	0	.0	0	.0	0	.0	0	.0	0	.0
	Rape	23	0	.0	0	.0	0	.0	0	.0	0	.0
	Robbery	38	1	2.6	0	.0	0	.0	1	100.0	0	.0
	Agg. Assault	175	3	1.7	0	.0	0	.0	2	66.7	1	33.3
1986	Murder	3	0	.0	0	.0	0	.0	0	.0	0	.0
	Rape	66	16	24.2	7	43.8	1	6.3	7	43.8	0	.0
	Robbery	68	20	29.4	3	15.0	1	5.0	7	35.0	5	25.0
	Agg. Assault	308	70	22.7	9	12.9	7	10.0	31	44.3	11	15.7
1987	Murder	8	1	12.5	1	100.0	0	.0	0	.0	0	.0
	Rape	49	8	16.3	4	50.0	1	12.5	3	37.5	0	.0
	Robbery	84	27	32.1	1	3.7	1	3.7	18	66.7	1	3.7
	Agg. Assault	358	72	20.1	21	29.2	6	8.4	28	38.9	8	11.1

SOURCE: Central Records Division of the Crime Reporting Section, Michigan Department of State Police.

*This includes black and white only.

Table 11-6. Number and Percentage of Violent Crime Arrests by Race* and Sex for Warren, 1978–1987

Year	Crime	Grand Total	Juvenile Total	Percent of Total	White Juveniles				Black Juveniles			
					Male	Percent	Female	Percent	Male	Percent	Female	Percent
1978	Murder	7	0	.0	0	.0	0	.0	0	.0	0	.0
	Rape	4	0	.0	0	.0	0	.0	0	.0	0	.0
	Robbery	72	17	23.6	16	94.1	0	.0	1	5.9	0	.0
	Agg. Assault	115	18	15.7	14	77.8	4	22.2	0	.0	0	.0
1979	Murder	4	0	.0	0	.0	0	.0	0	.0	0	.0
	Rape	14	2	14.3	2	100.0	0	.0	0	.0	0	.0
	Robbery	61	14	23.0	12	85.7	1	7.2	1	7.2	0	.0
	Agg. Assault	144	28	19.4	24	85.8	2	7.2	0	.0	0	.0
1980	Murder	2	0	.0	0	.0	0	.0	0	.0	0	.0
	Rape	4	1	25.0	1	100.0	0	.0	0	.0	0	.0
	Robbery	34	5	14.7	5	100.0	0	.0	0	.0	0	.0
	Agg. Assault	82	12	14.6	12	100.0	0	.0	0	.0	0	.0
1981	Murder	1	0	.0	0	.0	0	.0	0	.0	0	.0
	Rape	18	1	5.6	1	100.0	0	.0	0	.0	0	.0
	Robbery	76	22	29.0	9	40.9	5	22.7	8	36.4	0	.0
	Agg. Assault	155	43	27.7	40	93.0	0	.0	3	7.0	2	9.0
1982	Murder	3	0	.0	0	.0	0	.0	0	.0	0	.0
	Rape	19	4	21.1	1	25.0	0	.0	3	75.0	0	.0
	Robbery	81	14	17.3	13	92.9	0	.0	1	7.1	0	.0
	Agg. Assault	206	34	16.5	32	94.1	2	5.9	0	.0	0	.0

1983	Murder	0	0	.0	0	.0	0	.0	0	.0	0	.0
	Rape	12	1	8.3	1	100.0	0	.0	0	.0	0	.0
	Robbery	79	8	10.1	2	25.0	2	25.0	4	50.0	0	.0
	Agg. Assault	151	20	13.3	19	94.9	4	5.0	0	.0	0	.0
1984	Murder	0	0	.0	0	.0	0	.0	0	.0	0	.0
	Rape	23	3	13.0	3	100.0	0	.0	0	.0	0	.0
	Robbery	113	8	7.1	4	50.0	0	.0	4	50.0	0	.0
	Agg. Assault	239	29	12.1	28	96.6	1	3.5	0	.0	0	.0
1985	Murder	11	0	.0	0	.0	0	.0	0	.0	0	.0
	Rape	25	1	4.0	1	100.0	0	.0	0	.0	0	.0
	Robbery	93	9	9.7	8	88.8	0	.0	1	11.2	0	.0
	Agg. Assault	183	15	9.3	15	88.3	2	11.7	0	.0	0	.0
1986	Murder	12	1	8.3	0	.0	1	100.0	0	.0	0	.0
	Rape	9	5	55.6	3	60.0	0	.0	2	40.0	0	.0
	Robbery	76	19	25.0	17	89.5	0	.0	2	10.5	0	.0
	Agg. Assault	240	40	16.7	35	87.5	5	12.5	0	.0	0	.0
1987	Murder	0	0	.0	0	.0	0	.0	0	.0	0	.0
	Rape	19	3	15.8	3	100.0	0	.0	0	.0	0	.0
	Robbery	167	30	18.0	12	40.0	0	.0	18	60.0	0	.0
	Agg. Assault	226	18	8.0	14	77.7	4	22.2	0	.0	0	.0

SOURCE: Central Records Division of the Crime Reporting Section, Michigan Department of State Police.

*This includes black and white only.

Table 11-7. Number and Percentage of Narcotics Laws Violations Arrests by Year, by Race,* and by Sex, for all Five Cities, 1978–1987

					White Juveniles				Black Juveniles			
Year	Crime	Grand Total	Juvenile Total	Percent of Total	Male	Percent	Female	Percent	Male	Percent	Female	Percent
1978	Detroit	3,222	169	5.3	46	27.2	10	6.0	106	62.7	7	4.2
	Flint	350	36	10.3	21	58.3	2	5.5	13	36.0	0	.0
	Grand Rapids	245	51	20.8	41	80.4	5	9.8	3	5.9	1	2.0
	Lansing	95	3	3.2	2	66.8	1	16.2	0	.0	0	.0
	Warren	172	68	39.5	57	83.8	11	16.2	0	.0	0	.0
1979	Detroit	2,087	397	19.0	47	11.8	30	7.6	197	49.6	.122	30.8
	Flint	345	30	8.7	21		2		7		0	.0
	Grand Rapids	273	61	22.3	41	67.2	13	21.3	4	6.6	0	.0
	Lansing	24	2	8.3	1	50.0	1	50.0	0	.0	0	.0
	Warren	312	109	34.9	89	81.7	20	18.4	0	.0	0	.0
1980	Detroit	3,834	88	2.3	23	26.1	6	7.0	54	61.3	5	5.7
	Flint	430	27	6.3	13	48.1	1	3.7	12	44.4	1	3.7
	Grand Rapids	238	21	8.8	17	81.0	2	9.5	1	4.8	0	.0
	Lansing	17	1	5.9	1	100.0	0	.0	0	.0	0	.0
	Warren	198	42	21.2	37	88.1	5	11.9	0	.0	0	.0
1981	Detroit	4,570	188	4.1	16	8.5	4	2.2	161	85.6	7	3.7
	Flint	427	14	3.3	4	28.7	1	7.0	7	50.0	0	.0
	Grand Rapids	354	31	8.8	18	58.0	2	6.4	6	19.3	2	6.4
	Lansing	61	5	8.2	5	100.0	0	.0	0	.0	0	.0
	Warren	334	70	21.0	54	77.2	15	21.4	0	.0	1	1.4
1982	Detroit	5,277	430	8.2	10	2.3	1	.3	410	95.3	9	2.1
	Flint	266	12	4.5	7	58.3	0	.0	4	33.3	1	8.4
	Grand Rapids	496	44	8.9	29	66.0	7	16.0	7	15.9	1	2.3
	Lansing	34	1	2.9	1	100.0	0	.0	0	.0	0	.0
	Warren	159	25	15.7	18	72.0	7	28.0	0	.0	0	.0

1983	Detroit	4,793	396	8.3	5	1.2	4	1.0	379	95.8	8	2.1
	Flint	309	9	2.9	5	55.7	0	.0	3	.3	0	.0
	Grand Rapids	609	22	3.6	13	59.0	2	9.1	6	27.4	1	4.4
	Lansing	33	0	.0	0	.0	0	.0	0	.0	0	.0
	Warren	139	38	27.3	30	78.9	7	18.4	1	2.6	0	.0
1984	Detroit	4,032	309	7.7	7	2.2	3	.9	289	93.6	10	3.3
	Flint	484	28	5.8	5	17.8	0	.0	22	78.6	1	3.6
	Grand Rapids	416	15	3.6	8	53.2	0	.0	6	40.0	0	.0
	Lansing	67	0	.0	0	.0	0	.0	0	.0	0	.0
	Warren	142	22	15.5	21	95.5	1	4.5	0	.0	0	.0
1985	Detroit	4,285	329	7.7	9	2.7	1	.3	298	90.5	20	6.1
	Flint	390	25	6.4	5	20.0	2	4.1	16	36.0	0	.0
	Grand Rapids	551	65	11.8	38	58.5	9	13.8	13	20.0	2	3.1
	Lansing	94	5	5.3	4	80.1	0	.0	1	19.9	0	.0
	Warren	111	18	16.2	12	66.7	6	33.4	0	.0	0	.0
1986	Detroit	5,456	563	10.3	12	2.1	1	.2	528	93.8	22	3.8
	Flint	572	21	3.7	2	9.5	0	.0	16	76.3	2	9.5
	Grand Rapids	509	35	6.9	22	62.8	1	2.9	11	31.4	1	2.9
	Lansing	57	5	8.8	2	40.0	1	20.0	2	40.0	0	.0
	Warren	259	27	10.4	20	74.1	7	25.9	0	.0	0	.0
1987	Detroit	7,420	1,020	13.8	28	2.8	5	.5	933	91.4	54	5.3
	Flint	636	51	8.0	6	11.7	0	.0	43	82.3	3	5.9
	Grand Rapids	571	23	4.0	18	78.2	1	4.5	4	17.4	0	.0
	Lansing	121	12	9.9	4	33.4	3	25.0	2	16.6	1	8.4
	Warren	308	26	8.4	25	96.2	1	3.8	0	.0	0	.0

SOURCE: Central Records Division of the Crime Reporting Section, Michigan Department of State Police.

*This includes black and white only.

Of the 56 juveniles arrested for murder in 1978, 50 (or 89 percent) were black males, and 2 (or 3.6 percent) were black females. The percentage distribution of arrests by race and gender remained relatively constant over the ten-year period. Of the 183 juveniles arrested in 1987 for murder, 162 (or 88.5 percent) were black males, and 12 (or 6.5 percent) were black females (Table 11-2). In 1980, the black male juvenile population as a percentage of the total juvenile population was 37.2 percent, and the black female juvenile population was 36.8 percent (Table 11-1).

Rape—(Detroit)

The total number of arrests for rape increased from 565 in 1978 to 1,278 in 1987, or by 126.2 percent. Of the 565 arrests, 181 (or 32 percent) in 1978 were juveniles. The number of juveniles arrested for rape increased from 181 to 199 (or by 9.9 percent) over the ten-year period. The juvenile percentage of the total arrests was 32 percent in 1978 and declined to 15.6 percent in 1987.

Of the 181 juveniles arrested in 1978 for rape, 163 (or 90 percent) were black males, and 2 were black females. The percentage distribution of arrests by race and gender remained relatively constant over the ten-year period. Of the 199 juveniles arrested in 1987 for rape, 178 (or 89.5 percent) were black males, and 5 (or 2.5 percent) were black females (Table 11-2).

Robbery—(Detroit)

The total number of arrests for robbery increased from 1,692 in 1978 to 2,957 in 1987 (or by 74.8 percent). Of those arrested in 1978 for robbery, 720 (or 42.6 percent) were juveniles. Although the number of total arrests for robbery increased over the ten-year period, the number of juveniles arrested decreased from 720 in 1978 to 502 in 1987.

Of the 720 juveniles arrested in 1978 for robbery, 649 (or 90.2 percent) were black males, and 20 (or 2.8 percent) were black females. The percentage distribution of arrests by race and gender remained relatively constant over the ten-year period. Of the 502 juveniles arrested in 1987 for robbery, 456 (or 90.8 percent) were black males, and 21 (or 4.2 percent) were black females (Table 11-2).

Aggravated Assault—(Detroit)

The total number of arrests for aggravated assault increased from 1,449 in 1978 to 4,725 in 1987 (or by 226.1 percent). Of those arrested in 1978 for aggravated assault, 565 (or 39 percent) were juveniles. The number of juveniles arrested for aggravated assault increased from 565 to 810 (or by 43.4 percent) over the ten-year period. However, the juvenile percentage of total arrests decreased from 39 percent in 1978 to 17.1 percent in 1987.

Of the 565 juveniles arrested in 1978 for aggravated assault, 409 (or 72.4 percent) were black males, and 65 (or 11.5 percent) were black females. Of the 810 juveniles arrested in 1987 for aggravated assault, 657 (or 81.1 percent) were black males, and 82 (or 10.2 percent) were black females (Table 11-2).

Narcotics Laws Violations—(Detroit)

The total number of arrests for narcotics laws violations increased from 3,222 in 1978 to 7,420 in 1987, or by 130.3 percent. Only 169, or 5.3 percent, of those arrested for narcotics laws violations in 1978 were juveniles. The number of juveniles arrested for narcotics laws violations increased from 169 to 1,020, or by 503.6 percent, over the 10-year period. The juvenile percentage of total arrests nearly tripled from 5.3 percent of the total in 1978 to 13.8 percent of the total in 1987.

Of the 169 juveniles arrested for narcotics laws violations in 1978, 106 or 62.7 percent were black males. The percentage distribution of arrests by race and gender increased over the ten-year period. Of the 1,020 arrested for narcotics laws violations in 1987, 91.4 percent were black males (Table 11-7).

Flint

Murder—(Flint)

The total number of arrests for murder in Flint increased from 45 in 1978 to 50 in 1987, or by 11.1 percent. Only three, or 6.7 percent, of those arrested for murder in 1978 were juveniles. Although the number of juveniles arrested for murder also increased from 3 to 8, or by 167 percent, over the ten-year period, the juvenile percentage changed only slightly from 14.6 percent of the total in 1978 to 16 percent of the total in 1987.

Of the 3 juveniles arrested for murder in 1978, 3 or 100 percent were black males. The percentage distribution of arrests by race and gender decreased over the ten-year period. Of the 8 juveniles arrested for murder in 1987, 5 or 62.5 percent were black males (Table 11-3). In 1980, the black male juvenile population as a percentage of the total juvenile population was 26.2 percent (Table 11-1).

Rape—(Flint)

The total number of arrests for rape increased from 57 to 71 (or by 24.6 percent). Of those arrested in 1978 for rape, 9 (or 15.8 percent) were juveniles. The number of juveniles arrested for rape decreased from 9 to 8 (or by 11.2 percent) over the ten-year period. The juvenile percentage of total arrests decreased from 15.8 percent of the total in 1978 to 11.3 percent of the total in 1987.

Of the 9 juveniles arrested in 1978 for rape, 8 (or 89.0 percent) were black males, and no black females were arrested. Of the 8 juveniles arrested in 1987 for rape, 75 percent were black males, and no black females were arrested (Table 11-3).

Robbery—(Flint)

The total number of arrests for robbery decreased from 248 in 1978 to 211 in 1987 (or by −14.9 percent). Of those arrested in 1978 for robbery, 48 (or 19.4 percent) were juveniles. The number of juveniles arrested for robbery increased from 48 to 67 (or by 39.6 percent) over the ten-year period. The juvenile percentage of total arrests increased from 19.4 percent of the total in 1978 to 31.8 percent of the total in 1987.

Of the 48 juveniles arrested in 1978 for robbery, 34 (or 70.9 percent) were black males, and no black females were arrested. Of the 67 juveniles arrested in 1987 for robbery, 77.6 percent were black males, and 1 was a black female (Table 11-3).

Aggravated Assault—(Flint)

The total number of arrests for aggravated assault decreased from 501 in 1978 to 467 in 1987 (or by −6.8 percent). Of those arrested in 1978 for aggravated assault, 73 (or 14.6 percent) were juveniles. The number of juveniles arrested for aggravated assault increased from 73 to 84, or by 15.1 percent, over the 10-year period. The juvenile percentage of total arrests increased slightly from 14.6 percent of the total in 1978 to 18 percent of the total in 1987.

Of the 73 juveniles arrested in 1978 for aggravated assault, 44 (or 60.5 percent) were black males, and 9 (or 12.4 percent) were black females. The percentage distribution of arrests by race and gender remained relatively constant over the 10-year period. Of the 84 juveniles arrested in 1987 for aggravated assault, 53 (or 63.1 percent) were black males, and 13 (or 15.5 percent) were black females (Table 11-3).

Narcotics Laws Violations—(Flint)

The total number of arrests for narcotics laws violations increased from 350 in 1978 to 636 in 1987 (or by 82 percent). Of those arrested in 1978 for narcotics laws violations, 36 (or 10.3 percent) were juveniles. The number of juveniles arrested for narcotics laws violations increased from 36 to 51 (or by 41.7 percent) over the ten-year period. However, the juvenile percentage of total arrests declined from 10.3 percent in 1978 to 8 percent in 1987.

Of the 36 juveniles arrested in 1978 for narcotics laws violations, 13 (or 36 percent) were black males, and no black females were arrested. Of the 51 juveniles arrested in 1987 for narcotics laws violations, 43 (or 82.3 percent) were black males, and 3 (or 5.9 percent) were black females (Table 11-7).

Grand Rapids

Murder—(Grand Rapids)

The total number of arrests for murder in Grand Rapids increased from 11 in 1978 to 13 in 1987 (or by 18.2 percent). Only 1 of those arrested for murder in 1978 was a juvenile. The number of juveniles arrested for murder increased from 1 to 2 over the 10-year period. The juvenile percentage of total arrests went from 9.1 percent of the total in 1978 to 15.4 percent in 1987.

The one juvenile arrested for murder in 1978 was nonblack. Of the two juveniles arrested for murder in 1987, one was a black female (Table 11-4). In 1980, the black male juvenile population as a percentage of the total juvenile population was 12.1 percent, and the black female juvenile population was 12.2 percent (Table 11-1).

Rape—(Grand Rapids)

The total number of arrests for rape increased from 74 in 1978 to 81 in 1987 (or by 9.5 percent). Of those arrested in 1978 for rape, 19 (or 25.7 percent) were juveniles. The number of juveniles arrested for rape decreased from 19 to 16 (or by −15.8 percent) over the 10-year period. The juvenile percentage of total arrests decreased from 25.7 percent in 1978 to 19.8 percent in 1987.

Of the 19 juveniles arrested in 1978 for rape, 12 (or 63.2 percent) were black males, and no black females were arrested. Of the 16 juveniles arrested in 1987 for rape, 6 (or 37.5 percent) were black males, and no black females were arrested (Table 11-4).

Robbery—(Grand Rapids)

The total number of arrests for robbery decreased from 114 in 1978 to 109 in 1987 (or by −4.4 percent). Of those arrested in 1978 for robbery, 36 (or 31.6 percent) were juveniles. The number of juveniles arrested for robbery increased from 36 to 38 (or by 5.5 percent) over the 10-year period. The juvenile percentage of total arrests rose slightly from 31.6 percent in 1978 to 34.9 percent in 1987.

Of the 36 juveniles arrested in 1978 for robbery, 22 (or 61.1 percent) were black males, and 3 (or 8.3 percent) were black females. Of the 38 juveniles arrested for robbery in 1987, 63.2 percent were black males, and 3 (or 7.9 percent) were black females (Table 11-4).

Aggravated Assault—(Grand Rapids)

The total number of arrests for aggravated assault increased from 274 in 1978 to 371 in 1987 (or by 35.4 percent). Of those arrested in 1978 for aggravated assault, 53 (or 19.3 percent) were juveniles. The number of juveniles arrested for aggravated assault increased from 53 to 98 (or by 85 percent) over the 10-year period. The juvenile percentage of total arrests increased from 19.3 percent in 1978 to 26.4 percent in 1987.

Of the 53 juveniles arrested in 1978 for aggravated assault, 21 (or 39.6 percent) were black males, and one was a black female. Of the 98 juveniles arrested in 1987 for aggravated assault, 35 (or 35.7 percent) were black males, and 11 (or 11.2 percent) were black females (Table 11-4).

Narcotics Laws Violations—(Grand Rapids)

The total number of arrests for narcotics laws violations increased from 245 in 1978 to 571 in 1987 (or by 133.1 percent). Of those arrested in 1978 for narcotics laws violations, 51 (or 20.8 percent) were juveniles. The number of juveniles arrested for narcotics laws violations decreased from 51 to 23 (or by −45.1 percent) over the 10-year period. The juvenile percentage of total arrests dropped dramatically from 20.8 percent in 1978 to 4 percent in 1987.

Of the 51 juveniles arrested in 1978 for narcotics laws violations, 3 (or 5.9 percent) were black males, and one was a black female. Of the 23 juveniles arrested in 1987 for narcotics laws violations, 4 (or 17.4 percent) were black males, and no black females were arrested (Table 11-7).

Lansing

Murder—(Lansing)

The total number of arrests for murder in Lansing increased from 6 in 1978 to 8 in 1987 (or by 33 percent). No juveniles were arrested for murder in 1978. The juvenile percentage of total arrests rose from 0 percent in 1978 to 12.5 percent in 1987.

As was noted above, no juvenile was arrested for murder in 1978. The one juvenile arrested for murder in 1987 was a white male (Table 11-5). In 1980, the black male juvenile population as a percentage of the total juvenile population was 9.8 percent, and the black female juvenile population was 9.9 percent (Table 11-1).

Rape—(Lansing)

The total number of arrests for rape increased from 7 in 1978 to 49 in 1987 (or by 600 percent). None of those arrested for rape in 1978 was a juvenile. The number of juveniles arrested for rape increased from 0 to 8 over the 10-year period. The juvenile percentage of total arrests went from 0 percent in 1978 to 16.3 percent in 1987.

Of the 8 juveniles arrested in 1987 for rape, 3 (or 37.5 percent) were black males, and no black females were arrested (Table 11-6).

Robbery—(Lansing)

The total number of arrests for robbery increased from 44 in 1978 to 84 in 1987 (or by 91 percent). Of those arrested in 1978 for robbery, 13 (or 29.5 percent) were juveniles. The number of juveniles arrested for robbery increased from 13 to 27 (or by 108 percent) over the 10-year period. The juvenile percentage of total arrests for robbery rose from 29.5 percent in 1978 to 32.1 percent in 1987.

Of the 13 juveniles arrested for robbery in 1978, 7 (or 53.8 percent) were black males, and no black females were arrested. Of the 27 juveniles arrested in 1987 for robbery, 18 (or 66.7 percent) were black males, and 1 black female was arrested (Table 11-5).

Aggravated Assault—(Lansing)

The total number of arrests for aggravated assault increased from 129 in 1978 to 358 in 1987 (or by 177.5 percent). Of those arrested in 1978 for aggravated assault, 15 (or 11.6 percent) were juveniles. The number of juveniles arrested for aggravated assault increased from 15 to 72 (or by 380 percent) over the 10-year period. The juvenile percentage of total arrests for aggravated assault went from 11.6 percent in 1978 to 20.1 percent in 1987.

Of the 15 juveniles arrested in 1978 for aggravated assault, 4 (or 26.7 percent) were black males, and no black females were arrested. Of the 72 juveniles arrested in 1987 for aggravated assault, 38.9 percent were black males, and 8 (or 11.1 percent) were black females (Table 11-5).

Narcotics Laws Violations—(Lansing)

The total number of arrests for narcotics laws violations increased from 95 in 1978 to 121 in 1987 (or by 27.4 percent). Of those arrested in 1978 for narcotics laws violations, 3 (or 3.2 percent) were juveniles. The number of juveniles arrested for narcotics laws violations increased from 3 in 1978 to 12 (or by 300 percent) over the 10-year period. The juvenile percentage of total arrests more than tripled from 3.2 percent in 1978 to 9.9 percent in 1987.

Of the 3 juveniles arrested for narcotics laws violations in 1978, none were black. Of the 12 juveniles arrested in 1987 for narcotics laws violations, 2 were black males, and 1 was a black female (Table 11-7).

Warren

Murder—(Warren)

The total number of arrests for murder in Warren decreased from 7 in 1978 to 0 in 1987. The number of juveniles arrested for murder was 0 in 1978 and 0 in 1987 (Table 11-6). In 1980, the black male juvenile population as a percentage of the total juvenile population was .08 percent, and the black female juvenile population was also .08 percent (Table 11-1).

Rape—(Warren)

The total number of rapes in Warren increased from 4 in 1978 to 19 in 1987 (or by 375 percent). None of those arrested for rape in 1978 were juveniles. The number of juveniles arrested for rape increased from 0 in 1978 to 3 over the 10-year period. The juvenile percentage of total arrests increased from 0 in 1978 to 15.8 percent in 1987. Of the 3 juveniles arrested in 1987 for rape, all were white males (Table 11-6).

Robbery—(Warren)

The total number of arrests for robbery increased from 72 in 1978 to 167 in 1987 (or by 132 percent). Of those arrested in 1978 for robbery, 17 (or 23.6 percent) were juveniles. The number of juveniles arrested for robbery increased from 17 to 30 in 1987 (or by 76.5 percent) over the 10-year period. However, the juvenile percentage of total arrests declined from 23.6 percent in 1978 to 18 percent in 1987.

Of the 17 juveniles arrested in 1978 for robbery, 1 was a black male, and no black females were arrested. Of the 30 juveniles arrested in 1987 for robbery, 18 (or 60 percent) were black males, and no black females were arrested (Table 11-6).

Aggravated Assault—(Warren)

The total number of arrests for aggravated assault increased from 115 in 1978 to 226 in 1987 (or by 96 percent). Of those arrested in 1978 for aggravated assault, 18 (or 15.7 percent) were juveniles. In both 1978 and 1987, the number of juveniles arrested for aggravated assault was 18. This figure represented 15.7 percent of the total in 1978 and 8.0 percent in 1987.

Of the 18 juveniles arrested for aggravated assault in 1978, none were black. Of the 18 juveniles arrested for aggravated assault in 1987, none were black (Table 11-6).

Narcotics Laws Violations—(Warren)

The total number of arrests for narcotics laws violations increased from 172 in 1978 to 308 in 1987 (or by 79 percent). Of those arrested in 1978 for narcotics laws violations, 68 (or 39.5 percent) were juveniles. The number of juveniles arrested for narcotics laws violations decreased from 68 to 26 (or by 38 percent) over the 10-year period. The juvenile percentage of total arrests decreased markedly from 39.5 percent in 1978 to 8.4 percent in 1987.

Of the 68 juveniles arrested for narcotics laws violations in 1978, none were black. Of the 26 juveniles arrested in 1987 for narcotics laws violations, none were black (Table 11-7).

Composite for All Five Cities

Murder—(Composite)

The total number of arrests for murder increased from 499 in 1978 to 1,591 in 1987 (or by 219 percent). Of those arrested in 1978 for murder, 60 (or 12.2 percent) were juveniles. Although the number of juveniles arrested for murder increased from 60 in 1978 to 194 in 1987 (or by 206.7 percent) over the 10-year period, the juvenile percentage of total arrests remained relatively constant—from 12.02 percent of the total in 1978 to 12.19 percent of the total in 1987.

Of the 60 juveniles arrested in 1978 for murder, 53 (or 88.3 percent) were black males, and 2 were black females. Of the 194 juveniles arrested in 1987 for murder, 167 (or 87.9 percent) were black males, and 13 (or 6.8 percent) were black females. In 1980, the black male juvenile population as a percentage of the total juvenile population was 29 percent.

Rape—(Composite)

The number of arrests for rape increased from 707 in 1978 to 1,498 in 1987, or by 111.9 percent. Of those arrested in 1978 for rape, 209 (or 29.6 percent) were juveniles. The number of juvenile arrests increased from 209 in 1978 to 234 in 1987 (or by 11.9 percent) over the 10-year period. The juvenile percentage of the total arrests was 29.6 percent in 1978, and this figure declined to 15.6 percent in 1987.

Of the 209 juveniles arrested in 1978 for rape, 183 (or 87.6 percent) were black males, and 2 were black females. Of the 234 juveniles arrested in 1987 for rape, 193 (or 82.5 percent) were black males, and 5 were black females.

Robbery—(Composite)

The total number of arrests for robbery increased from 2,170 in 1978 to 3,528 in 1987 (or by 62.6 percent). Of that figure, 834 (or 38.4 percent) of those arrested for robbery in 1978 were juveniles. Although the number of total arrests for robbery increased over the 10-year period, the number of juveniles arrested decreased from 834 in 1978 to 624 in 1978.

Of the 834 juveniles arrested in 1978 for robbery, 713 (or 84.6 percent) were black males, and 23 (or 2.8 percent) were black females. Of the 664 juveniles arrested in 1987 for robbery, 567 (or 85.5 percent) were black males.

Aggravated Assault—(Composite)

The total number of arrests for aggravated assault increased from 2,468 in 1978 to 6,147 in 1987 (or by 149.1 percent). Of those arrested in 1978 for aggravated assault, 29.3 percent were juveniles. The number of juveniles arrested for aggravated assault increased from 724 in 1978 to 1,082 in 1987 (or by 49.4 percent) over the 10-year period. However, the juvenile percentage of total arrests decreased from 29.3 percent in 1978 to 17.6 percent in 1987.

Of the 724 juveniles arrested in 1978 for aggravated assault, 475 (or 65.6 percent) were black males, and 75 (or 10.4 percent) were black females. Of the 1,082 juveniles arrested in 1987 for aggravated assault, 773 (or 71.4 percent) were black males, and 75 (or 6.9 percent) were black females.

Narcotics Laws Violations—(Composite)

The total number of arrests for narcotics laws violations increased from 4,084 in 1978 to 9,056 in 1987 (or by 121.7 percent). Of those arrested in 1978 for narcotics laws violations, 327 (or 8 percent) were juveniles. The number of juveniles arrested for narcotics laws violations increased from 327 in 1978 to 1,132 in 1987 (or by 246 percent) over the 10-year period. The juvenile percentage of total arrests increased from 8 percent in 1978 to 12.5 percent in 1987.

Of the 327 juveniles arrested in 1978 for narcotics laws violations, 122 (or 37.3 percent) were black males. Of the 1,132 arrested in 1987 for narcotics laws violations, 86.7 percent were black males.

Comparison of the Five Cities

Before leaving this aspect of the discussion regarding arrest rates, a comparison of the various cities will be presented.

Murder—(Comparison)

With regard to murder, the number of juveniles arrested in Detroit increased from 56 in 1978 to 183 in 1987 (or by 226.8 percent). In Flint, the number of juveniles arrested increased from 3 in 1978 to 8 in 1987 (or by 167 percent). In Grand Rapids, there was 1 juvenile arrested for murder in 1978, and this number increased to 2 in 1987. In Lansing and Warren there were no juveniles arrested for murder in 1978. In Lansing, there was 1 arrest in 1987.

Rape—(Comparison)

For rape, the number of juveniles arrested in Detroit was 181 in 1978, and this figure increased to 199 (or by 9.9 percent) in 1987. In Flint, the number of juveniles arrested was 9 in 1978 and 8 in 1987, representing a decrease of −11.2 percent. In Grand Rapids, the number of juveniles arrested decreased from 19 in 1978 to 16 in 1987 (or by −15.8 percent). In Lansing, the number of juveniles arrested for rape was 0 in 1978, and this figure increased to 8 in 1987. In Warren, the number of juveniles arrested for rape increased from 0 in 1978 to 3 in 1987.

Robbery—(Comparison)

The number of juvenile arrests for robbery in Detroit was 720 in 1978, and this figure decreased to 502 in 1987 (or by −30 percent). In Flint, the number of juveniles arrested for robbery increased from 48 in 1978 to 67 in 1987 (or by 39.6 percent). In Grand Rapids, the number of juveniles arrested for robbery increased from 36 in 1978 to 38 in 1987 (or by 5.5 percent). In Lansing, the number of juveniles arrested for robbery increased from 13 in 1978 to 27 in 1987, or by 108 percent. In Warren, the number of juveniles arrested for robbery increased from 17 in 1978 to 30 in 1987 (or by 76.5 percent).

Aggravated Assault—(Comparison)

The number of juveniles arrested in Detroit for aggravated assault increased from 565 in 1978 to 810 in 1987, or by 43.4 percent. In Flint, the number of juveniles arrested for aggravated assault increased from 73 in 1978 to 84 in 1987 (or by 15.1 percent). In Grand Rapids, the number of juveniles arrested for aggravated assault increased from 53 in 1978 to 98 in 1987 (or by 85 percent). In Lansing, the number of juveniles arrested for aggravated assault increased from 15 in 1978 to 72 in 1987 (or by 380 percent). In Warren, the number of juveniles arrested for aggravated assault was 18 in both 1978 and 1987.

Narcotics Laws Violations—(Comparison)

The number of juveniles arrested for narcotics laws violations in Detroit increased from 169 in 1978 to 1,020 in 1987 (or by 503.6 percent). In Flint, the number of juveniles arrested for narcotics laws violations increased from 36 in 1978 to 51 in 1987 (or by 41.6 percent). In Grand Rapids, the number of juveniles arrested for narcotics laws violations decreased from 51 in 1978 to 23 in 1987 (or by −45.1 percent). In Lansing, the number of juveniles arrested for narcotics laws violations increased from 3 in 1978 to 12 in 1987 (or by 300 percent). In Warren, the number of juveniles arrested for narcotics laws violations decreased from 68 in 1978 to 26 in 1987 (or by −38 percent) (Table 11-7).

Relationship Between Juvenile Drug Arrests and Arrests for Violent Crime

In the literature and in various newspapers, there have been numerous articles concerning the relationship between drugs and violent crime. For an examination of this issue, the Pearson Product Moment Correlation Coefficient (r) has been used in this paper in correlating juvenile narcotics arrests with juvenile arrests for crimes of violence in each of the five cities studied.

Correlations were done for the juvenile population (black, white, and total) for each of the five selected cities, for all five cities combined, and for all cities excluding Detroit (Flint, Grand Rapids, Lansing, and Warren). In addition to calculating (r), the percentage of variance that can be explained by the independent variable (narcotics laws violations) and its relationship to the arrests for various violent crimes was calculated (r^2).

[This percentage is ascertained by first calculating r-squared, which is the coefficient of determination. This is the proportion of variance in the dependent variable (violent crime arrests) accounted for or explained by the independent variable (narcotics laws violations arrests). The correlation coefficient (r^2) is then multiplied by 100 in order to give the percentage (Table 11-8). The results of the correlation coefficient do not imply that a causal relationship exists. They simply indicate the statistical significance of the association between the independent and dependent variables.]

Detroit

In Detroit, black juvenile arrests for narcotics laws violations were significant when correlated with arrests of black juveniles for murder and aggravated assault. With regard to murder, it was significant at the .01 level, and 81.0 percent of the arrests for murder were associated with arrests for narcotics laws violations. For arrests for aggravated assault, it was significant at the .01 level, and 64.0 percent of the arrests for aggravated assault were associated with arrests for narcotics laws violations. For white juveniles, there was a significant correlation for aggravated assault. It was significant at the .05 level, and 50.4 percent of the arrests were associated with arrests for narcotics laws violations.

In turning to the total juvenile population of Detroit, there was a correlation between arrests for narcotics laws violations and arrests for murder and aggravated assault. Both were significant at the .01 level. Eighty-three percent of the arrests for murder and 67.2 percent of the arrests for aggravated assault were associated with arrests for narcotics laws violations.

Flint

In Flint, there were no significant correlations when narcotics laws violations juvenile arrests were correlated with juvenile arrests for murder, rape, robbery, and aggravated assault.

Grand Rapids

In Grand Rapids, there was an inverse correlation between arrests for narcotics laws violations and arrests for rape for white juvenile males. It was significant at the .05 level of confidence. It appears that in Grand Rapids, the use, rather than the sale, of narcotics was the dominant reason for narcotics-related arrests (Table 11-9).

Table 11-8. Correlation between Juvenile Arrests for Narcotics Laws Violations and Juvenile Arrests for Crimes Against the Person, by Race, for 1978 to 1987, in Selected Michigan Cities

	Murder Arrests						Rape Arrests						Robbery Arrests						Aggravated Assault Arrests					
	r			Percentage $(r)^2$ x 100			r			Percentage $(r)^2$ x 100			r			Percentage $(r)^2$ x 100			r			Percentage $(r)^2$ x 100		
City	White	Black	Total	White	Black	Total	White	Black	Total	White	Black	Total	White	Black	Total	White	Black	Total	White	Black	Total	White	Black	Total
Detroit	.51	.90**	.91**	26.01	81.00	82.81	.44	.43	.43	19.36	18.49	18.49	.13	.08	.02	1.69	.64	.04	.71*	.80**	.82**	50.41	64.00	67.24
Flint	−.22	.34	.19	4.84	11.56	3.61	−.22	−.31	−.39	4.84	9.61	15.21	.16	0.00	−.17	2.56	0.00	2.89	−.29	.14	−.10	8.41	1.96	1.00
Grand Rapids	.04	.55	.05	.16	30.25	.25	−.68*	.06	−.45	46.24	0.36	20.25	.59	.29	.41	34.81	8.41	16.81	.02	.58	.10	0.04	33.64	1.00
Lansing	.33	−.17	.49	10.89	2.89	24.01	.31	.54	.43	9.61	29.16	18.49	−.08	.82**	.57	.64	67.24	32.49	.61	75*	.67*	37.21	56.25	44.89
Warren	−.20	.00	−.20	4.00	0.00	4.00	−.28	−.23	−.32	7.84	5.29	10.24	.43	.80**	.43	18.49	64.00	18.49	.15	.03	.17	2.25	.09	2.89
All Cities	.02	.92**	.91**	.04	84.64	82.81	−.73*	.40	.43	53.29	16.00	18.49	.52	.14	.61	27.04	1.96	37.21	.58	.84	.89**	33.64	70.56	79.21
All Cities Excluding Detroit	−.34	.59	−.13	11.56	34.81	1.69	.11	.11	−.68	1.21	1.21	46.24	.70*	.41	.39	49.00	16.81	15.21	.19	.75*	.08	3.61	56.25	.64

SOURCE: Computed by author from data in previous tables.

*Significant at .05 level

**Significant at .01 level

Race = black and white only

Table 11-9. Number and Percentage of Juvenile Arrests for Narcotics Laws Violations, by Use and Sale, by Year, by Race* and by Sex, for the Four Out-State Cities, 1978–1987

					White Male				White Female				Black Male				Black Female			
Year	City	Grand Total	Juvenile Total	Percent of Total	Sale	%	Use	%	Sale	%	Use	%	Sale	%	Use	%	Sale	%	Use	%
1978	Flint	350	36	10.3	2	5.6	19	52.8	1	2.8	1	2.8	5	13.9	8	22.2	0	.0	0	.0
	Grand Rapids	245	51	20.8	0	.0	41	80.4	0	.0	5	9.8	0	.0	3	5.9	1	2.0	0	.0
	Lansing	95	3	3.2	1	33.3	1	33.3	1	33.3	0	.0	0	.0	0	.0	0	.0	0	.0
	Warren	172	68	39.5	11	16.2	46	67.6	2	2.9	9	13.2	0	.0	0	.0	0	.0	0	.0
1979	Flint	345	30	8.7	3	10.2	18	60.0	0	.0	2	6.7	0	.0	7	23.3	0	.0	0	.0
	Grand Rapids	273	61	22.3	2	3.3	39	63.9	3	4.9	10	16.4	0	.0	4	6.6	0	.0	0	.0
	Lansing	24	2	8.3	0	.0	1	50.0	0	.0	1	50.0	0	.0	0	.0	0	.0	0	.0
	Warren	312	109	34.9	32	29.4	57	52.3	13	11.9	7	6.4	0	.0	0	.0	0	.0	0	.0
1980	Flint	430	27	6.3	1	3.7	12	44.4	0	.0	1	3.7	5	18.5	7	25.9	0	.0	1	3.7
	Grand Rapids	238	21	8.8	0	.0	17	81.0	0	.0	2	9.6	0	.0	1	4.8	0	.0	0	.0
	Lansing	17	1	5.9	0	.0	1	100.0	0	.0	0	.0	0	.0	0	.0	0	.0	0	.0
	Warren	198	42	21.2	14	33.3	23	54.8	2	4.8	3	7.1	0	.0	0	.0	0	.0	0	.0
1981	Flint	427	14	3.3	2	14.3	2	14.3	0	.0	1	7.1	6	42.9	1	7.1	0	.0	0	.0
	Grand Rapids	354	31	8.8	1	3.2	17	54.8	1	3.2	1	3.2	1	3.2	5	16.1	0	.0	2	6.4
	Lansing	61	5	8.2	5	100.0	0	.0	0	.0	0	.0	0	.0	0	.0	0	.0	0	.0
	Warren	334	70	21.0	11	15.7	43	61.4	7	10.0	8	11.4	0	.0	0	.0	0	.0	1	1.4
1982	Flint	266	12	4.5	2	16.7	5	41.7	0	.0	0	.0	3	25.0	1	8.3	1	8.3	0	.0
	Grand Rapids	496	44	8.9	11	25.0	18	40.9	4	9.1	3	6.9	0	.0	7	15.9	0	.0	1	2.3
	Lansing	34	1	2.9	0	.0	1	100.0	0	.0	0	.0	0	.0	0	.0	0	.0	0	.0
	Warren	159	25	15.7	5	20.0	13	52.0	2	8.0	5	20.0	0	.0	0	.0	0	.0	0	.0

1983	Flint	309	9	2.9	1	11.1	4	44.4	0	.0	0	.0	2	22.2	1	11.1	0	.0	0	.0
	Grand Rapids	609	22	3.6	9	40.9	4	18.2	1	4.5	1	4.5	0	.0	6	27.3	0	.0	1	4.5
	Lansing	33	0	.0	0	.0	0	.0	0	.0	0	.0	0	.0	0	.0	0	.0	0	.0
	Warren	139	38	27.3	9	23.7	22	55.3	0	.0	7	18.4	0	.0	1	2.6	0	.0	0	.0
1984	Flint	484	28	5.8	0	.0	5	17.9	0	.0	0	.0	18	64.3	4	14.3	1	3.6	0	.0
	Grand Rapids	416	15	3.6	0	.0	8	53.3	0	.0	0	.0	0	.0	6	40.0	0	.0	0	.0
	Lansing	67	0	.0	0	.0	0	.0	0	.0	0	.0	0	.0	0	.0	0	.0	0	.0
	Warren	142	22	15.5	5	22.7	16	72.7	1	4.5	0	.0	0	.0	0	.0	0	.0	0	.0
1985	Flint	390	25	6.4	0	.0	5	20.0	1	4.0	1	4.0	7	28.0	9	36.0	1	4.0	0	.0
	Grand Rapids	551	65	11.8	26	40.0	12	18.5	5	7.7	4	6.2	4	6.2	9	13.8	0	.0	0	.0
	Lansing	94	5	5.3	2	40.0	2	40.0	0	.0	0	.0	1	20.0	0	.0	0	.0	0	.0
	Warren	111	18	16.2	0	.0	12	66.7	2	11.1	4	22.2	0	.0	0	.0	0	.0	0	.0
1986	Flint	572	21	3.7	0	.0	2	9.5	0	.0	0	.0	7	33.3	9	42.9	2	9.5	0	.0
	Grand Rapids	509	35	6.9	20	57.1	2	5.7	0	.0	1	2.9	6	17.1	5	14.3	0	.0	1	2.9
	Lansing	57	5	8.8	1	20.0	1	20.0	1	20.0	0	.0	1	20.0	1	20.0	0	.0	0	.0
	Warren	259	27	10.4	1	3.7	19	70.4	0	.0	0	.0	0	.0	0	.0	0	.0	0	.0
1987	Flint	636	51	8.0	2	3.9	4	7.8	0	.0	0	.0	26	51.0	16	31.4	1	2.0	2	3.9
	Grand Rapids	571	23	4.0	1	4.3	17	73.9	0	.0	1	4.3	1	4.3	3	13.0	0	.0	0	.0
	Lansing	121	12	9.9	2	16.7	2	16.7	1	8.3	2	16.7	1	8.3	1	8.3	0	.0	1	8.3
	Warren	308	26	8.4	4	15.4	21	80.8	0	.0	1	3.8	0	.0	0	.0	0	.0	0	.0

SOURCE: Central Records Division of the Crime Reporting Section, Michigan Department of State Police.

*This includes black and white only.

Lansing

In Lansing, there was a correlation between juvenile arrests for narcotics laws violations and juvenile arrests for robbery and for aggravated assault for blacks. In terms of the correlation with regard to robbery, it was significant at the .01 level, and 67.2 percent of the arrests for robbery were associated with arrests for narcotics laws violations. For aggravated assault, it was significant at the .05 level, and 56.3 percent of the arrests for aggravated assault were associated with narcotics laws violations. For the total juvenile population, there was a correlation between arrests for narcotics laws violations and for aggravated assault. It was significant at the .05 level and 44.9 percent of the arrests for aggravated assault were associated with arrests for narcotics laws violations.

Warren

In Warren, there was a correlation for black males between juvenile arrests for narcotics laws violations and juvenile arrests for robbery. It was significant at the .01 level, and 64.0 percent of the arrests for robbery were associated with arrests for narcotics laws violations.

All Five Cities

When all five cities were viewed in terms of their black juvenile population, there were significant correlations at the .01 level for arrests for murder. Of the arrests for murder, 84.6 percent were associated with arrests for narcotics laws violations. For white juveniles, there was a significant negative correlation (at the .05 level) for rape. This negative correlation phenomenon seems to be true for white (but not black) juveniles. With regard to the total juvenile population there were correlations for arrests for murder and for aggravated assault at the .01 level. Of the arrests for murder, 82.8 percent, and of the arrests for aggravated assault, 79.2 percent were associated with arrests for narcotics laws violations.

Four Out-State Cities

In viewing the four out-state cities, in terms of the black juvenile population, there was a correlation for aggravated assault at the .05 level. Of the juvenile arrests for aggravated assault, 56.25 percent were associated with arrests for narcotics laws violations. For white juveniles, there was a significant correlation for robbery. It was significant at the .05 level, and 49.0 percent of the arrests were associated with arrests for narcotics laws violations.

Conclusions

This chapter has presented a review of selected literature related to the problem of young black offenders—particularly those arrested for violent crimes. The review included research on the possible relationship between the general development of delinquency and such factors as unstable family environment, poor educational opportunities, poverty, and the usage and selling of drugs.

The literature review was followed by a presentation of information on the number of total arrests and of juvenile arrests in the five largest cities in the State of Michigan. Data on arrests of juveniles for narcotics laws violations and arrests of juveniles for violent crimes were examined to assess the possible relationships between the two types of criminal behavior.

For violent crimes, the number of arrests for both the total population and the juvenile population has been on the rise from 1978 to 1987 in the five largest cities in Michigan. For narcotics laws violations, the number of arrests has also shown an increase for the total population. The number of arrests for juveniles, however, has increased in Detroit and Flint and has decreased in Grand Rapids and Warren. The data also showed an increase in Lansing, although the number of arrests was relatively small (increasing from 3 in 1978 to 12 in 1987).

The problem of the young black offender must be addressed by both the public and the private sectors, using multiple strategies: strengthening the family, providing equal high-quality educational opportunities, reducing poverty, and controlling the usage and the sale of narcotics.

REFERENCES

Associated Press. "Traffic and Drugs: Dealers, Victims, Younger Every Day." *Lansing State Journal*, February 2, 1989, page 3A.

Benson, Robert C. and Oliver Schroeder, Jr. *Homicide in an Urban Community*. Springfield, Illinois: Thomas, 1960.

Beverly, Creigs C. "Black Crime in Michigan." *The State of Black Michigan*, Urban Affairs Programs, Michigan State University, East Lansing and the Michigan Council of Urban League Executives, 1988, p. 23.

Blau, Judith R. and Peter M. Blau. "The Costs of Inequity: Metropolitan Structure and Violent Crime." *American Sociological Review* 47, pp. 114–129, 1982.

Census of Population, 1980. General Population Characteristics, Vol. 1, Part 24, Table 25, Michigan.

Central Records Division of the Crime Reporting Section, Michigan Department of State Police.

Cernkovich, Steven A. and Peggy C. Giordano. "Family Relationships and Delinquency." *Criminology*, 25, 2, 1987, p. 297.

Chambers, Carl D. "Narcotic Addiction and Crime: An Empirical Review." In James A. Inciaridi and Carl D. Chambers (eds.), *Drugs and the Criminal Justice System*. Beverly Hills, CA: Sage Publications, 1974, pp. 125–142.

Daniels, Lee A. "Ranks of Black Men Shrink on U.S. Campuses." *New York Times*, February 5, 1989, pages 1 and 15.

Farnworth, Margaret. "Family Structure, Family Attributes, and Delinquency in a Sample of Low Income Minority Males and Females." *Journal of Youth and Adolescence*, Vol. 13, No. 4, 1984, pp. 362–363.

Featherman, D. "Schooling and Occupational Careers: Constancy and Change in Worldly Success." In Orville Brim, Jr., and Jerome Kagan (eds.) *Constancy and Change in Human Development*. Cambridge, Massachusetts: Harvard University Press, 1980.

Fiqueira-McDonough, Josefina. "School Context, Gender, and Delinquency," *Journal of Youth and Adolescence*, Vol. 15, No. 1, 1986.

Fischer, Donald G. "Parental Supervision and Delinquency." *Perceptual and Motor Skills*, 1983, 56, pp. 635–640.

Fischer, Donald G. "Family Size and Delinquency." *Perceptual and Motor Skills*, 1984, 58, pp. 532–533.

Gandossy, Robert P., Jay R. Williams, Jo Cohen, and Henrick J. Hardwood. *Drugs and Crime.* U.S. Government Printing Office, Washington, D.C., May 1980, p. 52.

Gannett News Service. "Washington Withers in Terror of Drugs, Violence," *Lansing State Journal*, February 20, 1989, p. 3A.

Garbarino, James and Charles Asp. *Successful Schools and Competent Students.* Lexington, Massachusetts: Lexington Books, 1981.

Glueck, Sheldon and Eleanor Glueck. *Unraveling Juvenile Delinquency*, New York: The Commonwealth Fund, 1950.

Good, David H., Maureen A. Peirog-Good, and Robin C. Scales. "An Analysis of Youth Crime and Employment Patterns." *Journal of Quantitative Criminology*, Vol. 2, No. 3, 1986, pp. 219–236.

Greenberg, Keith, Steven A. Jay, and Jeanne Dequine. "Drug Arrests Soar." *USA Today*, February 6, 1989.

Hawkins, Darnell F. "Black and White Homicide Differentials." Criminal Justice and Behavior, Vol. 10, No. 4, December 1983, p. 433.

Innes, Christopher A. "Drug Use and Crime." *Journal of Justice Statistics*, Special Report, U.S. Department of Justice, July 1988, p. 1.

Johnson, Richard E. "Mother's versus Father's Role in Causing Delinquency." *Adolescence*, Vol. XXII, No. 86, Summer 1987, p. 313.

Krohn, Marvin D. "Inequality, Unemployment and Crime: A Cross-National Analysis." *The Sociological Quarterly*, 17, Summer 1976, p. 313.

Loftin, Colin and Robert Nash Parker. "An Errors-In-Variable Model of the Effect of Poverty on Urban Homicide Rates." *Criminology*, Vol. 23, #2, p. 281, 1985.

Messner, Steven F. "Poverty, Inequity and the Urban Homicide Rate: Some Unexpected Findings." *Criminology*, 20, pp. 102–114, 1982.

Miller, W. P. B. "Lower Class Culture as a Generating Milieu of Gang Delinquency." *Journal of Social Issues*, 1959, 15, pp. 15–19.

Moynihan, Daniel P. *The Negro Family: The Case for National Action.* U.S. Department of Labor, Washington, D.C., 1959.

Nadelmann, Ethan A. "The Case for Legalization." *The Public Interest*, No. 2, Summer 1988, p. 16.

Roberts, Harrell B. *The Inner World of a Black Juvenile Delinquent.* Hillsdale, New Jersey: Lawrence Erlbaum Associates, Publishers, 1987, p. 116.

Robins, L. N., P. A. West, and B. Herjanic. "Arrests and Delinquency in Two Generations: A Study of Black Families and Their Children." *Journal of Child Psychology and Psychiatry*, 1975, 16, pp. 125–140.

Schmid, Calvin and Stanton E. Schmid. *Crime in the State of Washington.* Olympia, Washington: Washington Law and Justice Planning Office, Washington State Planning and Community Affairs Agency, 1972.

Shanock, Shelly S. and Dorothy O. Lewis. "Juvenile Court Versus Guidance Referral: Psychosocial and Parental Factors." *American Journal of Psychology*, 1977, 134, pp. 1130–1133.

Smith, Dwayne and Robert Nash Parker. "Type of Homicide and Variation in Regional Rates." *Social Forces*, 59, 1980, p. 136.

Steinberg, Laurence. *Adolescents.* Alfred A. Knopf, New York, 1985, p. 392.

Stern, Marilyn, John E. Lorthman, and Michael R. Vanslyck. "Father's Absence and Adolescent Problem Behavior: Alcohol Consumption, Drug Use, and Sexual Activity." *Adolescence*, 1984, 19, pp. 301–312.

Stevens, Richard C. and Rosalind D. Ellis. "Narcotics Addicts and Crime: Analysis of Recent Transperiod." *Criminology*, Vol. 12, 1975, pp. 474–488.

Thornberry, Terence P., Melanie Moore, and R. L. Christenson. "The Effect of Dropping Out of High School on Subsequent Criminal Behavior." *Criminology*, Vol. 23, No. 1., 1985.

Ventura, Stephanie J. "Selected Vital and Health Statistics in Poverty and Non-Poverty Areas of Nineteen Large Cities, United States, 1969–71." *Vital and Health Statistics*, Series 21, No. 26, Rockville, Maryland: U.S. Department of Health, Education and Welfare, 1975.

Wolfgang, Marvin E. *Patterns in Criminal Homicide*, Philadelphia: University of Pennsylvania Press, 1958.

Ward, Sam. "Cities High on Drug Violence." *USA Today*, February 6, 1989, p. 1.

CHAPTER 12

Black Crime in Michigan: Past and Present

Homer C. Hawkins

Introduction

Black crime in the 21st century continues to be a matter of grave concern for all Michigan residents. Blacks comprise 14.3% of Michigan's population, yet a disproportionate percentage of blacks is being arrested for crimes (U.S. Census Bureau 2000). This chapter assesses the nature and changes in black crime in Michigan between 1972 and 2004. Attention is given to the differences that exist between whites and blacks relative to crime. Special attention is paid to arrest rates, the victims of crime, the causes of crime, and treatment by the police and courts. In addition, the prison system is examined.

Arrest Rates

Tables 12-1 through 12-5 present data on the numbers and percentages of blacks arrested for index crimes[1] in Michigan. Numbers and percentages are examined for blacks for the time period 1972 through 2004[2] (Michigan State Police 1972, 1977, 1981, 1984, 1994, 1998, 2000, 2004).

The number of blacks and whites arrested for crimes involving murder showed a decline over this time period (Table 12-1). There was a very large decline in total murders between 2000 and 2004. This was reflected in substantial declines for both blacks and whites. The percentage of blacks arrested for murder went down from 2000 to 2004 and the percentage of whites went up. The number of arrests of blacks and whites for forcible

[1]Index crimes include the following: murder rape, robbery, aggravated assault, burglary, larceny, auto theft, and arson.

[2]There was not a racial breakdown available prior to 1972.

Table 12-1. Number of Persons, Black and White,[a] Arrested for Murder and Percentage of Total Persons, Black and White, Arrested for Murder in Michigan, 1972–2004

Year	Total	Black	% Black	White	% White
1972	714	476	66.7	230	32.2
1977	815	597	73.3	206	25.3
1981	873	667	76.3	195	22.3
1984	1,024	802	78.3	214	20.9
1994	1,674	1,342	80.2	311	18.6
1998	1,514	1,287	85.0	214	14.1
2000	1,316	1,136	86.3	175	13.3
2004	385	311	80.8	70	18.2

[a]Numbers and percentages for "other" minorities are not shown.

rape, robbery and aggravate assault declined over the time period. For rape there was a big decline in the percentage for blacks and a substantial increase for whites (Table 12-2). For robbery there was a moderate decline for blacks and whites (Table 12-3). Form a percentage standpoint there was a slight decline for blacks and a moderate increase for whites. For aggravated assault, the numbers and percentages dropped for blacks (Table 12-4). For, whites the numbers went up, as did the percentages. Turning to property crimes (larceny, burglary, auto theft and arson), the numbers for blacks declined over the time period, as did the percentages (Table 12-5). The numbers and percentages for whites remained fairly constant.

For the state as a whole, then, blacks were arrested for a higher number and percentage of violent crimes than whites (except for rape for whites) and whites were arrested for a higher number and percentage of property crimes. For all of these comparisons it should be remembered that blacks comprise 14.3% of the total population of Michigan.

Table 12-2. Number of Persons, Black and White,[a] Arrested for Rape and Percentage of Total Persons, Black and White, Arrested for Rape in Michigan, 1972–2004

Year	Total	Black	% Black	White	% White
1972	862	351	40.7	514	59.6
1977	1,347	707	52.5	622	46.2
1981	1,751	1,082	61.8	635	36.3
1984	2,373	1,382	58.3	967	40.6
1994	1,971	1,118	56.7	819	41.6
1998	1,574	749	47.6	792	50.3
2000	1,428	726	50.8	679	47.5
2004	1,160	358	30.7	766	66.0

[a]Numbers and percentages for "other" minorities are not shown.

Table 12-3. Number of Persons, Black and White,[a] Arrested for Robbery and Percentage of Total Persons, Black and White, Arrested for Robbery in Michigan, 1972–2004

Year	Total	Black	% Black	White	% White
1972	4,778	3,247	67.9	1,508	31.6
1977	4,310	2,890	67.1	1,389	32.2
1981	4,705	3,625	77.0	1,028	21.8
1984	5,383	4,267	79.2	1,093	20.3
1994	4,735	3,839	81.1	818	17.3
1998	3,343	2,554	76.4	759	22.7
2000	3,015	2,345	78.1	635	21.1
2004	2,376	1,696	71.4	657	27.7

[a]Numbers and percentages for "other" minorities are not shown.

Table 12-4. Number of Persons, Black and White,[a] Arrested for Aggravated Assault and Percentage of Total Persons, Black and White, Arrested for Aggravated Assault in Michigan, 1972–2004

Year	Total	Black	% Black	White	% White
1971	6,103	2,700	44.2	3,288	53.9
1977	6,987	2,935	42.4	3,950	56.5
1981	8,695	4,201	47.9	4,190	47.1
1984	9,644	4,813	49.9	4,650	48.2
1994	15,241	8,273	54.3	6,659	43.7
1998	14,682	8,385	57.1	6,078	41.4
1999	12,245	7,156	58.4	4,919	40.2
2004	11,205	5,925	52.9	5,974	53.3

[a]Numbers and percentages for "other" minorities are not shown.

Table 12-5. Number of Persons, Black and White,[a] Arrested for Property Crimes and Percentage of Total Persons, Black and White, Arrested for Property Crimes in Michigan, 1972–2004

Year	Total	Black	% Black	White	% White
1972	64,570	19,319	29.9	44,239	68.6
1977	62,441	20,199	32.3	42,296	67.7
1981	65,067	25,429	39.8	37,921	58.3
1984	60,999	24,057	39.4	35,495	58.2
1994	50,513	20,421	40.4	25,795	55.9
1998	38,906	15,403	39.6	22,459	57.7
2000	35,129	13,962	39.7	20,434	58.2
2004	37,639	13,087	34.8	22,649	60.2

[a]Numbers and percentages for "other" minorities are not shown.

Victims of Crime

People tend to commit crimes against persons who live closest to them. The housing situation in urban Michigan continues to be segregated. Thus, most blacks live in mostly black neighborhoods, and most whites in mostly white neighborhoods. Given this reality, it is clear why the victims and offenders are usually of the same race. In the case of blacks, close proximity, unemployment, and poverty interact to result in a higher percentage of black victims of crime.

The data for 1993 show that approximately 70% of the victims of confirmed murders in Michigan were black. In 2000, this figure remained constant (Michigan State Police 1994, 2000). This is in line with statistics nationwide. On the national level murder is the leading cause of death for young black males and one of the leading causes for young black females (Petersilla 1983). More than two decades later the situation that existed in 1983 in Michigan continues to be about the same. In 2004, 69.4 percent of the victims of murder were black (Michigan State Police 2004). The newspapers nationwide and in Michigan constantly focus on drive-by shootings and accidental shootings of individuals in the line of fire. What is clear to the author is that one can assume that in the case of drive-by shootings in our urban areas, the perpetrators will probably be black and the victims will also be black. Our urban areas are becoming killing grounds and the process seems to be a self-inflicted genocide. The biggest enemy for a young black male in our urban areas is usually another young black male. The drive-by shootings and random killings lead to other drive-by shootings and random killings in retaliation. Another fact that seems to come to the forefront is that the perpetrators of violence are getting younger and younger, and the weapon of choice is usually some form of handgun (Michigan State Police 2004, 16).

Our urban areas appear to be becoming war zones where gunfire is a daily occurrence. Most black youths either know or are related to someone who has been killed by a handgun. Homicide by handgun is becoming an epidemic in the black urban population. This is a problem for which no end is in sight.

What all this suggests is that individuals who are black, are poor, and live in the inner city have an increased probability of being victimized by violent crime. In addition, the victimizer in most cases will also be black.

Causes of Crime

The causes of crime have been explored and discussed many times. Issues such as unemployment, poverty, and lack of education are those most mentioned. There is an interaction among these factors, and they cannot be viewed as isolated phenomena. For people who are undereducated, the possibility of being unemployed is greatly increased. Quite naturally, unemployment leads to poverty. Deteriorating neighborhoods in the cities of Michigan and the United States are breeding grounds for crime. Crime evolves from the various kinds of discrimination that most affect the black population.

Urban crime is entwined with the socioeconomic situation that exists in our country. When people have no jobs, they do what they feel they have to do to survive. Often this means committing crimes. The unemployed are more highly motivated to commit crimes because they are out of work and have financial needs (Paternoster and Bushway 2001). A critical point is that blacks are at the bottom of the economic ladder. The kinds of jobs held by many urban blacks are those most affected by negative economic swings. These are the so-called service-related jobs. In these kinds of jobs, the work force tends not to be unionized and is subject to more layoffs when business slows. Minority populations disproportionately occupy unstable, low-wage jobs, and are most affected during economic downturns (D. M. Smith, Devine, and Sheley 1992). Blacks often fall victim to the sequence of last hired, first fired. In addition, urban blacks seem to be disproportionately affected by plant closings. This means that blacks are often faced with the fact that the possibility of employment does not exist.

At the present time, the unemployment situation in Michigan has improved for blacks but their rate of unemployment is still significantly higher than that for whites. Unemployment statistics reveal that the unemployment rate for the black population in Michigan is over two and a half times that for the white population. The gap between whites and blacks is still quite significant, but there has been some improvement over the last few years. The annual average unemployment rate in 1985 was 7.6% for whites and 27.8% for blacks. In 1991, the respective figures were 5.8% and 16.8% (U.S. Department of Labor, Bureau of Labor Statistics 1985, 1991). The respective figures were 4.7% and12.8% in 2000 (U.S Census Bureau 2000) and 5.8% and 14.4% in 2004 (U.S. Department of Labor, Bureau of Labor Statistics 2004). Thus the data indicate that the situation for whites has fluctuated slightly over the period discussed and the situation for blacks has improved; however, the gap between whites and blacks remains quite wide. Spohn and Holleran (2000) note that young black and Hispanic males face greater odds of incarceration than middle-aged white males, and unemployed black and Hispanics are substantially more likely to be sentenced to prison than employed white males. Other research has found that blacks, males, and offenders with low levels of education and income receive substantially longer sentences (Mustard 2001). Other research notes that criminal behavior is influenced by lack of income, job experiences, and perception of a blocked opportunity structure.

While labor market conditions and reactions to those conditions have some affect on crime, findings tend to suggest that long periods of unemployment, job experiences, and a lack of income work in tandem with anger and external to increase criminal activities (Baron and Hartnagel 1997). Numerous other studies focusing on sentencing suggest that race and ethnicity do play an important role in contemporary sentencing decisions. Black and Hispanic offenders, particularly those who are young, male, or unemployed, receive longer sentences or differential benefits from guidelines departures than do similarly situated white offenders (Free 1997; Spohn and Holleran 2000).

With respect to poverty in Michigan, blacks are far worse off than whites. In terms of numbers and percentages, in 1989 there were 717,111 whites below the poverty level, or 9.4%. For blacks, the number was 419,921, or 33.7%. The percentage of blacks below the poverty level was more than three and one-half times that of whites (U.S. Census Bureau 1990). In 1999 the respective figures were 338,492, or 25.2%, for blacks and 925,057, or 7.5%, for whites (U.S. Census Bureau 2000). Though the overall situation has improved, the difference between whites and blacks is quite evident.

The risks of incarceration are highly stratified by education. Among black men born between 1965 and 1969, 30% of those without a college education and nearly 60% of high school dropouts went to prison by 1999. The novel pervasiveness of imprisonment indicates the emergence of incarceration as a new stage in the life course of young, low-skilled black men. Mass imprisonment among recent birth cohorts of noncollege black men challenges one to include the criminal justice system among the key institutional influences on American social inequality (Pettit and Western 2004). Increasing crime among low-educated black and Hispanic men is often seen to result from declining economic opportunities for unskilled workers. Bourgois (1995) made this point in his study of gang activity. Using census and FBI data, Lochner and Moretti (2004) added to this when they found that schooling significantly reduced the probability of incarceration or arrest.

Environment has a great deal to do with an individual's life chances. In the areas of employment, income, and education, blacks are at a deficit compared to their white counterparts. These factors are interrelated and must be viewed in this context. A poor education leads to limited employment possibilities and limited income. Unemployment is a way of life for the undereducated black living below the poverty level. Many times individuals act in a desperate manner when they view their situation as being desperate. Young blacks in the ghetto feel that their chances of getting jobs and pulling themselves out of poverty are minimal. Oftentimes the young black person has less than a high school education, and this means that the only kind of job, if any, that can be secured is entry level. When the economic situation is not good, even this kind of job is hard to find.

The Criminal Justice System

In this examination of blacks in the criminal justice system, the focus is on the police, the court system, and the prison setting. These questions are addressed: Are there differences for blacks versus whites in treatment by police? Are there differences for blacks versus whites in the length of sentences for the same kinds of crimes? and What kinds of changes have taken place in the prison system in the last 20 years?

Police

Affirmative action programs have increased the percentage of black officers on police forces across the nation. This increase has led to a lessening of the discussion of the practice of racism by white police officers.

More attention is being focused on the prevention of crime in the black community than was the case a few years ago. It should be noted, however, that there is still some concern about the interaction between white officers and blacks in the ghetto. For example, a white police officer may have some unfavorable experiences with blacks on a few occasions and may, therefore, come to the conclusion that all blacks in the ghetto are dangerous. When police officers begin to think in this manner, their response to black suspects will be different. Differential treatment on the part of white police officers leads to difficulty between the white police officer and the black community.

With regard to this issue, some may argue that since there is more crime in the black community, a police officer must be aware of this and must view contact in the ghetto as being potentially more dangerous than contact in the suburban white community. Crime rates in the black community are high, and the police officer must act accordingly. This issue is a double-edged sword. The black community is concerned about police brutality, but it is also concerned about crime in our urban areas. The police prevent a continued escalation of black-on-black violence. It is clear that police brutality cannot be tolerated, but police interaction in the community is critical.

Police officers often feel that going into the black community is like going into a war zone, and they need to protect themselves. When a white police officer goes into the black community with this kind of posture, the response of blacks often will be negative. This negative response will then reinforce the police officer's view that blacks are dangerous. Brown and Frank (2005) note that black suspects are more likely than whites to be arrested in lieu of receiving a citation when the interaction with the officer is traffic-related. They go on to note that black suspects were more than 15 times more likely than whites to be arrested rather than cited. Citizens, particularly minority citizens, may be more likely to believe and make allegations that formal processing in the form of a citation is the result of police bias; indeed, the politicized nature of racial profiling has empowered citizens, and allegations of such conduct are acted on more often than in the past (Fridell et al. 2001). Although the process is cyclic and both sides are to blame, the pendulum probably swings more toward law enforcement's lack of tolerance when it comes to the negative feelings that exist between white police officers and the black community.

Sentencing Procedures

Are blacks treated differently from whites in the courts? Petersilla (1983) investigated the criminal justice systems of California, Michigan, and Texas and found that judges tend to impose heavier sentences on Hispanics and blacks than on whites convicted of comparable felonies and with similar criminal records. She found that in California, the average sentence was 5 months longer for Hispanics and 2.4 months longer for blacks than for whites. In Michigan the sentences averaged 1.7 months longer for blacks. (Petersilla did not give any data on Hispanics in Michigan because of the small sample size). In Texas sentences averaged 7.7 months longer for blacks and 8.1 months longer for Hispanics.

As we move into the 1990s the issue relative to sentencing may be changing, at least in California. Klein, Petersilla, and Turner (1990) note:

> Taken together, our findings indicate that California courts are making racially equitable sentencing decisions. The racial disparities apparent in the in/out decision are not evidence of discrimination in sentencing—once we control for relevant crime, prior record, and process variables. This finding held for of the six prime studies (assault, robbery, burglary, theft, and forgery). Drug crimes were the exception; Latinos faced a higher probability of imprisonment. We found no evidence of racial discrimination in the length of prison terms imposed for any of the crimes studied.

It is also clear that the other variables are not proxies for race—that is, they are not masking what are actually racially influenced decisions. Moreover, sentencing decisions were predictable, even though our database contained some of the many variables that can be considered legally in imposing criminal sentences.

The issue presented by the above authors presents a new viewpoint, but this view does not go unchallenged, as noted by Heaney (1992):

> It appears that three factors are important in the longer sentences for young black males. The first factor is the weight given to criminal history, even when the criminal history involves prior arrests for relatively minor offenses. Unfortunately, because of conditions in the inner city, a young black male is likely to have a longer criminal record than his white counterpart in the suburbs. Second, a gram of crack is given 100 times the weight as a gram of powder cocaine. . . . Even if crack is cheaper and more addictive, is it 100 times worse; because crack may be the inner city drug of choice, this distinction can reduce harsher sentences for black crack offenders than for white traffickers in powder cocaine. Third, many communities concentrate their law enforcement activities in the inner city. Certainly strict law enforcement in the inner city should be encouraged, but law enforcement in and of itself cannot solve the inner city drug problem.

The race effect and the disadvantage experienced by black defendants is often strongly represented in drug offenses and in property crimes that have relatively high white victimization rates (larceny, burglary) (Crawford, Chiricos, and Kleck 1998).

A lot has been written discussing the intersection of race and crime. In most of these discussions race signifies African American, and issues of disproportionate incarceration and arrests are the most familiar starting points (Wolpert 1999). Zimring, Eigen, and O'Malley (1976) suggest that society places a higher value on whites than on blacks. They note that blacks receive sentences of life imprisonment or death more than twice as often when the murder victim is white rather than black. In analyzing patterns of capital punishment in Louisiana, M. D. Smith (1988) found that a pattern of discrimination by race of victim, but not by race of offender, existed, even when a number of legal and extralegal factors were controlled. Amsterdam (1988) pointed out, in a study of the death penalty in Georgia, that it was less important to know whether or not an individual committed a homicide in the first place than to know whether, if he or she did kill, the victim was white or black. Forty percent of Georgia homicide cases involved white victims; in 87% of the cases in which a death penalty was imposed, the victim was white. White-victim cases are almost 11 times more likely to produce a death penalty than are black-victim cases. In 2000, there were 3,593 prisoners on death row. Of that number, 1,535, or 42%, were black. Again, this should be viewed in light of the fact that blacks comprise 14.3% of the population in the United States (Bureau of Justice Statistics, U.S. Department of Justice 2001).

In viewing sentencing guideline standards, blacks have experienced some adverse effects. The mandatory minimum statutes have had an adverse effect on blacks and this is corroborated by the literature. Research shows that blacks are more likely than whites to be convicted under mandatory minimum provisions in sentencing guidelines and more likely than whites to be sentenced to the indicated mandatory minimum or above. Much of this disparity is apparently a consequence of the differential treatment accorded crack cocaine offenders. The disparity in sentencing involving crack versus powder cocaine has recently been investigated by the U.S. Sentencing Commission (Free 1997).

Another study pointed to the fact that homicide cases involving black defendants and white victims fared worse than any other racial combination. They were more likely to result in first-degree murder charges and to proceed to capital trial (Sorensen and Wallace 1999). It was found that blacks convicted of cocaine offenses and Hispanics convicted of cocaine and marijuana offenses were sentenced more harshly than white offenders (Herbert 1997).

Unnever, Fraser, and Henretta (1980) suggest that bias can be found in some places and times and not in others, and it may be expressed outside the public view. They note that it is important for sociologists to take into account the possibility of discrimination in criminal courts and to be aware that recommendations by court officials can function as a way in which racial bias and sentencing is introduced. Armour (1998) reflects on the concept of a black tax in the American justice system. The prominence of stereotypes means that black people pay a price when they are in the presence of whites. The nonnegotiable inflation-proof cost borne by African Americans is discrimination. Hawkins (2006) noted some interesting findings in his comparison of sentencing data from 1996 and 2001. When all crimes as a group[3] were examined for both years, blacks received longer sentences than their white counterparts.

The Prison System

The Michigan prison system has changed a great deal over the last two decades. From an educational standpoint there has been a decline. The Department of Corrections budget has risen to more than $1.7 billion and the prison population has quadrupled over the past two decades. However, there has not been enough of a budgetary commitment to education. The education program expansion has not kept pace with the inmate population explosion. A brief look at the past two decades speaks to this issue.

1984

Recidivism has been a factor in the increase in the prison population. Recidivism is a problem that must be dealt with if the prison population is to be reduced. To lower the rate of recidivism, rehabilitation is necessary. The Michigan Department of Corrections had a number of programs, both academic and vocational, which were geared toward the rehabilitation of prison residents. (Michigan Department of Corrections 1984) (Table 12-6). Based on the number and kind of programs offered, it was clear that the Department of Corrections had a commitment to rehabilitation. It is clear, however, that programs for inmates did not keep pace with the increase in the prison population. There was a big increase in basic education, grades 0–8, and in GED (general education development; high school diploma equivalency) preparation. However, there has been a decline in the college academic program. Basic education, grades 0–8, has been the program that has kept pace with the increase in the prison population. Two aspects of the academic program that need special attention are GED preparation and the college components. In December 1984, the Michigan prison population was 14,604. Of that number, 1,274, or 8.7%, were in the GED preparation component

[3]All crimes are representative of every court disposition that resulted in a sentence.

Table 12-6. Michigan Department of Corrections Institutional Program Statistics: November 30, 1984

Program	Total Residents
Basic Education 0–8	1,286
GED Preparation	1,274
Life Role Competency	590
Chapter I. Remedial Math and Reading	340
College-Academic	1,646
Vocational	1,628
On-the-job training and apprenticeships	224

SOURCE: Michigan Department of Corrections (1984).

and 1,646, or 11.3%, were in the college academic component (see Table 12-7) (Michigan Department of Corrections 1984).

1991

In December 1991, the prison population was 36,019, and of that number, 2,213, or 6.1%, were in the GED preparation component and 2,237, or 6.2%, were in the college academic component, which represented a decline from 8.7% in 1984 (Michigan Department of Corrections 1991, 136–137). The GED preparation component was of critical importance because with a GED certificate a resident could be admitted into a degree program in a community college or a four-year college. There were a number of community colleges and four-year institutions that had academic programs in various correctional facilities across the state. Table 12-8 identifies each college and community college and the correctional facility that housed its programs. Community colleges and four-year institutions offered the prison resident the opportunity to obtain an associate and/or baccalaureate degree. The community colleges and four-year institutions were spread all over the state and served various camps and institutions on a statewide basis.

Table 12-7. Michigan Department of Corrections Institutional Program Statistics: November 1991

Program	Total Residents
Basic Education 0–8	3,069
GED Preparation	2,213
Life Role Competency	524
Chapter I. Remedial Math and Reading	210
College-Academic	2,237
Vocational	1,742
On-the-job training and apprenticeships	224

SOURCE: Michigan Department of Corrections (1991).

Table 12-8. Postsecondary Educational Institutions with Programs in Michigan Correctional Facilities, 1993

Educational Institution		Correctional Facility	
Name	Location	Name	Location
Jackson Community College	Jackson	State Prison of Southern Michigan	Jackson
		Egler Correctional Facility	Jackson
Kellogg Community College	Battle Creek	Crane Women's Facility	Coldwater
Kirtland Community College	Roscommon	Camp Lehman	Grayling
Montcalm Community College	Sidney	Marquette	Marquette
		Michigan Reformatory	Ionia
		Scott Correctional Facility	Plymouth
Spring Arbor College	Spring Arbor	State Prison of Southern Michigan	Jackson
		Egler Correctional Facility	Jackson
		Scott Correctional Facility	Plymouth
Western Michigan University	Kalamazoo	Scott Correctional Facility	Plymouth

SOURCE: G. Rivers, Administrator, Michigan Department of Corrections.

2004

By the end of 2004 the Michigan prison population had risen to 48,883. Of that number, 21,509, or 44%, were white and 25,908, or 53%, were black. The Department of Correction's total appropriations for fiscal 2004 was $1,705,772,500 (Michigan Department of Corrections 2004, 29, 66). It should also be noted that in fiscal year 2000 the Department of Corrections received 15.4% of the state general revenue funding, up from 3% in 1980 (Michigan Department of Corrections 2000).

The community college and four-year institution programs came to a halt in the mid-1990s. The Pell Grant Program that paid for inmates' tuition was discontinued (Home Box Office 1996). For all intents and purposes the associate and baccalaureate possibilities are almost nonexistent at this point in time. In 2000, approximately 22% of all offenders in prison and camps were enrolled in formal education, such as adult basic education (ABE), vocational training, and GED.

Michigan has a new program at the Newberry Correctional Facility in the Upper Peninsula. This school is one of the most prolific in the nation, graduating hundreds of prisoners each year with a GED diploma. In 2000, approximately 300 offenders earned the high school equivalency certificate. Newberry was designed as a specialized education prison when it opened, a place where the focus would be on guiding prisoners toward completion of their high school degrees, a major educational goal for the Michigan Department of Corrections. The Department of Corrections provides ABE and GED courses at all prisons; 6 of the 13 camps including the state's boot camps also offer ABE and GED. The Department overhauled its educational system in 1995, retooling its educational programs with an eye toward ensuring that all prisoners, with some exceptions, earn a high school degree or its equivalent before parole or discharge from parole. As a result, the number of prisoners earning a GED diploma has increased steadily. By department policy and with some exceptions, GED completion is required for parole or discharge from parole (Michigan Department of Corrections 2000).

Promoting the Idea of Educational Betterment

It is of critical importance for inmates to be aware of the fact that if they are to be rehabilitated, they must be the prime mover in this process. Education in the outside world is the key to economic security and employability. This is even more true in the prison setting. When inmates go to prison, they basically step off the world. The world continues to move and the inmates are stagnating in time. If inmates do not do something to improve their situation and to be better off at their release than they were when they came to prison, the probability of returning to prison is almost guaranteed. Oftentimes inmates coming into the prison setting are reading at the elementary level, but because individuals cannot read does not mean that they have no potential. With a great deal of time and effort inmates can move through an academic program that will culminate in the receipt of a GED diploma. It is important to impress on inmates that whatever their academic level was upon entry into prison, it behooves them to do anything possible to raise their educational level. The basic idea is that individuals must be able to do something at the time of release to earn a living and avoid a return to the kinds of behaviors that led to incarceration in the first place.

Diploma Attainment and Degree Completion

The incarcerated resident should be able to feel that receiving a high school diploma or completing a college degree can become a reality. However, college is out of reach of almost all inmates at this point in time. Practically every institution has a GED program. An inmate's being transferred usually does not mean the end of an educational experience but does usually mean that attainment of the GED will be delayed because the new institution has no openings at the time of the inmate's arrival. The problem lies in the resident's adjustment to a new set of teachers and expectations. If the individual is transferred too often, he or she may just give up and feel that the frustrations are not worth it.

From a pure economic standpoint, it benefits society if the individual becomes productive and does not return to prison. The taxpayer is footing the bill for the inmate in prison. One only has to look at the increase in the budget of the Michigan Department of Corrections over the past few years to see clearly that neither Michigan nor the United States as a country can continue to build prisons and pour money into the housing of prisoners. We as taxpayers cannot continue to withstand the massive budget increases that have been necessary to imprison individuals. If educational betterment is the key to reduce recidivism, then educational betterment for our children is the key to the future. It costs a lot less to send an individual to college than it does to send him or her to prison. Recommendations to reduce black crime and recidivism are provided in Chapter 19.

REFERENCES

Amsterdam, A. G. 1988. Race and the death penalty. *Criminal Justice Ethics W-S* 7(1):83–86.

Armour, J. 1998. Negrophilia and reasonable racism: The hidden costs of being black in prison (E. Gilbert, reviewer). *American Journal of Criminal Justice* 22(2):265.

Baron, S. W., and T. F. Hartnagel. 1997. Attributions, affect and crime: Street youths' reaction to unemployment. *Criminology* 35(3):409–434.

Bourgois, P. 1995. *In search of respect: Selling crack in el barrio.* New York: Cambridge Univ. Press.

Brown, R. A., and J. Frank. 2005. Police–citizen encounters and field citations: Do encounter characteristics influence ticketing? *Policies* 28(3):635–654.

Bureau of Justice Statistics. 2001. *Capital punishment.* Washington, DC: U.S. Department of Justice, Office of Justice Programs. December.

Crawford, C., T. Chiricos, and G. Kleck. 1998. Race, racial threat, and sentencing of habitual offenders. *Criminology* 36(3):481–511.

Free, M. D., Jr. 1997. The impact of federal sentencing reforms on African Americans. *Journal of Black Studies* 28(2):268–286.

Fridell, L., R. Lunney, D. Diamond, and B. Kubu. 2001. Racially biased policing: A principled response. *Executive Research Forum,* 551–572.

Hawkins, H. C. 2006. Race and sentencing outcomes in Michigan: 1996–2001. Paper presented at Hawaii International Conference on Social Sciences, Honolulu.

Heaney, G. W. 1992. Revisiting disparity: Debating building sentencing. *American Criminal Law Review* 29:792.

Herbert, C. S. 1997. Sentencing outcomes of blacks, Hispanic and white males convicted under federal sentencing guidelines. *Criminal Justice Review* 22(2):133–151.

Home Box Office. 1996. *Prisons and drugs.* January 27.

Klein, S., J. Petersilia, and S. Turner. 1990. Race and imprisonment decisions in California. *Science* 247(February):816.

Lochner, L., and E. Moretti. 2004. The effect of education on crime: Evidence from prison inmates, arrests and self reports. *American Economic Review* 94(1):155–189.

Michigan Department of Corrections. 1984. *Annual statistical report,* 42, 55–56.

———. 1991. *Annual statistical report,* 123–127, 136–137, 144, 189.

———. 2000. *Annual statistical report,* 66, 90, 95, 150.

———. 2004. *Annual statistical report,* 15, 16, 29, 66.

Michigan State Police. 1972. *Uniform crime report,* sec. 7.

———. 1977. *Uniform crime report,* sec. 10.

———. 1981. *Uniform crime report,* 9–12.

———. 1984. *Uniform crime report,* 38–40.

———. 1994. *Uniform crime report,* 22–46.

———. 1998. *Uniform crime report,* 23–48.

———. 2000. *Uniform crime report,* 17–35.

———. 2004. *Uniform crime report,* 15–30.

Mustard, D. B. 2001. Racial, ethnic and gender disparities in sentencing: evidence from the U.S. federal courts. *Journal of Law and Economics* XLIV(April):1–21.

Paternoster, R., and S. D. Bushway. 2001. Theoretical and empirical work on the relationship between unemployment and crime. *Journal of Quantitative Criminology* 17(4):391–497.

Petersilia, J. 1983. *Racial disparities in the criminal justice system.* Santa Monica, CA: Rand.

Pettit, B., and B. Western. 2004. Mass imprisonment and the life course: Races and class in equality in U.S. incarceration. *American Sociological Review* 69(April):151–169.

Smith, D. M., J. A. Devine, and J. F. Sheley. 1992. Crime and unemployment: Effects across age and race categories. *Sociological Perspectives* 35(Winter):551–572.

Smith, M. D. 1988. Patterns of discrimination in assessment of the death penalty: The case of Louisiana. *Journal of Criminal Justice* 15:279–366.

Sorensen, J., and D. H. Wallace. 1999. The effect of race on juvenile justice decision making in Nebraska: Detention, adjudications, and disparities 1988–1993. *Justice Quarterly* 16(3):445–478.

Spohn, C., and D. Holleran. 2000. The imprisonment penalty paid by young, unemployed black and Hispanic male offenders. *Criminology* 38(1):281–306.

Unnever, J. D., C. E. Fraser, and J. C. Henretta. 1980. Racial differences in criminal justice sentencing. *Sociological Quarterly* 21(Spring):197–205.

U.S. Census Bureau. 1990. *Current population reports: Consumer income*. Washington, DC: U.S. Department of Commerce.

———. 2000. *Michigan state and county quick facts*. Washington, DC: Data User Services Division.

———. 1992. *1990 census summary file 3 (SF3). State of Michigan*. Washington, DC: Data User Services Division.

———. 2002. *2002 census summary file 3 (SF3). State of Michigan*. Washington, DC: Data User Services Division.

U.S. Department of Labor, Bureau of Labor Statistics. 1985. *Current population surveys*. Washington, DC: U.S. Department of Labor.

———. 1991. *Current population surveys*. Washington, DC: U.S. Department of Labor.

———. 2004. *Current population surveys*, 36–37. Washington, DC: U.S. Department of Labor.

Wolpert, C. 1999. Considering race and crime: Distilling non-partisan policies from opposing theories. *American Criminal Law Review* 16(2):265–288.

Zimring, F., J. Eigen, and S. O'Malley. 1976. Punishing homicide in Philadelphia: Perspectives on the death penalty. *University of Chicago Law Review* 72(Winter):1072–1093.

CHAPTER 13

Black and White High School Dropout Rates in Michigan: The Inequality Persists

Percy Bates

Answers to specific questions about the severity of the dropout problem for black high school students in Michigan are as elusive as is the concept of dropout itself. The answers depend upon whom you ask, what measures are used, and the point of view of the respondent. Some sources (U.S. General Accounting Office, 1986) argue that the dropout rate nationally is actually improving, while others (U.S. Department of Education, 1989) argue that in many states, including Michigan, it is definitely getting worse. Nearly everyone seems to agree that the problem is particularly severe in large cities such as Detroit. Whom should we believe?

If the issue were not such an important one, it would not be necessary to believe anyone. We could take each bit of information and not worry about who is right and who is wrong. Unfortunately, that is not a luxury that we can afford at present. Time is wasting, and it may already be too late for some youngsters. What we know for sure is that the problem constitutes a major threat to the welfare of a sizable portion of black youth in Michigan.

Black Enrollment: A Growing Proportion

Black students are a growing proportion of the total enrollment in Michigan's schools. Between 1974 and 1986, the total enrollment in Michigan's public elementary and secondary schools fell from 2.1 million to 1.6 million. Black enrollment also declined, but the proportion of black students rose from 14 percent to 18 percent during this period. In contrast, the proportion of white students enrolled in public schools declined during this period from about 83 percent to 78 percent (Cain and Wing, July 1986).

According to the Michigan Department of Education's 1985–86 Racial/Ethnic Census, there were 1,593,200 students in Michigan's public elementary and secondary schools during 1985–86 (Cain and Wing, February 1986). Black students numbered 291,953, and they constituted 18.3 percent of the total public school enrollment. White students numbered 1,239,415, and they constituted 77.8 percent of the total public school enrollment.

As indicated, the proportion of black students in Michigan's public elementary and secondary schools has increased. Despite the increase in the proportion of black students enrolled in Michigan's public schools, the question is: What proportion of these black students are dropping out, and why? An analysis of Michigan black-white dropout rates may reveal some answers to these questions.

The Black High School Dropout Rate in Michigan

The most recent available data on dropout rates for all public school students in grades 9 to 12 in Michigan come from the 1985–86 Michigan Department of Education (MDE) dropout survey. The MDE has collected data and studied the problem of dropouts since 1962–63. These data were collected annually until 1981–82, and then they were collected every other year until 1985–86. At the time of this writing, 1987–88 data were not available.

Initially, the Michigan Department of Education collected and analyzed data on high school dropout rates only by sex and by local school district; but in 1976-77, the Department began to ask local school districts to report their student dropout data by five racial and ethnic categories: American Indian, Asian, black, Hispanic, and white. This change in collection, analysis, and reporting of the data made it possible to compare the dropout rates for each of these groups on a statewide basis and over time (see Table 13-1).

Table 13-1. Michigan Annual Percentage Dropout Rates by Racial/Ethnic Category, 1976–86, Grades 9 Through 12

Year	Black	White	Black/White Ratio	Am. Indian	Asian	Hispanic	Overall
1976–77	11.8	5.4	2.2	6.9	2.6	12.9	6.3
1977–78	10.9	5.8	1.9	6.4	3.5	11.3	6.5
1978–79	10.3	5.7	1.8	7.2	3.1	11.6	6.4
1979–80	13.4	5.5	2.4	5.9	4.4	10.7	6.5
1980–81	8.8	5.0	1.8	7.2	3.4	9.1	5.6
1981–82	7.8	4.7	1.7	6.8	2.6	9.6	5.2
1982–83	No	Report	———————	———	———	———	———
1983–84	11.7	4.2	2.8	6.3	3.7	10.2	5.4
1984–85	No	Report					
1985–86	12.0	4.5	2.6	5.9	2.3	10.9	5.8
Average	10.8	5.1	2.1	6.6	3.2	10.8	6.0

SOURCE: Michigan Department of Education Office of Research and Information Services (Chung, 1989). The averages and the black/white ratios were computed for this table.

As shown in Table 13-1, the annual dropout rate for black high school students in Michigan during 1985–86 was 12 percent, while the dropout rate for white high school students in Michigan during this same period was 4.5 percent, resulting in a black rate of 2.6 times the rate for whites. During the period from 1976–77 to 1985–86, the average dropout rate for black students was 10.8 percent, while the average rate for white students during the same period was 5.1 percent. Although there were variations in the dropout ratios between black and white Michigan high school students during the 10–year period reported in Table 13-1, black students dropped out at a rate that was on average twice that of white students.

According to the U.S. General Accounting Office (GAO) (1986), the black-white gap in high school completion rates has been growing progressively smaller nationally, but black dropout rates in Michigan have not confirmed the generally optimistic picture painted in the GAO report. The black annual dropout rate in 1985–86 was between 2 and 3 times the white annual dropout rate, just as it had been in 1976; and after a narrowing of the gap in 1980–81 and 1981–82, the gap widened again in 1983–84 and 1985–86 (Figure 13-1).

It is apparent from the data in Table 13-1 and Figure 13-1 that from 1976 to 1986 black high school students in the State of Michigan dropped out at a faster rate than their white counterparts. Although data for 1987–88 from the Michigan Department of Education are not presently available, it is likely that this information would not differ substantially from the 1985–86 data.

Despite their long history of use in Michigan, annual dropout rates can be misleading, because they do not take into account the question of how many students actually graduate. One might assume that if the annual dropout rate for black students is 12 percent, then 88 percent must graduate. This is not the case, however. A rule of thumb for estimating the four-year, longitudinal dropout rate from an annual dropout rate is to multiply by a factor of about three (Chung, 1989). Hence, the annual 12 percent dropout

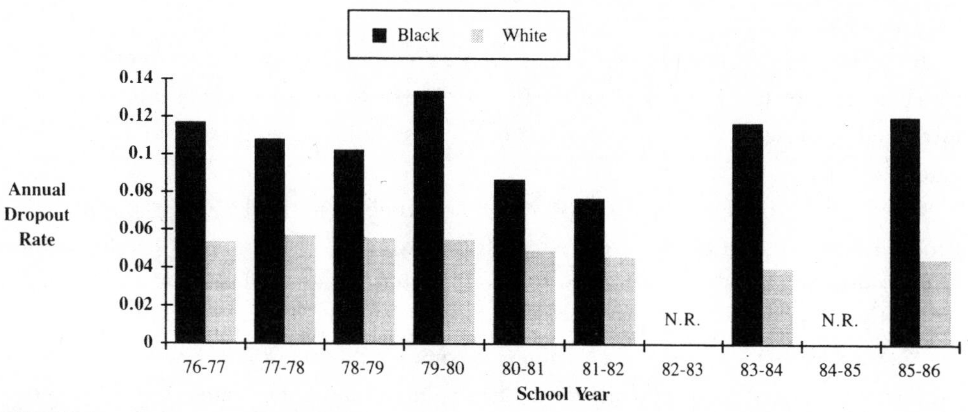

FIGURE 13-1

Annual Dropout Rates for Black and White Students in Michigan Public Schools, 1976–86

SOURCE: Based on data from the Michigan Department of Education Office of Research and Information Services (Chung, 1989). N.R. = No Report.

rate for black high school students in Michigan was probably somewhere near 36 percent in terms of a four-year longitudinal dropout rate, making the graduation rate for Michigan black high school students in 1985–86 somewhere near 64 percent (100 − 36 = 64). This estimate agrees very closely with an estimate from the U.S. Bureau of the Census (1988) of 64.5 percent graduation rate for Michigan's black students. By contrast, the graduation rate obtained by using this same formula is 86.5 percent for Michigan white high school students.

Although annual dropout rates may give parents and taxpayers a misleading picture of the dropout problem, they may, in fact, be more accurate than four-year longitudinal dropout rates, which can be distorted by changes in enrollment over time. Annual dropout rates are also more convenient for school districts to report, because all the necessary data come from a single school year (Michigan Department of Education, September 30, 1986). Annual dropout rates, then, can be considered useful for comparisons over time and between districts, but they should be used with caution.

The Black-White Dropout Gap and the Concentration of Blacks in Central Cities

According to the Michigan State Board of Education's *Racial Ethnic Census, 1985–86* (Cain and Wing, February 1986), only 30 school districts out of 525 accounted for 94 percent of all black enrollment, counting both elementary and secondary students in grades K-12, in Michigan public schools. Looking only at secondary students in grades 9–12, the Michigan Department of Education Office of Research and Information Services provided data from their Elementary and Secondary Information Access System (ESIAS) database for the adjusted enrollments by racial and ethnic categories for grades 9 to 12 for these same 30 Michigan school districts (Phelps and Ruddock, 1989). These enrollment data are listed in Table 13-2 and can be assumed to represent approximately 94 percent of Michigan black students in grades 9–12 in 1985–86. The 30 districts, which represent central city as well as suburban districts, range from 100 percent black (Highland Park) to 4.7 percent black (Wayne-Westland).

It is clear that black enrollment is not evenly distributed across the State of Michigan. One place to look for the reasons for the black-white dropout rate gap might be in the performance of those school districts that are responsible for serving this concentration of black students.

The annual dropout rates in 1985–86 for black students in the 30 Michigan school districts with the highest black enrollments ranged from less than 3 percent to more than 20 percent (Table 13-3). It is clear from these data that some districts are more successful than others in retaining students to graduation.

Another way of looking at the situation is to compare the statewide dropout rate with the dropout rate in the districts in which most black students are concentrated. Table 13-4 shows the annual dropout rates for the 29 districts (30 minus Detroit) with the largest numbers of black students; and for 23 of these 29 districts where the black dropout rate exceeds the statewide average dropout rate (4.5 percent) for white students. Table 13-4 also shows the annual dropout rates for Detroit pulled out and presented separately. A number of

Table 13-2. The Thirty Michigan School Districts with the Highest Black Adjusted Enrollment, Grades 9 to 12, by Racial/Ethnic Category, 1985–86

	Black		White		Am. Indian		Asian		Hispanic		Total
District	N	%	N	%	N	%	N	%	N	%	N
Detroit	44,758	91.6	2,957	6.1	102	0.2	211	0.4	810	1.7	48,838
Flint	3,578	67.2	1,532	28.8	80	1.5	21	0.4	114	2.1	5,325
Pontiac	2,609	57.8	1,435	31.8	34	0.8	35	0.8	401	8.9	4,514
Saginaw	2,375	51.0	1,707	36.7	50	1.1	24	0.5	499	10.7	4,655
Grand Rapids	1,694	34.6	2,853	58.2	22	0.5	127	2.6	207	4.2	4,903
Highland Park	1,529	100.0	0	0.0	0	0.0	0	0.0	0	0.0	1,529
Lansing	1,470	25.1	3,584	61.2	70	1.2	146	2.5	582	10.0	5,852
Benton Harbor	1,466	81.8	308	17.2	11	0.6	0	0.0	8	0.5	1,793
Southfield	890	33.6	1,689	63.8	0	0.0	54	2.0	15	0.6	2,648
Kalamazoo	821	29.6	1,838	66.3	40	1.4	38	1.4	37	1.3	2,774
Ann Arbor	786	18.0	3,292	75.5	19	0.4	201	4.6	63	1.5	4,361
Battle Creek	763	31.8	1,561	65.1	7	0.3	16	0.7	51	2.1	2,398
Muskegon Hgts.	731	94.0	40	5.1	1	0.1	0	0.0	6	0.8	778
Inkster	683	99.0	4	0.6	0	0.0	3	0.4	0	0.0	690
Oak Park	665	75.7	188	21.4	1	0.1	19	2.2	5	0.6	878
Beecher	650	82.6	102	13.0	9	1.1	8	1.0	18	2.3	787
Muskegon	567	40.4	755	53.8	21	1.5	6	0.4	54	3.8	1,403
Ypsilanti	542	32.7	1,077	65.1	2	0.1	21	1.3	13	0.8	1,655
Buena Vista	421	80.0	61	11.6	2	0.4	0	0.0	42	8.0	526
Jackson	387	24.6	1,073	68.3	60	3.8	19	1.2	33	2.1	1,572
River Rouge	363	46.7	394	50.6	10	1.3	0	0.0	11	1.4	778
Willow Run	340	35.2	612	63.4	8	0.8	4	0.4	2	0.2	966
Westwood	330	51.9	299	47.0	0	0.0	1	0.2	6	0.9	636
Mt. Clemens	325	33.6	616	63.7	7	0.7	3	0.3	16	1.7	967
Romulus	314	19.9	1,237	78.5	0	0.0	11	0.7	14	0.9	1,576
Van Buren Twp.	306	13.8	1,864	84.3	5	0.2	13	0.6	20	0.9	2,211
Albion	261	38.9	380	56.6	0	0.0	0	0.0	30	4.5	671
Wayne-Westland	250	4.7	4,886	92.5	61	1.2	32	0.6	53	1.0	5,282
Ecorse	242	63.2	111	29.0	0	0.0	1	0.3	29	7.6	383
Ferndale	205	15.5	1,071	81.1	0	0.0	38	2.9	7	0.5	1,321

SOURCE: Michigan Department of Education Office of Research and Information Services (Phelps and Ruddock, 1989).

Table 13-3. Black and White Dropout Rates for Thirty Michigan School Districts,* Grades 9–12, 1985–86

District	Black Rate	White Rate
Ecorse	20.7	38.7
Flint	15.0	19.5
Detroit	14.8	23.4
Mt. Clemens	13.5	15.1
Jackson	12.9	13.4
Willow Run	12.9	25.7
Lansing	12.8	9.4
Benton Harbor	12.1	7.8
The statewide dropout rate for all black students is 12.0%		
Ferndale	10.7	11.2
Kalamazoo	10.1	8.3
River Rouge	9.9	20.6
Romulus	9.6	5.9
Grand Rapids	8.6	8.6
Battle Creek	8.1	9.8
Westwood	7.3	13.0
Pontiac	6.7	17.5
Highland Park	6.5	0.0**
The statewide dropout rate for all students is 5.8%		
Ypsilanti	5.4	4.6
Oak Park	5.3	11.7
Beecher	5.1	15.7
Albion	5.0	5.8
Saginaw	4.9	4.8
Muskegon Hts.	4.8	7.5
Ann Arbor	4.7	2.9
The statewide dropout rate for all white students is 4.5%		
Wayne-Westland	4.0	4.8
Buena Vista	3.3	3.3
Muskegon	3.2	5.7
Van Buren Twp.	3.2	5.0
Inkster	2.8	0.0***
Southfield	2.5	3.1

SOURCE: Michigan Department of Education Office of Research and Information Services, Elementary and Secondary Information Access System (ESIAS) data base (Phelps and Ruddock, 1989).

*The thirty school districts with the highest black adjusted high school enrollment in Michigan.

**No white students.

***4 white students.

possible contributing factors to the dropout gap between black students and white students in Michigan are shown in Table 13-5.

When the statewide average dropout rates are compared with the dropout rates in the 29 districts (30 minus Detroit) with the largest numbers of black students, the mean dropout rate goes down for blacks (from 12.0 to 8.4) and up for whites (from 4.5 to 8.3).

Table 13-4. Annual Dropout Rates for Michigan and for Selected School Districts with the Highest Adjusted Black Enrollments, 1985–1986

Students	Statewide Dropout %	29 Districts* with Most Blacks, Dropout %	23 Districts* Where Black Dropout % > 4.5	Detroit Dropout %
All	5.8	8.4	9.4	15.4
Black	12.0	8.4	9.2	14.7
White	4.5	8.3	9.6	23.4

SOURCE: Michigan Department of Education Office of Research and Information Services (Phelps and Ruddock, 1989).

*Minus Detroit.

When Detroit is excluded, the dropout rate for blacks in the districts with the largest numbers of black students is the same as the average for all students, both black and white, in these districts.

A similar situation is observed in reference to the 23 concentrated districts (minus Detroit) with a dropout rate for blacks (9.2 percent) that exceeds the statewide dropout rate for whites (4.5 percent). The average figure for the three categories (all students, black students, and white students) would be about 9.3 percent in these 23 districts.

Table 13-5. Factors Potentially Affecting Dropout Rates

	Statewide	29 Districts*	23 Districts**	Detroit
SEV/Pupil[1]	$61,491	$54,312	$58,659	$51,062
% Families in Poverty[2]	8.2%	13.5%	14.5%	18.9%
% of Districts Located in:				
Urban,	21%	55%	52%	100%
Suburban, or	35%	45%	48%	0%
Rural Setting[3]	44%	0%	0%	0%
Instructional Exp./Pupil[4,5]	$2,049	$2,054	$2,074	$1,956
Average Teacher Salary[5]	$30,008	$31,394	$31,244	$30,793
Pupil-Teacher Ratio[5]	21.0	21.8	22.1	24
Mean Adjusted 9-12 Enrollment[1]	910	2,201	2,202	48,838
% Black Enrollment[1]	18.3%	47.7%	46.2%	88.4%

SOURCES:

[1]Michigan Department of Education Office of Research and Information Services (Phelps and Ruddock, 1989). SEV stands for State Equalized Valuation.

[2]U.S. Bureau of the Census, 1980, Table 57, Summary of Economic Characteristics. See references.

[3]Urban was defined as location within Michigan's one Standard Consolidated Statistical Area, the seven counties in Southeastern Michigan; suburban was defined as location within one of Michigan's Standard Metropolitan Statistical Areas; rural was defined as location in neither a SCSA nor a SMSA (U.S. Bureau of Census, 1980, page 13).

[4]Chen, 1988. See references. The statewide average is pupil weighted.

[5]Michigan State Board of Education, 1986. See references.

*Districts with the highest enrollments of blacks.

**Districts where the dropout rate is greater than the statewide average of 4.5 for whites.

In Table 13-4, the data for Detroit are presented separately because of its size relative to the other 29 districts. Detroit is an outlier and skews the sample in reference to black student dropouts in Michigan. Detroit, with 63.6 percent of the total black enrollment in Michigan's 30 districts with the largest black enrollments, accounts for 75.5 percent of the total black dropouts in these districts (Phelps and Ruddock, 1989).

Table 13-4 shows that in Detroit in 1985–86, the black dropout percentage was 14.7 percent, and the white dropout percentage was 23.4 percent. This relatively higher white rate probably includes a sizable number of students who leave the Detroit public schools to attend private schools.

Information presented thus far has called attention to the gap between black and white dropout rates in the State of Michigan. No clear pattern emerges, however, that explains the gap or why some districts are more successful than others at keeping black students in school. Researchers at the Michigan Department of Education hypothesize that at least a quarter of the variance in dropout rates can be explained by social and economic factors such as family income and number of parents in the home—factors that are outside a school district's control. These researchers concede, however, that one-half to three-fourths of the factors contributing to the dropout rate can be influenced by the school district (Hornbeck, 1987).

One investigator of the dropout problem (Pallas, 1986) believes that school-related factors (such as academic performance), which are more directly under the school's control than are social and economic factors, are the best predictors of who drops out of school.

The information in Table 13-5 supports the contention that the dropout issue is a complicated problem that defies an easy answer. Table 13-5 contains two measures of socioeconomic status: state equalized valuation (SEV) per pupil and percentage of families living in poverty. Both measures show that the communities where black students are concentrated are poorer than the average Michigan community, a factor that may contribute to their higher dropout rate. Susan Mayer and Christopher Jencks (1989) reviewed several studies and concluded that most of them demonstrate that "teenagers who live in high SES neighborhoods attain more schooling than teenagers from similar families who live in lower SES neighborhoods."

Table 13-5 also shows that the school districts serving the majority of black students in Michigan are concentrated in urban areas. Urban students are more apt to drop out than rural or suburban students, according to a U.S. Department of Education study (Gruskin, Campbell, and Paulu, 1987).

In addition, Table 13-5 includes four variables that measure school inputs that may be related to student progress. The first (instructional expenditures per pupil) shows that in the instructional area, less money is spent on Detroit students than on students statewide. A second variable (average teacher salary), however, did not indicate any disadvantage for the districts where black students are concentrated.

It seems clear from Table 13-5 that when compared with their white counterparts, most Michigan black students are in poorer school districts; have a higher percentage of families in poverty; live in large, racially identifiable, highly urbanized areas; and attend larger school districts. The extent to which these factors contribute to the higher dropout rate for black students is unclear; but they are not positive factors in retaining black students in school—at least not in the minds of many educators and policymakers (Rutter, 1983).

The dropout problem is troubling on a nationwide basis; and some school districts, both in and outside the State of Michigan, are attempting to respond to the problem. An article in the *New York Times* (Ayres, May 21, 1989) reported on a program in West Virginia that linked high school completion to receiving a driver's license. The school districts in West Virginia reported considerable success with the program. Students quoted in the article suggested that the need to drive was a stronger force for remaining in school than the desire to drop out. This approach, although reportedly having some degree of success, is not without its critics. Some argue that keeping students in school who do not want to be there makes for an unpleasant environment for students and teachers. Reactions are mixed, but the goal of reducing the dropout rate is being met. Similar programs may be implemented in Michigan and elsewhere.

The Michigan Department of Education's Operation Graduation (Bryson, 1989) reports a degree of success. Operation Graduation began in 1986 with a $700,000 per year allocation from the Michigan Legislature for a school dropout prevention program throughout the state. Nine school districts developed dropout prevention programs under this program: Beecher, Detroit, Flint, Kalamazoo, Lansing, Montrose, Muskegon City, Muskegon Heights, and Willow Run. (All of these districts except Montrose are among the 30 districts with high black enrollment listed in Tables 13-2 and 13-3.) These dropout prevention programs served some 650 youngsters, 79 percent of whom were black and 16 percent of whom were white.

The programs varied somewhat, but all of them included a paid work incentive experience and intensive counseling. At the end of 1987–88, after two years of operation, the dropout rate among participants in Operation Graduation was only 3.2 percent. This is considerably lower than the 5.8 percent annual dropout rate for the State of Michigan in 1985–86. This seems promising, considering that participants in the program were selected on the basis of being students at risk of dropping out (Bryson, 1989).

The data presented here describe the status of the dropout situation for an estimated 94 percent of the black high school students in Michigan in 1985–86. Dropout rates for local school districts vary dramatically. Annual dropout rates for the 30 Michigan school districts with the highest black enrollments ranged from a low of 2.5 percent in Southfield to a high of 20.7 percent in Ecorse. Clearly, the dropout problem is not the same for all local school districts in Michigan. The fact that some districts are doing relatively well in stemming the flow of dropouts from their schools suggests that the problem is not unsolvable.

On the whole, it appears that the State of Michigan has not succeeded in its responsibility to provide equal educational opportunities to all students. In 1981–82, the black dropout rate was 7.8 percent, and the white dropout rate was 4.7 percent, resulting in a black-white ratio of 1.7.

By 1985–86, the black dropout rate had increased to 12 percent, whereas the white dropout rate had declined to 4.5 percent, resulting in an increase in the black-white ratio to 2.6 (see Table 13-1).

With respect to black and white high school dropout rates in Michigan, the inequality persists.

Discussion

From the previous discussion and presentation of data, it becomes clear that questions about dropouts in Michigan may have complicated answers. For example: Who is a dropout? On the surface it would appear that a student dropout is anyone who, for whatever reason, is no longer in school on a regular basis. Although this may be a fairly simple method of determining dropout status, it can also be misleading and give a false view of the situation. While a student may not be in a given public school on a particular day, that does not mean that he or she may not be in a public or private school somewhere else.

A second question: How many black students drop out? The answer depends on whom you ask, the nature of the count, and the definition selected for a dropout. Although the answers may vary, the percentage of dropouts is substantial, no matter which estimates are used.

In out efforts to educate all of America's youth, it is important to keep students in school until they complete a high school education. Our youth must be well educated and well prepared, for the future will be more technological than at any time we have known previously.

Since black youths have historically experienced roadblocks and obstacles on their way to postsecondary activities to a greater extent than have white students, it is important to provide them with a quality education. That certainly cannot be done if they are not in school.

Looking across the entire state at the issue of dropouts provides limited useful information for the educational practitioner. Looking at specific school districts and at what may be happening in these districts, however, has greater potential in the effort to understand the nature of the dropout problem and what should be done to alleviate it.

For example, it appears that the bulk of black students in the State of Michigan are concentrated in central city school districts. Factors in central city environments may interact to impede the academic progress of black students, and these factors deserve additional investigation, analysis, and corrective measures.

Public schools in the State of Michigan seem to have greater difficulty retaining black students than white students. Schools must become more attractive and potentially useful places for black students. The rate that black students, compared with white students, are currently leaving school indicates that they would rather be somewhere else. To the degree that educators and other concerned citizens can reverse the present trend, we must do so. If we fail, there can only be disaster in the future for the schools, the students, and society.

Americans, black and white, must continue to search for ways to reduce the current dropout rate for black students and to provide a quality education for all of the nation's young people. We must pay particular attention to black youth, who experience more than their share of obstacles on their way to receiving a quality education and preparation for lifelong learning and the world of work.

Recommendations

1. Implement the Governor's proposed preschool education program for all children. This approach is preventive and tends to provide students with a solid social and academic base. Such a program is supported by the research findings from the Perry Preschool

Project, which worked exclusively with black youngsters and proved both educationally and economically successful (Berrueta-Clement et al., 1984).

2. Proceed with a school finance reform plan that will provide equal per pupil expenditure for instruction for all school districts in Michigan. This should include equalization of teacher and administrator compensation so that talented educators are not lured from the central cities to the suburbs.
3. Institute metropolitan school compacts that involve business and industry, unions, and government in creating job opportunities for students who succeed in graduating from local high schools. Where possible, create cooperative programs that offer work experience and entree to apprenticeship training.
4. Take desegregation beyond school district boundaries by providing opportunities for low-income, central-city students to attend suburban schools. Chicago, Indianapolis, Milwaukee, and Minneapolis are experimenting with this kind of metropolitan plan.
5. Take advantage of federal initiatives for economic redevelopment of urban communities. If low social and economic status appears to be related to dropping out, efforts should be made to improve not only the schools but the communities in which these potential dropout students live.
6. Increase efforts to develop more "effective schools," along the lines proposed by the late Dr. Ronald Edmonds (1979). Successful effective schools are attractive places for both teachers and students, particularly black students, and tend to have lower dropout rates.
7. Expand the Michigan Department of Education's Operation Graduation, which provides subsidized work experience and intensive counseling for students at risk of dropping out (Bryson, 1989).
8. Develop a think tank of scholars and other concerned citizens dedicated to the empowerment of black educators and students to find solutions to the problem of black dropouts in Michigan. Black educators and parents have historically been in the vanguard of efforts to improve the schooling of black students.
9. Expand research efforts in each school district and elevate the priority of the dropout problem. There is a need for more research that (a) clearly describes the nature and extent of the dropout problem in Michigan's public schools and (b) recommends policy changes to solve this problem.
10. Institute a program on an experimental basis, with adequate follow-up, modeled after the West Virginia plan, which links high school completion to receiving a driver's license.

REFERENCES

Ayres, B. Drummond. "West Virginia Reduces Dropouts by Denying Them Driver's License, "*New York Times*, Sunday, May 21, 1989, p. 1.

Berrueta-Clement, John R., Weikart, David P., and Crissey, Marie Skodak. *Changed Lives: The Effects of the Perry Preschool Program on Youths through Age 19.* Ypsilanti, MI: High/Scope Press, 1984.

Bryson, Naomi. "Operation Graduation: A School Dropout Prevention Program; A Report to the Michigan Legislature." Lansing: Michigan Department of Education Bureau of Educational Services (mimeographed), February 1989.

Cain, Eugene and Wing, Nancy. *Michigan Racial Ethnic Census, 1980–1984*. Lansing: Office of Equal Educational Opportunity, Michigan State Board of Education, July 1986, p. 2.

Cain, Eugene and Wing, Nancy. "Michigan Racial Ethnic Census, 1985–1986." Lansing: Office of Equal Educational Opportunity, Michigan State Board of Education, (microfiche), February 14, 1986, p. 998.

Chen, Li-Ju. "An Equity Analysis of Michigan's School Finance System." Ann Arbor, MI: Doctoral dissertation, The University of Michigan, 1988, p. 65.

Chung, Ki-Suck. Office of Research and Information Services, Michigan Department of Education, personal communications on February 12, 1989, and March 16, 1989.

Edmonds, Ronald. "Effective Schools for the Urban Poor," *Educational Leadership*, Vol. 37, No. 1, October 1979.

Gruskin, Susan J., Campbell, Mary A., and Paulu, Nancy. *Dealing with Dropouts: The Urban Superintendents' Call to Action*, Washington, D.C.: Office of Educational Research and Improvement, 1987.

Hornbeck, Mark. "State's System May Contribute to High Dropout Rate in Schools," *Ann Arbor News*, December 1, 1987, page C-5.

Mayer, Susan and Jencks, Christopher. "Growing Up in Poor Neighborhoods: How Much Does It Matter?" *Science*, Vol. 243 (March 17, 1989), pp. 1441–1445.

Michigan Department of Education Office of Research and Information Services. "Form RI-4701." Lansing: Author, September 30, 1986, pp. 3–4

Michigan Department of Education Office of Research and Information Services. "Michigan Public High School Dropouts by County and School District, 1985–86 (Grades 9–12)." Lansing: Author (mimeographed), June 29, 1987.

Michigan State Board of Education. *1985–86 Bulletin 1014: Michigan K-12 School Districts Ranked by Selected Financial Data*. Lansing, MI: Author, 1986.

Pallas, Aaron. "School Dropouts in the United States," *The Condition of Education. 1986 Edition*. Washington, D.C.: Department of Education, 1986, p. 161 and p. 164.

Phelps, James and Ruddock, Lewis. Data from the Elementary and Secondary Information Access System (ESIAS), provided by the Office of Research and Information Service, Michigan Department of Education, Lansing, MI, on February 13, 1989.

Rutter, Michael. "School Effects on Pupil Progress: Research Findings and Policy Implications," *Child Development*, Vol. 54 (1983), pp. 1–29.

U.S. Bureau of the Census. *1980 Census of the Population*. Volume 1, Characteristics of the Population, Chapter C, General Social and Economic Characteristics, Part 24, Michigan, PC80-1-C, Washington, DC: U.S. Government Printing Office, 1980.

U.S. Bureau of the Census. Current Population Reports. Series P-20, No. 428, *Educational Attainment in the United States: March 1986 and 1987*. "Errata" for pp. 53–55. Washington, D.C.: U.S. Government Printing Office, 1988.

U.S. Department of Education Office of Planning, Budget, and Information. "State Education Performance Chart: Student Performance, Resource Inputs, State Reforms, and Population Characteristics, 1982 and 1988" Washington, D.C.: Author, 1989.

U.S. General Accounting Office (GAO). *Dropouts: The Nature and Extent of the Problem*. Washington, DC: GAO/HRD-86-106BR, 1986.

CHAPTER 14

Blacks in Michigan Higher Education

Walter R. Allen

In the early morning hours of July 23, 1967, after the Sunday newspapers were already printed and distributed, Detroit exploded in what was to become the nation's bloodiest black urban rebellion.

The rebellion grew out of a history of injustice. An Associated Press survey of racial tensions in major Michigan cities published the week before chronicled complaints about persistent racial discrimination. The racial discrimination was expressed in employment, housing, and health care, among other areas. It was also expressed in educational opportunities.

The participation of black Americans in U.S. higher education was dismal in 1967, a full two years after the Higher Education Act of 1965. The goal of equal opportunity in higher education, sought by Congressional legislation in 1965, continued to elude the grasp of black Americans. Although blacks represented 11.2 percent of the national population in 1967, they were only 7.8 percent of the nation's high school graduates and a mere 6.1 percent of the nation's college students (Morris, 1979: 74). Twenty years later, when blacks are 13.5 percent of the national population, they represent 10.7 percent of the nation's high school graduates and 8.8 percent of the nation's college students (American Council on Education, 1986).

Black progress toward equity in higher education nationally has been slow and uneven. Moreover, where black students are enrolled in institutions of higher education, studies show them to experience disproportionately high rates of dropout, dissatisfaction with college, and academic underachievement, compared to whites (Allen, 1986; Fleming, 1984; Blackwell, 1981; Thomas, 1981). In higher education, twenty years after the Detroit riot, blacks continue to be extremely disadvantaged on the national level.

Black student protests occurred across the United States from 1969 through 1971, as students on hundreds of campuses engaged in vigorous protests that involved boycotts, mass demonstrations, and at times violent acts of resistance. At the heart of these protests was black student frustration with the persistence of racial discrimination on college campuses and in the society at large, years after the urban rebellions of the late 1960s. Black students were frustrated by the slow progress toward the goals of racial equality in the nation's cities and on campuses, despite the promises of President Johnson's Great Society and War on Poverty programs.

White students also mobilized during these years to protest U.S. involvement in the War in Vietnam and the continuing denial of equal rights to women. At key junctures in these parallel struggles, the black student movement supported, and was supported by, the membership of other movements for change in the society. At other junctures, the goals and priorities of these parallel movements for social change diverged, often to the disadvantage of black students.

Blacks in Institutions of Higher Education in Michigan

The Detroit riot of 1967 provides the beginning point for an analysis of the status of blacks in Michigan higher education. This chapter presents a description and assessment of historical trends in black student enrollment and degrees awarded over the twenty-year period. In addition, current patterns are examined, and questions are posed about future prospects for Michigan's black citizens in the state higher education system.

Public Colleges and Universities: Black Student Undergraduate Enrollment 1970–1986

Publicly supported state universities and colleges enroll the majority of black students in U.S. higher education. Generally speaking, these schools tend to be larger in size, are cheaper to attend, and have greater academic program diversity and less rigorous admissions requirements than is true for privately controlled institutions of higher education. Thus, black college students in the U.S. are more likely to attend state-supported or public institutions than they are to attend private institutions. The same pattern holds true for the State of Michigan, so we begin with a consideration of black student college enrollment and earned degree patterns for state-controlled institutions in Michigan.

In 1970, the 7,586 black students enrolled in Michigan's public universities were 5.3 percent of the total student enrollment. Asian, Hispanic, and Indian students together totalled 1,784 students, with each group accounting for less than .5 percent of the total student enrollment. Of all students in Michigan's public universities and colleges, 93 percent were white (Table 14-1).

By 1976, there were 15,521 black students on the public campuses of the State of Michigan—twice the number in 1970—representing 9.4 percent of total enrollment. White students were 86 percent of the total enrollment, and Indians, Asians, and Hispanics were respectively .5, .6, and .8 percent of total enrollment (Table 14-2).

As of 1986, the absolute number of black students in Michigan public institutions had grown to 16,550, although their percentage of total student enrollment had declined to 7 percent. The Asian (1.8 percent) and Hispanic (1.2 percent) fractions had also grown while

Table 14-1. Undergraduate Enrollment in Michigan Four-Year Public Colleges and Universities by Race/Ethnicity, Fall 1970

Institution	Black	American Indian	Asian	Hispanic	White	Total
Central Michigan University	140	16	18	39	12,467	12,680
Eastern Michigan University	608	14	24	43	13,594	14,283
Ferris State College	405	23	11	42	8,376	8,857
Grand Valley State College	46	19	14	8	2,794	2,881
Lake Superior State College	3	28	23	7	1,287	1,348
Michigan State University	1,424	9	93	227	27,498	29,251
Michigan Technological University	29	113	18	30	4,362	4,552
Northern Michigan University	103	8	8	10	6,696	6,825
Oakland University	344	11	16	24	4,522	4,917
Saginaw Valley State College	64	6	6	24	1,051	1,151
University of Michigan-Ann Arbor	732	41	150	25	18,123	19,071
University of Michigan-Dearborn	23	1	3	1	440	468
University of Michigan-Flint	90	5	8	4	1,285	1,392
Wayne State University	2,912	163	194	100	14,824	18,193
Western Michigan University	663	48	30	79	16,234	17,054
Total	7,586	505	616	663	133,553	142,923
Percentage of Grand Total	5.3%	.4%	.4%	.5%	93.4%	100%

SOURCE: Department of Health, Education, and Welfare, Enrollment Data, National Center for Educational Statistics, Fall 1976.

the Indian (.5 percent) and white student (85.2 percent) fractions remained basically stable (Table 14-3).

Five campuses have historically enrolled the majority of black students in Michigan public higher education; thus, these institutions deserve our special attention. In fall 1986, the five largest enrollments of black students in Michigan colleges were: Wayne State University (6,288), Michigan State University (2,518), University of Michigan—Ann Arbor (1,710), Eastern Michigan University (1,665), and Western Michigan University (1,165). Together these schools account for 81 percent of the total 1986 black Michigan public college enrollment (Table 14-3).

Wayne State University's enrollment alone represented 38 percent of the total black student enrollment in 1986. Since 1970, black enrollment has tripled at Eastern Michigan University and roughly doubled on the other campuses. To gain perspective on this significant growth, however, we must be reminded that the Asian student population has grown by 10 times at the University of Michigan and by 5 times at Wayne State since 1970. Similarly, since 1970 the white student enrollment on these campuses has grown between a half to a third (Tables 14-1–14-3).

In summary, black student enrollment in Michigan four-year public university undergraduate programs increased rapidly from 5 percent of total enrollment in 1970 to a peak of 11 percent in 1976, declining steadily since then to the 1986 level of 7 percent. In absolute

Table 14-2. Undergraduate Enrollment in Michigan Four-Year Purlic Colleges and Universities by Race, Ethnicity, and Sex, Fall 1976

	Non-resident Alien		Black		American Indian		Asian		Hispanic		White		Total		
Institution	Men	Women	Men	Women	Men	Women	Men	Women	Men	Women	Men	Women	Men	Women	Total
Central Michigan University	33	8	152	157	8	14	8	13	60	55	6,230	7,099	6,491	7,346	13,837
Eastern Michigan University	314	177	517	724	8	13	24	22	16	22	5,521	6,230	6,397	7,183	13,580
Ferris State College	26	5	316	251	6	6	16	12	13	7	5,780	3,442	6,157	3,723	9,880
Grand Valley State College	31	19	175	110	14	17	12	7	31	26	2,877	2,529	3,140	2,708	5,848
Lake Superior State College	77	32	4	3	18	18	1	1	3	0	991	764	1,094	818	1,912
Michigan State University	179	66	826	1,224	36	44	85	96	106	83	17,031	15,785	18,263	17,298	35,591
Michigan Technological University	122	5	20	7	19	7	16	7	10	4	4,442	1,205	4,629	1,235	5,864
Northern Michigan University	26	10	110	59	26	16	10	3	16	9	162	87	4,055	3,567	7,622
Oakland University	22	11	218	281	12	8	12	20	16	18	3,226	3,586	3,506	3,924	7,430
Saginaw Valley State College	0	0	130	162	4	5	4	1	39	31	1,260	1,025	1,437	1,224	2,661
University of Michigan-Ann Arbor	553	202	878	859	33	24	194	122	128	113	10,682	8,532	12,268	9,852	22,120
University of Michigan-Dearborn	58	29	92	131	12	11	8	6	20	14	2,444	1,489	2,634	1,680	4,314
University of Michigan-Flint	36	25	148	237	7	9	4	7	35	21	1,475	1,296	1,705	1,595	3,300
Wayne State University	1,018	690	2,904	3,590	292	135	124	97	210	175	8,659	5,516	13,207	10,203	23,410
Western Michigan University	394	93	569	667	15	22	17	21	58	39	8,009	7,144	9,062	7,986	17,048
Total	2,869	1,372	7,059	8,462	510	349	535	435	761	617	78,789	65,729	90,543	76,964	165,507
Percentage of Grand Total	2.6%		9.4%		.5%		.6%		.8%		86.1%		100%		

SOURCE: Department of Health, Education, and Welfare, Enrollment Data, National Center for Educational Statistica, Fall 1976.

Table 14-3. Undergraduate Enrollment in Michigan Four-Year Public Colleges and Universities by Race/Ethnicity, Fall 1986

Institution	Non-resident Alien	Black	American Indian	Asian	Hispanic	White	Race Unknown	Total
Central Michigan University	190	288	67	52	120	120	0	17,993
Eastern Michigan University	919	1,665	60	267	251	251	759	21,349
Ferris State College	97	475	33	37	61	10,571	3	11,277
Grand Valley State College	0	226	27	65	83	7,781	179	8,361
Lake Superior State College	531	42	71	5	11	2,006	0	2,666
Michigan State University	2,135	2,518	124	632	501	38,178	0	44,088
Michigan Technological University	244	27	25	67	28	5,935	0	6,326
Northern Michigan University	40	250	120	34	32	7,376	0	7,852
Oakland University	63	664	32	210	104	11,634	0	12,707
Saginaw Valley State College	28	310	26	35	165	4,425	388	5,377
University of Michigan-Ann Arbor	2,456	1,710	134	1,598	636	28,224	216	34,974
University of Michigan-Dearborn	12	422	43	190	127	6,326	0	7,120
University of Michigan-Flint	0	500	52	64	79	5,352	0	6,047
Wayne State University	844	6,288	278	904	501	19,949	0	28,764
Western Michigan University	1,022	1,165	47	105	167	19,241	0	21,747
Total	8,581	16,550	1,139	4,265	2,866	201,702	1,545	236,648
Percentage of Grand Total	3.6%	7.0%	0.5%	1.8%	1.2%	85.2%	0.7%	100.0%

SOURCE: Postsecondary Information Unit, Michigan Department of Education, Fall 1986.

terms, the number of black students attending these universities and colleges doubled (Tables 14-1–14-3). Despite clear and dramatic progress over the period as a whole, short-run trends and trends on specific campuses served to dampen the black community's optimism about black progress in Michigan higher education.

In 1970, three years after the Detroit riots, the University of Michigan at Ann Arbor was wracked by student upheaval. At the center of this turmoil was the Black Action Movement, a movement organized by black students to protest the underrepresentation of black people and their concerns on the Ann Arbor campus. Ultimately, the Black Action Movement led to a campus-wide general strike that forced university officials to negotiate a settlement. Among the concessions gained from the university administration was a commitment to achieve a 10 percent black enrollment by 1975, the establishment of a Black Studies program, and the creation of an academic support program.

Between 1970 and 1987, the University of Michigan at Ann Arbor experienced two other black student-led protests, the first of which was the Black Action Movement II in 1975. The second occurred during winter term 1987, in response to racist incidents on the campus. In the combined United Coalition Against Racism and the Black Action Movement III, black student-led demonstrations involved mass protests, occupation of the administration building, and disruption of Regents board meetings. The protest culminated in a negotiated settlement involving the shuttle diplomacy of Reverend Jesse Jackson. The University agreed to set a goal of 12 percent black enrollment, created an Office of Minority Affairs to be headed by a newly designated Vice Provost, created a senior black administrator position in the Affirmative Action Office, established a Presidential Advisory Committee on Minority Affairs, and authorized broadbased strategies to improve black student, faculty, and staff recruitment and retention at the University.

In both the 1975 and 1987 demonstrations, black students repeated their demands for an increased black presence and for greater sensitivity by the University to black concerns. These student demonstrations called attention to the persistence of the conditions and frustrations which gave rise to the initial strike in 1970. Although the other state-controlled campuses did not experience wide-scale black student demonstrations in these years, student frustration over slow progress in achieving equitable status for blacks on these campuses was a shared and constantly smoldering reality.

Private Colleges and Universities: Black Student Undergraduate Enrollment, 1970–1986

One-third of black college and university students attend independent institutions in Michigan. In 1970 black students represented 4.9 percent of the total student enrollment on private campuses; white students were 94 percent of the total; Asians, .5 percent; Indians, .2 percent; and Hispanics, .7 percent. In 1970, the proportion of racial and ethnic students enrolled in private institutions (Table 14-4) of higher education in Michigan was roughly equal to that of their counterparts in public institutions (Table 14-1).

In 1976, blacks were 10 percent of the private school enrollment and whites were 82 percent of the total, roughly equalling their proportions on public campuses. The proportion of Asians and Hispanics on private campuses (Table 14-5) was twice their proportion on public campuses (Table 14-2).

By 1986, the black ratio had shifted such that blacks were 11 percent of private campus enrollment (Table 14-6) compared to 7 percent on public campuses (Table 14-3), while the white ratio remained basically unchanged. The Asian student ratio shifted in the opposite direction, so that by 1986 Asian students were 1.8 percent of public campus enrollment (Table 14-3) and 2.4 percent of enrollment on private campuses (Table 14-6).

Predictably, four of the five independent Michigan colleges and universities with the highest black student enrollment are located in Detroit, where the majority of the state's black population is concentrated (Table 14-6). The five private institutions with the highest black enrollment in 1986 were: University of Detroit (1,008), Marygrove College (883), Mercy College (822), Andrews University (471), and Madonna College (320). Together these schools

Table 14-4. Undergraduate Enrollment in Michigan Independent Colleges and Universities by Race/Ethnicity, Fall 1970

Institution	Black	American Indian	Asian	Hispanic	White	Total
Adrian College	11	0	2	3	1,500	1,516
Albion College	61	0	2	18	1,701	1,782
Alma College	20	1	0	0	1,237	1,258
Andrews University	122	6	16	19	973	1,136
Aquinas College	DATA NOT AVAILABLE					
Baker Junior College	DATA NOT AVAILABLE					
Calvin College	12	2	2	3	3,216	3,235
Calvin Theological Seminary	DATA NOT AVAILABLE					
Central Bible College	DATA NOT AVAILABLE					
Chrysler Institute	DATA NOT AVAILABLE					
Cleary College	DATA NOT AVAILABLE					
Concordia College	3	0	4	0	492	499
Cranbrook Academy of Art	0	0	0	0	11	11
Center for Creative Studies	DATA NOT AVAILABLE					
Center for Humanistic Studies	DATA NOT AVAILABLE					
Davenport College of Business	77	14	6	15	741	853
Detroit Baptist Theological Seminary	DATA NOT AVAILABLE					
Detroit College of Business Admin.	99	5	2	8	467	581
Detroit College of Law	DATA NOT AVAILABLE					
General Motors Institute	39	4	14	6	3,014	3,077
Grace Bible College	DATA NOT AVAILABLE					
Grand Rapids Baptist College & Sem.	7	0	0	0	565	572
Great Lakes Bible College	DATA NOT AVAILABLE					
Hillsdale College	38	0	26	25	657	1,046
Hope College	58	3	18	7	1,875	1,961
Jordan College	DATA NOT AVAILABLE					
Kalamazoo College	56	2	7	2	1,295	1,362
Kendall School of Design	DATA NOT AVAILABLE					
Lawrence Institute of Technology	121	0	21	35	4,156	4,333
Lewis College of Business	DATA NOT AVAILABLE					
Madonna College	17	0	2	3	285	307
Marygrove College	117	2	1	12	521	653
Mercy College of Detroit	127	0	7	8	813	955
Michigan Christian College	7	1	0	0	190	198
Muskegon Business College	51	1	0	4	310	366
Nazareth College	6	0	0	4	362	372
Northwood Institute	36	0	3	29	820	888
Olivet College	45	0	2	3	736	786
Reformed Bible College	0	2	4	1	69	76
Sacred Heart Seminary College	4	0	0	0	156	160
Saginaw Business Institute	DATA NOT AVAILABLE					
Saint John's Provincial Seminary	DATA NOT AVAILABLE					
Saint Mary's College	0	0	0	0	89	89
Sienna Heights College	1	0	2	7	442	452
Spring Arbor College	20	0	3	1	654	678
SS. Cyril and Methodius Seminary	DATA NOT AVAILABLE					
Suomi College	17	0	2	0	373	392
Thomas M. Cooley Law School	DATA NOT AVAILABLE					
University of Detroit	495	20	13	31	3,765	4,324
Walsh College of Acct. & Bus. Admin.	6	0	0	0	37	43
Western Theological Seminary	DATA NOT AVAILABLE					
William Tyndale College	DATA NOT AVAILABLE					
Total	1,673	63	159	244	31,822	33,961
Percentage of Grand Total	4.9%	.2%	.5%	.7%	93.7%	100.0%

SOURCE: U.S. Department of Health, Education and Welfare, Enrollment Data, National Center for Educational Statistics, 1970.

Table 14-5. Undergraduate Enrollment in Michigan Independent Colleges and Universities by Race/Ethnicity, and Sex, Fall 1976

	Non-resident Alien		Black		American Indian		Asian		Hispanic		White		Total	
Institution	Men	Women	Men	Women	Men	Women	Men	Women	Men	Women	Men	Women	Men	Women
Adrian College	4	1	13	5	0	0	0	0	2	4	471	485	490	495
Albion College	6	2	23	16	0	0	6	1	5	3	904	704	944	726
Alma College	9	1	13	8	0	0	0	0	0	0	539	522	561	531
Andrews University	92	116	89	128	7	5	17	20	40	47	700	683	945	999
Aquinas College	21	17	37	37	1	0	4	2	7	6	729	715	799	777
Baker Junior College	DATA NOT AVAILABLE													
Calvin College	115	137	15	29	2	5	24	10	5	7	1,735	1,714	1,896	1,902
Calvin Theological Seminary	DATA NOT AVAILABLE													
Central Bible College	DATA NOT AVAILABLE													
Chrysler Institute	DATA NOT AVAILABLE													
Cleary College	0	0	22	53	0	0	7	12	0	0	98	167	127	232
Concordia College	12	4	1	0	0	0	0	0	2	0	206	328	221	332
Cranbrook Academy of Art	0	0	0	0	0	0	0	0	0	0	3	4	3	4
Center For Creative Studies	4	2	49	33	0	0	3	6	2	1	431	346	489	388
Center For Humanistic Studies	DATA NOT AVAILABLE													
Davenport College of Business	8	4	60	79	12	16	38	50	5	3	1,045	761	1,168	913
Detroit Baptist Theological Seminary	DATA NOT AVAILABLE													
Detroit College of Business	1	0	593	463	22	10	5	3	25	14	972	381	1,618	871
Detroit College of Law	DATA NOT AVAILABLE													
General Motors Institute	119	12	176	76	8	1	45	10	24	3	1,429	368	1,801	470
Grace Bible College	0	0	1	0	0	1	1	0	2	0	4	1	86	55
Grand Rapids Baptist College & Seminary	4	2	2	1	0	0	1	0	0	0	373	416	380	419
Great Lakes Bible College	0	0	2	2	0	0	0	0	0	0	134	85	136	87
Hillsdale College	28	23	17	13	0	0	3	2	5	2	513	423	566	463
Hope College	37	18	14	IS	0	0	2	6	11	12	1,038	947	1,102	998
Jordan College	DATA NOT AVAILABLE													

Kalamazoo College	9	7	16	17	0	0	0	2	3	1	784	624	812	651
Kendall School of Design	DATA NOT AVAILABLE													
Lawrence Institute Technology	208	11	232	34	21	5	26	1	25	4	3,579	285	4,091	340
Lewis College of Business	0	0	41	180	0	0	1	0	0	0	3	0	45	180
Madonna College	0	2	55	136	0	1	3	8	1	2	400	942	459	1,091
Marygrove College	2	2	33	182	0	1	0	2	1	6	67	319	103	512
Mercy College of Detroit	6	16	156	397	2	5	1	7	12	19	521	1,066	698	1,510
Michigan Christian College	2	0	9	16	0	0	5	2	1	2	125	166	142	186
Muskegon Business College	0	0	46	76	1	2	0	0	5	5	260	291	312	374
Nazareth College	0	1	1	20	0	5	0	2	0	4	52	311	53	343
Northwood Institute	0	0	53	19	0	0	10	1	3	4	886	384	952	408
Olivet College	6	3	22	12	0	0	0	0	1	1	423	281	452	297
Reformed Bible College	5	8	8	0	2	3	2	2	1	2	65	66	83	81
Sacred Heart Seminary College	0	0	7	2	0	0	0	0	1	0	123	32	131	34
Saginaw Business Institute	DATA NOT AVAILABLE													
Saint John's Provincial Seminary	DATA NOT AVAILABLE													
Saint Mary's College	7	1	0	0	0	1	0	0	1	0	56	27	64	29
Sienna Heights College	3	4	40	26	4	3	1	1	22	29	373	445	443	508
Spring Arbor College	11	4	13	8	1	1	0	0	0	0	346	411	371	424
SS. Cyril and Methodius Seminary	DATA NOT AVAILABLE													
Suomi College	1	0	28	11	3	2	33	8	1	0	163	151	229	172
Thomas M. Cooley Law School	DATA NOT AVAILABLE													
University of Detroit	119	42	490	654	15	8	24	9	36	11	1,798	1,255	2,482	1,979
Walsh College of Business	2	0	20	15	0	0	1	1	3	0	570	245	596	261
Western Theological Seminary	DATA NOT AVAILABLE													
William Tyndale College	DATA NOT AVAILABLE													
Total	841	440	2,397	2,763	101	177	949	168	247	439	21,918	16,351	26,453	20,338
Percentage of Grand Total	2.7%		11.0%		.6%		2.4%		1.5%		81.89%		100.0%	

SOURCE: Postsecondary Information Unit, Michigan Department of Education, Fall 1976.

Table 14-6. Undergraduate Enrollment in Michigan Independent Colleges and Universities by Race/Ethnicity, and Sex, Fall 1986

Institution	Non-resident Alien	Black	American Indian	Asian	Hispanic	White	Race Unknown	Total
Adrian College	6	56	6	13	26	1,079	0	1,186
Albion College	11	30	0	18	3	1,524	1	1,587
Alma College	3	17	0	6	8	996	0	1,030
Andrews University	560	471	14	143	222	1,643	0	3,053
Aquinas College	12	73	11	17	31	2,504	0	1,158
Baker Junior College	0	309	21	42	26	2,258	0	2,656
Calvin College	376	27	2	20	9	3,712	0	4,146
Calvin Theological Seminary	76	1	0	15	8	145	0	245
Center for Creative Studies	36	37	0	3	11	1,071	0	1,158
Center for Humanistic Studies	0	3	0	0	1	71	0	75
Central Bible College	DATA NOT AVAILABLE					68		68
Chrysler Institute	0	125	0	1	1	378	0	505
Cleary College	1	144	3	5	3	892	3	1,071
Concordia College	10	16	3	2	4	354	33	422
Cranbrook Academy of Art	21	3	2	6	2	100	0	134
Davenport College of Business	3	319	22	13	48	3,201	0	3,606
D'Etre University	0	81	9	0	12	55	0	157
Detroit Baptist Theological Seminary	DATA NOT AVAILABLE					54		54
Detroit College of Business Administration	1	1,170	18	14	66	2,470	0	3,739
Detroit College of Law	9	70	2	10	8	656	0	755
Ecumenical Theological Seminary	DATA NOT AVAILABLE					0		0
General Motors Institute	301	182	10	138	49	2,959	0	3,639
Grace Bible College	3	4	1	0	3	120	0	131
Grand Rapids Baptist College & Seminary	20	17	2	2	2	834	0	877
Great Lakes Bible College	0	0	0	0	0	148	0	148
Great Lakes Junior College—Business	0	167	3	1	58	576	0	805
Hillsdale College	12	11	0	0	0	989	40	1,052
Hope College	66	18	4	14	27	2,416	0	2,545

Jordan College	10	1,131	6	4	30	843	0	2,024
Kalatnazoo College	43	24	1	43	8	958	26	1,103
Kendall School of Design	3	19	10	3	13	690	0	738
Lawrence Institute of Technology	126	439	43	93	57	5,384	0	6,142
Lewis College of Business	DATA NOT AVAILABLE					251		251
Madonna College	64	320	13	22	48	3,467	0	3,934
Marygrove College	7	883	4	8	6	307	0	1,215
Mercy College of Detroit	38	822	5	18	17	1,429	0	2,329
Michigan Christian College	4	56	0	0	2	216	0	278
Midrasha College/Jewish Studies	DATA NOT AVAILABLE					606		606
Muskegon Business College	0	73	3	2	6	1,302	0	1,386
Nazareth College	0	24	1	0	2	862	1	890
Northwood Institute	39	134	0	3	3	1,645	0	1,824
Olivet College	0	85	0	4	7	635	0	731
Reformed Bible College	50	1	3	9	3	98	0	164
Sacred Heart Seminary College	0	19	1	7	17	424	0	468
Saint Mary's College	7	17	0	2	2	249	0	277
Sienna Heights College	34	118	7	8	38	1,406	0	1,611
Spring Arbor College	22	151	1	7	6	1,028	0	1,217
SS. Cyril and Methodius Seminary	DATA NOT AVAILABLE					63		63
Suomi College	0	106	37	10	8	454	0	615
Thomas M. Cooley Law School	2	32	5	11	11	849	0	910
University of Detroit	306	1,006	17	85	82	4,667	0	6,165
Walsh College of Accounting and Business Administration	7	65	12	38	6	2,090	0	2,218
Western Theological Seminary	4	4	0	1	0	166	0	175
William Tyndale College	2	111	0	4	4	258	0	379
Yeshivath Beth Yehudah	DATA NOT AVAILABLE					55		55
Total	2,219	7,849	292	851	970	62,022	1,201	75,404
Percentage of Grand Total	2.9%	10.4%	0.4%	1.1%	1.3%	82.3%	2.2%	100.0%

SOURCE: Department of Health, Education, and Welfare, Enrollment Statistics, National Canter for Educational Statistics, Fall 1986.

account for 45 percent of the black student enrollment in Michigan's independent colleges and universities. The long-term pattern for these colleges, unlike that at many public schools, has produced steady growth in black student enrollment since 1970. It is striking to note that the percentage of total black student college enrollment in Michigan's private schools grew from 1970 (18 percent) to 1986 (32 percent). It is clear that the private share of black college enrollments in Michigan has been increasing, as the public share decreases. The increase in private school enrollment has not been sufficient, however, to offset the dramatic decrease in public school enrollment.

In summary, the overall proportion of black students in independent institutions of higher education in Michigan doubled from 1970 to 1986. Unlike public institutions, private institutions have not shown swift, sharp declines in black student enrollment. Independent institutions like Andrews University, the University of Detroit, Sienna Heights College, and Marygrove College realized substantial gains in black student enrollment. For many private, four-year liberal arts colleges (e.g., Hope College, Kalamazoo College, Albion College, Adrian College), however, black student enrollment declined significantly from the 1970s.

Black Student Graduate Enrollment in Michigan, 1976–1985

The discussion of black graduate enrollment will be confined to public institutions, since the overwhelming majority of the state's black graduate students are enrolled on state-controlled campuses.

In 1976, the number of students in graduate education on public campuses was 46,261 (Table 14-7). By 1985, this number had declined to 37,140, a reduction of 20 percent. Over the same period, the black graduate student population dropped from 7 percent to 5 percent of the total enrollment (3,178 to 1,881 black students). In 1985 (Table 14-8) the campuses with the largest black graduate student enrollment were: Wayne State University (826), University of Michigan-Ann Arbor (375), Michigan State University (289), and Eastern Michigan University (153). Comparison of these enrollments with the 1976 figures provides dramatic illustration of the serious declines that have occurred in black graduate enrollment. The respective figures for 1976 were: Wayne State (1,092), University of Michigan-Ann Arbor (854), Michigan State University (573), and Eastern Michigan University (369). In a nine-year period (1976–1985), black student graduate enrollment at the University of Michigan, Michigan State, and Eastern Michigan dropped by more than half (Tables 14-7 and 14-8).

The future implications of such drastic declines in the number of black graduate students are staggering. Currently the shortage of black advanced degree holders is nearing crisis dimensions, as universities, government, and the corporate world compete for a shrinking pool of eligible graduates. The sparse number of black students presently enrolled in graduate education signals that the problem will worsen dramatically in the near future. Even if enrollments were sizably expanded immediately, there would still be a three-to-seven-year lag period before those new entrants were finished with their degrees and available to enter the labor force.

Black Student Enrollment in Michigan Two-Year Public Colleges, 1976–1984

National patterns reveal black Americans to be disproportionately represented among students who attend two-year junior or community colleges. Many students in two-year public

Table 14-7. Graduate Enrollment in Michigan Four-Year Public Colleges and Universities by Race, Ethnicity, and Gender, Fall 1976

Institution	Non-resident Alien		Black		American Indian		Asian		Hispanic		White		Total	
	Men	Women	Men	Women	Men	Women	Men	Women	Men	Women	Men	Women	Men	Women
Central Michigan University	28	15	24	10	2	0	2	4	4	6	1,844	2,102	1,904	2,137
Eastern Michigan University	109	55	141	228	5	5	15	17	3	15	2,107	2,800	2,380	3,120
Ferris State College	DATA NOT AVAILABLE													
Grand Valley State College	2	1	3	6	0	1	1	1	5	2	220	169	231	180
Lake Superior State College	0	0	0	0	0	0	0	0	0	0	0	1	0	1
Michigan State University	761	200	253	320	14	5	69	33	60	55	4,771	4,658	5,928	5,271
Michigan Technological University	27	0	0	0	2	0	1	0	0	0	188	19	218	19
Northern Michigan University	17	7	5	0	0	2	1	0	1	0	404	441	428	450
Oakland University	4	2	25	67	2	7	5	6	4	3	531	1,899	571	1,984
Saginaw Valley State College	0	0	4	12	1	0	0	0	3	2	90	280	98	294
University of Michigan-Ann Arbor	843	235	376	478	12	11	90	48	91	59	4,653	3,232	6,065	4,063
University of Michigan-Dearborn	11	0	3	2	0	0	2	0	1	0	198	51	215	53
University of Michigan-Flint	DATA NOT AVAILABLE													
Wayne State University	304	235	376	716	43	33	160	56	36	41	2,830	2,035	3,749	3,116
Western Michigan University	177	70	59	70	1	7	2	4	49	49	1,572	1,726	1,860	1,926
Sub-Total	2,283	820	1,269	1,909	82	71	348	169	257	232	19,408	19,413	23,647	22,614
Total	3,103		3,178		153		517		489		38,821		46,261	
Percentage of Grand Total	6.7%		6.9%		.33%		1.1%		1.1%		83.9%		100%	

SOURCE: Department of Health, Education, and Welfare, Enrollment Data, National Center for Education Statistics, Fall 1976.

Table 14-8. Graduate Enrollment in Michigan Four-Year Public Colleges and Universities by Race, Ethnicity, and Gender, Fall 1985

	Non-resident Alien		Black		American Indian		Asian		Hispanic		White		Total		
Institution	Men	Women	Men	Women	Men	Women	Men	Women	Men	Women	Men	Women	Men	Women	Total
Central Michigan University	60	30	8	9	2	0	4	2	3	5	952	1,375	1,029	1,403	2,432
Eastern Michigan University	146	120	47	106	2	2	25	15	9	11	806	1,398	1,098	1,761	2,859
Ferris State College	0	0	0	0	0	0	0	0	0	15	16	15	16	31	47
Grand Valley State College	1	2	6	13	1	1	2	0	1	4	280	324	291	344	635
Lake Superior State College	20	9	0	0	0	0	0	0	0	0	8	4	28	13	41
Michigan State University	1,079	421	117	172	13	14	53	50	50	46	2,809	3,246	4,121	3,949	8,070
Michigan Technological University	94	8	0	0	1	0	5	1	1	0	189	65	290	74	364
Northern Michigan University	1	3	1	4	6	4	3	2	1	0	229	308	241	321	562
Oakland University	272	4	8	37	1	4	26	22	10	8	762	1,362	834	1,437	2,271
Saginaw Valley State College	3	0	6	5	0	1	3	2	2	6	188	314	202	328	530
University of Michigan-Ann Arbor	1,519	375	157	218	16	17	171	122	80	88	3,423	2,909	5,389	3,744	9,133
University of Michigan-Dearborn	2	1	6	11	1	2	11	4	3	5	330	237	353	260	613
University of Michigan-Flint	0	0	1	11	1	1	3	1	6	5	152	111	163	129	292
Wayne State University	419	105	195	631	24	27	84	64	34	63	2,208	2,393	2,964	3,283	6,247
Western Michigan University	249	103	36	76	3	3	6	3	9	11	1,049	1,515	1,349	1,711	3,060
Total	3,617	1,181	588	1,293	71	76	396	288	209	252	13,400	15,559	18,367	18,773	37,140
Percentage of Grand Total	12.9%		5.1%		0.4%		1.8%		1.2%		78.6%		100.0%		

SOURCE: Postsecondary Information Unit, Michigan Department of Education, Fall 1985.

colleges do not actually complete the requirements for an Associate of Arts degree. The instances where these students transfer into four-year degree programs are also rare since the articulation between two- and four-year institutions is limited. Thus, students enrolled in two-year public colleges experience some disadvantage relative to their peers on four-year campuses. They are generally weaker academically, come from poorer economic backgrounds, and tend not to earn degrees beyond the high school diploma. It is therefore significant that such a large number of black students who are in higher education are enrolled in two-year colleges.

From 1976 to 1984, the number of students enrolled in Michigan two-year public colleges grew by 52,363 or 38 percent (Tables 14-9 and 14-10). Certainly a sizable portion of students in two-year colleges can be characterized as "displaced," that is, as students who, given the choice (i.e., admission, available finances, proximity), would have instead enrolled in four-year colleges or universities. In 1976, black students were 14 percent of total enrollment at two-year public colleges; by 1984, black students were 11 percent of the total. For both years, black students' proportion of total enrollment on two-year public campuses exceeded their proportion of enrollment on four-year public campuses by over 3 percentage points. Through whatever combination of circumstances, Michigan black students in higher education are more likely to attend two-year institutions. By comparison, Asian, Hispanic, and white students are equally as likely to attend four-year colleges as they are to attend two-year colleges.

Black Earned Degrees from Michigan Colleges and Universities, 1976–1986

The final area of statistical comparison for this study of blacks in Michigan higher education is earned degrees: Bachelor's, Master's, Doctor's, First Professional, and Associate's degrees awarded by Michigan colleges and universities both public and private in 1976 and 1986 (Tables 14-11 and 14-12). Comparing 1976 to 1986, the number of Bachelor's degrees awarded by Michigan institutions was roughly equivalent (37,026 to 38,132), while the number of Master's degrees dropped substantially (16,005 to 11,804), and the number of Doctor's degrees also decreased (1,498 to 1,259). On the other hand, there was an increase from 1976 to 1986 in the number of First Professional degrees awarded (2,354 to 2,722), and a sizable increase in Associate degrees (20,535 to 27,866).

Black earned degrees declined in every category from 1976 to 1986 except for Associate's degrees, which increased by 140 degrees (Tables 14-11 and 14-12). This increase was not sufficient to offset the decline of 458 Bachelor's degrees, 438 Master's degrees, 58 Doctor's degrees, and 227 First Professional degrees. In short, blacks earned a total of 1,041 fewer degrees from Michigan colleges and universities in 1986 than in 1976. For the same ten-year period, Asians roughly doubled their number of degrees earned in each degree category, and whites were also successful over the period in increasing their number of earned degrees. The fact that the declines in the number of degrees awarded to blacks have been across the board refutes explanations which attribute declines in Master's and Doctorates awarded blacks to shifting interests. The across-the-board pattern also challenges the argument that a sizable proportion of black students who would have earned graduate degrees earlier now choose instead to earn professional degrees.

Table 14-9. Fall Headgount Enrollment in Two-Year Public Colleges by Race, Ethnicity, and Gender, Fall 1970

	Non-resident Alien		Black		American Indian		Asian		Hispanic		White		Total		
Institution	Men	Women	Men	Women	Men	Women	Men	Women	Men	Women	Men	Women	Men	Women	Total
Alpena Community College	2	0	28	9	6	4	6	5	1	0	1,055	639	1,098	657	1,755
Bay de Noc Community College	0	0	0	0	5	0	0	0	0	0	589	478	594	478	1,072
Charles S. Mott Community College	9	7	646	920	40	32	17	16	40	31	3,379	3,212	4,131	4,218	8,349
Delta College	202	14	323	495	12	15	30	13	96	77	3,196	3,494	3,859	4,108	7,967
Glen Oaks Community College	2	0	17	12	0	0	1	2	1	0	492	413	513	427	940
Gogebic Community College	0	0	56	0	4	3	0	0	0	0	582	447	642	450	1,092
Grand Rapids Junior College	4	2	2	1	0	0	1	0	0	0	373	416	380	419	799
Highland Park Community College	5	3	1,055	1,947	0	0	1	2	1	6	26	49	1,088	2,007	3,095
Jackson Community College	4	1	418	84	4	5	3	1	32	12	1,831	1,103	2,292	1,206	3,498
Kalamazoo Valley Community College	79	19	10G	135	68	71	30	12	43	23	1,507	1,714	1,833	1,974	3,807
Kellogg Community College	9	3	86	120	8	13	9	5	11	7	1,461	2,554	1,584	2,702	4,286
Kirtland Community College	1	1	22	0	2	2	0	0	1	3	720	431	746	437	1,183
Lake Michigan College	8	6	207	290	4	13	5	4	17	10	1,562	1,301	1,803	1,624	3,427
Lansing Community College	149	71	400	400	46	42	58	55	161	134	7,475	7,442	8,289	8,144	16,433
Macomb County Community College	0	0	146	93	58	39	43	28	41	29	10,411	6,790	10,699	6,979	17,678
Mid Michigan Community College	8	0	1	0	7	2	0	1	2	3	508	525	526	531	1,057

Monroe County Community College	0	0	4	4	0	0	0	1	1	1	1,050	967	1,055	973	2,028
Montcalm Community College	2	1	169	0	5	2	0	0	8	0	608	447	792	450	1,242
Muskegon Community College	0	0	192	160	15	10	0	0	26	14	2447	1,804	2,680	1,988	4,668
North Central Michigan College	4	1	1	0	6	3	0	0	1	0	702	815	714	819	4,533
Northwestern Michigan College	12	3	6	1	10	4	2	2	5	7	1,253	1,300	1,288	1,317	2,605
Oakland Community College	0	0	436	505	35	27	25	31	94	50	7,828	9,369	8,418	9,982	18,40D
Saint Clair County Community College	7	2	37	34	2	0	0	1	17	10	1,506	1,530	1,569	1,577	10,981
Schoolcraft College	18	12	67	30	49	36	30	26	40	52	3,751	3,724	3,955	3,880	7,835
Southwestern Michigan College	5	0	58	50	6	8	2	3	2	0	926	1,047	999	1,108	2,107
Washtenaw Community College	0	0	505	425	8	7	33	33	14	15	3,059	2,494	3,619	2,974	6,593
Wayne County Community College	35	13	2,908	5,774	75	122	17	20	39	37	867	1,317	3,941	7,280	11,221
West Shore Community College	0	0	9	9	1	0	2	0	0	0	445	356	457	365	822
Total	565	724	7,905	11,498	476	460	315	261	694	521	58,559	56,178	69,564	69,074	138,638
Percentage of Grand Total	0.9%		14.0%		0.7%		0.4%		0.9%		82.8%		100.0%		

SOURCE: Department of Health, Education, and Welfare, Enrollment Data, National Center for Education Statistics, Fall 1970.

Table 14-10. Fall Headcount Enrollment in Two-Year Public Colleges by Race, Ethnicity, and Gender, Fall 1984

Institution	Non-resident Alien		Black		American Indian		Asian		Hispanic		White		Total		
	Men	Women	Men	Women	Men	Women	Men	Women	Men	Women	Men	Women	Men	Women	Total
Alpena Community College	1	0	32	14	1	1	5	2	8	5	860	949	907	971	1,878
Bay de Noc Community College	2	0	0	0	17	23	1	2	0	5	684	1,067	704	1,097	1,801
Charles S. Mott Community College	12	2	522	1,054	52	69	24	38	74	97	3,826	5,388	4,510	6,648	11,158
Delta College	4	2	259	566	15	28	21	25	135	162	3,804	5,222	4,238	6,005	10,243
Glen Oaks Community College	17	0	5	15	1	2	4	2	4	2	513	648	544	669	1,313
Gogebic Community College	0	0	345	0	7	6	2	1	12	0	702	525	1,068	532	1,600
Grand Rapids Junior College	46	1	259	325	29	17	52	73	60	89	4,013	3,949	4,459	4,454	8,913
Highland Park Community College	21	11	630	1,694	0	0	1	2	0	3	11	43	663	1,753	2,415
Jackson Community College	3	6	509	104	18	16	75	30	30	14	2,445	2,824	3,079	2,992	6,071
Kalamazoo Valley Community College	122	27	292	405	20	17	34	35	27	45	3,064	4,193	3,559	4,722	8,281
Kellogg Community College	26	2	132	259	9	15	14	18	19	22	1,445	2,592	1,645	2,908	4,553
Kirtland Community College	20	0	1	5	0	0	4	4	509	789	535	798	1,333	1,596	2,929
Lake Michigan College	18	17	118	272	1	5	17	22	11	32	1,152	1,534	1,317	1,882	3,199
Lansing Community College	147	70	456	615	62	72	162	100	145	196	7,350	9,782	8,322	10,835	19,157
Macomb County Community College	37	15	350	234	58	83	161	115	77	113	14,676	14,971	15,359	15,533	30,892
Mid Michigan Community College	9	7	1	6	7	4	2	0	1	3	684	1,038	704	1,058	1,762

Monroe County Community College	1	0	6	13	3	3	4	5	6	10	1,144	1,683	1,166	1,714	2,880
Montcalm Community College	0	0	152	0	4	0	4	1	9	0	588	640	757	641	1,398
Muskegon Community College	0	0	132	175	30	54	14	14	27	22	1,828	2,327	2,031	2,592	4,623
North Central Michigan College	1	2	1	1	14	25	1	4	3	5	569	1,066	589	1,103	1,692
Northwestern Michigan College	17	2	2	1	15	10	4	3	8	1	1,462	1,697	1,508	1,714	3,222
Oakland Community College	107	65	557	1201	55	61	102	79	174	206	10,110	13,888	11,105	15,500	26,605
Saint Clair County Community College	6	5	10	36	3	4	5	2	5	10	1,447	2,352	1,476	2,409	3,885
Schoolcraft College	1	0	71	64	8	15	40	38	7	14	3,754	4,500	3,881	4,631	8,512
Southwestern Michigan College	8	4	80	85	10	15	7	2	6	12	840	1,296	951	1,414	2,365
Washtenaw Community College	11	21	461	521	27	38	93	82	28	19	3,170	3,387	3,790	4,068	7,858
Wayne County Community College	279	106	2,267	5,282	26	81	65	53	57	101	1,614	2,477	4,308	8,100	12,408
West Shore Community College	0	0	3	5	2	3	0	4	3	2	403	658	411	672	1,083
Total	897	365	7,674	12,947	495	672	914	752	940	1,194	72,667	91,485	83,586	107,415	191,001
Percentage of Grand Total	0.7%		10.8%		0.6%		0.9%		1.1%		85.9%		100.0%		

SOURCE: Pastsecondary Information Unit, Michigan Department of Education, Fall 1984.

Table 14-11. Earned Degrees by Race, Ethnicity, and Sex, Michigan Colleges and Universities, 1976

	Non-Resident Alien		American Indian Alaskan Native		Black Non-Hispanic		Asian or Pacific Islander		Hispanic		Total Minority		White Non-Hispanic		
	Number	%	Number	%	Number	%	Number	%	Number	%	Number	%	Number	%	Total
Bachelor's Degree (51)	667	1.8	81	.2	2,420	6.5	204	.6	289	.8	2,994	8.1	33,365	90.1	37,026
Female	190	1.2	32	.2	1,382	8.5	86	.5	122	.8	1,662	10.0	14,447	88.9	16,259
Male	477	2.3	49	.2	1,038	5.0	118	.6	167	.8	1,372	6.6	18,918	91.1	20,767
Master's Degree (21)	1,112	6.9	24	.1	1,217	7.6	117	.7	141	.9	1,499	9.4	13,394	83.7	16,005
Female	295	4.1	13	.2	806	11.3	47	.7	61	.9	927	13.0	5,908	82.9	7,130
Male	817	9.2	11	.1	411	4.6	70	.8	80	.9	572	6.4	7,486	84.3	8,875
Doctor's Degree (7)	183	12.2	3	.2	132	8.8	20	1.3	28	1.9	183	12.2	1,132	75.6	1,498
Female	31	8.2	2	.5	46	12.2	2	.5	5	1.3	55	14.6	292	77.2	378
Male	152	13.6	1	.1	86	7.7	18	1.6	23	2.1	128	11.4	840	75.0	1,120
First Professional Degree (10)	51	2.2	1	.0	343	14.6	10	.4	37	1.6	391	16.6	1,912	81.2	2,354
Female	13	3.4	0	.0	52	13.8	2	.5	2	.5	56	14.8	309	81.7	378
Male	38	1.9	1	.1	291	14.7	8	.4	35	1.8	335	17.0	603	81.1	1,976
Associate's Degree (68)	156	.8	31	.2	2,269	11.0	74	.4	196	1.0	2,570	12.5	17,809	86.7	20,535
Female	27	.3	13	.1	1,274	12.9	30	.3	79	.8	1,396	14.1	8,478	85.6	9,901
Male	129	1.2	18	.2	995	9.4	44	.4	117	1.1	1,174	11.0	9,331	87.7	10,634

SOURCE: Department of Health, Education, and Welfare, Earned Degrees Data, National Center for Education Statistics, 1976

( ) = Number of institutions reporting.

Table 14-12. Earned Degrees by Race, Ethnicity, and Gender, Michigan Colleges and Universities, 1986

	Non-Resident Alien		American Indian Alaskan Native		Black Non-Hispanic		Asian or Pacific Islander		Hispanic		Total Minority		White Non-Hispanic		
	Number	%	Number	%	Number	%	Number	%	Number	%	Number	%	Number	%	Total
Bachelor's Degree (52)	1,227	3.2	121	.3	1,962	5.1	431	1.1	306	.8	2,820	7.4	33,941	89	38,132
Female	361	1.9	63	.3	1,270	6.7	176	.9	164	.9	1,673	8.9	16,711	88.8	18,825
Male	866	4.5	58	.3	692	3.6	255	1.3	142	.7	1,147	5.9	17,230	89.2	19,307
Master's Degree (29)	1,587	13.4	44	.4	779	6.6	236	2.0	131	1.1	1,190	10.1	8,908	75.5	11,804
Female	372	6.7	20	.4	489	8.8	89	1.6	73	1.1	671	12.1	4,468	80.3	5,567
Male	1,215	19.5	24	.4	290	4.6	147	2.4	58	.9	519	8.3	4,440	71.2	6,237
Doctor's Degree (10)	257	20.4	2	.2	74	5.9	30	2.4	20	1.6	126	10.0	876	69.9	1,259
Female	41	10.4	1	.3	36	9.1	10	2.5	6	1.5	53	13.4	301	76.2	395
Male	216	25.0	1	.1	38	4.4	20	2.3	14	1.6	73	8.4	575	66.6	864
First Professional Degree (12)	39	1.4	6	.2	116	4.3	26	1.0	34	1.2	182	6.7	1,726	63.4	2,722
Female	6	.7	4	.5	44	5.2	10	1.2	6	.7	64	7.5	553	65.0	851
Male	33	1.8	2	.1	72	3.8	16	.9	28	1.5	118	6.3	1,173	62.7	1,871
Associate's Degree (67)	270	1.0	149	.5	2,409	8.6	183	.7	303	1.1	3,044	10.9	23,669	84.9	27,866
Female	101	.6	90	.5	1,578	9.6	70	.4	177	1.1	1,915	11.7	13,898	84.7	16,412
Male	169	1.5	59	.5	831	7.3	113	1.0	126	1.1	1,129	9.9	9,771	85.3	11,454

SOURCE: Postsecondary Information Unit, Michigan Department of Education, 1986.

( ) = Number of institutions reporting.

Unfortunately, statistics on black student enrollment in Michigan professional schools were not available. Therefore, it is not possible at this point to resolve the issue of whether declines in black student graduate enrollments in Michigan universities have been compensated by increased enrollments in professional schools. Related data suggest, however, that this is not the case. For instance, rather than increasing, the proportion of First Professional degrees awarded to blacks in Michigan has decreased significantly since 1976 (14.6 percent to 4.3 percent). This fact suggests that black student enrollment in Michigan professional schools has declined in line with general declines in black student enrollment in Michigan higher education.

Discussion and Implications: An Agenda for Action

This year marks the thirty-third anniversary of *Brown v. the Topeka Board of Education* and the twenty-second anniversary of the Higher Education Act of 1965. Both the Supreme Court's epic decision outlawing segregation in public schools and the U.S. Congress' subsequent decision to foster equal opportunity in college education helped to change the higher education experience for black Americans. The Civil Rights Movement of the 1950s and 1960s and the Black Liberation Movement of the 1960s and 1970s were also influential in redefining the college experience for black Americans. The number of black college students enrolled in higher education has more than doubled since 1960 (Thomas, 1981); and for the first time in history, black students are more likely to matriculate at predominantly white as opposed to traditionally black institutions (Deskins, 1983).

Over the long run, there has been substantial improvement in the college attainment of black Americans. On the surface, our society would seem to have made important progress toward dismantling the two-tiered "separate and unequal" higher education system based on race. Yet there are persistent problems, problems that potentially threaten or undercut black gains in higher education.

College-educated black males have higher unemployment rates than white male high school graduates; similarly, college-educated black males earn less than white male high school drop-outs (Farley and Allen, 1987). There has also been a steady, precipitous decline in black college enrollment and degree attainment since 1975. So dramatic are these declines that the substantial gains in college access made by blacks during the late 1960s and early 1970s are in danger of complete reversal. In short, the struggle continues.

The pattern of black enrollment and degree attainment in Michigan institutions of higher education parallels the national trend. On balance, blacks have lost ground since 1976, after dramatic increases from 1970 to 1975. Five factors are of particular significance in explaining these declines.

1. ***The reduced availability of financial aid from government sources.*** Cutbacks in federal and state funding of college education for low-income students have had devastating consequences for black enrollment and degree attainment. Because of their disproportionately low economic status, black students are dependent on financial aid in order to pursue advanced education. When this money is not available, the access of large numbers of black students to college is effectively blocked.

2. ***Weaker enforcement of Equal Opportunity and Affirmative Action regulations.*** A vast reservoir of racial prejudice, discrimination, and animosity persists in this society in the form of individual and institutional racism. Therefore, it is essential that there be systematic review and enforcement of government regulations requiring implementation of equal opportunity and affirmative action practices. When the federal and state governments opted for a more laissez-faire position in the enforcement of these regulations, the result was to encourage institutions and individuals to revert to traditionally exclusionary practices.
3. ***The redirection of university priorities from an emphasis on diversity to an emphasis on more restrictive admissions criteria.*** When universities moved to more restrictive admissions criteria in response to concerns about the declining quality of U.S. higher education, the result was to exclude sizable numbers of black students. Most devastating for black students, in this case, was the tendency to overemphasize scores on standardized tests in the admissions decision.
4. ***The higher number of black family heads who are unemployed or who are outside the labor force.*** Deterioration in the economic status of black families has indirectly, but powerfully, influenced black student access to post-secondary education in Michigan. Low-income students are less able to finance a college education, they tend to score lower on standardized tests, they are likely to have received weaker academic preparation in high school, and they are more often forced to enter the job market prematurely.
5. ***The high number of black youngsters who fail to graduate and the high number who graduate with weak educational foundations.*** Urban school systems are in crisis because urban communities are in crisis. These schools often represent the last bastion of defense against the poverty, despair, violence, and deprivation bred of the apartheid structure of life for this country's poor, black urban dwellers who have been written off as a non-salvageable underclass. Urban schools in this state and in the country are underfunded, understaffed, and sometimes lacking in the necessary will and direction to function effectively. The result is that black elementary and secondary school students continue to drop out at alarming rates and to be educationally handicapped.

The problem of black underrepresentation in higher education is not insoluble. Despite a mythology that suggests otherwise, the universities and colleges in this state have it in their power to substantially increase the number of black students enrolled and earning degrees. The problem of black access to Michigan colleges and universities cannot be easily resolved, however. Concerted, dedicated action will be required by colleges and universities, as well as by other actors, if the situation is to improve.

Recommendations

The following recommendations outline strategies that should be developed and actions that should be taken to improve the status of black people in Michigan higher education. For purposes of this chapter, these recommendations are restricted to the role of universities and colleges. It should be noted, however, that the public schools, the larger black community, black families, and the students themselves all have important roles to play in achieving the goal of expanded black participation in higher education.

Universities and colleges should:

1. Develop financial aid programs that more effectively address the needs of black students and result in increased black participation in higher education. The support should be provided at a level to insure that the representation of black students is at least equal to the proportion of blacks in Michigan's population (about 12 percent). It is particularly important that financial aid packages deemphasize the excessive indebtedness resulting from student loans in favor of other alternatives (e.g., scholarships, grants, work study).
2. Adjust the criteria on which decisions to admit black students are based, so as to give less weight to standardized test scores and more weight to other factors such as high school grades, motivation, work experience, and letters of reference.
3. Institute or expand special programming focused on the needs and circumstances of black students. Such programs might include activities in areas such as pre-college enrichment, academic remediation, and comprehensive support services.
4. Involve college faculty more extensively in the process of black student recruitment and retention. As the institution's "human link" between policy statements and performance, faculty play a critical role. They can either assist or debilitate the college experience of black students.

In short, Michigan institutions of higher education must make genuine and sustained efforts to recruit and retain black students and to improve the quality of their educational experiences. In the absence of serious institutional commitment, little progress will result. Colleges and universities need to design coordinated programming that is sensitive to black student needs at each stage in the process leading to successful attainment in higher education—that is, from the pre-college years, through college recruitment, admission, matriculation, and graduation. Without systematic planning and implementation of special strategies and incentives which reward institutional success, and punish failure, the situation will not improve significantly (Governor's Commission on the Future of Higher Education, December 1984). Inaction can only lead to further "dreams deferred." And as Langston Hughes wrote, "Such dreams lag like a heavy load and may even explode."

Twenty years ago, Detroit exploded, and the results of persistent deprivation, festering resentment, and frustrated dreams spilled over into an urban crisis. Today most of those problems are still with us, and many have worsened. In 1970, in 1975, and again in 1987, we experienced explosions on Michigan's campuses, as black students rose up to protest the denial of the American dream of sustained progress and upward mobility.

Unless and until the legitimate aspirations of black people in this state and in the nation are addressed, we shall all live in an uneasy quietude, nervous about when the next explosion will occur, and certain that there will be a next explosion . . . and another . . . and another . . . until black people are admitted into full citizenship, with all the rights and privileges implied.

REFERENCES

Allen, Walter. *Gender and Campus Race Differences in Black Student Academic Performance, Racial Attitudes and College Satisfaction.* Atlanta; Georgia: Southern Education Foundation, 1986.

American Council on Education. *Minorities in Higher Education Fifth Annual Status Report,* 1986. Washington, DC: American Council on Education, 1986.

Blackwell, James E. *Mainstreaming Outsiders: The Production of Black Professionals.* Bayside, New York: General Hall, 1981.

Deskins, Donald. *Minority Recruitment Data.* Totawa, New Jersey: Rowman and Allanheld, 1983.

Farley, W. Reynolds and Allen, Walter R. *The Color Line and the Quality of Life: Problem for the Twenty-First Century.* New York, New York: Russell Sage Foundation, 1987.

Fleming, Jacqueline. *Blacks in College.* San Francisco, California: Jossey-Bass, 1984.

Governor's Commission on the Future of Higher Education. "Putting Our Minds Together: New Directions for Michigan." Lansing, Michigan: Governor's Office, December 1984.

Morris, Lorenzo. *Elusive Equality: The Status of Black Americans in Higher Education.* Washington, D.C.: Howard University Press, 1979.

Thomas, Gail E. *Black Students in Higher Education: Conditions and Experiences.* Westport, Connecticut: Greenwood, 1981.

CHAPTER 15

Racial Disparities in Michigan's Educational System in 2006

Joe T. Darden

Introduction

Percy Bates concluded in the 1989 *The State of Black Michigan* report (reprinted in this volume as Chapter 13) that the State of Michigan has not succeeded in its responsibility to provide equal educational opportunities to all students. According to Bates, in 1981–1982, the black dropout rate was 7.8%, resulting in a black-white ratio of 1.7. However, by 1985–1986, the black dropout rate had increased to 12%, whereas the white dropout rate had declined to 4.5%, resulting in an increase in the black-white ratio to 2.6 (Bates 1989).

Also, in a previous *The State of Black Michigan* report (reprinted in this volume as Chapter 14), Walter Allen concluded that three years after the civil disorders and five years after the Higher Education Act of 1965, the participation of blacks in higher education in Michigan was dismal. Black student enrollment in Michigan's public universities had been declining from 1976 to 1986. Consistent with the decline in black student enrollment, the number of blacks earning degrees also declined from 1976 to 1985 (Allen 1987).

This chapter reexamines the status of blacks in education using the most recent data available. It focuses on racial disparities in high school graduation rates, dropout rates, enrollment in degree-granting institutions, and awarding of degrees by higher education institutions.

Racial Disparities in High School Graduation and Dropout Rates

Most blacks attend public schools in Michigan's large central cities. These schools are highly segregated by race and class. In fact, public schools in Michigan are among the most racially segregated in the nation (Logan, Stowell, and Oakley 2002). Among the 50 largest metropolitan areas, school children in Metropolitan Detroit attend the most racially segregated public schools, with an index of dissimilarity of 88.5 in 1999 (Logan, Stowell, and Oakley 2002). An index of 100 is complete segregation of the races, compared to an index of 0, which is complete desegregation.

Such urban school districts, where most blacks attend school, are also the poorest. Segregation by race and class impacts the dropout rates. The ability of Michigan to address the educational needs of the black population is critical for creating a better-educated workforce and maintaining or increasing Michigan's standing relative to other states with respect to educational attainment and personal income (Kelley 2005).

Since some studies calculate the graduation and dropout rate differently, I present here the way the graduation rate was calculated by Greene and Winters (2006), on which the discussion is based. The method is as follows: graduation rate = regular diplomas in spring of 2003/(estimated number of students entering ninth grade in 1999) * (1 + population change between 14 year olds in the summer of 1999 and 17 year olds in the summer of 2002).

Unlike many other high school graduation rate calculations, the estimates using the above method can be manipulated to interpret the high school dropout rate as well (Greene and Winters 2006). The high school dropout rate is found by subtracting the high school graduation rate from 100. That is, a graduation rate of 70% implies a dropout rate of 30% (Greene and Winters 2006).

In the nation as a whole, about 78% of white students and only 55% of black students graduated with a regular diploma in the class of 2003, a difference of 23 percentage points. Moreover, at 48%, black male students reported the lowest graduation rates of any subgroup nationally. Black females graduated at a rate of 59%, compared to a white female rate of 79%, the highest of any subgroups (Greene and Winters 2006).

Among large public school districts, Detroit, with a total student enrollment of 173,742 in 2003, had the highest dropout rate (58%) of any school district with 100,000 students or more (Greene and Winters 2006). Moreover, among 100 school districts in the nation ranging in size from 44,000 to more than 1 million students, Detroit tied with San Bernardino, California, as the district with the highest dropout rate (Greene and Winters 2006).

Black-White Graduation and Dropout Rates in Michigan

Table 15-1 shows that only 57% of blacks graduated from public schools in 2003, compared to 80% of whites, a difference of 23 percentage points. Those least likely to graduate were

Table 15-1. Black-White Differences in Public High School Graduation Rates in Michigan, 2003

	Total (%)	Total Black (%)	Total White (%)	Difference Gap
Overall	77	57	80	−23
Male	71	50	77	−27
Female	80	65	84	−19

SOURCE: Calculated by the author from data obtained from Greene and Winters (2006).

Table 15-2. Black-White Differences in Public High School Dropout Rates in Michigan, 2003

	Total	Total Black (%)	Total White (%)	Difference Gap	Black vs. White Ratio
Overall	23	43	20	+23	2.15
Male	29	50	23	+27	2.17
Female	20	35	16	+19	2.18

SOURCE: Calculated by the author from data obtained from Greene and Winters (2006).

black males. Only 50% graduated, compared to 77% of white males, resulting in the widest difference gap of any subgroup (27 percentage points). The racial gap was smaller (19 percentage points) between black and white female students (Table 15-1).

The dropout rate is reported in Table 15-2. Black students were more than twice as likely as white students to drop out of high school. In fact, the black dropout rate for both males and females was more than twice the rate for whites.

Changes in Dropout Rates, 1986–2003

Based on data from Michigan's Department of Education Survey, analyzed by Bates (1989), the dropout rate for Michigan was 12% for blacks and 4.5% for whites in 1985–1986. The racial difference gap was 7.5. However, based on data for 2003 from the Manhattan Institute, the black dropout rate was 43%, compared to a white dropout rate of 20%, a difference of 23 percentage points.

In Detroit in 1985–1986, the black dropout rate was 14.8%, compared to a white dropout rate of 23.4%, a dropout rate lower for blacks than for whites. In 2003, the dropout rate for blacks was 57% compared to a white dropout rate of 67%, a difference of 10 percentage points in favor of blacks. In the Detroit public schools, it is clear that the dropout rate increased to 3.85 times the rate in 1985–1986 for blacks and 2.86 times the rate for whites.

In sum, the black-white ratio for high school dropouts in Michigan changed little from 1986 to 2003. In 1986, the ratio was 2.60. By 2003, the ratio was 2.15 (Table 16-2), a difference of only 0.45.

Racial Disparities in Higher Education

Blacks in Michigan are disproportionately low income and disproportionately underserved by higher educational institutions 40 years after the civil disorders of 1967. Michigan, like other states, has a wide gap in black and white higher educational attainment. While 33.7% of all whites aged 25–64 had a college degree (associate or higher), only 20.4% of all blacks in that same age range had achieved this level of education in 2000 (U.S. Census Bureau 2004). The difference gap between blacks and whites was 13.3 percentage points. Whites were 1.65 times more likely to have a college degree compared to blacks.

Education is the most effective intervention available for improving the state's social and economic future. A high school education is not enough given the changes in the economy from manufacturing to service. State-level policy-making is crucial to providing greater

Table 15-3. Fall Enrollment in Michigan's Degree-Granting Institutions by Students' Race/Ethnicity, 2005–2006

Number White, Non-Hispanic	Number Black, Non-Hispanic	Total
448,017	76,295	626,751

% White	% Black
71.4	12.2

% of Population Aged 25–64 in 2000

White	Black
80.0	13.2

SOURCES: (1) National Center for Education Statistics. 2004. Integrated post secondary survey data (http://nces.gov/programs/digest/do5/tables/xla/tabno208.xls). (2) U.S. Census Bureau. 2004. Public use micro-data files.

access to all students (low income), from all geographic areas of the state (cities, rural areas, and suburbs).

Table 15-3 reports the Fall enrollment in degree-granting institutions in Michigan for black and white students during 2005–2006. The white percentage was 71.4%, compared to the black percentage of 12.2%. This percentage was slightly below the black percentage of the population aged 25–64 in 2000, which was 13.2% (Table 15-3).

Table 15-4 reports the changes in degrees awarded to black and white students from 1976 to 2006. The number of blacks receiving degrees has increased from 6,249 in 1976 to 10,295 in 2006, or by 64.7%. The number of whites receiving degrees increased from 67,612 to 81,947, or by 21.2%, in that same time period. However, the black percentage of total degrees changed little over this time period. According to Allen (1987; also Chapter 14 of this volume), the black percentage of total degrees awarded, which was 8.1% in 1976, declined to 6.5% in 1986. The most recent data show an increase to 9.3% by 2005–2006. Thus, in terms of the black percentage of total degrees awarded, the increase was only 1.2 percentage points between 1976 and 2005–2006.

Table 15-4. Higher Education Degrees Awarded to Black and White Students in Michigan, Fall 2005/Spring 2006 Compared to 1976–1986

Year	Total Degrees Awarded	Number Black	% Black	Number White	% White
1976	77,418	6,249	8.1	67,612	87.3
1986	81,783	5,340	6.5	69,120	84.5
2005/06	110,999	10,295	9.3	81,947	73.8

SOURCES: (1) Allen, W. 1987. Blacks in Michigan higher education. In *The state of black Michigan, 1987*, ed. F. Thomas, 53–68. East Lansing: Michigan State University Urban Affairs Programs. (2) U.S. Department of Education, National Center for Education Statistics, Integrated Postsecondary Education Data System (IPEDS), Fall 2005 and Spring 2006. Used with permission.

Conclusions

Racial disparities persist in Michigan's educational system 40 years after the civil disorders in 1967. This racial disparity is reflected in the high school dropout rates, which have changed little. There has also been little change in the black percentage of total degrees awarded from 1976 to 2006. However, the number of blacks receiving degrees increased by 64.7% from 1976 to 2006. Given the recent passage of Proposal 2, approved by 58% of Michigan voters, both black enrollment in Michigan's higher education institutions and the percentage of degrees awarded to blacks are expected to decline in the future. The proposal amended the state constitution to ban all state agencies and institutions from operating Affirmative Action programs that grant preferences based on race, color, ethnicity, national origin, or gender. The measure was to take effect December 23, 2006 (June 2007). Recommendations for addressing the racial disparities in education are presented in Chapter 19.

REFERENCES

Allen, W. 1987. Blacks in Michigan higher education. In *The state of black Michigan, 1987*, ed. F. Thomas, 53–68. East Lansing: Michigan State Univ. Urban Affairs Programs.

Bates, P. 1989. Black and white high school dropout rates in Michigan: The inequality persists. In *The state of black Michigan, 1989*, ed. F. Thomas, 19–27. East Lansing: Michigan State Univ. Urban Affairs Programs.

Greene, J. P., and M. Winters. 2006. Leaving boys behind: Public high school graduation rates. Civic Report 48. New York: Manhattan Institute for Policy Research.

June, A. W. 2007. Federal appeals court overturns extension for Michigan universities on complying with preference ban. *Chronicle of Higher Education*. January 3.

Kelley, P. 2005. *As America becomes more diverse: The impact of state higher education inequality*. Boulder, CO: National Center for Higher Education Management Systems.

Logan, J. R., J. Stowell, and D. Oakley. 2002. *Choosing segregation: Racial imbalance in American public schools*. Albany, NY: Mumford Center. http://mumford.albany.edu/census/SchoolPop/SPReport/page1.html.

U.S. Census Bureau. 2004. Public use microdata samples: Five percent samples for each state based on the 2000 census. http://www.census.gov.

PART 4

Political Conditions

CHAPTER 16

Black Political Participation in Michigan

Curtis Stokes

Throughout the 1980s, black Americans continued to support the Democratic Party. This was as true in the State of Michigan as in the nation. Beginning in the last two years of the Carter Administration and developing with intensity during the Reagan years, deep cuts in social spending had a negative impact upon the life chances of African Americans. In Michigan, despite the decline in living standards in the black community under a state government that was largely Democratic, there was no substantial decrease during the 1980s in black support for the Democratic Party at either the state or the national level.

This chapter will discuss electoral progress and problems of blacks during the 1980s; will present findings from an opinion survey of selected black public officials concerning their views on the spending priorities for the State of Michigan; will review the circumstances of the reelection in November 1989 of Coleman Young for a fifth term as mayor of Detroit; and will consider the possible future direction of black political activity in Michigan.

Electoral Progress and Problems of Blacks During the 1980s

Nationally, African Americans have made important electoral gains (measured in terms of voter registration, voting, and the number of elected officials) in the last twenty-five years. Problems remain, however. "The ability of black Americans to have their concerns heard and addressed in the halls of government has increased dramatically since the passage of the Voting Rights Act of 1965. . . . Despite this progress, there are still significant barriers to black political empowerment and representation" (Chambers, 1990, p. 15).

In pursuit of black empowerment, not only are there explicitly political barriers (such as the use of at-large elections), but there are also social and economic obstacles, like poverty and unemployment. After the progress of the late 1960s and the early 1970s, black electoral advance nationally tended to slow down in the 1980s. During this period, the annual rate of increase in the ranks of black elected officials was in general decline nationally (Jaynes and Williams, 1989, p. 238).

In Michigan, the number of black elected officials increased during the late 1970s and 1980s. There were 245 black elected officials in 1976; and by 1988, blacks held 316 of the 19,403 elective offices in the state. These 316 included two U.S. representatives, two state senators, thirteen state representatives, and one statewide elected official—the Secretary of State (*Black Elected Officials*, 1989, p. 219). These numbers, however, do not fully reveal the extent of black political influence in the state. In 1988, blacks were 10.1 percent of the state legislature; Detroit, the nation's seventh largest city, reelected a black mayor in 1989; and the two black U.S. representatives from Michigan are influential in Washington.

Moreover, Michigan seems to be faring reasonably well in the number of black female elected officials. Indeed, this appears to be part of a national trend. "While the pattern of growth and distribution of black females elected to office follows that of black elected officials as a whole, the number of black female officeholders, comprising 22.4 percent [nationally in 1984 and 1985] of all black elected officials, continues to increase at a faster annual rate than [the rate for] all black officials combined" (Preston, Henderson, and Puryear, 1987, p. 122).

In 1988, Michigan had 93 black female elected officials, ranking fifth in the nation behind Illinois, the District of Columbia, Mississippi, and California (*Black Elected Officials*, 1989, p. 15). Nevertheless, both nationally and in Michigan, black women have a long way to go before reaching parity with black men in the electoral arena—at least in regard to holding elective office.

In the areas of voter registration and election turnout during the 1980s, blacks continued to show improvement in closing the gaps between themselves and whites. The turnout rate at the national level was typical of this continued movement. "A first level of mobilization is registering to vote, and here blacks have made substantial progress compared to whites. . . . The gap between black and white turnout rates narrowed dramatically in the 1980s, from 10.4 percentage points in 1980 to only 5.6 percentage points in 1984, the lowest gap ever recorded" (Preston, Henderson, and Puryear, 1987, pp. 103 and 109). There was a reversal of this national trend in 1988, as the gap between black and white turnout widened to 7.6 percent (Jaynes and Williams, 1989, p. 235). Whether this will be a temporary reversal remains to be seen.

While the electoral political gains that African Americans have made over the last decade in the state should not be minimized, much more remains to be accomplished. In 1988, blacks were about 14 percent of the state's population and about 12 percent of the voting age population. Yet blacks held only 1.6 percent of the 19,403 elective offices in the state (*Black Elected Officials*, 1989, p. 9). Although the 1.6 percent is an improvement over the 1.1 percent in the late 1970s and is comparable to the national percentage for black elected officials, it falls far short of what has been attained in some states, especially in the South, relative to the black percentage of the voting age population. For example, Alabama, with a black voting age population of 22.9 percent, had 10.6 percent black representation in a total of 4,160 elected officials. (*Black Elected Officials*, 1989, pp. 9–10). As Table 16-1 shows, in the years between 1984 and 1988, Michigan blacks have stayed the same in four elective offices, lost ground in seven, and made gains in only four.

Proportional black representation in elective offices is important, and it is also important that citizens be informed concerning the viewpoints of the black officials presently serving in office.

In order to collect information in this area, an opinion survey was taken of Michigan black elected officials. (A copy of the survey instrument is presented in an Appendix to this chapter.)

The Opinion Survey of Michigan Black Elected Officials

Population and Sample

Between February 14 and April 9, 1990, an opinion survey of the 316 Michigan black elected officials was conducted by questionnaires sent through the mail. Four of the survey questionnaires appeared to be not deliverable. Of the 312 black elected officials who received questionnaires, 121 (or 38.5 percent) responded. No names were requested, and the assurance of anonymity was given.

Although this sample does not necessarily constitute a random sample of black elected officials in Michigan, it is nevertheless sufficient to provide meaningful descriptive statistics on the general perceptions of black elected officials regarding the issues addressed in the survey. According to Cochran (1977), this sample would achieve an error bound of 0.64 with a 0.95 confidence level. This means that the statistics computed from this sample could differ from the actual value by no more than plus or minus 0.64 with probability 0.95.

Methodology

Respondents were asked to indicate their viewpoints on the direction in which state appropriations from the general purpose fund should move for the upcoming fiscal year (1990–91), as compared with appropriations for the 1989–90 fiscal year. To guide the respondents, figures were provided on appropriations for eight departments/programs for the 1989–90 fiscal year (Table 16-2 and Appendix).

The black elected officials were also provided with seven statements addressing selected issues for which they were asked to rate their level of agreement or disagreement (Table 16-3 and Appendix).

Findings

Table 16-2, which provides the percentages and means for the eight expenditure categories, indicates that except for expenditures on corrections, the majority of black elected officials supported increased funding for each of the departments/programs on which the survey requested an opinion. For corrections, the majority believed that the expenditures should remain about the same.

In the areas of civil rights and education (especially school aid for K-12 education), there was support for a "substantial increase" in state spending. Only a few respondents supported any kind of decrease in state spending in the eight categories.

Table 16-1. Population Data and Data on Distribution of Black Elected Officials,* State of Michigan, 1984 and 1988

Population Data

	Total 1984	Black 1984		Total 1988	Black 1988		Percentage Change in Black Representation 1984–1988
		Number	Percentage		Number	Percentage	
General Population	9,262,078	1,199,023	13.0	9,075,000	1,232,385	14.0	+1.0
Voting Age Population	6,554,000	767,000	12.0	6,530,000	803,000	12.3	+.3
Registered Voters	4,739,000	553,000	11.6	4,819,000	603,000	13.0	+1.4
Elected Officals	19,403	297	1.5	19,403	316	1.6	+.1

Data on Distribution of Black Elected Officials*

	Total 1984	Black 1984		Total 1988	Black 1988		Percentage Change in Black Representation 1984–1988
		Number	Percentage		Number	Percentage	
Federal							
Representative	18	2	11.0	18	2	11.0	0.0
State							
Senator	38	3	7.8	38	2	5.0	−2.8
Representative	110	14	12.7	110	13	12.0	−.7
Secretary of State	1	1	100.0	1	1	100.0	0.0
County (83 counties)							
Commissioner	722	23	3.1	722	24	3.3	+.2
Clerk/Register	27	1	3.7	27	1	3.7	0.0
Register	56	1	2.0	56	1	2.0	0.0
Municipal (1,242 townships, 534 cities and villages in 1984; 1,245 townships, 532 cities and villages in 1988)							
City, Village, Township Governing Board Members	3,110	74	2.3	3,700	78	2.1	−.2

Mayor/Supervisor	1,777	14	0.8	1,776	13	.7	−.1
Clerk		11		1,701	8	.5	
Treasurer		9		1,701	9	.5	
Judicial							
Supreme Court Judges	7	0	0.0	7	1	14.0	+14.0
Court of Appeals Judges	18	2	11.1	15	1	5.5	−5.6
Circuit Court Judges	165	5	3.0	167	7	4.2	+1.2
Recorders Court Judges	29	16	55.0	29	15	52.0	−3.0
**District Court Judges			253	26	10.3		
**Probate Court Judges			111	2	1.8		
Education							
State Board of Education		1		8	1	12.5	
University or College Board Member (29 Community College districts and 13 State-supported 4-year colleges and universities, usually with 7 board members each)	294	16	5.4	294	13	4.4	−1.0
Local School Board Member (599 districts, usually with 7 board members each)	4,193	72	1.7	3,955	89	2.3	+.6

SOURCE: The data for this table were drawn primarily from the 1984 and 1988 editions of the national rosters of *Black Elected Officals* published by the Joint Center for Political Studies. Other data were supplied by several governmental offices/institutions in the State of Michigan (including the Michigan Association of Counties, the Michigan Secretary of State Bureau of Elections, the Administrative Secretary's Office of the Board of Education for the State of Michigan, the Michigan Townships Association, and the Michigan Municipal League).

*Note: This table includes only those elective offices in which blacks were represented.

**There were 29 black District Court judges and 1 black Probate Court Judge in 1984. Totals were not reported in the source.

Table 16-2. Percentages and Means on Survey Responses of Michigan Black Elected Officials Who Responded to Survey on Funding of Selected State of Michigan Departments/Programs 1990

Department/ Program	Appropriations* 1989–90	Substantial Decrease (%)**	Slight Decrease (%)	About the Same (%)	Slight Increase (%)	Substantial Increase (%)	Mean***
Social Services	$2,338,746,300	8.4	5.0	31.9	26.1	28.6	3.61
Higher Education	1,195,518,900	4.1	2.5	20.7	30.6	42.1	4.04
Mental Health	873,185,600	3.4	4.2	33.9	28.8	29.7	3.77
Corrections	713,902,000	11.0	17.8	35.6	17.8	17.8	3.14
School Aid (K-12 Education)	612,502,100	4.1	0.8	3.3	19.8	71.9	4.55
Community Colleges	212,490,500	3.3	3.3	33.3	33.3	26.7	3.77
Public Health	137,352,200	2.5	3.3	31.4	39.7	23.1	3.78
Civil Rights	10,707,900	3.3	3.3	20.8	31.7	40.8	4.03

SOURCES: *State appropriations figures were excerpted from the State of Michigan Executive Budget: 1990–91 Fiscal Year, Introduction, page b-2.

**Percentages were computed from data obtained from survey responses of black elected officials in Michigan.

***Note: A mean value near 5.00 indicates "substantial increase."

A mean value near 3.00 indicates "about the same."

A mean value near 1.00 indicates "substantial decrease."

Table 16-3. Percentages and Means on Survey Responses of Michigan Black Elected Officials Who Responded to Survey on Selected State Issues 1990

Level of Agreement*

Issue	SA (%)	A (%)	U (%)	D (%)	SD (%)	Mean**
1. State income tax should be made progressive.	28.7	25.2	23.5	13.9	8.7	3.5
2. State income tax should be the primary source of revenue to be increased to fund priority departments/programs.	13.9	15.7	17.4	31.3	21.7	2.7
3. State sales tax should be the primary source of revenue to be increased to fund priority departments/programs.	19.7	25.6	14.5	25.6	14.5	3.1
4. Public schools should not be funded by the property tax.	39.3	26.5	9.4	17.1	7.7	3.7
5. Michigan should outlaw state-funded abortions.	9.2	5.0	10.9	22.7	52.1	2.0
6. The Blanchard Administration has done an effective job in reducing the black-white unemployment gap.	4.3	8.5	21.4	41.9	23.9	2.3
7. Under the Blanchard Administration, the unemployment situation for blacks has substantially improved.	2.5	7.6	17.6	49.6	22.7	2.2

SOURCE: Percentages were computed from data obtained from survey responses of black elected officials in Michigan.

*SA = Strongly Agree; A = Agree; U = Undecided; D = Disagree; SD = Strongly Disagree.

**A mean value near 5.00 indicates "strong agreement."

A mean value near 3,00 indicates "uncertain."

A mean value near 1.00 indicates "strong disagreement."

Table 16-3, which provides the percentages and means for the seven statements addressing selected issues in Michigan, indicates that the majority of the respondents disagreed/strongly disagreed with the statements on three of the selected state issues (two involving unemployment among blacks and the other on state-funded abortions). A majority (52 percent) of the respondents strongly disagreed and 22.7 percent disagreed with the statement, "Michigan should outlaw state-funded abortions." Fifty percent of the respondents disagreed and 23 percent strongly disagreed with the statement, "Under the Blanchard Administration, the unemployment situation for blacks has substantially improved." Furthermore, 42 percent of the respondents disagreed and 24 percent strongly disagreed with the statement, "The Blanchard Administration has done an effective job in reducing the black-white unemployment gap."

On the issue of school taxes, 26 percent of the respondents agreed and 39 percent strongly agreed that "public schools should not be funded by the property tax" (Table 16-3).

The Reelection of Mayor Coleman Young

Coleman Young was reelected for a record fifth term in November 1989 as mayor of Detroit. He defeated accountant Thomas Barrow, who was making his second attempt to unseat Young. The mayor received 56 percent of the vote to Barrow's 44 percent—a margin of victory that was narrower than the 61 percent that Mayor Young had received in 1985 during Barrow's first challenge.

The smaller margin of victory in 1989 may have been more a reflection of the personal and political difficulties the mayor faced than a reflection of the improved candidacy of Tom Barrow. Among the mayor's difficulties were a paternity suit by a former city employee and the allegation that inappropriate use of city funds had occurred in regard to the new Chrysler Jefferson Avenue plant.

The mayor was believed to be so vulnerable in 1989 that several prominent politicians (including City Councilwoman Erma Henderson and Congressman John Conyers) sought to unseat him during the mayoral primary. Young's victory over all of his challengers in 1989 can be attributed to better organization, enormous financial resources (Young's campaign chest totaled about 5 million dollars, compared with some $250,000 for Barrow), and his combative style.

Another dimension of the mayoral contest, and not surprisingly so, was the fact that voting was sharply divided along racial lines. Young received 68 percent of the black vote and only 13 percent of the white vote, while Barrow got 87 percent of the white vote and only 32 percent of the black vote (Farrell, 1989, p. 14A).

The goals of Mayor Young's 1989 campaign did not appear to be fundamentally different from those of 1985. He promised to continue to promote the development of the downtown and riverfront areas, to encourage more movement on the city airport project, and to seek to attract businesses to the city through the use of various tax incentives.

During his tenure as mayor, Coleman Young has integrated city government, pushed through an ambitious affirmative action agenda in the police and fire departments, opened up opportunities for black businesses, and been a source of pride for many of the city's blacks. Nevertheless, the question remains as to whether the mayor's basic strategy for the revitalization of the city will lead to improvements in the life chances of the most disadvantaged segments of the black population.

In general, the social and economic conditions for blacks in Detroit appear to have worsened in the last 10 years, relative to those for whites in the surrounding suburbs. In 1980, for example, blacks in Detroit were 2.4 times more likely to be unemployed than were whites in the area. By 1989, blacks were 2.9 times more likely than whites to be unemployed. Furthermore, between 1980 and 1989, the black family median income fell from 60 percent to 49 percent of the white family median income (Rosenstone, 1989, pp. 5 and 20).

Still, whatever the defects in Mayor Young's "downtown" as opposed to "neighborhood" strategy for the revitalization of Detroit, the real problems that the city currently faces may have less to do with the mayor than with economics and racial polarization. Likewise, the future of Detroit will be affected by decisions undertaken by the big three automakers (Chrysler, Ford, and General Motors) and by the effects of residential segregation (Widick, 1989, pp. 231–268).

Conclusions

This chapter has discussed the electoral progress and problems of Michigan blacks during the 1980s; has presented findings from an opinion survey of Michigan black elected officials concerning their views on state spending priorities and on selected issues of public policy; and has considered the circumstances of Mayor Coleman Young's reelection in November 1989.

It was shown that while African Americans made modest electoral gains in the State of Michigan during the 1980s, especially in the last five years of the decade, much remains to be accomplished.

Black elected officials who responded to the opinion survey indicated their preferences with respect to funding certain departments/programs. The majority of the respondents supported increased funding for each of the departments/programs (with the exception of corrections) on which the survey requested an opinion. For corrections, the majority believed that the expenditures should remain about the same. In the areas of civil rights and education (especially school aid for K-12 education), there was support for a "substantial increase" in state spending.

With respect to the statements regarding seven issues on which opinions were solicited, the majority of the respondents disagreed with the statements on three of the selected state issues (one on state-funded abortions and two involving unemployment among blacks). The majority disagreed with the view that the Blanchard Administration has done an effective job in reducing the black-white unemployment gap; and they also disagreed with the view that under the Blanchard Administration, the unemployment situation for blacks has substantially improved.

Finally, the circumstances of Coleman Young's reelection as major of Detroit were considered. It was suggested that the record of Mayor Young's tenure during the 1980s leaves open to question the matter of whether his administration has led to improvements in the life chances of the most disadvantaged segments of the black population. It was further suggested that the problems in Detroit may have more to do with the effects of residential segregation and the decisions of the big three automakers than with the presence of a black mayor.

Discussion

The annual report on the *State of Black Michigan* in 1987 concluded that the "social and economic inequalities [in health care, higher education, jobs, ownership of businesses, and income] that existed between blacks and whites in 1967, when several Michigan cities exploded, are still prevalent today" (Darden, 1987, p. 81). Black electoral gains during the 1980s seem to have had little, if any, impact upon improving the life chances of the most disadvantaged African Americans.

Despite these developments, black political preferences in the state continue to be strongly associated with the Democratic Party. Many black voters, both nationally and in the State of Michigan, apparently believe their interests are served best by identifying with Democratic candidates (Walton, 1985, pp. 129 and 165). They may also believe that the social and economic problems that Michigan blacks face reflect less on the Democratic Party than on national failures. Certainly the performance of the Reagan Administration did nothing to dispel this view.

Social critic Harold Cruse has contended that "the only hope left for the political, economic, and cultural survival of blacks into the next century is self-organization" (Cruse, 1987, p. 382). Whether this view is correct remains to be seen, but Michigan blacks, and indeed blacks nationally, must begin to think creatively about the possibility of some form of independent political activity. Michigan blacks showed their independence in their rejection of black Republican gubernatorial candidate William Lucas in 1986 and in their earlier support for Republican William Milliken during 1981–1982. This kind of flexibility, both inside and outside of the two-party system, needs to be deepened and perhaps accorded some form of organizational base in the African American community.

REFERENCES

Black Elected Officials: A National Roster, 1984, Washington, D.C.: The Joint Center for Political Studies. 1965.

Black Elected Officials: A National Roster, 1986. Washington, D.C.: The Joint Center for Political Studies, 1989.

Chambers. Julius L. "Black Americans and the Courts: Has the Clock Been Turned Back Permanently?" *The State of Black America*: 1990. New York, New York: The National Urban League, 1990.

Cochran, W. G. *Sampling Techniques*, 3rd edition. New York, New York: John Wiley & Sons, 1977.

Cruse, Harold. *Plural But Equal.* New York, New York: William Morrow and Company, 1987.

Darden, Joe T "Racial Disparities in Michigan since the Civil Disorders of 1967: Summary and Conclusions," *The State of Black Michigan*: 1987. East Lansing, Michigan: Urban Affairs Programs and the Michigan Council of Urban League Executives, 1987.

Farrell, David. "Detroiters Voted Along Racial Lines," *The Detroil News*, November 9, 1989.

Jaynes, Gerald David and Williams, Robin M., Jr., eds. *A Common Destiny: Blacks and American Society*. Washington, D.C.: National Academy Press, 1989.

Preston, Michael B., Henderson, Lenneal J., Jr., and Puryear, Paul L., eds. *The New Black Politics: The Search for Political Power*. New York, New York: Longman, 1987.

Rosenstone, Steven J. (principal investigator). *Separate and Unequal: The Racial Divide*. Ann Arbor, Michigan: A Report to the Detroit Tri-County Area by The University of Michigan Detroit Area Study, 1989.

Walton, Hanes, Jr. *Invisible Politics: Black Political Behavior*. Albany, New York: The State University of New York Press, 1985.

Widick, B. J. *Detroit: City of Race and Class Violence.* Detroit: Wayne State University Press, 1989.

APPENDIX
SURVEY OF BLACK ELECTED OFFICIALS QUESTIONNAIRE

Survey 1
Black Elected Officials
February 1990
Please return this questionnaire in the enclosed stamped addressed envelope by **February 28, 1990,** to:

Office of the Dean
Urban Affairs Programs
Room 117, Owen Graduate Center
Michigan State University
East Lansing, Michigan 48824

SURVEY OF BLACK ELECTED OFFICIALS IN MICHIGAN

1. For the following items, please check (x) to indicate your viewpoint on the direction in which state appropriations from the general purpose fund should move for the upcoming fiscal year (1990–91), as compared with appropriations in the 1989–90 fiscal year.

		Your preference for 1990–91				
State of Michigan Funding far:	Appropriations 1989–90*	Substantial Decrease	Slight Decrease	About the Same	Slight Increase	Substantial Increase
Social Services	$2,338,746,300					
Higher Education	1.195.518,900					
Mental Health	873,185.600					
Corrections	713,902.000					
School Aid (K–12 Education)	612,502,100					
Community Colleges	212.490,500					
Public Health	137,352,200					
Civil Rights	10,707,900					

*SOURCE: Excerpted from the State of Michigan Executive Budget: 1990–1991 Fiscal Year, Introduction, page b-2.

Survey
Black Elected Officials
February 1990

2

II. Please circle the category which best expresses your feelings about the following items:

Scale: SA = Strongly Agree
A = Agree
U = Uncertain
D = Disagree
SD = Strongly Disagree

1. The state income tax should be made progressive.	SA	A	U	D	SD
2. The state income tax should be the primary source of revenue to be increased to fund the priorities listed above.	SA	A	u	D	SD
3. The state sales tax should be the primary source of revenue to be increased to fund the priorities listed above.	SA	A	U	D	SD
4. Public schools should not be Funded by the property tax.	SA	A	U	D	SD
5. Michigan should outlaw state-funded abortions.	SA	A	U	D	SD
6. The Blanchard Administration has done an effective job in reducing the black-white unemployment gap.	SA	A	U	D	SD
7. Under the Blanchard Administration, the unemployment situation for blacks has substantially improved.	SA	A	U	D	SD

Please return completed questionnaire by **February 28, 1990**, to:

Office of the Dean
Urban Affairs Programs
Room 117, Owen Graduate Center
Michigan State University
East Lansing, Michigan 48824

CHAPTER 17

Black Political Participation in Michigan, 15 Years Later

Curtis Stokes

Introduction

During the last 15 years, African Americans have made significant progress in electoral politics, nationally and in Michigan. Whether Democratic or Republican administrations and legislatures are dominant, this overall positive political trend has remained the same. On the other hand, the general social and economic conditions of the black population, especially in Michigan, have not improved qualitatively and indeed have worsened for large segments of black Michigan. Though the social and economic well-being of all Michiganians has been negatively impacted by the continuing and generalized economic crisis gripping the state's economy, black Michiganians have been disproportionately impacted. This chapter examines the contemporary political status of black Michigan, contrasting it with blacks' increasingly weakened socioeconomic status, and points toward the need to construct a new black politics, one that is historically defined, simultaneously practical and visionary, and multidimensional.

Politics as Electoralism

Dating back to the Reconstruction era, the 1905 Niagara Movement, and, importantly, the establishment of the National Association for the Advancement of Colored People in 1909, African American politics has largely been dominated by a kind of single-minded electoralism. Apart from the momentary intervention of a Booker T. Washington or Marcus Garvey, or the limited influence of a radical left movement, black leaders from Frederick Douglass to Martin Luther King, Jr., and beyond have repeatedly emphasized the pivotal link between attaining the electoral franchise and empowering black America. King said, "If the Negro achieved the ballot throughout the South, many of the problems which we faced would be solved" (Walters 2005, 6). Furthermore, according to Ronald Walters, a well-respected political scientist: "It is clear that the Voting Rights Act of 1965 was essential to the political empowerment of the black community. More specifically it became the means by which blacks began to influence national politics by making a difference in the selection of presidents of the United States" (26).

The question here is not whether the adoption of the Voting Rights Act of 1965 was a crucial milestone in the black freedom struggle; it clearly was, and blacks are better off, especially politically, because of its existence. The issue at stake concerns the need to distinguish between having "access" to power and exercising "actual" power. "Power is not simply the ability to get something done, but to get it done despite the resistance and opposition of others" (Sowell 1983). Or, as Jennings (1992, 38–39) says: Empowerment

> does not mean merely influence in certain policy areas or accessibility to decision makers . . . [but] the capacity to question and upset the ownership, management, and distribution of wealth in both public and private sectors. This is a much more important political resource than proximity or access to public and private decision makers—no matter how liberal or supportive they may be about issues of concern to blacks.

Though this has not always been so, contemporary African American politics in Michigan is consistent with the national pattern. In 2001, blacks comprised 14.3% of Michigan's population and 13.1% of its voting-age population but held 16.4% of the seats in Michigan's 110-person House of Representative and 13.2% of the seats in the 38-person Michigan Senate. As is the case nationally, black women continue to make impressive gains and thus are closing the historic gender gap in elective offices, now holding 33.3% and 40% of the seats in the Michigan House and Senate, respectively. There are also six black mayors, including Detroit's Kwame M. Kilpatrick, in Michigan cities of at least 50,000 people. New Jersey is the only other state with more black mayors in cities of at least 50,000 people (Joint Center for Political and Economic Studies 2003). Blacks have also continued to support the Democratic Party, with more than 80% of African Americans routinely voting for the Democratic ticket. In 2006, for example, 94% of black Michiganians voted for Governor Jennifer Granholm and 88% supported U.S. Senator Debbie Stabenow. Michigan blacks have continued to send two black Detroiters to the U.S. House of Representatives, Democrats John Conyers, Jr., and Carolyn C. Kilpatrick (*Detroit News* 2006b; Joint Center for Political and Economic Studies Blacks 2006).

Despite voter-approved term limits in 1992, which went into effect in 1998 and 2002 for Michigan elected officials, and the dominance of the Republican Party during most of the past 15 years, blacks in Michigan have made some impressive electoral gains. True, we should not minimize the fact that 41 years after the adoption of the Voting Rights Act of 1965 blacks, 14.3% of the state's population hold only 1.8% of all elective offices in Michigan. When one looks at the state legislature, however, where the numerical racial gap in legislative representation has effectively been overcome, as well as the broad participation of ordinary blacks in the electoral process, it is apparent that African Americans have made use of the Voting Rights Act of 1965.

The main problem with relying too heavily on electoral activism in the way African Americans have done, nationally and in Michigan, is that electoral gains, however promising they may appear as a vehicle for meaningful socioeconomic changes, can be easily undermined by a range of factors, including being taken for granted by the Democratic Party; white and, increasingly, black out-migration from the central cities; de-industrialization and outsourcing of economic resources; a national retreat from any meaningful support for the reconstruction of cities; conflict between a rising black middle class and poor blacks; tensions between native blacks and recent immigrants from Latin America, Asia, and even other parts of the global black world; and old-fashioned institutionalized white racism.

This can easily be seen with a quick look at the national picture. In 2005, African Americans, 12.3% of the nation's population, held 2.5% of the nation's net worth and far less of its financial assets, own 5.2% of the nation's businesses but barely 0.4% of the business revenues, have a per capita income that is 58% of the white per capita income, and have a poverty rate three times the white poverty rate (Kennickell 2002; U.S. Census Bureau 2006b). These statistics are very similar to what they were some 40 years ago even though the number of black elected officials, nearly 10,000 in 2005, is more than six times what it was in 1970. Similarly, in Michigan the social and economic conditions of blacks, especially contrasted with the well-being of white Michiganians, are just as difficult as those faced by blacks nationally, if not worse because of the economic challenges the state currently faces. For example, in 2005, nearly one third of Michigan blacks are poor, which is three times the white impoverishment rate, and just under 50% of adult black males in Detroit were unemployed in 2000 (Saenz 2005; *Detroit News* 2006a; Joint Center for Political and Economic Studies 2006; U.S. Census Bureau 2006a, 2006b). Black elected officials in the Michigan House have sponsored important pieces of legislation, including laws regarding health care, antidiscrimination in the workplace, and jobs (Brown 1993, 40). However the bottom line is, notwithstanding how progressive or liberal black legislators are, conventional politics by itself cannot overcome the limits of electoral politics.

Toward a New Black Politics

In light of the growing divide between increasing electoral success and socioeconomic decline among blacks, nationally and in Michigan, a question needs to be posed: Which way forward? The reigning approach for empowering the black community is correctly undergoing withering criticism by a growing number of African American political scientists: "Just as the number of black elected officials reached record numbers, the utility of electoral politics as a vehicle to promote further advancement is in question. Rather than extending the advancements made earlier, electoral politics in many ways has become a tool for stifling black progress, particularly at the national level" (Jones 2003, 8). Mack Jones concludes somewhat pessimistically, saying that any kind of one-dimensional electoralism can at best "only serve as a device for slowing retrogression" (8). Similarly Jerry Watts (2005) writes:

> Scholars of black politics need to begin asking questions concerning the viability of urban electoral politics as a mechanism for generating upward mobility of impoverished populations. We

> may discover that electing black mayors has had a minute impact, if any at all, on the upward mobility of the poor. . . . What has been the impact of these black elected officials on the living conditions of their poor communities?

Watts asks and answers his own question: essentially, failure. This is a message that should be taken seriously by all African American leaders, including those in Michigan.

Leadership is more than about representation. It involves having a sense of history, having knowledge of one's community as it evolves, understanding the interactive dimensions of momentary and long-term objectives, and designing appropriate strategies and tactics to effectuate the best outcome for African Americans locally and nationally. In 2006 the struggle around the anti–Affirmative Action amendment, Proposal 2, in Michigan is illustrative of the inside-outside or multidimensional approach to politics being recommended here. The voter-approved proposal, now article 1, section 26, of the Michigan Constitution, stipulates that "the state shall not discriminate against, or grant preferential treatment to, any individual or group on the basis of race, sex, color ethnicity, or national origin in the operation of public employment, public education, or public contracting." Blacks (86%) and Hispanics (69%) opposed the proposal by wide margins, while whites (56%) supported Proposal 2 (*Detroit News* 2006b). Though opponents of Proposal 2 were unsuccessful in defeating the amendment, the kind of organizing centered at the grassroots and among leaders is the kind of approach that was instrumental in attaining important improvements in the lives of blacks during the Civil Rights era.

What is needed in the nation and locally is the birth of "independent politics," subservient to neither the two major political parties, especially the Democratic Party, nor leftist utopianism. Instead, a grassroots, communitarian, protest model politics that values examining both internal and external aspects of the problems confronting African Americans, and with a vision toward a more democratic and just America, should be constructed.

REFERENCES

Brown, Ronald E. 1993. African-American voters and black political representation in the state of Michigan. In *The state of black Michigan*. East Lansing: Urban Affairs Programs, Michigan State University.

Detroit News. 2006a. Bigger share of blacks than whites feels pinch. August 30.

———. 2006b. Ballot proposals and how Michigan voted. November 8.

Jennings, James. 1992. *The politics of black empowerment: the transformation of black activism in urban America*. Detroit: Wayne State University Press.

Joint Center for Political and Economic Studies. 2003. Black elected officials: a statistical summary, 2001. www.jointcenter.org.

———. 2006. Blacks and the 2006 midterm elections. www.jointcenter.org.

Jones, Mack H. 2003. Expanding the boundaries of electoral politics as a vehicle for fundamental change. *NCOBPS Newsletter* 18:No. 1.

Kennickell, Arthur B. 2003. A rolling tide: changes in the distribution of wealth in the U.S., 1989–2001. Federal Reserve Board. www.federalreserve.gov.

Saenz, Rogelio. 2005. Beyond New Orleans: the social and economic isolation of urban African Americans. Population Reference Bureau. www.prb.org.

Sowell, Thomas. 1983. *The economics and politics of race: an international perspective.* New York: William Morrow.

U.S. Census Bureau. 2006a. Income, poverty, and health insurance coverage in the United States: 2005. www.census.gov.

———. 2006b. Black-owned firms: 2002 www.census.gov.

Walters, Ronald W. 2005. *Freedom is not enough: black voters, black candidates and American presidential politics.* New York: Littlefield.

Watts, Jerry G. 2005. What use are black mayors? An open letter to the National Conference of Black Political Scientists. *Black Commentator.* November 17. www.blackcommentator.com.

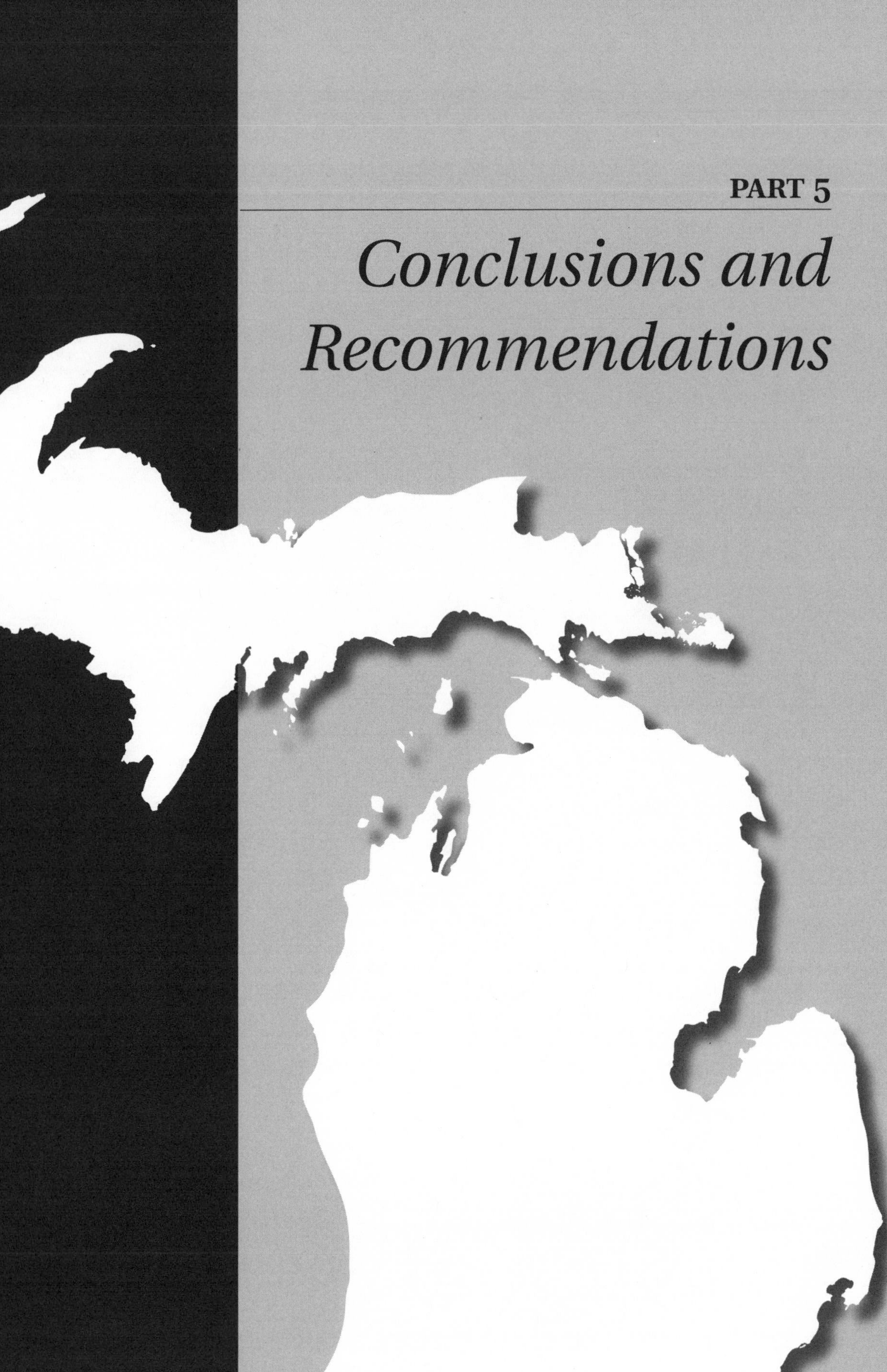

PART 5

Conclusions and Recommendations

CHAPTER 18

Summary of Past Conclusions and Recommendations to Improve Black Michigan, 1985–1993

Joe T. Darden, Curtis Stokes, and Richard W. Thomas

The State of Black Michigan: 1985

Executive Summary

Introduction

This publication, the second in what is expected to be a series of annual reports on *The State of Black Michigan*, presents factual material and interpretive discussions concerning the status of black Michigan residents compared with white Michigan residents, in the areas of politics, housing, education, family life, teenage pregnancy, and economic/community development.

Black Political Awareness and Political Participation

Major Ideas

1. Michigan black voters, overwhelmingly Democratic, have been successful in electing black politicians in a variety of offices.
2. In general, however, black politicians are questioning the leadership of Democratic Governor James Blanchard whom they see as trying to please suburbanites and Republicans at the expense of low-income citizens, particularly blacks and other minorities, most of whom live in Michigan's central cities.
3. Problems within the Democratic Party are increasingly apparent. There is a growing gap between labor leaders and union members. The liberal-labor-civil rights coalition divides on issues such as affirmative action, taxes, and foreign policy. The new generation of Democrats have a different agenda from that of old-line leaders.

4. White conservatives have managed to convert black issues into non-racially-oriented economic growth issues. This has at least partially neutralized overall concern with those issues now identified with blacks—e.g., welfare, low-income housing, and public works jobs.

Implications

In the next gubernatorial election, blacks may desert the Democratic Party if the opportunity is provided for them to vote for a black Republican candidate. If this should happen, the traditional political alliances in Michigan may be dramatically altered.

The Housing Situation of Blacks in Metropolitan Areas of Michigan

Findings

1. Blacks in metropolitan areas of Michigan do not have equal access to non-segregated housing. In 1980, residential segregation was above 50 percent in seven of Michigan's twelve metropolitan areas. The high cost of housing in non-segregated areas was not the primary reason for the blacks' lack of access.
2. Blacks in metropolitan areas of Michigan do not receive an equal share of the conventional mortgage loans and home improvement loans.
3. A higher percentage of blacks, compared to whites, live in older, overcrowded housing. In 1980, blacks in owner-occupied housing in metropolitan areas were 3.5 times more likely than whites to live in overcrowded housing. In renter-occupied housing, the ratio was 2.3 times.

Recommendations

1. The enforcement of fair housing laws must be strengthened through closer monitoring of the flow, accuracy, and completeness of the information real estate brokers pass on to black and white homeseekers about housing availability throughout the metropolitan areas of Michigan.
2. Lending institutions should be required by the Federal and/or State Governments to insure that equity in the distribution of mortgage loans occurs.
3. Efforts should be made to increase the rate of black homeownership. One approach would be to pressure Congress to modify present housing legislation to permit the option of a 30-year, no-downpayment mortgage for single-family home purchases.

Equity and Excellence in Education for Blacks in Michigan: Where Are We?

Findings

1. Access of blacks to all phases of education is inferior, compared to that for whites.
2. In terms of process, or treatment of students by educators, blacks were more likely than whites to be reprimanded harshly for the same behavior. Blacks were also overrepresented in programs for the educable mentally impaired and underrepresented in certain other programs.
3. Blacks did not record academic achievement at rates comparable to whites. In 1984, the mean SAT scores for blacks were the lowest scores of all Michigan racial groups.

4. Michigan black students were not always able to transfer secondary education into post-secondary education and jobs. In 1983, for example, only 42 percent of black high school graduates were enrolled in college degree programs, and unemployment rates for black youth remained high. In 1984, over 70 percent of the school districts in Michigan did not have any black professional staff. The eleven school districts with black superintendents (1.9 percent) employed 74.2 percent of the black instructional staff.

Recommendations

1. Black parents must take the initiative to correct present inequities.
2. Community organizations and school officials must work with parents to lobby for targeting of state and federal funds to districts with large enrollments of black students.
3. School officials and parents should monitor tracking and labeling of black students, cultural biases in curriculum and instruction, and the placement of black students in programs for the gifted. Inservice training programs for school personnel should be provided when needed.

Black Families in Michigan

Major Ideas

1. Many white Americans view the black population in negative terms. The black family is blamed for such problems as teenage pregnancy, female-headed households, and unemployment, instead of focusing on the larger social system that impinges upon the family unit.
2. Because of their socio-economic status in Michigan, black families are more vulnerable than whites to the impact of negative social and economic forces.
3. Michigan black households have the lowest median income ($13,695) of all ethnic groups. The white median is $19,983.

Recommendations

1. Public and private organizations should intensify efforts to increase employment opportunities for blacks in Michigan.
2. Social services programs must be strengthened.

Teenage Pregnancy

Findings

1. There has been an increase in premarital sexual activity without effective birth control among all elements of the teenage population, regardless of race, socioeconomic status, residence, and religious affiliation. This increase has been accompanied by a decrease in marriage rates among teenagers.
2. Of total live births in Michigan, the percent mothered by nonwhite teenagers (22.8 percent) was twice as high as the percent mothered by white teenagers (11.8 percent). Black women are 13 percent, and white women are 84 percent of the total female population.
3. The incidence of black children living in single-parent households has increased in recent years. For example, in 1980, 63,021 black Detroit households had female heads and children under 18.

Recommendations

1. All concerned citizens must work together to develop and implement prevention programs involving teenagers of both sexes.
2. Social systems must be established to support the teenager during pregnancy and to encourage avoiding unintended pregnancies.

Toward a Strategy for Economic Development in the Black Community

Findings

1. Black unemployment rates continue to be approximately three times those of whites.
2. The "economic recovery" has not greatly increased the number of people leaving the public assistance rolls in largely black areas.
3. These and other economic indicators demonstrate that the current economic recovery is not removing the tremendous gap in black-white economic status.

Proposed Strategy

1. Black professionals and members of civil rights organizations, black churches, black sororities and fraternities and other groups should develop a preferred set of effective national, state, and local governmental policies and should lobby for them vigorously and effectively.
2. The process should include a survey of resources and a delegation of tasks. Financing should involve largely volunteer and organizational efforts, although at a later point external foundation and other support would help.
3. Three areas of focus should be targeted.
   a. Youth development
   b. Economic status of households
   c. Community development

Summary and Conclusions

Although community development efforts could bring improvement, they may not be capable of reversing problems whose roots lie beyond the reach of community activism. The overall conclusions of this report—that for blacks political power is precarious, housing segregated, education unequal, family life besieged, and economic status poor—can only lead one to conclude that the black community in Michigan is in a crisis state. Observers have evoked the "crisis" image so much that it rarely causes reaction, yet escalating levels of segregation and impoverishment among Michigan blacks can be called little else.

In the final analysis, it will be up to the nation as a whole to reverse current trends. New, creative policies must be initiated and old, effective ones must be sustained. Such policies must promote racial equality, social welfare, and economic stability for all needy Americans. Michigan is only the shadow of a nation that has refused to carry out these policy responsibilities. It is imperative that all concerned citizens press for improved federal as well as state urban and social initiatives.

The State of Black Michigan: 1986

Executive Summary

Introduction

This publication, the third in a series of annual reports on *The State of Black Michigan*, presents factual material, interpretive discussions, and recommendations concerning the status of black Michigan residents, In the areas of business development, self-help, employment in Michigan state government, crime, and political progress.

Enhancing Michigan's Black Business Development

Findings

1. Although black business ownership increased by 77.8 percent between 1969 and 1982, all of the increase was attributed to the establishment of small firms—i.e., firms without paid employees.
2. Larger black-owned firms—i.e., firms with paid employees—actually declined, and so did the sales of all black-owned firms in terms of dollars of constant purchasing power.
3. Although currently constituting only a small percentage of all black-owned firms, the larger firms remain the backbone of the black economy. Such firms provided for 72 percent of the total sales in 1982.
4. Black business development continues to suffer from overconcentration of firms in retail trade and from the absence of black-owned financial institutions to provide the needed capital. Thus, in spite of the increase in small black-owned firms between 1969 and 1982, blacks have made only a small step toward racial equality in the business world.
5. Michigan's black-owned firms are located primarily in areas where the black population is concentrated, and therefore these firms depend heavily on black support for economic survival. Yet in 1982, Michigan's blacks spent only about 7 percent of their estimated $7.0 billion personal income in black-owned firms.

Conclusions

If the black community is to accelerate its business development, it must use effective entrepreneurial approaches. The current large flow of funds out of the black community must be curtailed, and the community's economic resources must be brought to bear in an organized way to help solve its economic problems. This will require strategic planning on a large scale, with the involvement of both the community's leadership and its technicians. A community economic development coalition should be organized. Such a coalition should consider a variety of approaches, including capital formation, market opportunities, and management development.

Recommendations

1. Develop strategies for black churches and other organizations to pool their banking for placement in institutions which respond by lending money to black community businesses and institutions, and by providing other needed services.

2. Develop models for the effective involvement of black churches and black organizations (lay, professional, fraternal, business, union, and community) in community economic development The challenge is to develop the strategy and secure the united effort of persons who can commit the resources, give the leadership, and motivate the cooperation of the masses—especially those with buying power and the ability to save and invest.
3. Create a community development fund that would be a partnership of private sector corporations and community residents. A match of corporate dollars against those raised by the community would provide significant funds for the development of both community-owned businesses and other non-business development projects. Just as the black community encourages corporate America's support of institutions such as the NAACP, the United Negro College Fund, and the Urban League, so should it encourage white corporate America to support a self-determined capital creation movement within the black community.
4. Insist that funds deriving from the community and invested with insurance companies and other financial institutions be invested in significant part in black companies. Also insist that a portion of the pension and profit-sharing dollars of black pensioners be invested in black firms. In Michigan, blacks should demand that some of the state pension and profit-sharing funds traditionally used for equity investment in non-black businesses be specifically earmarked for black business development.
5. Lobby the State Legislature and the Governor to increase the amount of the $2.5 million provided to the Strategic Fund in 1985 for loans to minority businesses. This should be an annual appropriation until the fund reaches at least $25 million.
6. Monitor closely the state's performance in goal-setting and reporting under its program to encourage agencies to purchase from qualified minorities.
7. Expand corporate purchasing programs to give more than token work to minority firms. Major corporations should sponsor minority firms and should work to develop black firms into major suppliers.
8. Establish joint ventures by majority firms with black and other minority businesses for providing minority firms entry into markets heretofore unattainable. The joint venture is an excellent vehicle for contracts where bonding and large-scale financing are needed.
9. Encourage black churches and other black-controlled institutions to study their purchases of commodities and services and to batch them for orders from black businesses or distributors. Where no appropriate businesses exist and the orders are large enough, businesses should be organized. When such purchases are made through majority institutions, batching should enable quantity discounts; and some leverage benefiting the community should be sought, including improved employment practices.
10. Increase the number of minority engineering, science, and business school graduates, at both the undergraduate and graduate levels. Blacks and other minorities must be helped to see that their personal aspirations can be fulfilled in business as well as in other professions. Such efforts must start at kindergarten and must stress skills in science and mathematics. Economic education in the schools must also be emphasized.

11. Enhance affirmative actions within corporate America for developing a larger cadre of well-trained, experienced black management. More blacks need to be on the corporate fast track, even though they may leave to take positions with black companies or to start firms of their own. Further, more majority corporations should seek minority members for their boards of directors. A study of board memberships and employment practices of Michigan-based firms should be completed expeditiously.

Black Self-Help in Michigan

Major Ideas

1. Black self-help efforts are not new. The tradition originated in black churches, and in fraternal, professional, and business organizations.
2. Black self-help projects have provided the foundation for the major economic, social, and political gains made by blacks in Michigan.
3. Only with increased black support and participation can problems of black business development, teenage pregnancy, drug addiction, and crime in black communities be effectively addressed.

Recommendations

1. Black self-help of all kinds should be encouraged, especially among poor, black youth.
2. A statewide newsletter of black self-help organizations should be published.
3. Systematic research on the most successful past and current black self-help organizations, projects, and activities should be conducted from which models can be developed. A course on the history of black self-help organizations should be developed for community groups and adult education classes. Such a course should also be taught in public schools.
4. A national and international hookup of all black organizations engaged in any form of self-help should be established.
5. Black self-help must not be allowed to divert attention from the lingering effects of historical racism. Black self-help has always been part of the larger struggle against racism, and it has never been, nor is it now, a retreat from confronting racism.

Black Employment in State Government: The Michigan Example

Findings

1. As has been true for jobs in manufacturing industries, the number of jobs in the public sector has declined since 1980. Both blacks and whites were employed in fewer numbers in state government in 1984 than in 1980.
2. Despite fewer total jobs in state government, blacks made small gains overall between 1980 and 1984. Black full-time classified state employees increased from 17.6 percent in 1980 to 19.0 percent in 1984, exceeding the established utilization standards for the total workforce (12.4 percent in 1980 and 12.9 percent in 1984).
3. Problems of racial inequality remain in state government hiring practices. Some departments continue to hire few blacks. As a result, only 7 of 22, or 31.8 percent of the departments, were above utilization standards in both 1980 and 1984. Almost half of the

departments (10 of 22) were below utilization standards in 1980 and remained below standards in 1984.

4. Three departments have hired disproportionate percentages of blacks: Civil Rights, Mental Health, and Social Services. In addition to over-concentration in certain departments, blacks are also disproportionately concentrated in the lower level occupations, e.g., paraprofessionals and service/maintenance positions.
5. One of the most critical problems confronting blacks in state government is the underrepresentation of black men. There is a glaring deficit of black men employed in state government compared to white men, white women, and black women. Serious attention must be given to ways to employ more black men in Michigan state government if racial equality is to be achieved.

Recommendations

Greater effort will be required by many departments if they are to meet the established utilization standards. The following recommendations are offered for consideration by state government departments generally and by targeted departments specifically:

1. Develop, or increase the use of, internship programs designed to interest black students in careers in state government.
2. Improve and expand management training and other grooming opportunities for blacks already in state service. Tuition reimbursement and other incentive programs should be offered for participating in professionally related courses at colleges and universities.
3. Continue to implement early retirement programs to create additional vacancies. For departments where blacks are underutilized, establish a formal program that sets a goal of hiring three blacks for every two whites.
4. Expand the role of the Michigan Equal Employment and Business Opportunity Council to include the reviewing of appointments downward to level 12 in all departments.

Black Crime in Michigan

Findings

1. A higher percentage of blacks compared to whites were arrested for murder, forcible rape, and robbery between 1981 and 1984. Furthermore, the percentage of arrests of blacks for murder and robbery increased, while it decreased for whites during the three-year period.
2. The percentage of arrests of blacks for forcible rape decreased while it increased for whites.
3. There was little change in the percentage of arrests for property crimes for whites and blacks from 1981 to 1984. A higher percentage of whites compared to blacks continued to be arrested for property crimes.
4. In general, the victims of violent crimes continue to be disproportionately low-income and black. The reasons for such disproportionate crimes against blacks seem to be related to the higher rates of poverty and unemployment, and the lower educational level of the people in the areas where most blacks live.
5. When blacks and whites are arrested for the same crimes, the criminal justice system usually treats them differently, i.e., judges tend to impose longer sentences on blacks than on whites convicted of comparable felonies and with similar criminal records.

Recommendations

It is clear that definite changes need to take place, both in the community and in the prison setting. The reduction of crime and of recidivism is of paramount importance.

Education is an important key to reducing crime. Special efforts must be made to improve the educational opportunities for black children in ghetto schools. The kind of education the black child receives in an inner-city school does not match what is offered in suburban schools. There is a need to close the gap that exists between suburban and inner-city schools. Improving educational opportunities for black youngsters will increase the probability of their being more employable as adults and their ability to work in the kinds of jobs that will keep them above the poverty level.

In the prison setting, a critical key is more education. Although control will always be the primary goal in the correctional setting, it is hoped that providing residents with more educational opportunities will become more valued within the Department of Corrections. Specifically, there needs to be an expansion of the GED preparation component so that more residents can receive high school diploma equivalencies. This, in turn, will increase the number of residents eligible for community college and four-year college programs. In addition, there is a need for a Department of Corrections institutional center for education at each Department of Corrections facility. This would lead to greater coordination of college level courses. Increased coordination would mean more graduates. All in all, additional funding is needed for the non-college, college, and institutional programs to raise the skill levels of incarcerated residents.

Black Political Progress in Michigan During the Mid-Eighties

Findings

1. Little recent progress has been made in increasing the number of black elected officials. Between 1984 and 1986, only three black elected officials were added to the 297 total of 1984. Most incumbent black officials were reelected. Some were replaced by other blacks. Most of the recently elected black officials are liberal Democrats and represent no change in black political bargaining power.
2. Significant on the eve of the 1986 gubernatorial election is the fact that in 1984 the black percentage of registered voters exceeded the white percentage of registered voters. In 1984, 75.1 percent of blacks and 74.3 percent of whites were registered to vote.
3. Black voter turnout also increased substantially between 1980 and 1984. In 1980, black voter turnout was 59.4 percent, and the white turnout was 65.1 percent. By 1984,65.4 percent of black voters cast votes, compared with 62.6 percent for whites. With the entry of new black voters and increased black voter turnout, both black and white politicians recognize the emerging potential influence black voters may have on the statewide 1986 election.
4. In 1986, black voters may participate in one of the most important gubernatorial elections in Michigan's history. Should William Lucas, a black candidate, win the Republican primary, both black and white voters will be faced with a challenge never presented before in a general election in Michigan. The 1986 election will test the importance of race and party loyalty in the campaign for governor. For some whites, the challenge will

be whether race is more important than the candidate's stand on the issues. For some blacks, the challenge will be whether party loyalty is more important than race. For others (both black and white), neither race nor party loyalty will be as important as the issues each candidate articulates.

5. Party loyalty remains high among some black opinion leaders. The strength of such loyalty, however, may be faced with its most critical test in the November election of 1986. Should William Lucas lose the Republican primary, however, black voting patterns in Michigan will be predictable.

Summary and Conclusions

The overall conclusions of this report are that racial disparities in the social, economic, and political arenas remain wide, and progress toward reducing racial inequality is extremely slow. If the rate of black progress is to increase, blacks must rely more on the support of other blacks.

Increased black support is necessary if progress is to be achieved in black economic development and black self-help projects. Pressure must be exerted by black individuals and groups if racial inequality in the occupational structure of state government is to be reduced and if blacks are to receive fair treatment by the criminal justice system. Finally, black political participation must be increased if public officials are to be elected who will be responsive to black needs and aspirations.

The State of Black Michigan: 1987

Executive Summary

Introduction

This publication is the fourth in a series of annual reports on the State of Black Michigan. Since 1987 marks the 20th anniversary of the black rebellion in Michigan cities, this special issue is devoted to assessing the changes in the conditions of Michigan's black population since the civil disorders of 1967. The various chapters address some of the most critical issues that have continued to face blacks in Michigan. The focus is on the changing economic status of blacks, the status of blacks in private industry, black ownership of business franchises, black unemployment, health of blacks, and black representation in Michigan's institutions of higher education. The extent of civil rights enforcement is also examined.

Changing Economic Status of Blacks

Findings

1. The economic status of blacks, as measured by occupational representation, improved between 1966 and 1975.
2. Between 1975 and 1984, the economic status of blacks generally worsened. The growth of jobs in the current recovery has been primarily in nonblack areas in the state.

3. If the economic status of blacks is to improve significantly, the nine-year period from 1984 to 1993 must reflect progress similar to that blacks made in white-collar occupations in the nine-year period from 1966 to 1975.

Blacks in Private Industry

Findings

1. Among 178 Michigan-based corporations, representing 1,500 directorships, only 30, or 2 percent, of the directors were black in 1984.
2. Blacks remain underrepresented in various occupations within private industries in Michigan. Blacks were most underrepresented among officials, managers and professionals, technicians and sales persons, and craft workers.
3. In most white-owned companies, the top-ranking blacks, if any, are in middle-management and are concentrated in public relations, community relations, or affirmative action. These positions are the first to be cut during budget reductions.
4. It is unlikely that blacks will rise soon to top-operating positions in even a few white-owned firms. Most blacks are simply not high enough in the career ladder, nor are they on a career path with line responsibility which leads to top-management positions.

Recommendations

1. A broad-based strategy must be initiated with the commitment of significant resources to address these problems.
2. The broad-based effort will require coordination across racial lines.
3. The leadership in the black community must come together, form coalitions, and establish a long-term agenda.

Black Ownership of Business Franchises

Findings

1. Although franchising offers an excellent opportunity for persons who desire to run their own companies, very few franchises are held by blacks.
2. Exact information on the extent of the under-representation of blacks in the franchising business is not available, due to a lack of data-gathering by race by any state, federal, or private agency.

Recommendations

1. Since franchising offers the opportunity to operate a successful business, it is recommended that a state association of owners be formed. They could meet at least once a year to discuss common problems and share successful business strategies. Such an organization could help those who already have established their companies, and it could also disseminate information to individuals seeking a franchise. Information concerning techniques and problems involved in the financing of these businesses might be made available to prospective franchisees.

2. A statewide association of franchise owners or the State of Michigan's Department of Civil Rights should collect annual data on franchise owners by race and sex as part of their affirmative action efforts.

Black-White Unemployment Patterns

Findings

1. Four years after Detroit and other Michigan cities exploded, the black unemployment rate in the state was still 14.0 percent compared to a white rate of 6.9 percent.
2. Since 1971, the black unemployment rate has steadily increased, reaching its peak of 33.4 percent in 1982 and declining to 22.3 percent in 1986. The white rate, on the other hand, rose to 13.3 percent in 1982 and dropped to 7.1 percent in 1986.
3. The gap between black and white unemployment rates has been increasing since 1971.
4. Over a 15-year period (1971–1986), the black unemployment rate has remained at least twice the rate for whites except for the years 1975 and 1976.
5. Since 1984, the black unemployment rate has been three or more times the rate for whites.

The Health of Blacks

Findings

1. Among males, the life expectancy gap between nonwhites and whites increased between 1960 and 1985. On the other hand, there was a slight improvement in the life expectancy of nonwhite females compared with that of white females over the same time period.
2. In the age group of 15–24 years, the health status of nonwhite females, compared with that of white females, remained virtually unchanged from 1975 to 1985, with mortality rate ratios for the category "all causes" (all leading causes combined) of 1.86 and 1.76 respectively. (A ratio of 1.00 would indicate equality.)
3. In the age group of 15–24 years, the health status of nonwhite males, compared with that of white males, became worse, with mortality rate ratios for all leading causes (combined) of 1.86 for 1975 and 2.43 for 1985.
4. For nonwhite females in the middle-aged group of 35–49 years, the mortality rate ratio for the combination of all leading causes was about 2½ times that for white females in both 1975 and 1985.
5. For males in the middle-aged group, the mortality rate ratio increased in 1985, when compared with 1975, rising from 2.37 to 3.19.
6. The rate of infant mortality of blacks increased relative to the white rate from 1974 to 1985. Over the eleven-year period, the infant mortality rate ratio rose from 2.03 to 2.42—that is, from 2 to almost 2½ times the white rate.
7. The general conclusion to be drawn from these findings is that since the civil disorders of 1967, the health status of blacks in Michigan has not improved relative to that of whites.

Recommendations

1. The Michigan Department of Public Health must collect more comprehensive and detailed data on the health of the minority population of Michigan.
2. The presentation of data in the Michigan Health Statistics Annuals should include figures for both unadjusted and adjusted epidemiological risk factors for mortality.

3. Morbidity data should also be presented in the Health Statistics Annuals, as mortality data usually do not fully capture the health profile of a population.
4. Intensive studies of health-related behaviors and epidemiological risk factors among the black population of Michigan are needed to adequately assess their impact on health status.
5. The lack of improvement in the health status of nonwhites relative to whites demands further investigation and policies designed to address the problem.
6. Aggressive action should be taken to educate the Michigan population (especially the black population) about the potentially fatal impact of intravenous drug use that may cause the spread of AIDS and premature death.

Blacks in Institutions of Higher Education

Findings

1. Three years after the disorders of 1967 and five years after the Higher Education Act of 1965, the participation of blacks in higher education in Michigan was dismal.
2. Black undergraduate student enrollment in Michigan public universities has been declining from a peak of 11 percent in 1976 to 7 percent in 1986.
3. Unlike the enrollment of blacks in public universities, which declined to 7 percent, black enrollment in private institutions stood at 10 percent in 1986.
4. Black enrollment in Michigan's graduate schools has been declining since 1976.
5. Consistent with the decline in black graduate student enrollment, the number of blacks earning degrees also declined from 1976 to 1985.

Recommendations

Universities and colleges should:

1. Develop financial aid programs that more effectively address the needs of black students and result in increased black participation in higher education. The support should be provided at a level to insure that the representation of black students is at least equal to the proportion of blacks in Michigan's population (about 12 percent).
2. Adjust the criteria on which decisions to admit black students are based, so as to give less weight to standardized test scores and more weight to other factors such as high school grades, motivation, work experience, and letters of reference.
3. Institute or expand special programming focused on the needs and circumstances of black students. Such programs might include activities in areas such as pre-college enrichment, academic remediation, and comprehensive support services.
4. Involve college faculty more extensively in the process of black student recruitment and retention. As the institution's "human link" between policy statements and performance, faculty play a critical role. They can either assist or debilitate the college experience of black students.

The Status of Civil Rights

Findings

1. Most complaints today are still race-related and result from alleged employment discrimination.

2. Total complaints of discrimination have generally increased over the years. There has been an annual reduction of staff each year, however, from 1979–80 through 1984–85.

Recommendations

1. Although the commission has the constitutional authority to enforce civil rights, its effectiveness could be strengthened by stronger support from the state's political leadership; by increased budget and staff to carry out its mandate, and by leadership by commissioners who have statewide visibility and clout to command attention from the public and private sectors.
2. The commission must take a stronger advocacy role in the fight against persistent discrimination.

Conclusions

The social and economic inequalities that existed between blacks and whites in 1967, when several Michigan cities exploded, are still prevalent today. Until racial inequality and discrimination are reduced, the possibility of history repeating itself might be only one spark away.

The State of Black Michigan: 1988

Executive Summary

Introduction

This publication, the fifth in a series of annual reports on the *State of Black Michigan*, presents factual material, interpretive discussions, and recommendations concerning the status of black Michigan residents. The topics include black-white unemployment patterns by gender, the impact of Michigan's restructured automotive industry on black employment, black crime, the use of deadly force by the Detroit police, and the impact of social welfare programs on Michigan blacks.

Michigan's Black-White Unemployment Patterns, 1971–1986: Differences by Gender

Findings

1. During 1971–1986 in Michigan, the ratio of black male to white male unemployment has varied from as low as 1.5 times greater for blacks than for whites in 1976 to 3.7 times greater in 1985.
2. In the case of females, the ratio has varied from 1.3 times greater for blacks than for whites in 1975 to 3.5 times greater in 1985.
3. The unemployment gap between blacks and whites has been wider in the Detroit Standard Metropolitan Statistical Area (SMSA), where the maximum ratio in 1985 reached 4.67 times greater for black males and 4.0 times greater for black females.
4. In the City of Detroit, where black political control exists in various forms, the black-white unemployment gap has remained wide, although narrower than in the Detroit SMSA and in the state as a whole.
5. Given the persistent black-white unemployment gap, it appears that increasing numbers of whites are finding better employment opportunities by migrating to the suburbs,

leaving their black counterparts to search for employment in the city, where opportunities are fewer.

The Impact of Michigan's Restructured Automobile Industry on Black Employment

Findings

1. The Detroit Metropolitan Statistical Area (MSA) accounted for 70.3 percent of the state's losses in automotive manufacturing between 1978–1984.
2. The impact of these losses on Michigan's black population is critical, considering that 98.5 percent of Michigan's blacks are located in the state's MSAs, where 90.8 percent of the job loss has been experienced.
3. Auto job losses are the greatest in the MSAs where the black population is most heavily concentrated.
4. Since blacks have been so dependent on automobile manufacturing jobs, their economic well-being is deteriorating as a consequence, with no apparent alternative source of new jobs offering comparable wages and benefits to offset this economic loss.
5. Furthermore, new plant ventures in the state are not having a positive impact on black employment, due in part to the fact that most new plants are located at such great distances from the centers of black concentration that the accessibility of these plants to potential black workers is severely limited.

Recommendations

1. Implement first-choice-of-employment programs for displaced autoworkers when new auto plants come on the line.
2. Assure that displaced workers receive retraining that is appropriate for new jobs requiring higher levels of technical skills.
3. Establish a vigorous out-placement program, once workers are retrained.
4. Require an "Employment-Potential Impact Statement" for each proposed plant site.
5. Increase the Equal Employment Opportunity Commission's monitoring procedures so that existing plants are annually reviewed to determine whether they are in compliance.

Black Crime in Michigan

Findings

1. Between 1982 and 1986, the percentage of arrests of blacks increased for crimes involving murder, robbery, and aggravated assault. On the other hand, the percentage of arrests of whites decreased for these same crimes over the four-year period.
2. Decreases in the percentage of arrests of blacks have occurred for rape and property crimes, while the percentage of arrests of whites for these same crimes increased over the four-year period.
3. In 1986, approximately 7 out of every 10 murder victims were black as compared with approximately 3 out of 10 for whites.
4. The rate of murder victimization for blacks increased by nearly 10 percentage points between 1982 and 1986, and decreased by 8.2 percentage points for whites over the same time period.

5. When these trends are assessed in relation to national victimization data, declining prospects for economic advancement through gainful employment, and the disproportionate percentage of high school dropouts among blacks, particularly black males, the situation is even more discouraging.

Recommendations

1. Every child should be guaranteed access to a high quality preschool program.
2. Every student should be guaranteed a job upon successful completion of high school.
3. With the exception of use by law enforcement officials, Michigan should ban all handguns in the state.
4. Neighborhood self-help and revitalization programs should receive strong support and encouragement from city and state governments.
5. Finding effective solutions to the problem of illicit drugs must become a priority for the federal, state, and city governments.

Deadly Force and Racial Composition in the Detroit Police Department

Findings

1. It was acceptable in 1976 to use deadly force to effect the arrest or prevent the escape of an individual alleged to have committed felonious breaking and entering. This was not acceptable in 1986.
2. In 1976, robbery was a crime that allowed an officer to use deadly force to effect an arrest or prevent an escape. In 1986, the crime committed had to be armed robbery rather than just robbery.
3. These changes in policies concerning the use of deadly force are related to the increasing black representation on the Detroit police force.
4. Increased black representation on the Detroit police force has been related to the sharp decline in the number of citizens killed by Detroit police officers between 1971 and 1986.
5. The central most important factor in a reduction in the use of deadly force appears to be a sound formal policy supported by the police chief. Black political power and the election of a black mayor, or a sensitive nonblack mayor, can contribute to a climate in which a police chief is appointed who will formulate a restrictive policy regarding the use of deadly force.

Recommendations

1. A police officer should be required to appear before a Board of Review whenever he/she discharges his/her weapon.
2. When there are allegations of criminal misconduct brought against a police officer, there should be a separate monitoring committee made up of two attorneys in private practice and an attorney representing the ACLU.
3. When a police officer uses deadly force, he/she must be held accountable.
4. In cases where criminal misconduct is found, the police officer should be tried like any other citizen.

Social Welfare and Blacks in Michigan

Findings

1. Persistent high rates of black unemployment have made blacks in Michigan disproportionately dependent on social welfare programs.
2. Programs that are considered to be "entitlement," such as Social Security and Medicare, have generally been supported by policy makers as "earned" and essential to the well-being of the entire population. These programs have disproportionately white recipients.
3. Programs based on means-testing or categorical eligibility, however, such as Aid to Families with Dependent Children (AFDC), have continually been attacked for promoting familial "irresponsibility." As a result, those categorical programs are treated differently in times of fiscal restraint. Such programs have disproportionately black recipients.
4. Although there is a strong desire on the part of AFDC recipients to work, programs such as Michigan's Opportunity and Skills Training (MOST), which was designed to encourage labor force participation of persons receiving AFDC and General Assistance benefits, did not contain adequate provisions for child care, transportation, or specialized training.
5. Future social welfare programs in Michigan must be transformed from programs that merely maintain the poor at a level below poverty to programs that enable the poor to break out of poverty and achieve upward social mobility.

Recommendations

1. Guarantee an adequate income for all residents. At the very least, income support should equal the official poverty level of the nation.
2. Implement the five-year plan to reduce infant-mortality and mother-mortality rates, as recommended in 1987 by the Task Force on Infant Mortality.
3. Develop strategies to reverse the current distribution of funding for black children remaining in the home with their parents.
4. Improve the access of Michigan's teenaged residents to educational and employment opportunities that will make them contributors to the economic base of the state's future.
5. Assure opportunities for black parents to be employed in jobs with career ladders and with services that support rather than jeopardize the family.

Summary and Conclusions

The overall conclusions are that the black-white unemployment ratio has grown significantly for both males and females; the opportunity for black employment is declining since new plants are locating at greater distances from black residential areas; the rate of black murder victims has increased; the use of deadly force in Detroit has declined with the increasing representation of blacks on the police force; and the social welfare system has not provided adequate assistance for the poor, nor has it provided the poor with the tools to break out of poverty.

The economic situation of blacks compared with that of whites continues to deteriorate. Furthermore, the prospects for improvement through greater employment opportunities for blacks do not look promising. Urgent action by both the private and public sectors is needed now.

The State of Black Michigan: 1989

Executive Summary

Introduction

This publication is the sixth in a series of annual reports on the *State of Black Michigan*. The various chapters address some of the most critical issues facing blacks in Michigan. The situation of black youth and women is the major focus of this year's report. Highlighted are: black children and the child welfare system; disparities in black-white youth unemployment; black-white high school dropout rates; the problem of the young black offender; and issues related to the black female offender. The political preferences of blacks in the 1988 elections are also examined.

Michigan's Black Children and the Child Welfare System

Findings

1. The present organizational structure of Michigan's child welfare services leaves the providers and the recipients of the services confused, and the efficiency and effectiveness of child welfare services are diminished.
2. A review of Michigan's child welfare system reveals that the future does not look encouraging for black children. There is evidence of marked racial discrepancies in the identification of problems, proposed corrective interventions, provision of services, and expected outcomes.
3. Although there is some evidence that the Michigan system is indeed addressing child welfare needs, many black and other minority children are victimized by the system that was created to ensure the protection and care of all children.
4. Although the legal basis for developing and providing child welfare services is fairly clear, the appropriations and the process to ensure the monitoring and evaluation do not exist. As a result, the accountability that is required to confirm program efficiency and effectiveness, as well as cost-effectiveness, does not occur.

Recommendations

1. Ensure sufficient appropriations to fund the design, development, and implementation of cost- and program-effective services that highlight prevention and that address the special needs of black and other minority children.
2. Create an autonomous State Department of Children, Youth, and Families, to be staffed by professionally trained child welfare personnel who represent education, labor, public health, social services, and all other mandated areas of child welfare.
3. Develop and implement a statewide ethnically and culturally sensitive training curriculum as a requirement for all persons providing child welfare services.
4. Employ resources to ensure maximum information management, including the use of technology and training, so that information is available to the legislature, to professionals, and to the community-at-large. Such efforts should ensure appropriate monitoring of outcomes and hold all areas accountable to the needs of children.

5. Increase community/public education to emphasize the importance of children as our future. Children need strong advocates for their rights if the child welfare system is to be improved.
6. Develop a state policy on children, parents, and families, using public/private child welfare professionals to develop standards, accountability procedures, and appropriate legislation. Permanency planning efforts must also be addressed and monitored. The focus of child welfare services must be on prevention, including the use of family-focused interventions.
7. Provide adequate economic and other resources to poor black families. Equal access to opportunities and resources for poor black families will increase their ability to better manage their lives and will be the best protective resource for black children.

Black-White Youth Unemployment in Michigan, 1971–1987

Findings

1. Black youth unemployment rates in the State of Michigan have ranged from 33 percent (1979) to 68 percent (1983). In contrast, the range for white youths has been from 14 percent (1979) to 25 percent (1982).
2. Over the period 1971–1987, black youths in the labor force in the State of Michigan were on average 2¾ times more likely to be unemployed than their white youth counterparts.
3. Black youth unemployment in Michigan grew on average by 1.7 percent per year over the 1971–1987 period. In contrast, white youth unemployment grew only 0.1 percent per year over the same period.
4. In 1987, young blacks were almost 4 times more likely than young whites to be unemployed.

Black and White High School Dropout Rates in Michigan: The Inequality Persists

Findings

1. The annual dropout rate for black high school students in Michigan during 1985–86 was 12 percent, while the dropout rate for white high school students during this same period was 4.5 percent, resulting in a black rate that was 2.6 times the rate for whites.
2. During the period from 1976–77 to 1985–86, the average dropout rate for black students was 10.8 percent, while the average rate for white students during the same period was 5.1 percent, resulting in an average dropout rate for black students that was twice that of white students.
3. Dropout rates for local school districts vary dramatically. Annual dropout rates for the 30 Michigan school districts with the highest black enrollments ranged from a low of 2.5 percent in Southfield to a high of 20.7 percent in Ecorse.
4. On the whole, it appears that the State of Michigan has not succeeded in its responsibility to provide equal educational opportunities to all students. The black dropout rate increased from almost two times the rate for whites in 1981–82 to almost three times the rate for whites in 1985–86.

Recommendations

1. Implement the Governor's proposed preschool education program for all children. This approach is preventive and tends to provide students with a solid social and academic base. Such a program is supported by the research findings from the Perry Preschool Project, which worked exclusively with black youngsters and proved both educationally and economically successful (Berrueta-Clement et al., 1984).
2. Proceed with a school finance reform plan that will provide equal per pupil expenditure for instruction for all school districts in Michigan. This should include equalization of teacher and administrator compensation so that talented educators are not lured from the central cities to the suburbs.
3. Institute metropolitan school compacts that involve business and industry, unions, and government in creating job opportunities for students who succeed in graduating from local high schools. Where possible, create cooperative programs that offer work experience and entree to apprenticeship training.
4. Take desegregation beyond school district boundaries by providing opportunities for low-income, central-city students to attend suburban schools. Chicago, Indianapolis, Milwaukee, and Minneapolis are experimenting with this kind of metropolitan plan.
5. Take advantage of federal initiatives for economic redevelopment of urban communities. If low social and economic status appears to be related to dropping out, efforts should be made to improve not only the schools but the communities in which these potential dropout students live.
6. Increase efforts to develop more "effective schools," along the lines proposed by the late Dr. Ronald Edmonds (1979). Successful effective schools are attractive places for both teachers and students, particularly black students, and tend to have lower dropout rates.
7. Expand the Michigan Department of Education's Operation Graduation, which provides subsidized work experience and intensive counseling for students at risk of dropping out (Bryson, 1989).
8. Develop a think tank of scholars and other concerned citizens dedicated to the empowerment of black educators and students to find solutions to the problem of black dropouts in Michigan. Black educators and parents have historically been in the vanguard of efforts to improve the schooling of black students.
9. Expand research efforts in each school district and elevate the priority of the dropout problem. There is a need for more research that (a) clearly describes the nature and extent of the dropout problem in Michigan's public schools and (b) recommends policy changes to solve this problem.
10. Institute a program on an experimental basis, with adequate follow-up, modeled after the West Virginia plan, which links high school completion to receiving a driver's license.

The Young Black Offender in Michigan

Findings

1. The total number of arrests for murder, rape, robbery, aggravated assault, and narcotics laws violations increased in Michigan's largest cities—Detroit, Grand Rapids, Flint, Lansing, and Warren, between 1978 and 1987. For example, in the five cities combined, the

total number of arrests for murder increased from 499 in 1978 to 1,591 in 1987 (or by 219 percent). Of those arrested in 1978 for murder, 60 (or 12.2 percent) were juveniles. The juvenile population in the five cities constituted 30 percent of the total population in 1980.

2. Although the number of juveniles arrested for murder increased from 60 in 1978 to 194 in 1987 (or by 206.7 percent) over the ten-year period, the juvenile percentage of the total arrests remained relatively constant—from 12.02 percent of the total in 1978 to 12.19 percent of the total in 1987.
3. Although the black male juvenile population as a percentage of the total juvenile population was about 30 percent in 1980, of the 60 juveniles arrested in 1978 for murder, 53 (or 88.3 percent) were black males. Of the 194 juveniles arrested in 1987 for murder, 167 (or 87.9 percent) were black males.
4. Much attention recently has been given to narcotics laws violations as a possible link to the increase in murder and other violent crimes. In the five largest cities in Michigan, the total number of arrests for narcotics laws violations increased from 4,084 in 1978 to 9,056 in 1987 (or by 121.7 percent). Of those arrested in 1978 for narcotics laws violations, 327 (or 8 percent) were juveniles.
5. The number of juveniles arrested for narcotics laws violations increased from 327 in 1978 to 1,132 in 1987 (or by 246 percent) over the ten-year period. The juvenile percentage of total arrests increased from 8 percent in 1978 to 12.5 percent in 1987.
6. Of the 327 juveniles arrested in 1978 for narcotics laws violations in the five cities, 122 (or 37.3 percent) were black males. Of the 1,132 arrested in 1987 for narcotics laws violations, 86.7 percent were black males. As mentioned previously, the black male juvenile population in 1980 was 30 percent.

The Black Female Offender in Michigan

Findings

1. The rate of arrests of black females is overwhelmingly in excess of their representation in the general population of the State of Michigan.
2. Although black females are less likely murder victims than black males, their risk ratio exceeds that for white females by a large margin. Of all homicide deaths in 1986, black females accounted for 12.6 percent, compared with 8.5 percent for white females.
3. The differential in black/white ratios (that is, disparities in arrest rates) is more acute for black females for the three violent crimes of murder, aggravated assault, and robbery, when compared with nonpersonal crimes such as burglary and embezzlement.
4. New, faster, more lucrative, and easier money-generating activities have been replacing traditional activities for black females. For example, there has been a decreasing arrest trend for black females for prostitution and an increasing trend of arrests for embezzlement, fraud, and narcotics-related offenses.

Recommendations

1. Educational Programs

   Appropriate mechanisms must be developed to identify children who experience school or learning problems. Adequate and, where necessary, alternative educational packages must be developed. They must be needs-based—that is, tailored to fit not only the individual learning needs of pupils but also the social circumstances and needs of the larger community. Often children's interest for school and education is affected by what happens at home. Educational programs must also be targeted at adults. Dropout prevention programs must be developed so that potential dropouts can be identified and appropriate programs developed for them.

2. Training Programs

   Training programs must be designed to prepare women to compete in today's labor market. This applies also to those confined in correctional facilities. Sewing, cooking, and hairdressing are examples of skills that perpetuate the sex-role expectations of females, but hardly prepare the inmates for a successful adjustment into society. Innovative and diversified educational and training programs must be developed, especially in the area of computer or other skills more attuned to the demands of today's economy.

3. Teen Pregnancy and Parenting Programs

   Teenagers must be provided with realistic sex education programs, undertaken early enough to be effective in avoiding teenage pregnancies. The education programs must be directed at both the young men and young women. Sex education is often reduced to lessons on contraceptive use. The message must focus on the family, on marriage, and therefore on responsible parenthood. Those caught in the teen pregnancy dilemma can be provided with parenting educational programs involving both teen parents and emphasizing health care, nutrition, and sex education for responsible parenthood and family planning.

4. Drug Education Programs

   A drug education program expressed exclusively in the "Say No to Drugs" cliche is doomed to failure because it ignores the supply side of the equation and, therefore, the substantial financial rewards accruing from this illicit underground business. The minimum-wage job and drug sale calculus is in favor of the latter. Appropriate social policy is needed to boost the educational and legitimate employment skills and earning power of the inner-city underclass. Traditional job-training programs often lead to low-paying, dead-end jobs and to chronic poverty and eventually to the search for illegitimate but more lucrative expedients. Efforts must be targeted at training for today, for the future, and for a higher earning power.

The Political Preferences of Michigan Blacks in the 1988 Elections

Findings

1. Black voter turnout in 1988 slipped from 1984 levels.
2. At the national and state levels in 1988, blacks continued to express a negative image of the Republican Party.
3. In spite of growing uneasiness with the Democratic party on the part of many blacks, the Republican Party faces a formidable challenge in attracting black converts at the local, state, and national levels.
4. Perceived lack of interest in black concerns will limit the Republican Party's ability to capitalize on the unrest among black Democrats.

Racial Disparities in Michigan in 1989: Summary and Conclusions

The overall conclusions of this report are that the racial and economic gap between blacks and whites continues to widen, exacerbating an already established two-tier system, where:

- black children, more often than white children, are victimized by a child welfare system that was created to insure the equal protection of all children;
- young blacks are nearly 4 times more likely than young whites to be unemployed;
- black students are more than 2½ times more likely than white students to drop out of high school.

As the quality of life of two of the most vulnerable populations in Michigan— black youth and black women—continues to worsen, arrest rates have also increased, resulting in additional pressure on Michigan's already overcrowded criminal justice system.

Unequal social and economic conditions, on the basis of race, lead to unequal outcomes. If the outcomes are to be equalized, the social and economic conditions must be equalized.

The State of Black Michigan: 1990

Executive Summary

Introduction

This publication is the seventh in a series of annual reports on *The State of Black Michigan*. The various chapters discuss some of the most critical issues facing blacks in Michigan.

Among the questions addressed in the 1990 report are the following:

- How did Michigan blacks fare in the area of unemployment, both absolutely and relatively to whites, under Democratic and Republican governors during the period 1971 to 1988?
- What political progress did Michigan blacks achieve during the 1980s? What are the views of black elected officials concerning spending priorities for the State of Michigan?
- What was the extent of occupational segregation between blacks and whites in Michigan mass media industries in the 1980s?
- What is the status of life expectancy for blacks, as compared with whites, in Michigan? What has been the significance of AIDS in black mortality?
- Are a disproportionate number of Michigan black children, compared with white children, being waived to adult courts for trial?
- What is the extent of psychiatric disorders among adult prisoners, both black and white, in Michigan?

Black Unemployment in Michigan Under Democratic and Republican Governors

Findings

1. Both the degree of unemployment and the trends in unemployment differed under the Republican and Democratic administrations.
2. Black rates of unemployment were higher, and the unemployment gap between blacks and whites was wider under the Democratic administration of Governor Blanchard (1983 to 1988) than under the Republican administration of Governor Milliken (1971 to 1982).

3. For both males and females, the black unemployment rate was roughly 2¼ times the white rate during the 1971–1982 Republican regime, and about 3 times the white rate during the subsequent Democratic administration (1983–1988). For youths, black unemployment was greater by 2½ times in the Republican regime and by 3¼ times in the Democratic regime.
4. Trends in unemployment rates showed an increase for all groups during the Republican administration, while the trends showed a decrease under the Democratic administration that followed. However, the rates of unemployment were never lowered to the level of the rates under the Republican administration.
5. The black-white unemployment gap remained relatively constant during the Republican governorship, but the gap appears to have widened under the Democratic governorship, because the unemployment rate fell proportionately more for whites than for blacks under Governor Blanchard's administration during the period 1983–1988.

Recommendation

1. Eliminating the black-white unemployment gap would require specifically targeted policies to reduce black unemployment. If policies to close the gap are to be effective, then when reductions in unemployment occur, the rate of decrease should not be less for blacks than for whites.

Black Political Participation in Michigan

Findings

1. In Michigan, the number of black elected officials increased during the late 1970s and 1980s. There were 245 black elected officials in 1976; and by 1988, blacks held 316 (1.6 percent) of the 19,403 elected offices in the state.
2. In 1988, Michigan had 93 black female elected officials, ranking fifth in the nation behind Illinois, the District of Columbia, Mississippi, and California.
3. In the areas of voter registration and election turnout during the 1980s, blacks continued to show improvement in closing the gaps between themselves and whites.
4. Except for expenditures on corrections, the majority of black elected officials supported increased funding for each of the departments/programs on which a special May 1990 survey requested an opinion. In the areas of civil rights and education (especially school aid for K-12 education), there was support for a "substantial increase" in state spending.
5. Fifty percent of the survey respondents disagreed and an additional 23 percent strongly disagreed with the statement, "Under the Blanchard Administration, the unemployment situation for blacks has substantially improved." Furthermore, 42 percent of the respondents disagreed and an additional 24 percent strongly disagreed with the statement, "The Blanchard Administration has done an effective job in reducing the black-white unemployment gap."

Occupational Segregation Between Blacks and Whites in Michigan Mass Media Industries

Findings

1. The white-black representation in the broadcasting industry in both 1984 and 1988 was close to approximating the statewide pattern of representation in the Michigan labor

force. However, the racial distribution across occupational levels within the broadcasting industry was not even.

2. In 1984, white males were more than twice as likely as black males to be employed as officials and managers. Overall, the situation in the broadcasting industry improved for black men between 1984 and 1988, as the proportions of black officials and managers and sales-workers increased.
3. At the officials and managers level, the percentage of black women increased to a greater degree (10.3 to 15.0 percent) than the percentage of white women (17.8 to 18.7 percent) from 1984 to 1988.
4. In 1988, the office and clerical workers category accounted for 40.2 percent of all black women employed in the broadcasting industry, compared with 30.7 percent of white women, 4.0 percent of black men, and 1.4 percent of white men.
5. The representation of blacks in newspaper firms in five selected Michigan cities was measured against the black representation in the labor force of each city. An analysis revealed that blacks were severely underrepresented in Detroit (by 40-plus percentage points), moderately underrepresented in Battle Creek (by 9 percentage points), and slightly underrepresented in Lansing (by 1 percentage point). In Bay City and Kalamazoo, blacks were slightly overrepresented (by 1.9 and 1.0 percentage points, respectively).

Recommendations

1. Mass media industry officials should develop internship programs designed to attract more blacks into the industry.
2. Mass media industry officials should hire black males and females in jobs and positions that can lead to upward mobility and financial rewards.
3. Personnel directors should buy advertising space and time on black-owned media to reach potential job applicants.

Michigan's Black-White Mortality Gap: The Impact of Drugs and AIDS

Findings

1. In Michigan, the life expectancy gap between blacks and whites increased from 1960 to 1987. The gap widened because the life expectancy for whites increased faster than the life expectancy for blacks. From 1982 to 1987, life expectancy for blacks actually decreased, while life expectancy for whites continued to increase.
2. A review of the life expectancy gap between Michigan's black residents and white residents from 1960 to 1987 reveals that the gap was most narrow in 1960. Between 1960 and 1987, the gap increased from a difference of 4.9 years to a difference of 6.8 years (whites, 75.3; blacks, 68.5). In 1988, infant mortality for blacks in Michigan was more than 2½ times that for whites.
3. Michigan black residents had higher death rates than did white residents from diabetes, homicide, and chronic liver disease/cirrhosis in 1987.
4. The leading cause of death in 1988 for black males aged 25–34 was homicide, with the rate being approximately 22 times higher than the rate for white males. Drug use, particularly cocaine, appears to have played an important role in many black homicides.

5. In 1988, AIDS appeared as the fifth leading cause of death for black males between the ages of 25 and 34. During the period 1980 to 1989, 48 percent of adults with AIDS were black, although blacks made up only about 13 percent of Michigan's population. Of the adult males with AIDS, 44 percent were black; of the adult females, 81 percent were black. Black children made up 64 percent of Michigan's children with AIDS. This disproportionate representation of blacks appears to be related to the disproportionate use of intravenous drugs by blacks.

Recommendations

1. The Michigan Office of Substance Abuse Services (OSAS) must spearhead the development of an aggressive drug abuse treatment program that is available, accessible, affordable, and appropriate for blacks, especially pregnant women. Black churches must be involved to insure spiritual focus.
2. The Michigan Office of Substance Abuse Services (OSAS) and the Michigan Department of Public Health (MDPH) must coordinate and/or foster community-wide anti-drug efforts linking churches, schools, and community organizations such as the Urban League and the NAACP.
3. The Michigan Department of Education, local school districts, and the Michigan Department of Labor must improve educational and economic opportunities for black young people.
4. The Michigan Department of Public Health, with the support of black churches and community organizations, must implement effective anti-smoking campaigns and demonstrate zero tolerance for the targeting of the black community by the tobacco and alcohol industries.
5. Local school boards must address the need to increase AIDS education (beginning in elementary schools) that targets the black community, particularly males.
6. Accessible, available, affordable, and quality prenatal care for black women must be increased via cooperation among Medicaid, local medical societies, medical schools, and local businesses or philanthropic foundations.

The Incarceration of Black Children and Youth in Michigan

Findings

1. The study findings indicate that a disproportionate number of blacks in the juvenile justice system were receiving waivers to adult courts (that is, being tried as adults), when compared with the percentage that blacks represented in the total state population for this age range.
2. Of those waivers where children and youth actually went to trial and received a sentence, a greater proportion of whites compared with blacks had charges reduced or dropped.
3. Among the 47 children committed to Michigan prisons in 1987, the greatest number (35) were black males. In addition, there were 2 black female children, 9 white male children, and 1 "other" minority male child. By 1989, the number of children committed to prison in Michigan had almost doubled—from 47 to 89, an increase of 89 percent. Of these, 57 (or 64.0 percent) were black males, and 29 (or 32.6 percent) were white males. (Female

children, whether black or white, are not usually committed to prison, although there was one of each in 1989.)

4. As of March 1989, the Michigan prison population included a total of 562 children, of whom 366 (65 percent) were black; 182 (32 percent) were white; and 14 (3 percent) were classified as "other."
5. Although fewer black children than white children are found in the general population in Genesee, Ingham, Muskegon, Wayne, and Washtenaw Counties, black children in the corrections population outnumbered white children in the sentencing courts of these five counties.

Recommendations

1. The Department of Social Services and the Department of Corrections should review and reassess the results of incarcerating children in terms of the long-term financial costs created for these state-dependent persons.
2. The Michigan State Legislature should appoint a commission to examine the racial disparity in the incarceration of Michigan children to determine whether there is institutional racism in the criminal justice system.
3. The Michigan State Legislature should reduce and contain the costs of corrections. They should furthermore redirect fiscal resources and efforts toward the rehabilitation and treatment of children to prepare them for functional independence. The legislature should increase spending in other state departments responsible for the welfare of children and families, in order to address basic needs involving family services and educational and employment opportunities.
4. The Department of Corrections and the Department of Social Services should use automation to improve procedures for monitoring and tracking individuals within the corrections system. The focus should be on improved outcomes for all services through evaluation and quality assurance.
5. Government officials and agencies responsible for the welfare of Michigan juveniles should take steps to insure equal access to community corrections programs.

Psychiatric Disorders Among African-American Prisoners in Michigan

Findings

1. The most frequent psychiatric disorders found in a 1987 study of Michigan prisoners were *antisocial personality, alcohol abuse/dependence, psychosexual dysfunction, generalized anxiety*, and *simple phobia.*
2. The frequency of psychiatric disorders among black prisoners differed from the frequency found among white prisoners. A higher percentage of white prisoners than black prisoners had psychiatric disorders of all types except for *organic brain syndrome* and *agoraphobia.*
3. White prisoners were found to have *alcohol abuse/dependence disorders* at a rate of 69.3 percent—more than twice the rate (30.0 percent) for black prisoners. A majority (58.4 percent) of the white prisoners in the sample were found to exhibit *antisocial personality disorders,* compared with 44.3 percent for black prisoners.

4. The 1987 prison study showed that the psychiatric disorders of males in the sample of all Michigan prisoners differed from those of female prisoners. Male prisoners were more than twice as likely as females to have *antisocial personality disorders* (51.5 percent, compared with 21.9 percent). Males were also more than twice as likely as females to have *alcohol abuse/dependence* (47.9 percent, compared with 19.9 percent). Females, on the other hand, were more than twice as likely as males to have *psychosexual dysfunction* (57.8 percent, compared with 21.2 percent).
5. Psychiatric disorders can have a substantial impact on whether a prisoner can adjust to parole or to alternative forms of incarceration. Therefore, in the interests of both the prisoners and society, it is imperative that parole and probation programs, as well as alternative forms of incarceration, include effective mental health treatment programs.

Recommendations

1. The federal court should continue to monitor the state's implementation of a treatment program for psychiatrically disordered prison residents to insure that the program conforms to general community standards of care.
2. State and federal legislators should make certain that the state's prison population is included in any future national health and mental health system and national health insurance.
3. Whenever feasible, the DOC should develop community-based mental health treatment programs and should contract for mental health services from local mental health service organizations.
4. The DOC should locate new psychiatric facilities for mentally ill prisoners near university campuses to facilitate closer university-DOC collaboration.
5. The DOC should promote and fund university-based research in correctional mental health issues.
6. The DOC should promote and fund correctional mental health training programs at state universities in order to create a supply of clinicians to work with mentally ill prisoners.
7. The DOC should develop and fund programs to subsidize tuition and living expenses of professional students who agree to work in correctional settings upon graduation.
8. The DOC should create a state/university-sponsored center for teaching, research, and clinical service in correctional mental health and other correctional care issues.

Summary and Conclusions

The overall conclusions are that the political gains made by blacks during the last decade have not been translated into economic and social progress.

The black-white unemployment gap, which remained relatively constant under Governor Milliken's Republican administration, appears to have widened under Governor Blanchard's Democratic administration. Unemployment was reduced proportionately more for whites than for blacks under the Democratic administration. This widening of the unemployment gap was occurring even as Michigan blacks continued their high level of support for the Democratic Party.

Black representation in Michigan broadcasting industries was found to be uneven in terms of distribution across job categories. For example, blacks were underrepresented at the level of officials and managers and overrepresented in the clerical and service categories. An analysis of black representation in the newspaper firms of five selected Michigan cities showed that blacks were underrepresented in three of the five cities studied.

The life expectancy gap between whites and blacks has increased, inasmuch as the life expectancy of whites has increased faster than the life expectancy of blacks. The impact of drug abuse and AIDS on the life expectancy of blacks is cause for deep concern.

As unemployment and health problems continue and worsen, a higher proportion of blacks compared with whites are being incarcerated—including many juveniles who are receiving waivers to adult courts and are ultimately being incarcerated with adults.

Incarcerated individuals may have serious psychiatric problems that need identification and treatment. This segment of the population, the majority of whom are black males, require attention and appropriate action.

As Michigan enters the decade of the 1990s, black citizens must continue to press for equality. So long as gaps exist in critical areas of the common life, such as employment and health care, the State of Black Michigan is in jeopardy.

The State of Black Michigan: 1991

Executive Summary

Introduction

This publication is the eighth in a series of annual reports on *The State of Black Michigan*. Through the years, the various chapters have discussed some of the most critical issues facing blacks in Michigan.

In addition to presenting a review of the range of topics discussed in past issues and a review of past recommendations for constructive steps that could be taken, the 1991 edition addresses two aspects of the economic status of Michigan's black citizens: (1) black-white unemployment and (2) black business development.

Among the questions addressed in the 1991 report are the following:

Regarding Unemployment Trends (1971–1989):

1. How have unemployment rates in Michigan compared with rates in the nation as a whole?
2. What has been the trend in the black-white unemployment gap for males, females, and youths in Michigan and in the U.S.?
3. What has been the trend in the black-white unemployment growth rate for males, females, and youths in Michigan and in the nation as a whole?

Regarding Trends in Black-Owned Business Development (1982–1987):

1. What has been the trend of black business development in Michigan and in the nation as a whole?
2. How does the representation of Michigan's black business ownership compare with the representation of black business ownership in the nation (based on the percentage of blacks in the population)?

3. How has Michigan ranked as a state in terms of black-owned firms with paid employees and in terms of total receipts?
4. Of the total firms in Michigan, what percentage were black-owned?
5. Which counties in Michigan had the largest number of black-owned firms with paid employees between 1982 and 1987?
6. Which Michigan cities had the greatest amount of growth in the number of black-owned firms with paid employees between 1982 and 1987?

The State of Black Michigan: Review and Analysis of Contents of Previous Issues, 1984–1990

The research findings presented in previous issues of *The State of Black Michigan* have consistently confirmed the existence of a widening socioeconomic gap between Michigan blacks and whites. In view of the continuing similarity of the overall conclusions, it might appear that the reports have addressed a narrow range of topics and have repeated the same information year after year.

An examination of the Tables of Contents of all previous issues will demonstrate the range of topics that were discussed from 1984 to 1990.

Past issues of *The State of Black Michigan* have presented chapters addressing 10 major areas of concern affecting the welfare of Michigan's black citizens. These 10 areas are (1) civil rights (2) crime (3) economic issues (4) education (5) employment/unemployment (6) family (7) health (8) housing (9) media (10) political participation.

Twenty-eight authors from Michigan State University, University of Michigan, Oakland University, and Wayne State University have contributed 40 chapters dealing with current problems involving the status of Michigan's black citizens. When possible, comparisons have been made between the status of Michigan's black citizens and that of Michigan's white citizens.

The State of Black Michigan: Review and Analysis of Past Recommendations, 1985–1989

The 1985–1989 issues of *The State of Black Michigan* presented a total of 88 recommendations focusing on various social and economic areas of concern: civil rights, crime, economic issues, education, employment, family issues, health, and housing.

Legislative action and other approaches designed to reverse the relative decline in the social and economic conditions facing Michigan's black citizens are needed.

In 1990, a forum of critical thinkers in the State of Michigan was assembled for the free exchange of ideas focusing on a review of the recommendations in *The State of Black Michigan* annual reports of 1985–1989. The purpose of the think tank discussions was to develop an updated set of recommendations based on those presented in the annual reports.

Twenty-one persons (public officials and other community leaders from various parts of the state) attended at least one of the six sessions of the think tank.

Revised and updated recommendations were formulated, as the think tank participants reviewed the past recommendations presented in the 1985–89 issues of *The State of Black Michigan*.

These recommendations, if translated into legislation or otherwise implemented, could strengthen the movement toward self-sufficiency and empowerment for Michigan's black citizens.

Patterns of Black-White Unemployment in Michigan Versus the Nation, 1971–1989

Findings

1. Unemployment rates averaged at higher levels in Michigan than in the nation as a whole for both blacks and whites over the 1971–1989 period.
2. The Michigan-U.S. unemployment differential was higher for blacks than for whites. This led to a slightly larger average black-white unemployment gap (measured as the mean ratio of black to white unemployment rates) in Michigan (2½ times for both males and females and 3 times for youths) than in the nation (2⅓ times for males, 2 times for females, and 2½ times for youths).
3. In Michigan, black male unemployment grew at a rate about triple that for white males. While black female unemployment rose at 1.7 percent per year on average, unemployment for white females exhibited a decline. Similarly, the trend of black youth unemployment was upward, while that of white youth was downward.

Unemployment grew more rapidly for both black and white males in Michigan than in the nation. However, the male black-white unemployment gap increased twice as fast in Michigan as in the U.S.

Unemployment grew faster for black females in Michigan than in the United States; it fell more slowly in Michigan than in the nation for white females. The female black-white unemployment gap rose about 1½ times more rapidly in Michigan than in the United States.

Black youth unemployment increased faster in Michigan than in the United States. White youth unemployment, however, exhibited a downward trend in Michigan but was trendless in the U.S. The youth black-white unemployment gap grew about 8 times faster in Michigan than in the United States.

Black-Owned Businesses in Michigan, 1982 to 1987, and the Top 31 in 1989

Findings

Note: Items 1–14 below are based on the latest available U.S. Census data (1987) for this kind of information, which is published every five years. This explains the time period of 1982 to 1987. The next round of data on black business development is scheduled to be gathered in 1992, for publication in 1995.

1. Michigan's level of business ownership has lagged behind the nation as a whole, once population size is taken into account. In 1987, the U.S. had a total of 140 firms with paid employees per 10,000 of the total population, compared with 110 for Michigan; and 24 black-owned firms nationally per 10,000 of the black population, compared with 17 for Michigan.

   The growth between 1982 and 1987 in the number of black-owned firms with paid employees in the U.S. (87.1 percent) exceeded that in Michigan (58.3 percent) by half, when the state's black-owned firms with paid employees reached 2,241.
2. While blacks in 1990 were 13.9 percent of Michigan's population and 11.1 percent of the nation's, in 1987 they owned only 2.1 percent of the firms with paid employees in the state, compared with 2.0 in the nation.

3. Among the 16 states with over 2,000 black-owned firms with paid employees, Michigan ranked 15th, and had the same rank after controlling for population. It was exceeded by California, New York, Illinois, Ohio, and 10 Southern states. Michigan ranked 10th in total receipts ($525 million) received by these firms, but 4th in average receipts per black-owned firm.
4. Of the 426.7 thousand firms located in Michigan in 1987, only 13.7 thousand (or 3.2 percent) were black-owned firms. These black-owned firms accounted for $701 million in receipts, or merely 1.1 percent of the total ($63.9 billion) for all firms in the state.
5. The counties with the largest number of black-owned firms with paid employees in Michigan are Wayne, with two-thirds of these firms, followed by Oakland, Genesee, Washtenaw, Kent, and Ingham. Oakland and Ingham Counties led in the growth in the number of these firms from 1982 to 1987, with Wayne County ranking lowest among the six counties. Oakland County led in average receipts per firm ($536,000) which was over three times the average for black-owned firms in Wayne County.
6. Southfield and Lansing led Michigan cities in the growth of the number of black-owned firms between 1982 and 1987. Southfield's growth rate was 140 percent, and Lansing's growth rate was 118 percent.
7. Average receipts per firm ($149.8 thousand) for all firms in Michigan were about three times those for black-owned businesses ($51.2 thousand).
8. In 1987, about 16.3 percent of black-owned firms had paid employees, in contrast to 24.2 percent of all firms in the state.
9. Michigan had 103.4 thousand firms with paid employees in 1987; only 2.2 percent of the firms were owned by blacks.
10. All firms in Michigan with paid employees had average receipts per firm of $544.1 thousand, compared with $234.1 thousand for black-owned firms. These amounts for both groups were modestly higher than the corresponding averages for the nation as a whole.
11. Black-owned firms have scarcely begun to enter the U.S. mainstream. The entire *Black Enterprise* "Top 100" nationally had sales of $4.1 billion in 1987, whereas a single firm, ranking 109th in the *Fortune 500* for the same year, Scott Paper, had similar sales.
12. When standardized against the black population, California ranks 1st with 34 black-owned firms per 10,000, and Michigan ranks 15th among the top 16 states.
13. The larger black-owned firms in the state expanded their sales more rapidly than the firms without paid employees in the five-year period ending in 1987. Of the $369 million increase in sales, firms with paid employees accounted for $325 million. The growth rate substantially exceeded the rate of inflation causing a significant growth in sales measured in dollars of constant purchasing power.
14. Classified by industry, about 53 percent of Michigan's black-owned firms in 1987 were in services; when firms in retail sales are added, 70 percent are accounted for; when finance, insurance, and real estate are included, the total reaches 76.5 percent. Few firms with paid employees were in construction (233), manufacturing (46), and wholesale trade (32).

* * * *

15. The previously discussed findings from the Census data do not adequately represent the larger firms. The top 31 firms in Michigan in 1989, as listed in *Black Enterprise* or in *Crain's Detroit Business*, had combined sales of $831 million, a substantial increase from 1987. The smallest had $5.0 million in sales. The average of the 31 firms was $26.3 million. In 1989, they employed almost 8,000 persons, or an average of 257 persons per firm.
16. Those large black-owned firms in 1982 that continued to be listed in *Black Enterprise* in 1989 increased their sales in the 7-year period by almost 20 percent annually, a respectable growth rate in current dollars, as well as in inflation-adjusted dollars.
17. Data from the most recent issue of *Black Enterprise* for 1990 (published in 1991) show 28 Michigan black-owned firms among the "Top 100" in the nation. Reflecting the damage from the current recession, this is down from the 31 in 1989. Included for 1990 are 15 industrial/service firms, 12 auto dealers, and 1 commercial bank. No savings and loan or life insurance company was large enough to be included.
18. Barden Communications, Inc. preserved a place for Detroit in the highest 6 of the *Black Enterprise* "Top 100"—a place that was once held by Motown, Inc. Wesley Industries in Flint was recognized as the "BE's Company of the Year" for 1990.

Recommendations

1. Further research should be conducted by the Michigan Department of Commerce on the obstacles to launching, expanding, and sustaining black-owned businesses and on effective measures for surmounting those obstacles that can be overcome.
2. Promising programs (such as the New Detroit Business Partnership and the Greater Detroit BIDCO) should be evaluated by the Michigan Department of Commerce and/or local Urban League chapters, and expanded if found to be effective.
3. New mechanisms for filling gaps in financing must be expanded or initiated by the Michigan Department of Commerce and by commercial banks.
4. A seed capital company for black entrepreneurs should be established by private investors in cooperation with the Michigan Department of Commerce.
5. The Department of Commerce should be encouraged to design and implement programs to provide low-cost management and technical assistance to emerging minority companies.
6. Supporters of business development should urge the Governor and the Legislature to rethink certain budget cuts that would weaken minority business development; and supporters should also inform appropriate parties of how helpful certain agencies have been.
7. More resources should be directed by civil rights and church organizations and other community groups to promoting purchasing opportunities for consumers and other buyers in minority communities, particularly in central cities.
8. Public corporations should be encouraged to have a wider racial diversity of directors on their boards; and civil rights and other community groups should expose the racial composition of selected corporations in Michigan and consider boycotting those corporations that have all-white boards.
9. Retail and other black-owned firms serving only blacks should explore reaching a wider market to take advantage of higher household incomes.

10. The positive outcomes from community reinvestment agreements with Detroit-based financial institutions should be strengthened, monitored closely, and progress verified by independent sources.
11. Supporters of black economic development must give high priority to worker mobility and to enhancements in the education and training of black Americans and be conscious of the damage done to older and declining areas as well as to the metropolitan fringe as a result of urban sprawl.

The State of Black Michigan: 1992

Executive Summary

Introduction

This publication is the ninth in a series of annual reports. Using the most recent data available, the economic and social conditions of Michigan's black population are assessed. The various chapters discuss some of the most critical issues facing blacks in Michigan.

Among the questions addressed in the 1992 report are the following:

What role did the decline in employment in the manufacturing and automobile industries play in the unemployment patterns of Michigan blacks compared with whites over the 1971–1990 period?

What has been the pattern of reductions, if any, that have occurred in black residential segregation since antidiscrimination provisions in housing policies were introduced?

What changes occurred between 1971 and 1990 in the health status of blacks in Michigan in relation to the health status of whites?

What effects has crack cocaine had on the health status of black and white women and children in Michigan?

What patterns of segregation exist in Michigan's metropolitan area schools?

How has the African-American student population fared in the State's early reading instructional program (kindergarten through grade 3) as measured by the State's assessment program?

What is the relationship between the level of African-American student achievement and the financial status of the school districts where African-American children attend school?

Industrial Change and Black-White Unemployment Patterns in Michigan, 1971–1990

Findings

1. Reductions in industrial employment have had deleterious effects on black workers. The strongest impacts have been among black males who have traditionally been overrepresented in the manufacturing sector.
2. The unemployment rate among black males in the State is estimated to have increased by an average of about .6 of a percentage point per year for every 10,000 job reductions in manufacturing employment. This finding translates to an increase in the unemployment rate of 12 percentage points over the 1971–1990 period.
3. For white males, the estimated increase in the unemployment rate is .2 of a percentage point per year attributable to a similar reduction in manufacturing employment of 10,000

jobs. The annual increase is .3 of a percentage point for black females and .1 of a percentage point for white females.

4. Shifts in employment away from the industrial sector over the 1971–1990 period in Michigan contributed substantially to the rise of both the levels of unemployment for blacks and the black-white unemployment gap.
5. Although the declining levels of employment in both the manufacturing and the automobile industries raised the unemployment rates of both blacks and whites, the effect of such declines has been disproportionately larger for blacks. The black-white unemployment gap has therefore been widened by the declines in the levels of employment in these industrial sectors.

Recommendations

Two recommendations to reduce the black-white unemployment gap seem to emerge from the present findings: (1) the continuing deindustrialization of Michigan must be arrested; and (2) attempts must be made to ease employment of blacks in the alternate nonindustrialized sector.

Residential Segregation of Blacks in Metropolitan Areas of Michigan, 1960–1990

Findings

1. Black movement to the suburbs of Michigan's metropolitan areas greatly increased after passage of the Federal Fair Housing Act in 1968, especially in Bay City, Lansing, Grand Rapids, Kalamazoo, Muskegon, and Flint. Black representation in the total suburban population remains small, however.
2. Additionally, between 1960 and 1990, the average level of black residential segregation declined in the suburbs, central cities, and standard metropolitan statistical areas in the state. The greatest average decline occurred in the central cities (–24.1 percentage points) and the least average decline occurred in the suburbs (–8.1 percentage points).
3. During the thirty-year period (1960–1990), blacks in central cities became less residentially segregated than blacks in the suburbs. In 1990, blacks in the suburbs of Detroit, Muskegon, and Jackson were the most segregated of all Michigan suburbs.
4. In 1990, the mean level of segregation in the various metropolitan areas of the state was 68.8 percent, reflecting an increase in segregation in six of the twelve metropolitan areas between 1980 and 1990. The greatest increases were in Muskegon and Lansing.
5. The Detroit Metropolitan area remained (in 1990) the most racially segregated metropolitan area in the state with an index of 87.4 percent (virtually the same level that existed in 1960, i.e., before passage of the Federal Fair Housing Act and Michigan's Elliott-Larson Civil Rights Act). Apparently, these two pieces of legislation have had virtually no impact on reducing the high level of residential segregation in metropolitan Detroit.

Recommendations

The recommendations that follow are divided into two parts: (1) incentives to desegregate; and (2) disincentives to discriminate.

Incentives to Desegregate

1. The federal and state governments should provide substantial tax deductions to any family that purchases a home in an area where members of its racial group are underrepresented.
2. The state and local governments should provide low (i.e., below market rate) interest loans to any family that purchases a home in an area where members of its racial group are underrepresented.
3. The federal, state, and local governments should provide tax deductions to real estate firms according to the proportion of sales made to families in areas of racial underrepresentation.

Disincentives to Discriminate

1. The federal, state, and local governments should provide sufficient financial support to fair housing centers so that they may be able to employ full-time professional testers or inspectors to detect violators in the housing industry.
2. Fair housing centers, in cooperation with attorneys and plaintiffs (i.e., victims of discrimination), should file a sufficient number of lawsuits, using the data gathered through testing, so that the suits will serve as a deterrent against acts of unlawful discrimination.
3. The State of Michigan's Department of Licensing and Regulation should vigorously enforce regulations that would lead to revoking licenses of real estate brokers found guilty of discrimination.

Disparities in Health Between Blacks and Whites in Michigan

Findings

1. In Michigan, the infant death rate declined for both blacks and whites between 1970 and 1990, but the decline was greater for whites than for blacks, thus widening the inequality gap from a rate of 1.7 in 1970 to 2.7 in 1990. The black/white infant death ratio was highest in Flint and Lansing and narrowest in Grand Rapids, Pontiac, and Saginaw.
2. Death by homicide in 1990 demonstrated the largest disparity in death rates between Michigan blacks and whites, when all categories among the top ten leading causes of death are compared.
3. The widest racial disparity in male mortality from heart disease occurred in the age category of 20–24, where black males were more than seven times more likely than white males to die from heart disease.
4. The widest racial disparity in female mortality from heart disease occurred in the age category of 35–39, where black females were almost nine times more likely than white females to die from heart disease.

Recommendations

1. The State Legislature should develop a statewide health insurance plan that targets groups at risk—especially low-income groups that are uninsured and cannot afford the usual private sources of health care.

2. The State Legislature should approve the pending legislation to establish an Office of Black Affairs. One of the priorities of this Office should be to develop ways to improve access to health care.
3. The State Health Department, through its Office of Minority Health, should coordinate advocacy groups for comprehensive health care.
4. The Michigan Association for Local Public Health should develop a statewide directory of clinics which serve low-income populations in the black communities. These clinics should have sliding fee scales or other means to help the most needy or those without health insurance.
5. Black leaders, black organizations, and black community groups should work together to educate black citizens regarding better health care. Educational programs regarding AIDS, prenatal care, early cancer detection, nutrition, and other aspects of health care should be organized and presented in schools and churches and to neighborhood groups.

Racial Disparities Among Victims of Crack Cocaine in Metropolitan Areas of Michigan

Findings

1. In 1986, cocaine equaled and thereafter surpassed heroin, marijuana, and other drugs to become the number one drug of concern in Michigan.
2. Data regarding admissions to state-funded treatment programs show an increasing use of cocaine.
3. Those admitted to state-funded programs are disproportionately black.
4. The percentage of black males admitted to state-funded programs, compared to the percentage of black males in the population, was greatest in Grand Rapids (Kent County) and Saginaw.
5. The number of pregnant women admitted to state-funded treatment programs is increasing. There were 573 pregnant women admitted to state-funded treatment programs over the first six months of fiscal year 1990–91, compared with 502 cases in the last six months of fiscal year 1989–90.

Recommendations

These recommendations are two-pronged: (1) measures designed to prevent children being born addicted to drugs; and (2) measures designed to deal with those children who have been born to crack-using mothers.

1. A state-funded class, dealing with the dangers of drugs, should be made compulsory in each school district throughout the state.
2. Every elementary school teacher should be required to attend a yearly workshop designed to enlarge understanding of the special needs of children born to drug-abusing mothers. Special attention should be given to the problems of children exposed to crack.
3. Each elementary school should have a well-designed program oriented toward children with developmental problems related to exposure to drugs at birth.
4. Each school in the state should have a plan in place that will focus on two categories of students: those with mental health problems related to maternal abuse of drugs, and those with behavioral problems associated with ongoing drug use.

The Extent of School Desegregation in Metropolitan Areas of Michigan

Findings

1. The distribution pattern of Michigan's black students reveals significant and persistent racial isolation.
2. Over half of all black students in Michigan attend intensely segregated schools.
3. Only 22 percent of black students in Michigan attended schools that were predominantly white in 1989–90, i.e., virtually the same percentage as in 1976. Thus, the overall racial isolation of black students in Michigan remained virtually unchanged from 1976 to 1989.
4. In 1989–90, 94 percent of all black students in Michigan attended school in 40 school districts out of a total of 530, and the black-white achievement gap between districts remained wide.
5. Achieving meaningful desegregation is very discouraging once black enrollment in a district exceeds 50 percent.

Recommendations

1. The State Board of Education should explore voluntary metro desegregation measures in Detroit like those that are being used in other metropolitan areas such as Milwaukee and Indianapolis.
2. The State Board of Education should require school districts to justify racially distinguishable rates of suspensions, expulsions, and dropouts that may contribute to declining student participation in the predominantly minority districts. Challenging such discrimination is the legally mandated role of the U.S. Office for Civil Rights under Title VI of the 1964 Civil Rights Act.
3. The State Board of Education should address the achievement gap by increasing the percentage of minority professional-instructional staff in predominantly minority school districts to provide role models, raise expectations, and provide a diverse and multicultural learning environment.
4. The recruiting of minority teachers and administrators must involve a broad coalition of individuals associated with university teacher education programs, state departments of education, teacher unions, and local school districts.
5. The State Board of Education should develop a closer link between teacher performance and student outcomes. This will involve building administrators with the support of their superintendents and elected board members.

Disparities in Funding Patterns and Reading Outcomes in Selected Michigan School Districts

Findings

1. In 1989–90, more than 75 percent of Michigan's African-American students attended school in central city school districts that received at least half their operating revenue from the State. These districts tended to have high tax rates and declining tax bases, a combination of factors which argue that increases in local assessments will tend to further erode their revenue-raising ability.
2. Average achievement on the grade 4 reading test was very low in the districts servicing these students, compared with achievement in the more wealthy suburban school districts.

3. The districts where most African-American students attended school in 1989–90 were 11 percentage points below the achievement mean for the State.
4. Like achievement, the average fiscal capacity for districts where most African-American students attended school was substantially less than the capacity for districts in the State as a whole.
5. For the cohort of 30 districts enrolling the highest percentages of African-American students, the 30-district average ($39,177) was exceeded by the State average ($98,183) by $59,006. Fiscal disparities are commonly judged to have some effect on instructional impact and secondarily on pupil performance outcomes. Although other factors also contribute to student outcomes, abundant fiscal resources clearly provide educational options or enhancements that cannot be provided in dependent or impoverished districts.

Recommendations

To reduce fiscal inequities and to improve student reading outcomes, the following actions are recommended:

1. The State should (a) integrate the tax bases for public education within each Intermediate School District immediately; and (b) over a five-year period, remove per-pupil allocation differences between the various Intermediate Districts.
2. Each district must recruit more minority professionals as teachers, counselors, psychologists, and school administrators.
3. Institutions of higher education must assure the availability of sufficient numbers of minority men and women for such school positions.
4. The Intermediate School Districts must undergo reform to meet the needs of changing times. This can be accomplished by bringing Intermediate Districts directly under the control of the Chief State School Officer. This officer should recommend to the State Board of Education the names of persons in business, education, and the professions best suited to develop policies for bringing about necessary change, and best suited to serve as members on ISD Boards. ISD Boards should be advisory to the State Board of Education.
5. Parents must strengthen the relationship between home and school. Home-and-school linkage and parenting skills should be a primary focus for all Intermediate School Districts.

Summary and Conclusions

The overall conclusions are that the State of Black Michigan remains severely depressed, economically and socially. Reductions in manufacturing employment, especially in the automobile industry, have had deleterious effects on black employment. The strongest impacts have been among black males who have traditionally been overrepresented in the manufacturing sector in the State. Such decline in manufacturing employment has primarily been responsible for the persistent high unemployment rate among black males.

Although whites were also impacted by the economic downturn, the stress has not been as severe, since whites have been more able to find work in other sectors. As a result, the white male unemployment rate showed no overall increasing trend, and the unemployment rate for white females actually exhibited a slight downward trend between 1971–1990, thereby widening the gap between the races.

Black movement to the suburbs of Michigan's metropolitan areas greatly increased between 1960 and 1990, and residential segregation declined overall. However, over the last decade, residential segregation actually increased in six of the twelve metropolitan areas. Furthermore, metropolitan Detroit, where most blacks in the State reside, has remained as rigidly segregated in 1990 as it was in 1960. Thus, the Federal Fair Housing Act and Michigan's Elliott-Larson Civil Rights Act have been virtually ineffective in impacting the rigid separation of the races in metropolitan Detroit.

Racial disparities in health in the State have continued to widen. The infant death rate, for example, declined for both blacks and whites between 1970 and 1990, but the decline was greater for whites than for blacks, thus widening the inequality gap.

Racial isolation and economic despair have led some blacks to turn to crack cocaine as a form of escape. In 1986, cocaine equaled and thereafter surpassed other drugs to become the number one drug of concern in the State.

The severe economic depression and racial desperation have also affected the status of black education. Public schools in the State remain largely racially segregated despite the *Brown* vs. *Board of Education* decision in 1954. The majority of black students attend school in 30 of 530 K–12 school districts. Most of these districts are located in central cities and are usually poorer than other districts and more dependent on state aid. Reading achievement levels are shown to be usually lower in the poorer districts than in the more affluent districts.

The knowledge that social and economic problems persist in black Michigan has been revealed, and recommendations have been offered to address them. The issue, therefore, is not a lack of knowledge, but a lack of will. What is at stake is a future of continuing apartheid with the probability of increased racial conflict or a future with more equality and the prospect of racial harmony.

The State of Black Michigan: 1993

Executive Summary

Introduction

This report on *The State of Black Michigan: 1993* is the 10th consecutive report in this annual series. As in previous reports, the authors have used the most recent data available to assess the extent of inequality between blacks and whites in the State.

Among the questions addressed in the 1993 report are the following:

- What, if any, progress has been made for African-American children and youth since the eighties?
- What are the issues surrounding health care policy, and how will proposed federal approaches to health care impact the disparity in health status between blacks and whites?
- Why does AIDS disproportionately affect blacks?
- What is the extent of disparities in demographic and socioeconomic characteristics between Michigan's black and white older populations?
- How effective are African-American state and congressional legislators in shaping public policies that improve the overall economic and social well-being of African-American citizens?

The Young African-American Population in Michigan: A Black-White Progress Report

Findings

1. Although the infant death rates for the State have been on a slight decline since 1981, the death rate for African-American infants remains more than double the rate for white infants.
2. Infant death rates are related to poverty rates. In 1990, Michigan's black children had a poverty rate of 46.3 percent as compared with 12.4 percent for white children.
3. Despite the continuing research on children and youth, the status of African-American children in Michigan did not improve over the last decade. Instead, according to several indicators, the welfare of all children in the State has declined, with a disproportionate decline among African-American children.

Recommendations

1. State legislators and the Governor should work in concert, using the model developed by the National Association of Black Social Workers, to enact legislation that will insure the preservation of families, particularly minority families.
2. Legislators should create a nonpartisan joint-select committee to develop culturally competent policies which will address the needs of children, youth, and families adversely affected by the impact of poverty, substance abuse, and unemployment; this committee should be advised by citizens, clients/consumers, and professionals of the community.
3. State legislators and government officials should redirect the priorities in state budget spending from corrections to departments and programs that will insure the costs for medical, educational, and social service needs of children and families.
4. All funders and providers of services should use program evaluation and research methods when developing, funding, and implementing family preservation programs.
5. African-American parents, professionals, and civic and religious leaders should demonstrate a stronger leadership role in teaching black youth how to avoid the disadvantages of early pregnancy and drug use.

Black-White Health Disparity in Michigan: A Commentary on Issues of Equity

Findings

1. Managed care health strategies have failed to address the state-level disparities in health status between blacks and whites. The racial disparities continue to exist—whether the focus is on mortality, morbidity, or utilization of health services.
2. The presently proposed competitive market approach (managed competition) as a strategy for both cost containment and equity in access may exacerbate the disparity in health status between blacks and whites.
3. While Michigan has done better than most states in providing health care to the poor, access to health care for poor families with children has diminished in the last decade.
4. The health care status of blacks in Michigan is continuing to decline as we approach the 21st century, and there is little hope of closing the gap between blacks and whites.

Recommendations

1. The Office of Minority Health, in addition to serving its present role in the Department of Public Health, should be expanded under the auspices of the Governor to advise and assist the Department of Social Services and the Department of Mental Health.
2. The State of Michigan should develop a universal access plan to broaden health care access to black and other minority residents; this plan should include strategies to require providers to accept publicly funded patients as a condition of licensure and relicensure in Michigan.
3. Health status data for black Michigan residents should be published annually by the Office of Minority Health.
4. Black health care providers should collaborate with the Office of Minority Health in developing comprehensive strategies to address the health status of Michigan's black males, who, as a group, have the poorest access to publicly funded basic health services.
5. The Office of Minority Health should take the lead in establishing "One-Stop Shopping" information centers throughout the State to enable patients and providers to gain basic up-to-date information on all available services, locations, and eligibility criteria.

The First Decade of AIDS in Michigan: The Impact on Blacks and Whites

Findings

1. Blacks made up 14 percent of Michigan's population in 1990, but they comprised 50 percent of the 1990 AIDS cases and 52 percent of the 1992 cases.
2. The rate of AIDS was 5.3 times higher for blacks than for whites in 1990 and 6.6 times higher in 1991.
3. In 1988, AIDS was the fifth leading cause of death in Michigan for black males aged 25–44, with a rate of 20.7 per 100,000. Two years later, AIDS became the second leading cause of death for black males in that same age group with a rate of 48.3 per 100,000. For white males aged 25–44, AIDS was the fourth leading cause of death in 1990 with a rate of 10.7 per 100,000.
4. Of the 385 reported cases (1981–1992) of women with AIDS, 196 (or 77 percent) were black.
5. The primary explanation as to why AIDS disproportionately affects blacks can be found in transmission behaviors. Intravenous drug use by males accounted for 33 percent of AIDS cases for blacks versus 4 percent for whites; for females, the corresponding figures were 63 percent for blacks versus 23 percent for whites.
6. Most disheartening is the fact that the methadone treatment programs for heroin addiction in Michigan have decreased from 58 in 1980, the beginning of the AIDS epidemic, to fewer than 25 at the end of 1992. Of Michigan's ten largest counties, five have no methadone treatment programs.

Recommendations

1. The Center for Substance Abuse Services should expand methadone treatment and should insure that the regional authorities make treatment available and accessible to the uninsured; treatment should be long-term and comprehensive, with a link to good

primary health care; the special issues and needs of women, such as child care, pregnancy, and domestic violence, must be addressed.

2. The Center for Substance Abuse Services should expand and upgrade substance-abuse treatment for those in the criminal justice system, with emphasis on long-term aftercare and community-based addiction treatment.
3. African-American leaders and communities should institute or increase mentoring programs for young people in community-based organizations/institutions, such as Scouts, YMCA, YWCA, churches, NAACP, and Urban League—and in other organizations, such as fraternities and sororities; these mentors should model responsible sexual behavior and promote drug-free lifestyles for youth.
4. African-American leaders and communities should promote the formation of peer support groups (similar to Alcoholics Anonymous and Narcotics Anonymous) for adults engaging in high-risk behaviors.
5. African-American leaders and neighborhood groups should form more neighborhood organizations (Block Clubs) to promote drug-free neighborhoods and to reduce the availability of drugs in black neighborhoods.

Black-White Disparities in Michigan's Changing Older Population

Findings

1. Blacks in the 65-plus age category were more than twice as likely as their white counterparts to be poor (23.9 percent vs. 9.2 percent) in 1990.
2. In the 65-plus age category, black women are nearly twice as likely to be poor or near-poor as are black men and 1.4 times more likely to be poor than are white women. Black women are nearly 5.5 times more likely to be poor than are white men.
3. For those 65 years of age or older with no work disability, nearly 16 percent of all blacks were in the labor force, compared with 14 percent of all whites. Within the percentages, fewer blacks (88.8 percent) than whites (95.7 percent) were actually employed. Similar to the situation among the non-elderly populations, black men, who comprised the highest percentage (15.0) of persons without disabilities who are in the labor force, were the least likely to be employed.
4. In the 65–75 age category, black women were nearly twice as likely as black men and white women, and three times as likely as white men, to have mobility limitations.

Recommendations

1. The Michigan Office of Services to the Aging (or some other agency) should undertake state-level surveys that focus only on the black populations; detailed information—rather than the less specific information found in larger and more general studies—is needed regarding the economic circumstances, living arrangements, family structure, and health characteristics of the elderly black population in Michigan.
2. Michigan legislators should revise the Supplemental Security Income Program by raising the economic "safety net" beyond 75 percent of the poverty level; such action can improve the economic status of all older adults, including Michigan's black elderly.
3. Black churches and other black organizations should conduct outreach efforts to identify persons eligible for, but not currently receiving, SSI and other benefits; elderly

potential social service recipients are often unaware of the benefits for which they may be eligible.

4. The Michigan Office of Services to the Aging should institute services such as nutrition programs, day-care facilities for the elderly, and homemaker programs, targeted particularly for low-income elderly populations which tend to be located in central city areas.

African-American Voters and Black Political Representation in Michigan

Findings

1. Political cynicism and alienation are eroding the trust that African-American voters have in the political system. However, African-Americans in the Michigan General Assembly have served on committees that allow them to stand for the black electorate.
2. Evidence suggests that the overall public-policy agenda of African-Americans in the Michigan House and Senate reflects an empathy with the demands of African-American voters.
3. All three black members of the Senate have supported such legislation as extended health care for children, a seven-day wait for the purchase of handguns, and a graduated state income tax. Black House members have been generally supportive of legislation that would provide child-care support for working mothers and Medicare payments for the needy.
4. Despite attempts by black legislators to be responsive, the majority of African-American voters demonstrated frustration by voting for a proposed state constitutional amendment limiting the terms of elected officials.
5. The message that black voters are sending is that public officials must do a better job of explaining their job performance and the functioning of government.

Recommendations

The following steps can help to increase the trust that African-Americans have toward the political system:

1. Individual black elected officials should organize black "community cabinets" to get input from individuals and from social and civic groups—input directed toward the formulation of a viable black public policy agenda.
2. Black elected officials and other concerned citizens should inform the public, by formal and informal methods of communication, of the existence of these "community cabinets."
3. Black elected officials should inform voters of legislation that is pending, and should present information about the political standing of the Governor, the President, and other political leaders and officials on such legislation.
4. State and federal legislators should travel across the state and conduct public forums and workshops to provide citizen activists with information regarding such developments as laws which protect victims of crime, programs that aim to reduce infant mortality, and grants and contracts that seek to improve the economic climate in black communities.

Conclusions

The overall conclusions are that black children born in the State of Michigan can expect to experience inequality at every stage in the life cycle—as children, as youth, and as older adults. Such inequality persists despite the fact that black lawmakers have stood for and fought for policies that would improve the social and economic well-being of their predominantly black constituents. New political strategies must be found to reduce persistent racial inequality.

Although the infant death rates for the State have been on a slight decline since 1981, the death rate for African-American infants remains more than double the rate for white infants. Despite continuing research on children and youth in general, the social and economic condition of African-American children did not improve over the last decade.

Racial disparities among black children and adults continue to exist—whether the focus is on mortality, morbidity, or utilization of health services. Although Michigan has done better than most states in providing health care to the poor, access to health care for poor families with children has diminished in the last decade. Furthermore, the health care status of blacks in Michigan is continuing to decline as we approach the 21st century, with little actual impact on closing the gap between blacks and whites.

The differential impact of AIDS is a primary example. Blacks made up 14 percent of the Michigan population in 1990, but they comprised 50 percent of the 1990 AIDS cases and 52 percent of the 1992 cases. The rate of AIDS was 5.3 times higher for blacks than for whites in 1990 and 6.6 times higher in 1991. The primary explanation for the extent of the differential was found to be in transmission behavior.

Blacks in the 65-plus age category were more than twice as likely as their white counterparts to be poor (23.9 percent vs. 9.2 percent). By far, the poorest of all elderly persons are black women, who are 1.4 times more likely than white women to be poor and 5.5 times more likely than white men to be poor.

Evidence suggests that the overall public-policy agenda of African-American lawmakers in Michigan's House and Senate has reflected empathy with the concerns of most African-Americans. The black lawmakers have supported legislation, for example, that extended health care for children, child-care support for working mothers, and Medicare payments for the needy. But since many African-Americans perceive most non-African-American lawmakers as more concerned with budget cuts than with the programs that affect urban communities, political cynicism and alienation are eroding the trust that many African-American voters have in the entire political system.

CHAPTER 19

Assessment of the Michigan Legislature Response to Past Recommendations and Future Actions Needed

Joe T. Darden

Public Acts by the Michigan Legislature, 1985–2004: Their Importance to the Black Condition

An investigation was conducted of all acts passed by the Michigan House and Senate from 1985 to 2006. These acts were then examined for their connection with the recommendations made in the annual *State of Black Michigan* reports from 1985 to 1993.

There were several public acts passed by the Michigan Legislature from 1985 to 2004 that were related, directly or indirectly, to improving the conditions of low- and moderate-income residents in particular, many of whom were black. Consistent with recommendations made by researchers of the *State of Black Michigan* reports, some legislation was focused on blacks directly. Public acts were created in the following areas: education, health, crime and corrections, civil rights, anti–mortgage lending discrimination, urban economic development, redevelopment, affordable housing, and urban homesteading.

Education

In 1985, no acts were passed that were directly or indirectly related to recommendations in the *State of Black Michigan* report of that year. In 1986, however, the Michigan legislature passed the Martin Luther King, Jr.–Rosa Parks Scholarship Program. This program was intended to increase the pool of minority candidates pursuing academic careers in postsecondary education in Michigan (Michigan Public Acts of 1986, No. 219, 1122). Funds were included in the appropriations for each nondoctoral degree-granting public college and university in Michigan (Michigan Public Acts of 1986, No. 219, 1123). The state legislature also funded a Martin Luther King, Jr.–Rosa Parks Fellowship Program. Funds were appropriated for each doctorate degree-granting public college and university in Michigan (Michigan Public Acts of 1986, No. 219, 1123).

In 1986, the Michigan legislature passed an act to establish a Michigan educational opportunity grant program for resident qualified students enrolled in eligible postsecondary public schools. This program was intended to help eligible students meet educational expenses (Michigan Public Acts of 1986, 273, 1315).

Finally, in 1986 the legislature passed an act creating a Michigan Education Trust. This act was intended to provide students and their parents with financial assistance for post-secondary education at a Michigan institution of higher education of their choice. The trust was intended to provide affordable access to state institutions of higher education (Michigan Public Acts of 1986, No. 316, 1466). Since black students and parents in the state generally have lower incomes than whites, these educational support programs had the potential to benefit black families disproportionately.

In 1987, the legislature passed an act that appropriated funds for the academic/vocational programs for certain correctional facilities (Michigan Public Acts of 1987, No. 143, 957). The goal was to improve ex-offenders' employability and reduce recidivism. While a direct link between the recommendations in the *State of Black Michigan* reports and certain public acts cannot be demonstrated, the acts described here are very consistent with such recommendations.

In 1989, the Michigan legislature introduced a school completion program that was administered by the Department of Social Services. The intent of the program was to provide incentives for low-income Michigan residents to graduate from high school (Michigan Public Acts of 1989, No. 42, 116). The program provided payment for tuition for up to 80 credits at any community college in the state. Also in 1989, the state legislature passed HB 4337, which contained a section (303) that provided funds for the Office of Minority Equity in Post-Secondary Education. This office had the responsibility of reviewing and making recommendations for enhancing the state's progress in responding to the educational needs of minorities (Michigan Public Acts of 1989, No. 171, 771). The needs of handicappers and women in postsecondary education were also included. The office served as an ombudsman to investigate and resolve reports of barriers to minority access on state university campuses.

In 1997, the Michigan legislature passed an act that provided a tax credit for tuition paid for any student to attend an institution of higher education. The claimant was required to have an adjusted gross income of $200,000 or less and to be a resident of the state. For the 1998 tax year and each subsequent tax year 8% of the sum of all fees and tuition paid, not to exceed $375 for each student for each tax year, was the credit amount allowed (Michigan Public Acts of 1997, No. 82, 276).

In 2000, the state legislature created the Michigan Post-Secondary Access Student Scholarship (PASS) program. A student is eligible for a PASS award for the equivalent of two years of full-time college enrollment. One of the criteria for a scholarship is that the student be eligible for a federal PELL grant (Michigan Public Acts of 2000, No. 272, 984). Thus the PASS program favored low-income students. Such students are disproportionately black.

Health

In 1987, among the recommendations of the *State of Black Michigan* reports was that aggressive actions should be taken to educate the Michigan population (especially the black population) about the potentially fatal impact of intravenous drug use that may cause the spread of AIDS and premature death (see Chapter 18). It was also in 1987 that the legislature appropriated funds to develop and implement AIDS provider education activities (Michigan Public Acts of 1987, No. 130, 650). The focus was on AIDS prevention and control. Community service grants were also provided to local agencies for low-income prenatal care. Prenatal outreach programs were funded to support residents in River Rouge, Inkster, Ecorse, and Highland Park. These municipalities are predominantly black, with a large low-income population. The legislature also funded school drug education and prevention programs intended to provide technical assistance to local school districts (Michigan Public Acts of 1987, No. 133, 778).

In 1994, the state legislature amended a section of the Public Health Code. The amendment dealt with individuals arrested and charged with certain crimes. These individuals were given confidentially administered examinations and tests for venereal diseases and received counseling regarding hepatitis B infections, HIV infections, AIDS, and AIDS-related complex, covering information about treatment, transmission, and protective measures. Test results were required to be provided to victims who might have been exposed to a body fluid during the course of a crime (Michigan Public Acts of 1994, 72, 286).

In 1995, the state legislature amended the Public Health Code by prohibiting health maintenance organizations from denying enrollment to an enrollee's child on any of the following grounds: (a) the child was born out of wedlock, (b) the child is not claimed as a dependent on the enrollee's federal income tax return, or (c) the child does not reside with the enrollee or in the health maintenance organization's service area (Michigan Public Acts of 1995, No. 240, 1968).

In 2004, the Michigan legislature passed an act creating a childhood lead poisoning prevention and control commission within the Department of Community Health. The Childhood Lead Poisoning Control Commission is required to conduct at least two public hearings to seek input from the general public and organizations or individuals that have an interest in childhood lead poisoning prevention and control (Michigan Public Acts of 2004, No. 431, 188). Lead poisoning occurs most frequently in poor urban areas, where a disproportionate share of the black population resides.

Crime and Corrections

In 1986, the *State of Black Michigan* report recommended more education programs to raise the skill levels of incarcerated residents. In 1987, the legislature passed an act that appropriated funds for the academic/vocational programs for certain correctional facilities (Michigan Public Acts of 1987, No. 143, 957). The goal was to improve ex-offenders' employability and reduce recidivism.

Civil Rights

In 1991, the state legislature passed a law requiring the chief of police of each city or village and each township with a police department and the sheriff of each county to report to the

Department of State police information related to crimes motivated by prejudice or bias based on race, ethnic origin, religion, gender, or sexual orientation (Michigan Public Acts of 1991, No. 172, 1117). Blacks are disproportionately victims of such crimes.

In 1992, the state legislature amended the Elliott-Larsen Civil Rights Act of 1976. The sections amended were 301 and 303 of act number 453 of 1976. These sections apply to private clubs. If a private club allows use of its facilities by one or more adults per membership, the use must be equally available to all adults who are under membership. All classes of membership shall be available without regard to race, color, gender, religion, marital status, or national origin (Michigan Public Acts of 1992, No. 70, 200). Some private clubs may have excluded blacks before this Act.

Additionally, the state legislature amended section 602 of Public Act 453 of the Michigan Elliott-Larsen Civil Rights Act. The amendment related to persons conducting business with the state or an agency. If a person who is conducting business or seeking to conduct business with the state or an agency, the Department of Civil Rights can request a review of the person's equal employment opportunity practices for the purpose of determining the person's compliance with a covenant entered into or willingness to comply with a covenant to be entered into. Under the amendment, the Department of Civil Rights may conduct the review (Michigan Public Acts of 1992, No. 258, 1427).

Anti–Mortgage Lending Discrimination

In 1996, the Michigan legislature amended Public Acts of 1977 to prohibit certain mortgage lending practices by credit-granting institutions. The amendment required that notices be posted informing loan applicants that it is illegal to establish a minimum mortgage amount of more than $10,000 or a minimum home improvement loan of more than $1,000. It is also illegal to deny a loan or vary the terms and conditions of a loan because of racial or ethnic trends or characteristics of the neighborhood or age of the structure, but not because of its physical condition (Michigan Public Acts of 1996, No. 338, 1052).

Urban Economic Development, Redevelopment, and Urban Homesteading, Affordable Housing

To assist the unemployed, who were disproportionately black, in 1989 the legislature passed a job start pilot program for unemployed, employable persons 18–25 years of age residing in the Genesee, Ingham, Kalamazoo, Muskegon, Oakland, and Wayne county districts (Michigan Public Acts of 1989, No. 200, 1290).

In 1992, the state legislature passed a law creating urban redevelopment corporations for the purpose of clearing, rehabilitating, modernizing, beautifying, and reconstructing substandard and unsanitary areas and to provide for the powers and duties of urban redevelopment corporations and certain units of local government (Michigan Public Acts of 1992, No. 138, 546).

In 1993, the state legislature amended Public Acts of 1980. The amendment established an act to prevent urban deterioration and encourage economic development activity, neighborhood revitalization, and historic preservation by providing for the establishment of tax increment finance authorities (Michigan Public Acts of 1993, No. 322, 2014).

In 1994, the state legislature amended the State Housing Development Authority Act of 1966 by exempting housing projects that serve low-income residents from taxes. The amendment declared the following:

> If a housing project is owned by a nonprofit housing corporation, consumer housing cooperative, limited dividend housing corporation, mobile home park corporation, or mobile home park association financed with a federally aided or authority aided mortgage or advance or grant from the authority, then the housing project is exempt from all ad valorem property taxes imposed by the state or by any political sub-division, public body or taxing district in which the project is located. (Michigan Public Acts of 1994, No. 363, 1808).

The benefits of any tax exemption granted by this amendment were to be allocated by the owner of the housing project exclusively to low-income persons or families in the form of reduced housing charges (Michigan Public Acts of 1994, 363, 1809).

In 1999, the Michigan legislature passed legislation creating an Urban Homestead Program. The act permitted by resolution local governmental units to operate or contract with a community organization to operate and administer an urban homestead program that makes property available to qualified buyers to rent and purchase. Also by resolution, the local governmental unit was required to designate whether the local governmental unit or a nonprofit community was to be administered under the act. The local governmental unit was required to provide an appeals process to applicants, that is, qualified buyers who were adversely affected by a decision of the administrator (Michigan Public Acts of 1999, No. 127, 844).

The legislature also created an urban homestead program for single-family public housing. The act allowed local governmental units to authorize a housing commission within that local governmental unit or a nonprofit community organization to operate an urban homestead program in single-family public housing that makes single-family public housing properties available for purchase to eligible buyers (Michigan Public Acts of 1999, No. 128, 848).

Finally, the legislature passed an urban homestead act that allowed local governmental units to operate an urban homestead program for vacant land that made parcels of vacant property available to individuals to purchase under the act (Michigan Public Acts of 1999, No. 129, 851).

Conclusions

This assessment of public acts passed by the Michigan legislature since 1985 revealed that several acts had the potential to positively impact low-income residents, urban residents, and indirectly black residents. Some of the acts were directly or indirectly consistent with the recommendations in the *State of Black Michigan* reports. It is highly likely that some of the legislation had positive benefits for a certain percentage of blacks. It is fair to say that had the legislation not been passed, the racial inequality that presently persists may have been worse. However, since the data clearly show that the social and economic gap between blacks and whites on most indicators has increased since the civil disorders of 1967, more legislative and other action must be taken in the future if racial equality is to become a reality in Michigan.

Recommendations for Future Action

Although future action is needed in several areas, three areas are the most important: (1) improving the quality of education in the public schools and providing greater access to institutions of higher education, (2) reducing black crime and recidivism, and (3) increasing black business ownership and black economic development. Thus, specific recommendations are made for improvements in these areas.

Recommendations for Improving the Quality of Public Education and Increasing the Access to Institutions of Higher Education

To address the persistent racial disparities in education in Michigan, policy makers should implement new legislation or positive actions (1) to address the high level of racial segregation in the public schools, (2) to reduce the disparity in funding between school districts and individual public schools, (3) to reduce the inequity in college preparation programs between schools in predominantly black and concentrated poverty neighborhoods and schools in white and middle- and upper-class suburban neighborhoods, and (4) to add more resources and focus more on reducing high school dropout rates. Providing incentives for increasing high school completion rates should be considered.

Those students who do finish high school must be supported financially to a greater extent in order for them to enroll in and finish college. The governor's $4,000 scholarship for all students is a step in the right direction. As college tuition continues to increase, the governor and legislature may want to consider raising the amount in the near-future. In other words, affordability must be the priority in order to increase college access for those who are disproportionately attending schools that are poor, located in the urban core and rural areas of the state. Financial aid programs must be based more on need and less on merit alone since the cost of college is rising so fast (National Center for Public Policy and Higher Education 2003).

Since poor students (who are disproportionately black) fail to complete college even after enrolling, colleges should explore both support services and financial incentives to foster academic skills and motivation. Research based on the Student Achievement and Retention Project (STAR) suggests that incentives in the form of both support services and financial awards for performance may impact retention rates (August, Lang, and Oreopoulos 2006).

Recommendations for Reducing Black Crime and Recidivism

The recommendations presented on black crime and recidivism were contributed by Homer Hawkins based on his findings in Chapter 12. According to Hawkins, changes need to take place, both in the community and in the prison setting. Reduction of crime and of recidivism is of paramount importance.

Education is an important key to reducing crime. Special efforts must be made to improve the educational opportunities for black children in ghetto schools. The kind of education the black child receives in an inner-city school does not match what is offered in suburban schools. There is a need to close the gap that exists between suburban and inner-city schools. Improving educational opportunities for black youngsters will increase the probability of their being more employable as adults and their ability to work in the kinds of jobs that will keep them above the poverty level.

In the prison setting, a critical key is more education. Although control will always be the primary goal in the correctional setting, it is hoped that providing residents with more educational opportunities will become more valued within the Department of Corrections. Specifically, there needs to be an expansion of the GED preparation component so that more residents can receive high school diploma equivalencies. The fact that most inmates no longer have a real opportunity to obtain an associate or bachelor's degree is a major setback. There is a need to reinstate the Pell Grant that pays for the college education of inmates.

The GED program is quite important; however, the fact that the community college and four-year programs have been eradicated is a major step backward. The GED program should have as one of its major components to act as a feeder into an associate degree program that can result in a degree and also lead to enrollment in a four-year institution. This was available in the late 1980s and early 1990s and is a necessary component to help individuals who return to the community to succeed and not return to prison. Education was important in the 1980s and it is even more important today. However, inmates coming out of prison today are even less prepared than their counterparts of the 1980s. Education is key to being a success in life. More financial aid needs to be directed into inner-city schools. Crime prevention directed at our youth is less expensive than prison for adults at a later stage in life.

Recommendations for Increasing Black-Owned Businesses and Economic Development

The recommendations that follow address ways to strengthen black businesses and economic development. They build on the recommendations made by Karl Gregory in 1991 (see Chapter 2).

(1) *Black residents of Michigan, via some appropriate organizational structure, must pool a portion of their income for investment in capital- and knowledge-intensive black-owned businesses. Most individual black entrepreneurs do not have sufficient wealth (Olson 2006).*

Capital- and knowledge-intensive black-owned businesses differ from "traditional" black-owned businesses, which operate with a small amount of capital under the ownership of people with less than a college education. These businesses commonly consist of personal services such as beauty parlors, barber shops, and funeral establishments. Due largely to their small financial and human capital, these traditional businesses (a) are small-scale, (b) have high failure rates, (c) generate few jobs, and (d) have little growth potential (Bates 1989). These businesses also have little potential for improving the economic well-being of the black population as a group (Boyd 1990).

On the other hand, capital-intensive and knowledge-intensive black-owned businesses are businesses owned and managed by college-educated blacks, preferably blacks with master's degrees in business administration. Since they have greater financial and human capital, they tend (a) to be larger, (b) to have lower failure rates, (c) to generate more jobs, and (d) to have more growth potential, which will benefit greatly not only the owner and manager but the employees where the business is located.

(2) *The newly established capital- and knowledge-intensive black-owned businesses must serve a broad geographic and racially diverse market extending beyond the traditional predominantly black central city.*

The 2002 data on black-owned businesses show that the black business participation rate in suburban municipalities is on average higher than the rate in central cities in Michigan (Chapter 3, Table 3-6). This may be evidence that some newly established black-owned businesses are already following the "broad geographic and racially diverse" approach in their operation. The research has shown that these businesses are more stable, are more profitable, and reflect the "growth businesses" of the future (Boyd 1990).

(3) *Blacks who operate the "new capital- and knowledge-intensive" business must ensure that a new generation of family and community members receives apprenticeship-type entrepreneurial training. Such training must be a top priority.*

Such training programs could be put in place via cooperative agreements with public schools or other community organizations. Fairlie and Robb (2004) argue strongly that, to break the vicious cycle of low rates of black business ownership, there must be policies and practices to improve apprenticeship-type training programs.

(4) *There must be a paradigm shift among black leaders and black members of the labor force involving a change in the excessive black dependence on public employment for economic survival.*

Historically, blacks have relied on the public sector more than any other group. They have done so in part because the public sector has given blacks more opportunity to advance economically than the private sector (Boyd 1990). Government agencies were among the first to adopt standards for hiring and promotions. Through civil service examinations, many black workers in the 1940s were able to obtain clerical positions in the postal service and eventually advance economically (Landry 1987). Blacks have also received greater returns on their human capital in government occupations.

However, the continued excessive reliance on government employment makes blacks more vulnerable economically since the future will bring smaller government at the federal and state levels. The slow or nonexistent growth of state and local government employment projected for the future will reduce the chances of black economic advancement through public sector jobs.

Black leaders and black-led organizations must begin now to shift to a plan that establishes priorities and aspirations that support the creation and expansion of new types of black-owned businesses. Such businesses should be established in construction; real estate and rental firms; retail trade; manufacturing; wholesale trade; and professional, scientific, and technical services. These businesses would best address the limited employment opportunities experienced by blacks, especially those in the central city (Bates and Dunham 1992).

Research has shown that blacks have a better chance of being hired and promoted by black-owned businesses. That is why most black-owned firms have a higher percentage of black workers than white-owned firms. Research has also shown that a black business presence grants the group power and status needed to reduce white racism and facilitate black economic progress (Villemez and Beggs 1984). After all, a major weakness in many black areas in Michigan is a lack of economic progress. Therefore, another paradigm shift is needed.

(5) *There must be a shift toward the establishment of black-owned banks, thereby keeping the billions of dollars now held by blacks to be invested according to an economic development plan.*

It is not a lack of resources that delays both the establishment of more black-owned businesses and the establishment of more black-owned banks, since black consumers in Michigan spend millions or perhaps billions of dollars each year. Instead, the challenge may be a lack of more effective leadership in designing and implementing an economic development plan.

Thus, the greatest challenge to black organizations, churches, and leaders is to raise the consciousness of the black masses and move toward a paradigm shift. Beginning a plan that will lead to the creation of more businesses and banks will enhance black economic development. The results will be the creation of more jobs for the working-class and poor constituents. Such changes will lead to a new level of mobility, resulting in a reduction of poverty and uneven development.

REFERENCES

August, J., D. Lang, and P. Oreopoulos. 2006. Lead them to water and pay them to drink: An experiment with services and incentives for college achievement. National Bureau of Economic Research Working Paper Series 12790. http://papers.nber.org/papers/w12790.

Bates, T. 1989. The changing nature of minority business: A comparative analysis of Asian, non-minority, and black owned businesses. *Review of Black Political Economy* 18(2):25–42.

Bates, T., and C. R. Dunham. 1992. Facilitating upward mobility through small business ownership. In *Urban labor markets and job opportunity*, ed. G. Peterson and W. Vroman. Washington, DC: The Urban Institute.

Boyd, R. L. 1990. Black business transformation, black well-being, and public policy. *Population Research and Policy Review* 9:117–132.

Fairlie, R., and A. Robb. 2004. Why are black owned businesses less successful than white owned businesses? The role of families, inheritances, and business human capital. Discussion Paper Series 1ZADP No. 1292. http://www.IZA.org/publications/dps/.

Landry, B. 1987. *The new black middle class*. Berkley: Univ. of California Press.

National Center for Public Policy and Higher Education. 2003. College affordability in jeopardy. San Jose, CA: NCPPHE. http://www.highereducation.org/reports/affordability_supplement/index.shtml.

Olson, E. 2006. Small business: New help for the black entrepreneur. *New York Times*. October 27.

Villemez, W., and J. J. Beggs. 1984. Black capitalism and black inequality: Some neglected sociological considerations. *Social Forces* 63:117–144.

About the Authors

The authors are listed alphabetically.

Walter Allen is Professor of Education and Information Studies in the Graduate School of Education and Information Studies at the University of California, Los Angeles. He is a former Professor at the University of Michigan.

Percy Bates is Professor of Education and Director of Programs for Educational Opportunity in the School of Education at the University of Michigan.

Clifford Broman is Professor of Sociology in the Department of Sociology at Michigan State University.

Renee B. Canady is Assistant Professor of Nursing in the College of Nursing at Michigan State University.

Joe T. Darden is Professor of Geography in the Department of Geography at Michigan State University.

Karl Gregory is Distinguished Emeritus Professor of Economics in the School of Business Administration at Oakland University.

Homer Hawkins is Associate Professor of Criminal Justice in the School of Criminal Justice at Michigan State University.

Curtis Stokes is Professor of Political Philosophy and African American Politics in James Madison College at Michigan State University.

Richard W. Thomas is Professor of History in the Department of History at Michigan State University.

Index

Note: tables indicated with *t* after page number

ABSW. *See* Association of Black Social Workers
academic scholarships. *See* scholarships
acquired immune deficiency syndrome. *See* AIDS/HIV
Adams, Charles G., 84
Ad Hoc Committee for Fair Banking Practices, 67
adult basic education (ABE), in prisons, 225, 227
Affirmative Action, 222, 303; threat to, 5, 265, 273, 292
age/aging, 339–40; of housing, 8, 8*t*, 11, 121–23; and mortality rate, 162, 164*t*, 165–66, 173–74, 308; and poverty, 339, 341; senior citizens, 21, 86
aggravated assault, arrests for, 200, 201–2, 203, 204, 205, 206, 209*t*; black-white comparison, 188*t*–197*t*, 218, 219*t*
AIDS/HIV, 171, 173*t*, 176*t*, 338, 341, 345; and intravenous drug use, 167, 169, 172, 175, 309, 322, 338
Alabama, black vote in, 278–79
Alba, R., 157
Albion Black Alumni Association (ABAA), 90
alcohol abuse, 172, 174, 323. *See also* drug and substance abuse
Allen, Walter, 5, 243, 269, 272
American Council on Education, 183
Amsterdam, A. G., 224
Am-Tech Export Trading Co., Inc., 56*t*, 60
Ann Arbor, Michigan: age of housing in, 122, 122*t*; black-owned firms in, 51, 52*t*, 53, 54*t*, 63, 75; black suburbanization in, 132, 133*t*, 134, 135*t*; housing costs in, 118–19; rental housing in, 124; residential segregation in, 115, 116*t*, 117*t*, 118*t*, 136–37*t*, 148*t*
Anti-Redlining Act (Michigan, 1977), 119, 126
Armour, J., 225
Asians, 162, 232*t*, 235*t*; higher education of, 244, 245*t*–247*t*, 249*t*–253*t*, 255*t*–256*t*, 258*t*–263*t*; and residential segregation, 148–50*t*
Asp, Charles, 181
Associated Press, 185, 243
Association of Black Social Workers (ABSW), 89, 90, 101, 337
automobile dealerships, 26, 32, 55*t*–57*t*, 58, 59, 60
automobile industry, 64, 311

Barden Communications, Inc., 55*t*, 59, 64
Barfield, Clementine, 105, 107–8
Barrow, Thomas, 284
Bates, Percy, 5, 231, 269, 271

Bates, T., 69
Battle Creek, Michigan, 53, 54*t,* 75–76, 88; age of housing in, 122, 122*t;* black suburbanization in, 133*t,* 134; residential segregation in, 116*t,* 117*t,* 118*t,* 136–37*t,* 149*t,* 150
Bay City. *See* Saginaw-Bay City-Midland
Benton Harbor, Michigan, 53, 54*t,* 85, 88; black suburbanization in, 133*t,* 134; housing issues in, 118–19, 122, 122*t,* 123; residential segregation in, 114, 114*t,* 115, 116*t,* 117*t,* 118*t,* 136–37*t,* 148*t*
Beverly, Creigs C., 182
BIDCO. *See* Greater Detroit BIDCO (Business and Industrial Development Corporation)
Birmingham, Michigan, 139
birth control, 93. *See also* pregnancy, prevention of
Black Action Movement, 247–48
black crime, 220–28, 311–12; arrest rates, 217–19*t;* causes of, 220–22; and criminal justice system, 222–28; and police, 222–23; and prevention programs, 91–92, 304–5; and prison system, 225–28; sentencing procedures, 223–25; victims of, 220, 224, 225, 311. *See also* young black offenders; violent crime; *specific crimes*
black empowerment, obstacles to, 277–78, 290, 291
Black Enterprise " Top 100," 25–26, 38, 41–42, 53, 61, 63, 328; auto dealers in, 26, 32, 57, 59, 60
Black Family Development, Inc. (BFDI), 89–90, 101–2
Black Liberation Movement, 264
black-owned business. *See* business trends, black-owned
Black United Fund (BUF) of Michigan, 99–101
black upwardly mobile professionals, 18
black-white inequality. *See* racial disparity
black women, 327; arrests of, 317; as business owners, 60; causes of death for, 173–74, 175, 332; college education of, 182–83; as elected officials, 278, 320; labor force participation rates for, 22–23; in media industry, 321; self-help organizations of, 83, 86–88, 102–4; single mothers, 86–87, 103, 299; and teenage pregnancy, 82, 86–87, 299–300, 318
black youths. *See* youth, black self-help and
Blanchard, James, 87, 283, 285, 297, 320, 324
Blau, Peter and Judith Blau, 183
blue-collar workers, 28, 28*t,* 30–31
Booker T. Washington Business Association, 26
Bourgois, P., 222
Broman, Clifford L., 5, 161
Brown, Deborah, 88
Brown, R. A., 223
Brown, Walter L., 85
BUF. *See* Black United Fund (BUF) of Michigan
Bureau of Census. *See* Census Bureau, U.S.
business, outmigration of, 15–16, 17
business trends, black-owned, 32, 37–78, 349–51; (1987-2002), 69–78; automobile dealerships, 26, 32, 55*t*–57*t,* 58, 59, 60; *Black Enterprise* 100, 25–26, 328, 329; business participation rate (BPR), 73, 74*t,* 75, 75*t,* 76, 77, 77*t;* changes in (1987-2002), 71–76; characteristics of business owners (CBO), 70; churches and, 85; by city, 48–50, 75–76, 75*t;* compared to all business in Michigan, 71–73; by county in Michigan, 46–48, 73, 74*t;* employees and location patterns, 77–78; franchising, 307–8; historical legacy of, 69–70; by industry, 50–51, 51*t;* larger firms (1982-1989), 53–59; larger firms (1990), 59–61; "ma and pa" firms, 25, 66; in majority-black cities, 76; by metropolitan area (1987), 51–53, 52*t;* in Michigan and U.S. compared, 38*t,* 39–40, 41*t,* 44–46; in other states compared to Michigan, 41–44; recommendations for 1991, 65–67, 349–51; share of sales and receipts, 71*t,* 73, 74*t;* subchapter S category, 38; summary and recommendations, 61–65, 301–2, 325–26, 327–30; survey of, 37–39
"Buy in Detroit" program, 66

California: black-owned business in, 41, 42*t,* 43*t,* 44, 59; sentencing in, 223
Canady, Hortense Golden, 86–87
Canady, Renee, 5, 171
cancers, 161, 164*t,* 165, 172, 173*t*
cardiovascular disease. *See* heart (cardiovascular) disease
Census Bureau data, U.S., 19; on black business, 37, 38, 39, 57, 58, 327–28; on housing, 118, 130; on suburbanization, 138; *Summary File 3A (1990),* 153; *Summary Tape File 4,* 152; *2002 Survey of Business Owners,* 71
Center for Substance Abuse Services, 338–39. *See also* drug and substance abuse
cerebrovascular disease (stroke), 163, 164*t,* 165*t,* 172, 173*t*

Cernkovich, Steven A., 180
children/childcare, 85, 333; and black self-help, 89; and lead poisoning, 345; infant mortality, 166–67, 166*t*, 174, 174*t*, 308, 332, 337, 341; and single mothers, 86–87. *See also* education; pregnancy; youth
child welfare system, 313, 314–15, 319, 337
churches, and black self-help, 84–85, 93, 101
cirrhosis, 163, 164*t*, 165, 172
cities, black business participation rates for, 75–76, 75*t*. *See also* standard metropolitan areas; *specific* cities
civil disorders (1967), 3, 15, 97
civil rights, 309–10, 345–46
Civil Rights Act of 1964 (U.S.), 27, 130
Civil Rights Act of 1968 (U.S.), 130
Civil Rights Act (1977, Michigan). *See* Elliot-Larsen Civil Rights Act of 1977 (Michigan)
Civil Rights Movement, 264
Clark, Kenneth B., 33
cocaine/crack cocaine, 185, 224–25, 333, 336. *See also* drug and substance abuse
Cochran, W. G., 279
colleges and universities. *See* higher education; *specific* institutions
Commerce Department (Michigan), 59, 65, 66, 121, 329
Commission on Accreditation of Rehabilitation Facilities (CARF), 102
community development, 92, 302, 339
Concerned Black Women's Roundtable, 87–88
Conference on Negro Problems, 83
Consumer Price Index, 44, 48
Conyers, John, Jr., 290
counties: black-owned firms by, 46–48, 73, 74*t*; residential segregation by, 150–51, 151*t*. *See also specific county*
crack cocaine. *See* cocaine/crack cocaine
Crain's Detroit Business Book of Lists, 38, 53, 59, 61, 63–64, 329; new information in, 67–68
crime prevention, 91–92, 304–5. *See also* black crime; young black offender
criminal justice system, 222–28, 304
Crisis Intervention Program, 105
Cruse, Harold, 286
Current Population Surveys, 24. *See also* Census Bureau data

DABO. *See* Detroit Association of Black Organizations (DABO)
Daniels, Lee A., 182–83
Danziger, S., 153
Darden, Joe T., 3, 4, 69, 113, 129, 147, 152, 269
Dearborn, Michigan, 75
death rates. *See* mortality (death) rates
deliquency, factors in, 179–86. *See also* young black offender
Delta Sigma Theta Sorority, 86–87, 102–4
Democratic Party, 277, 285–86, 290, 297, 298, 318; and unemployment rate, 319–20, 324
Departments, state government. *See under* Michigan Department of
Detroit, city of, 17–18, 67; black college students in, 248; black-owned firms in, 48, 49, 49*t*, 52, 52*t*, 63, 76; black self-help in, 82–83, 90–92; black women and self-help in, 86–87, 102; civil disorder in (1967), 3, 15, 97; high school dropout rate in, 234, 238, 270; juvenile population in, 187*t*; juveniles and violent crime in, 186, 188–89*t*, 200–201, 209*t*; New Detroit Business Partnership Plan for, 26, 59, 64; police department in, 222–23, 312; poverty rate in, 154; residential segregation in, 115*t*, 155, 156*t*; unemployment in, 23*t*, 24, 32, 154; Young as mayor of, 105, 284; youth violence prevention in, 104–8
Detroit Association of Black Organizations (DABO), 66, 90–92
Detroit Association of Black Social Workers (DABSW), 89, 90, 101
Detroit Free Press, 47, 139
Detroit metropolitan area (SMSA): age of housing in, 122, 122*t*; black-owned firms in, 51, 52–53, 52*t*, 54*t*, 63; black suburbanization in, 133*t*, 134; labor force participation data for, 22*t*, 23, 32; racial steering in, 137–40, 157–58, 159; rental housing costs in, 119; residential segregation in, 114*t*–118*t*, 136–37*t*, 148*t*, 150, 151–57, 157*t*, 331, 336; socioeconomic and demographic changes in (1990-2000), 153–54; unemployment rates in, 23*t*, 24. *See also* Macomb County; Oakland County; Wayne County
Detroit News, 107
Detroit Tribune, 84
diabetes, 162, 163, 164*t*, 172, 173*t*
dissimilarity index. *See* index of dissimilarity
D. L. & J. Services, Inc., 41–42
DOC. *See* Michigan Department of Corrections (DOC)

drug and substance abuse, 86, 318, 338–39; and AIDS, 169, 172, 175, 309, 322, 338; alcohol abuse, 172, 174, 323; among prisoners, 323–24; crack cocaine, 185, 224–25, 333, 336; and violent crime/homicide, 184–85, 208–12, 321; and young black offender, 184–86, 198–99*t*, 218–12. *See also* narcotics law violations
DuBois, W. E. B., 81, 83

Eastern Michigan University, 245, 246*t*, 247*t*, 258
economic development, 92, 300, 330; black-owned business and, 349–51. *See also under* business
economic status, trends in, 15–33, 306–7, 316; conclusions on, 31–33; general trends, 16–18; occupational participation, 27–31; outmigration following 1967 riots, 15–16; population growth, 18, 18*t*; unemployment rate, 23–25. *See also* poverty rates; socioeconomic inequality
Edmonds, Ronald, 316
education, 298–99, 317–18; and black self-help, 103, 104; business, 302; and incarceration risk, 222; prison programs for, 225–28, 305, 349; racial disparities in, 269–73; reading outcomes and funding, 334–35; and residential segregation, 156–57; and school desegregation, 334; training programs, 87, 318, 350; and youth crime, 181–83, 348–49. *See also* higher education; high school drop out rate; Michigan Department of Education; scholarships
Educational Progress in the Community (EPIC), 90
Efforts for Social Betterment Among Negro Americans (DuBois), 81
Eigen, J., 224
elderly/older population. *See* age/aging
elected officials, black, 16, 17, 278, 291, 340; survey of, 279, 280–83*t*, 285, 287–88, 320. *See also* political participation
Elementary and Secondary Information Access System (ESIAS), 234
Elliot-Larsen Civil Rights Act of 1977 (Michigan), 113, 130, 132, 139, 147, 336, 346
Ellis Electronic, Inc., 56*t*, 60
employment. *See* labor force participation rates; unemployment rates
empowerment, obstacles to, 277–78, 290, 291
Engler, Governor, 66
Equal Employment Opportunity Commission (EEOC) U.S., 27, 36*t*, 265
Executive Order 11063, 130

Fair Housing Act of 1968 (U.S.), 113, 132, 139, 147, 331, 336
Fair Housing Center, 139
Fairlie, R., 70
families: and black self-help, 89–90, 101–2; and higher education, 265; incomes, 7, 7*t*, 11, 19, 19*t*, 20, 347; and juvenile delinquency, 179–81; single mother households, 86–87, 103, 299. *See also* children/childcare
Farley, R., 153
Farnsworth, Margaret, 181
fast-food industry, 24–25
Featherman, D., 181
federal government, 86, 264; housing policies of, 113, 125, 129–30, 132
Federal Housing Adminstration (FHA), 129
Ferndale, Michigan, 75, 76
FHA/FmHA/VA loans. *See* home improvement loans
Figueira-McDonough, Josefina, 182
financial aid, for college students, 264, 266, 348. *See also* scholarships and financial aid
First Independence National Bank of Detroit, 26, 60
fiscal disparities, 335. *See also* economic status; income level; poverty rates
Fischer, Donald G., 180
Flint, Michigan: black-owned firms in, 48, 49*t*, 50, 51, 52*t*, 53, 54*t*, 63, 76; black suburbanization in, 133*t*, 134; black women and self-help in, 87; juvenile population in, 187*t*; juveniles and violent crime in, 190–91*t*, 201–2, 208, 209–11*t*, 212; residential segregation in, 114, 114*t*, 115, 116*t*, 117*t*, 118*t*, 136–37*t*, 148*t*, 151
Flint Association of Black Social Workers, 89
Florida, black-owned business in, 41, 42, 42*t*, 43*t*
Fortune magazine, 42, 328
Frank, J., 223

Gandossy, Robert P. et al., 184
Gannett News Service, 185–86
Garbarino, James, 181
Garvey, Marcus, 83, 289
GED programs, in prison, 225–28, 305, 349

GEMS: Growing and Empowering Myself Successfully, 103–4
gender: in elected offices, 290; and life expectancy, 172–74; and unemployment, 310. *See also* black women
General Motors Corporation, 26
Genesee County, black-owned business in, 46*t*, 47, 48*t*, 62
Gilreath Manufacturing, Inc., 67
Giordano, Peggy C., 180
Glueck, Sheldon and Eleanor Glueck, 180
Good, David H. et al., 183
government employment, 15, 350. *See also* elected officials; federal government; Michigan; state government
graduation equivalent diploma. *See* GED programs, in prison
Grand Rapids, Michigan, 87, 89, 122, 122*t*; black-owned business in, 48, 49*t*, 50, 52, 52*t*, 54*t*, 63; black suburbanization in, 132, 133*t*, 134; juvenile population in, 187*t*; juveniles and violent crime in, 192–93*t*, 202–3, 208, 209–11*t*; residential segregation in, 116*t*, 117*t*, 118*t*, 136–37*t*, 148*t*
Granholm, Jennifer, 290
Greater Detroit BIDCO (Business and Industrial Development Corporation), 59, 64, 65
Greene, J. P., 270
Gregory, Karl D., 4, 92, 349
Gumbleton, Thomas J., 107–8

Hankerson, Barry L., 99
Hartford Memorial Baptist Church, 84–85, 93
Havens Realty Company v. Coleman (1982), 143
Hawkins, Darnell, 184
Hawkins, Homer C., 5, 179, 217, 225, 348
health care organizations, 58
health issues, 83, 161–77, 308–9, 345; behavior-related, 167; black-white disparities, 332–33, 337–38, 341; causes of disparities in, 176; data and methodology, 162–63; death rate and, 161, 162, 163–67, 172–74; and drug abuse treatment, 322; and life expectancy, 161; overall patterns in U.S., 171–72; and socioeconomic inequality, 161–62, 167, 168*t*, 176; statewide patterns for, 172–74. *See also* AIDS/HIV
Heaney, G. W., 224
heart (cardiovascular) disease, 161, 163, 164*t*, 165, 172, 173, 332
Herjanic, B., 180
higher education, 17, 243–66, 299, 335; agenda for action on, 264–65; college degrees earned, 257, 262–63*t*, 272; gender ratio in, 182–83; graduate enrollment, 254; in prison system, 225–27, 228; in private colleges and universities, 248–54; professional schools, 264; in public colleges and universities, 244–48, 255–56*t*; racial disparities in, 271–72; recommendations for, 265–66, 309; scholarships and aid for, 86, 88, 90, 104, 264, 343–44, 348; and student protests, 243–44, 247–48; in two-year public colleges, 254, 257, 258–61*t*
Higher Education Act of 1965 (U.S.), 243
Highland Park, Michigan, 52, 53
high school dropout rate, 182, 231–41, 312, 348; black-white comparison, 233–38, 233*t*, 269–71, 315; in Detroit, 234, 238, 270; discussion and reccommendations, 240–41, 315–16; factors affecting, 237*t*; and growing black enrollment, 231–32; and incarceration risk, 222; in Michigan, 232–34; prevention programs, 239, 318
Hispanics, 148–50*t*, 232*t*, 235*t*, 292; criminal behavior of, 221, 222, 223, 225; health risks to, 162, 175; higher education for, 244, 245*t*–247*t*, 249*t*–253*t*, 255*t*–256*t*, 258*t*–263*t*
HIV. *See* AIDS/HIV
Holleran, D., 221
Holman, M. Carl, 82
Holzer, H., 153
home improvement loans, 119–21, 298, 346
homeownership, access to, 9, 11, 123–25, 298
home purchase loans. *See* mortgage loans
homicide/murder, 162, 164*t*, 172, 311, 332; arrests for, black-white comparison, 188*t*–197*t*, 217, 218*t*; and narcotics violations, 184, 185–86, 208, 209*t*, 212, 321; and poverty, 184; prevention programs, 105–8, 201–5; sentencing for, 224, 225; and young blacks, 104, 165, 166, 173, 174*t*, 186, 201, 202, 203, 204, 205, 209*t*, 220, 317
Hope United Methodist Church, 85
housing: accessibility of non-segregated, 113–19; age of, 8, 8*t*, 11, 121–22; cost of, 118–19; in metropolitan areas, 113–27; overcrowding in, 122–23; quality of, 121–23; racial disparities in, 8–10, 11, 122*t*, 123*t*, 124*t*, 125*t*; rental, 9–10*t*, 119, 123, 124, 138, 139–40; state legislation for, 347; values of, 9, 9*t*, 11. *See also* residential segregation

Housing and Community Development Act, 143
Housing and Urban Development (HUD), U.S. Department of, 138, 143
"How to Stop the Mis-education of Black Children" (Holman), 82
Hughes, Langston, 266
human immunodeficiency virus. *See* AIDS/HIV

illegal drug use. *See* drug and substance abuse
Illinois, black-owned business in, 41, 42*t*, 43*t*
income level: family, 7, 7*t*, 11, 19, 19*t*, 20, 347; and health, 161, 176; and poverty rates, 8, 21–22, 21*t*; racial inequality in, 7–8, 19–20; and residential segregation, 153, 155–56, 155*t*; trends in distribution, 19–20, 19*t*, 32
index of dissimilarity: in black-owned business, 73; and family incomes, 7, 7*t*; in housing rents, 9–10; in occupational structure, 6–7, 6*t*; in residential segregation, 113–14, 130–32, 136*t*, 137, 147, 148–49*t*, 150–57
inequality. *See* socioeconomic inequality; racial disparity
infant mortality, 166–67, 166*t*, 174, 174*t*, 308, 332, 337, 341
Ingham County, black-owned business in, 46*t*, 47, 48*t*, 62, 328
Inkster, Michigan, 52, 138
Inner City Business Improvement Forum (ICBIF), 26, 65
Inner City Sub-Center (ICSC), 98, 106
Innes, Christopher A., 184
integration incentive plans, 141–44
Internal Revenue Service, U.S., 38
Islam, Nation of, 83, 106
IV (intravenous) drug abuse. *See* drug and substance abuse

Jackson, Hugh, 85
Jackson, Michigan, 53, 54*t*, 136–37*t*; age of housing in, 122, 122*t*; black suburbanization in, 133*t*, 134, 135*t*; residential segregation in, 116*t*, 117*t*, 118*t*, 149*t*
Jargowsky. P. A., 154
Jencks, Christopher, 238
jobs. *See under* occupational; unemployment rate
Johnson, Richard E., 180
Jones, Mack, 291
juvenile justice system, 322–23. *See also* young black offender

Kalamazoo, Michigan, 53, 54*t*, 76, 88; black suburbanization in, 132, 133*t*, 134, 135*t*; residential segregation in, 115, 116*t*, 117*t*, 118*t*, 134, 136–37*t*, 149*t*, 150
Kamel, S. M., 152
Kent County, black-owned business in, 46*t*, 47, 48*t*
Kerner Commission Report (National Advisory Commission on Civil Disorders), 8, 18, 33
Keys Group, Inc., 55*t*, 60, 64
Kilpatrick, Carolyn C., 290
Kilpatrick, Kwame, 290
King, Martin Luther, Jr., 289, 290
Klein, S. et al., 223
Krohn, Marvin D., 183–84

labor force participation rates, 22–23, 22*t*, 27–31, 32, 320. *See also* unemployment rates
Lansing, Michigan, 124, 187*t*; black-owned firms in, 48, 49*t*, 50, 51, 52*t*, 54*t*, 63, 76, 328; black suburbanization in, 132, 133*t*, 134; juveniles and violent crime in, 194–95*t*, 203–4, 209–11*t*, 212; residential segregation in, 115, 116*t*, 117*t*, 118*t*, 136–37*t*, 149*t*
Levin, Carl, 107
Lewis, Dorothy O., 180
life expectancy, 163, 171, 172, 174, 177, 308, 321, 325. *See also* mortality (death) rates
loans denied, to black business owners, 69–70. *See also* mortgage loans
Lochner, L., 222
Loftin, Colin, 183
Logan, J. R., 157
low-income families, 347. *See also* poverty rates
Lucas, William, 286, 305, 306

M. A. Hanna (firm), 42
Macomb County, 73, 138, 139
Martin Luther King, Jr.-Rosa Parks Scholarship Program, 343–44
mass media, occupational segregation in, 320–21, 325
Mayer, Susan, 238
Messner, Steven E., 183
Metropolitan Anti-Crime Coalition (MACC), 91–92
metropolitan areas. *See* Detroit SMSA; standard metropolitan statistical areas (SMSAs); *specific urban area*

Michigan Association of Black Social Workers (MABSW), 89, 90
Michigan Chronicle, 84
Michigan Council of Urban League Executives, 4
Michigan Department of Civil Rights, 346
Michigan Department of Commerce, 59, 65, 66, 121, 329
Michigan Department of Corrections (DOC), 225–28, 323, 324, 349. *See also* prison system
Michigan Department of Education, 232, 234, 238, 271, 322; Operation Graduation, 239, 316
Michigan Department of Public Health, 169, 322
Michigan Education Trust, 344
Michigan legislature, 343–51; and black-owned business, 349–51; and civil rights, 345–46; and education, 343–44, 348–49; and health, 345; and housing programs, 346–47; recommendations for action by, 348–51
Michigan Office of Minority Health, 338
Michigan Office of Services to the Aging, 339–40
Michigan Office of Substance Abuse Services, 322. *See also* drug and substance abuse
Michigan State Board of Education, 334
Michigan State University, 245, 246*t*, 247*t*, 258
Michigan Strategic Fund, 64, 65–66
middle class, 20, 154, 155, 181
Midland, Michigan. *See* Saginaw-Bay City-Midland
Miller, W. P. B., 180
Milliken, William, 286, 324
minimum wage, 25
Mississippi, black-owned business in, 41, 42*t*, 43, 44
Moretti, E., 222
mortality (death) rates, 83, 161, 163–67, 172–74; accidental death, 173*t*, 174; and age group, 162, 164*t*, 173–74, 308; infant mortality, 166–67, 166*t*, 174, 174*t*, 308, 332, 337, 341. *See also* homicide/murder; life expectancy
mortgage loans, 119–21, 125, 129, 158, 298, 346; and pro-integrative incentives, 143–44
Motown, Inc., 59–60, 106, 329
Moynihan, Daniel P., 180
Muhammad, Elijah, 83
Muhammad, Warith Deem, 83
murder. *See* homicide/murder
Muskegon-Muskegon Heights, Michigan, 53, 54*t*, 87; black suburbanization in, 133*t*, 134; residential segregation in, 116*t*, 117*t*, 118*t*, 136–37*t*, 148*t*
Nadelmann, Ethan A., 185
narcotics laws violations, 198–99*t*, 200–201, 202, 203, 204, 205, 206, 207; and violent crime, 184–86, 208–12, 316, 317; *See also* drug and substance abuse
National Advisory Commission on Civil Disorders (Kerner Commission), 3, 18, 33
National Association for the Advancement of Colored People (NAACP), 66, 84, 289
National Association of Black Social Workers, 89, 337
National Association of Colored Women, 83
National Association of Negro Business and Professional Women's Clubs (NANBPW), 88
National Colored Convention, 82–83
National Housing Discrimination Study (1991), 140
National Negro Health Week, 83
National Scholarship Service for Negro Students, 90
National Urban League, 82, 93
Nation of Islam, 83, 106
Negro Business League, 83
New Detroit Business Partnership, 59, 64, 65
New Detroit Inc., 26, 59, 98
New Jersey, black-owned business in, 41, 42*t*, 43*t*
newspaper firms, blacks in, 321, 324
New York, black-owned business in, 41, 42–43, 42*t*, 43*t*, 59

Oakland County, 73, 138, 139; black-owned business in, 46*t*, 47, 48*t*, 62, 328
Oak Park, Michigan, 52, 138
occupational participation, 27–31, 36. *See also* labor force participation; unemployment rate
occupational structure, 6–7, 11
Ohio Bonus for Integrative Moves, 143–44
O'Malley, S., 224
Operation Get Down (ODG), 98–99
Operation Graduation, 239, 316
outmigration, 18, 18*t*; following 1967 riots, 15–16. *See also* suburbanization

parents, and teen pregnancy, 82, 318. *See also* families
Parker, Bernard, Jr., 99
Parker, Robert Nash, 183
Pearson Product Moment Correlation Coefficient, 208

Petersilia, J., 223
Pilgrim Rest Baptist Church, 85
police, 222–23, 312
political participation, 277–92, 297–98, 305–6, 340; and black empowerment, 277–78, 290, 291; conclusions and discussion, 286–86; in 1988 elections, 318; electoral progress in 1980s, 277–79; following 1967 riots, 16; and new black politics, 291–92; and politics as electoralism, 289–91; survey of elected officials, 279, 280–83*t*, 287–88, 320; Young as mayor of Detroit, 284, 285
Pontiac, Michigan, 23, 85, 138; black-owned business in, 47, 52, 53
population growth, 18, 18*t*, 32
Post-Secondary Access Student Scholarship (PASS) program, 344
poverty rates, 176, 337; among black elderly, 339, 341; and black elected officials, 291; in city of Detroit, 154; and crime, 183, 221, 222; and homicide, 184; racial inequality in, 8, 11, 21–22, 21*t*, 32
pregnancy: and drug addiction, 333; prevention of, 82, 86, 93, 103; teenage, 82, 86–87, 299–300, 318
prison system, 322–23, 345; educational programs in, 225–28, 305, 349; psychiatric disorders in, 323–24, 325; recidivism rate in, 225, 344, 349
"A Process for Black Community Development" (Gregory), 92
property crimes, arrests for, 218, 219*t*
Proposal 2 (Michigan), 5, 273
psychiatric disorders, among prisoners, 323–24, 325
Public Acts of 1977 (1996 Amendment), 346
Public Acts of 1980 (1993 Amendment), 346

racial disparity, 3–11, 319; in educational attainment, 8; in family incomes, 7, 7*t*, 11; in housing, 8–10, 11; in labor participation, 29–31; in occupational structure, 6–7, 6*t*, 11; in poverty rates, 8, 11, 21–22, 21*t*, 32; in vehicle availability, 10–11, 10*t*. *See also* index of dissimilarity; socioeconomic inequality
Racial Ethnic Census (Michigan State Board of Education), 234
racial steering, 137–40, 157–58, 159
rape, arrests for, 200, 201, 202, 203, 204–5, 209*t*; black-white comparison, 188*t*–197*t*, 218
Reagan administration, 27, 81, 277, 286
recidivism, in prisons, 225, 344, 349
rental housing, 9–10, 10*t*, 124; costs of, 119; overcrowding in, 123; racial discrimination in, 138, 139–40
Republican Party, 318, 319–20
residential segregation, 4, 17, 113–59, 220, 298; and black access to homeownership, 123–25; and black suburbanization, 115–18, 132–34, 135*t*, 136*t*, 138; in central cities (2000), 151–52; changes in (1990-2000), 147–59; by county, 150–51, 151*t*; in Detroit metro area, 114*t*–118*t*, 136–37*t*, 148*t*, 150, 152–57, 336; and dissimilarity index, 113–14, 130–32, 136*t*, 137, 147, 148–49*t*, 150–57; and education level, 156–57; and housing costs, 118–19; and housing quality, 121–23; and income levels, 153, 155–56, 155*t*; and integration incentives, 141–44, 332; in metropolitan areas, 113–25, 126, 131, 134–37*t*, 147–59, 331–32; and mortgage loan accessibility, 119–21, 125, 129; and racial steering in Detroit SMSA, 137–40, 157–58, 159; and socioeconomic status, 152–53, 154, 157; technical limits to measuring, 131–32. *See also* housing
restrictive convenants, 129. *See also* residential segregation
retail trade, 50, 62
Robb, A., 70
robbery, arrests for, 200, 201, 202, 204, 205, 206, 209*t*; black-white comparison, 188*t*–197*t*, 219*t*
Roberts, Harrell B., 181
Robins, L. N., 180

Saginaw-Bay City-Midland, 53, 54*t*; black suburbanization in, 132, 133*t*, 134; residential segregation in, 114, 114*t*, 115, 116*t*, 117*t*, 118*t*, 136–37*t*, 149*t*, 151
Save Our Sons and Daughters (SOSAD), 104–8
scholarships and financial aid, 264, 266, 343–44, 348; and black self-help, 86, 88, 90, 104
school desegregation, 334–35. *See also* education; high school dropout rate
Scott Paper of Philadelphia, 42, 328
self-help, black, 81–108, 303; (1967-2007), 97–108; Black Family Development, Inc., 89–90, 101–2; Black United Fund of Michigan, 99–101; and black women, 83, 86–88, 102–4; building networks of, 88–93; building on

tradition of, 82–84; and churches, 84–85, 93, 101; Operation Get Down, 98–99; in post-urban disorder period, 97; and scholarships, 86, 88, 90, 104; spiritual foundation for, 93; status and activities of, 84–85; and youth violence, 104–8
senior citizens, 21, 86. *See also* age/aging
service workers, 30, 49, 50, 63, 70, 221
sex education, 318. *See also* pregnancy
Shanock, Shelly S., 180
Smith, M. D., 224
SMSA. *See* standard metropolitan statistical area
Social Security records, 38
social welfare. *See* child welfare system
socioeconomic inequality, 5–11, 284, 291, 299; and black health, 161–62, 167, 168*t*, 176, 176*t*; and crime, 220–21; and residential segregation, 152–53, 154, 157; unemployment rate and, 5–6. *See also* economic status, trends in; income level; poverty rates; unemployment rate
Southfield, Michigan, 103, 138; black-owned business in, 47, 48, 49*t*, 50, 52, 53, 62, 76, 328
Southfield Alumni Chapter (SAC), 103
spiritual education, 93
Spohn, C., 221
Stabenow, Debbie, 290
standard metropolitan statistical area (SMSA): black-owned firms in, 51–53, 54*t*; home improvement loans in, 120–21*t*; housing quality in, 121–23; residential segregation in, 113–25, 131, 134–37*t*, 147–59. *See also* Detroit SMSA; *specific urban area*
state equalized valuation (SEV), 238
state government, 26, 125, 323; black employment in, 303–4. *See also under* Michigan
State Housing Development Authority Act of 1966, 347
The State of Black Michigan, 4; (1985), 82, 297–300; (1986), 26, 37, 301–6; (1987), 285, 306–10; (1988), 310–13; (1989), 269, 314–19; (1990), 319–25; (1991), 325–30; (1992), 330–36; (1993), 336–40
Steinberg, Laurence, 182
Stern, Marilyn et al., 180
Stokes, Curtis, 5
stroke. *See* cerebrovascular disease (stroke)
Student Achievement and Retention (STAR), 348
student protests, 243–44, 247–48. *See also* education; higher education
student aid and scholarships. *See* scholarships
Substance Abuse Services, 322, 339. *See also* drugs and substance abuse
suburbanization, black, 115–18, 132–34, 135–36*t*, 138; and business, 75, 77; in Detroit SMSA, 154–57, 336. *See also specific suburbs*
Sullivan, Leon, 26
Summa-Harrison Metal Products, Inc., 56*t*, 60
Superb Manufacturing, 56*t*, 60
survey, of black elected officials, 279, 280–83*t*, 287–88
Survey of Minority-Owned Enterprises—Black 1987, 37–38, 50

T.A.S. Graphic Communications, Inc., 67
Thomas, Richard, 74, 81, 97, 297
Thornberry, Terence P. et al., 182
training programs, 87, 318, 350. *See also* education
Trans Jones, Inc./Jones Transfer Company, 55*t*, 60, 64
Turner, M. et al., 158
Turner, S., 223

unemployment rate, 17, 58, 176, 308, 310–11, 346; black-white disparity in, 5–6, 11, 16, 310–11, 315, 319–20, 324, 325, 327, 330–31; and black youth, 24–25, 183–84, 327; in city of Detroit, 23*t*, 24, 32154; and crime, 183–84, 220–21; and industrial decline (1971-1990), 311, 330–31, 335; under Republican *vs.* Democratic governors, 319–20; trends in, 23–25, 30, 32
United Coalition Against Racism, 248
United States, black-owned business in, 39–40, 39*t*, 41*t*, 44–46
Universal Negro Improvement Association, 83
Universal Software, 56*t*, 60
University of Michigan—Ann Arbor, 245, 246*t*, 247–48, 247*t*, 258
Urban Affairs Programs at Michigan State University, 4
urban areas, black business participation rates in, 75–76, 75*t*. *See also* standard metropolitan statistical area (SMSA); *specific cities*
Urban Homestead Program, 347
Urban League, 82, 93
urban redevelopment corporations, 346

vehicle availability, 10–11, 10*t*
violent crime, 304; black-white comparison of, 188*t*–197*t*; and drug abuse, 184–86, 208–12, 321. *See also* aggravated assault; black crime; homicide/murder; rape; robbery
voter registration/turnout, 278, 305, 320
Voting Rights Act of 1965, 277, 290

Walters, Ronald, 290
Warren, Michigan, 76, 187*t*; juveniles and violent crime in, 196–97*t*, 204–5, 209–11*t*, 212
Washenaw County, black-owned business in, 46*t*, 47, 48*t*, 62
Washington, Booker T., 83, 289
Watts, Jerry, 291–92
Wayne County, 138, 139, 151; black-owned business in, 46*t*, 47, 48*t*, 62, 328
Wayne State University, 245, 246*t*, 247*t*, 254; and Inner City Sub-Center, 98
Wesley Industries, Inc., 55*t*, 60, 64, 329
West, P. A., 180
Western Michigan University, 245, 246*t*, 247*t*
West Virginia, high school completion in, 238, 241, 316
white-collar occupations, 27–31, 32–33
white racism, 3. *See also* racial disparity
Williams, Joyce, 88
Williams, Melvin, 85
Winters, M., 270
women. *See* black women
working class, 181. *See also* blue–collar workers

X, Malcolm, 98, 99

Young, Coleman, 105, 284, 285
young black offenders, 179–213, 221; arrests in Detroit, 186, 188–89*t*, 200–201, 208; arrests in Flint, 190–91*t*, 201–2, 208; arrests in Grand Rapids, 192–93*t*, 202–3, 208; arrests in Lansing, 194–95*t*, 203–4, 212; arrests in select cities (1978-1987), 186–207; arrests in Warren, 196–97*t*, 204–5, 212; composite and comparison of crimes by, 205–7; education of, 181–83, 222, 348–49; factors in delinquency, 179–86; and family, 179–81; imprisonment of, 322–23; and narcotics violations, 184–86, 198–99*t*, 200–201, 202, 203, 204, 205, 206, 207, 208–12, 316, 317; and poverty, 183–84; and violent crime, 184–86, 200–212, 316–17 (*See also specific crimes*)
youth: and black self-help, 90, 93, 98–99, 103–8; and homicide, 165, 166, 173; unemployment rates for, 24–25, 183–84, 327. *See also* children/childcare; education; teenage pregnancy

Zimring, F. et al., 224